MS. MARVEL

OPERATION LIGHTNING STORM

WRITER: **BRIAN REED**

PENCILS: **ROBERTO DE LA TORRE (ISSUES #11-12)**

& AARON LOPRESTI (ISSUES #13-17)

INKS: **JON SIBAL (ISSUES #11-12)**

& MATT RYAN (ISSUES #13-17)

COLORS: **CHRIS SOTOMAYOR**

LETTERS: **DAVE SHARPE**

COVER ART: **GREG HORN WITH TRAVEL FOREMAN (ISSUE #11)**

ASSISTANT EDITOR: **ALEJANDRO ARBONA**

EDITOR: **BILL ROSEMANN**

COLLECTION EDITOR: **JENNIFER GRÜNWALD**

ASSISTANT EDITORS: **CORY LEVINE & MICHAEL SHORT**

ASSOCIATE EDITOR: **MARK D. BEAZLEY**

SENIOR EDITOR, SPECIAL PROJECTS: **JEFF YOUNGQUIST**

SENIOR VICE PRESIDENT OF SALES: **DAVID GABRIEL**

PRODUCTION: **JERRON QUALITY COLOR & JERRY KALINOWSKI**

VICE PRESIDENT OF CREATIVE: **TOM MARVELLI**

EDITOR IN CHIEF: **JOE QUESADA**

PUBLISHER: **DAN BUCKLEY**

MS. MARVEL VOL. 3: OPERATION LIGHTNING STORM. Contains material originally published in magazine form as MS. MARVEL #11-17. First printing 2007. Hardcover ISBN# 978-0-7851-2890-8. Softcover ISBN# 978-0-7851-2449-8. Published by MARVEL PUBLISHING, INC., a subsidiary of MARVEL ENTERTAINMENT, INC. OFFICE OF PUBLICATION: 417 5th Avenue, New York, NY 10016. Copyright © 2007 Marvel Characters, Inc. All rights reserved. Hardcover: $19.99 per copy in the U.S. and $32.00 in Canada (GST #R127032852). Softcover: $14.99 per copy in the U.S. and $24.00 in Canada (GST #R127032852). Canadian Agreement #40668537. All characters featured in this issue and the distinctive names and likenesses thereof, and all related indicia are trademarks of Marvel Characters, Inc. No similarity between any of the names, characters, persons, and/or institutions in this magazine with those of any living or dead person or institution is intended, and any such similarity which may exist is purely coincidental. **Printed in the U.S.A.** ALAN FINE, CEO Marvel Toys & Publishing Divisions and CMO Marvel Entertainment, Inc.; DAVID GABRIEL, Senior VP of Publishing Sales & Circulation; DAVID BOGART, VP of Business Affairs & Editorial Operations; MICHAEL PASCIULLO, VP Merchandising & Communications; JIM BOYLE, VP of Publishing Operations; DAN CARR, Executive Director of Publishing Technology; JUSTIN F. GABRIE, Managing Editor; SUSAN CRESPI, Production Manager; STAN LEE, Chairman Emeritus. For information regarding advertising in Marvel Comics or on Marvel.com, please contact Joe Maimone,

PREVIOUSLY:

After many years as a super hero, Carol has come to the realization that she should be doing more with her life. She could be more than just another hero — she could be the best of the best.

But recent weeks have been rough on Ms. Marvel. After fending off an invasion by the extraterrestrial Brood, battling insane sorcerer Warren Traveler, and combating former Avenger Julia "Arachne" Carpenter, our hero found herself fighting for her life against Warbird, a Carol Danvers from an alternate reality.

During the fight, which also included X-Men member Rogue, Ms. Marvel realized that she had been hiding her true feelings about the mutant, who nearly killed Carol many years ago. Ms. Marvel believed she had forgiven Rogue, until, in the heat of battle, Carol lashed out, injuring Rogue badly enough to require hospitalization.

The only bright spot during Ms. Marvel's recent days has been meeting William Wagner, the attractive owner of a small cafe near Carol's apartment. Of course, she met him during her battle with Warbird, which greatly damaged his restaurant...

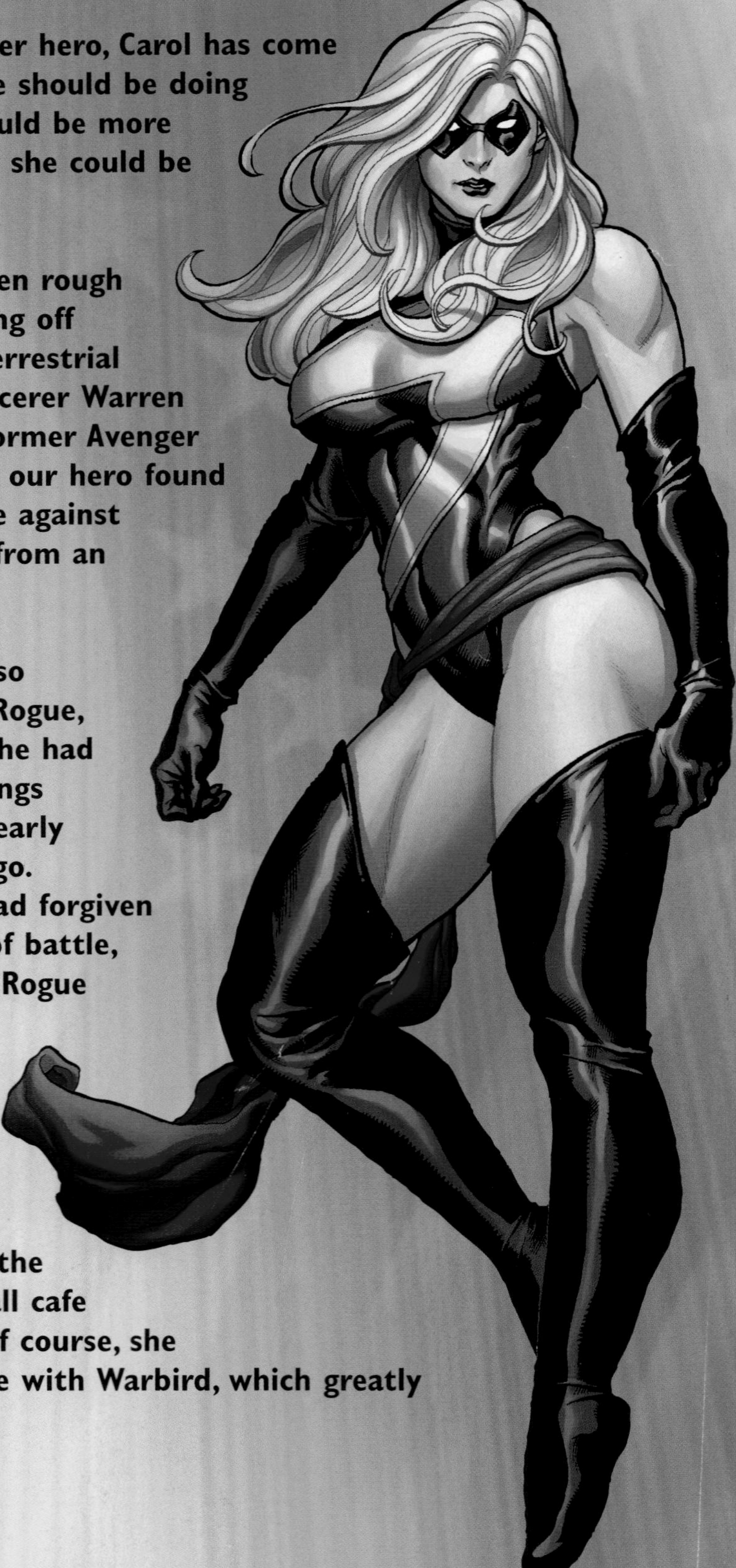

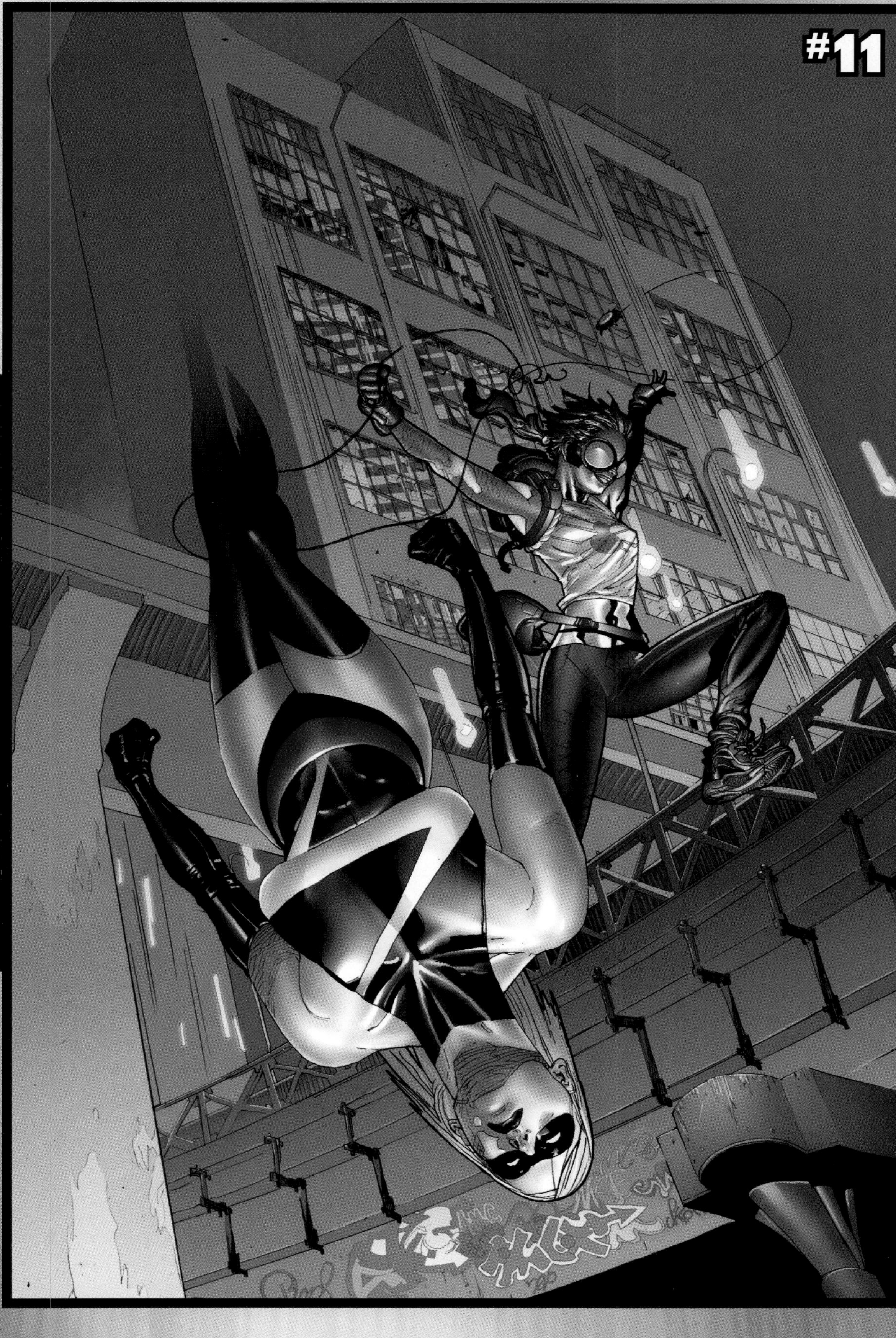
#11

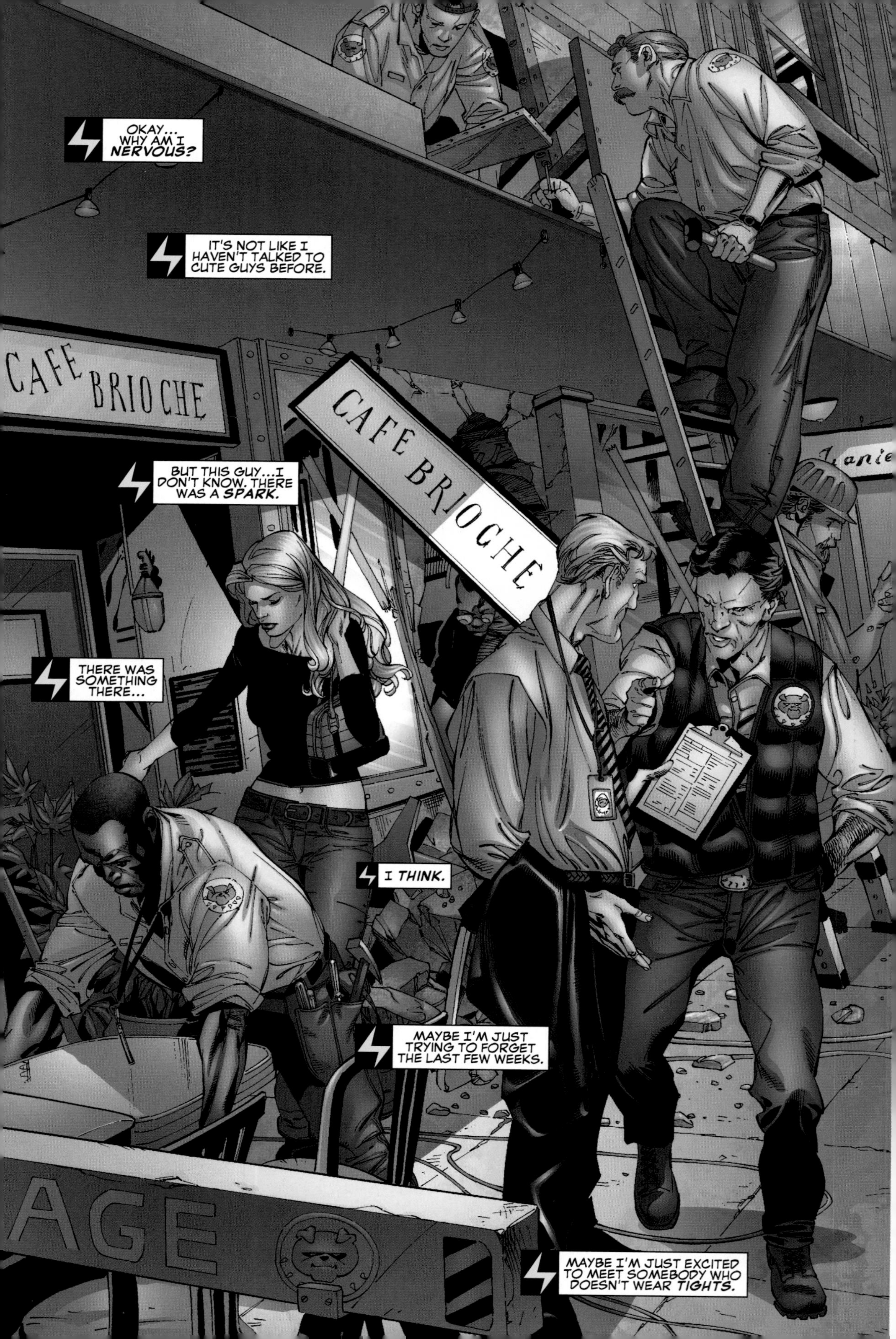
OKAY... WHY AM I NERVOUS?
IT'S NOT LIKE I HAVEN'T TALKED TO CUTE GUYS BEFORE.
BUT THIS GUY...I DON'T KNOW. THERE WAS A SPARK.
THERE WAS SOMETHING THERE...
I THINK.
MAYBE I'M JUST TRYING TO FORGET THE LAST FEW WEEKS.
MAYBE I'M JUST EXCITED TO MEET SOMEBODY WHO DOESN'T WEAR TIGHTS.
CAFE BRIOCHE
CAFE BRIOCHE
AGE

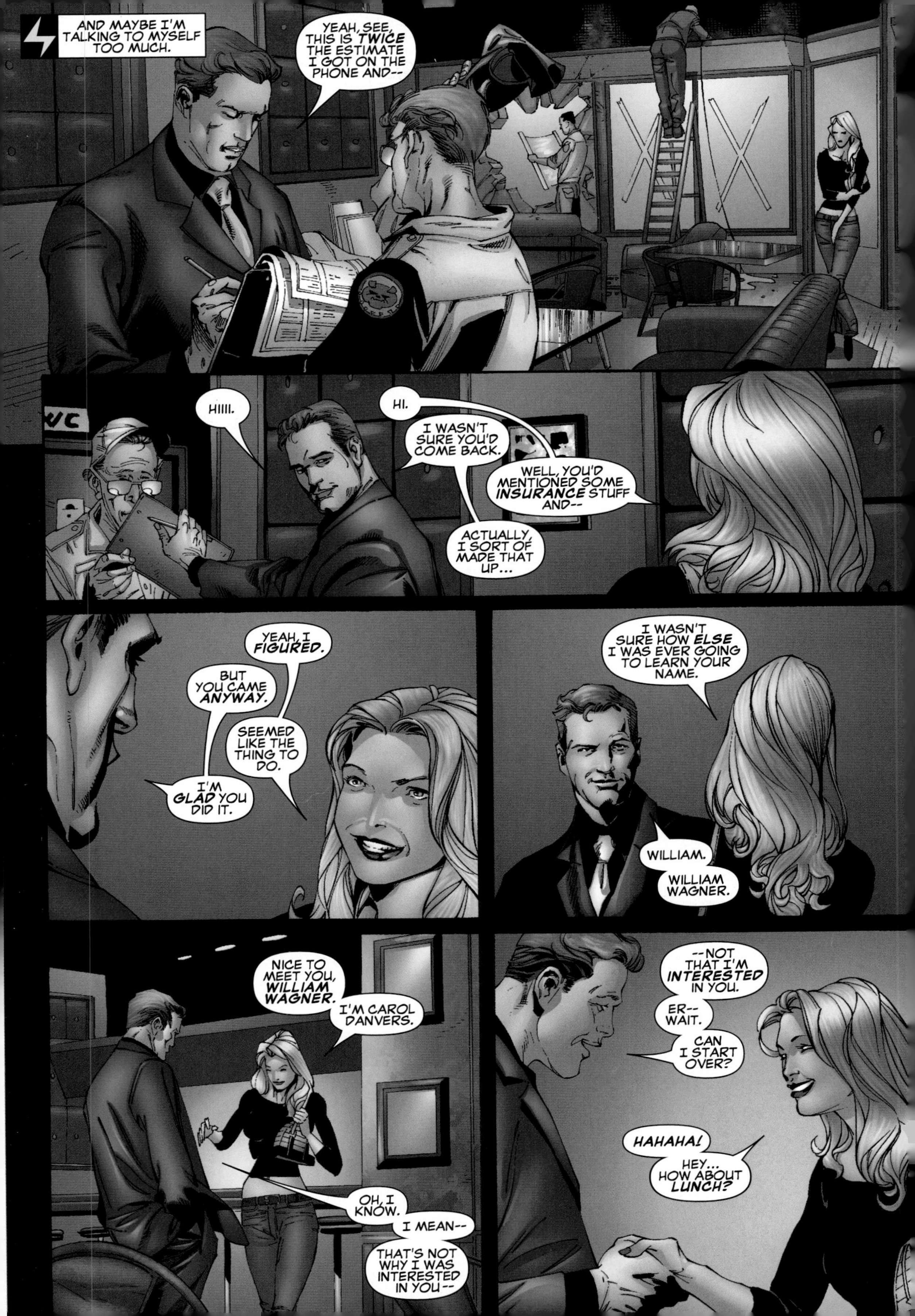
AND MAYBE I'M TALKING TO MYSELF TOO MUCH.
YEAH, SEE, THIS IS *TWICE* THE ESTIMATE I GOT ON THE PHONE AND--
HIIII.
HI.
I WASN'T SURE YOU'D COME BACK.
WELL, YOU'D MENTIONED SOME *INSURANCE* STUFF AND--
ACTUALLY, I SORT OF MADE THAT UP...
YEAH, I *FIGURED.*
BUT YOU CAME *ANYWAY.*
SEEMED LIKE THE THING TO DO.
I'M *GLAD* YOU DID IT.
I WASN'T SURE HOW *ELSE* I WAS EVER GOING TO LEARN YOUR NAME.
WILLIAM.
WILLIAM WAGNER.
NICE TO MEET YOU, *WILLIAM WAGNER.*
I'M CAROL DANVERS.
OH, I KNOW.
I MEAN--
THAT'S NOT WHY I WAS INTERESTED IN YOU--
--NOT THAT I'M *INTERESTED* IN YOU.
ER-- WAIT.
CAN I START OVER?
HAHAHA!
HEY... HOW ABOUT *LUNCH?*

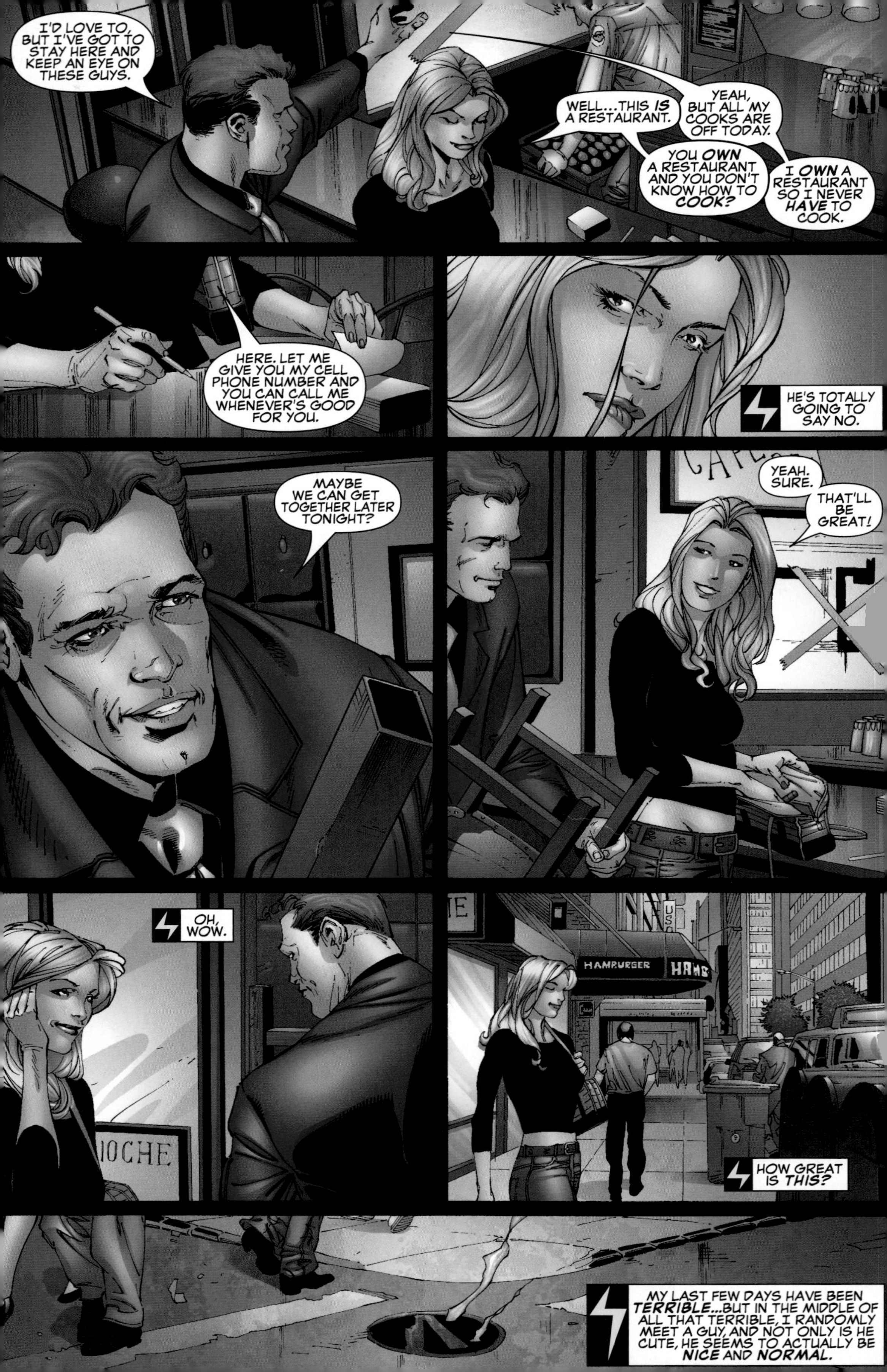
I'D LOVE TO, BUT I'VE GOT TO STAY HERE AND KEEP AN EYE ON THESE GUYS.
WELL...THIS IS A RESTAURANT.
YEAH, BUT ALL MY COOKS ARE OFF TODAY.
YOU OWN A RESTAURANT AND YOU DON'T KNOW HOW TO COOK?
I OWN A RESTAURANT SO I NEVER HAVE TO COOK.
HERE. LET ME GIVE YOU MY CELL PHONE NUMBER AND YOU CAN CALL ME WHENEVER'S GOOD FOR YOU.
HE'S TOTALLY GOING TO SAY NO.
MAYBE WE CAN GET TOGETHER LATER TONIGHT?
YEAH. SURE.
THAT'LL BE GREAT!
OH, WOW.
HAMBURGER
HOW GREAT IS THIS?
MY LAST FEW DAYS HAVE BEEN TERRIBLE...BUT IN THE MIDDLE OF ALL THAT TERRIBLE, I RANDOMLY MEET A GUY, AND NOT ONLY IS HE CUTE, HE SEEMS TO ACTUALLY BE NICE AND NORMAL.

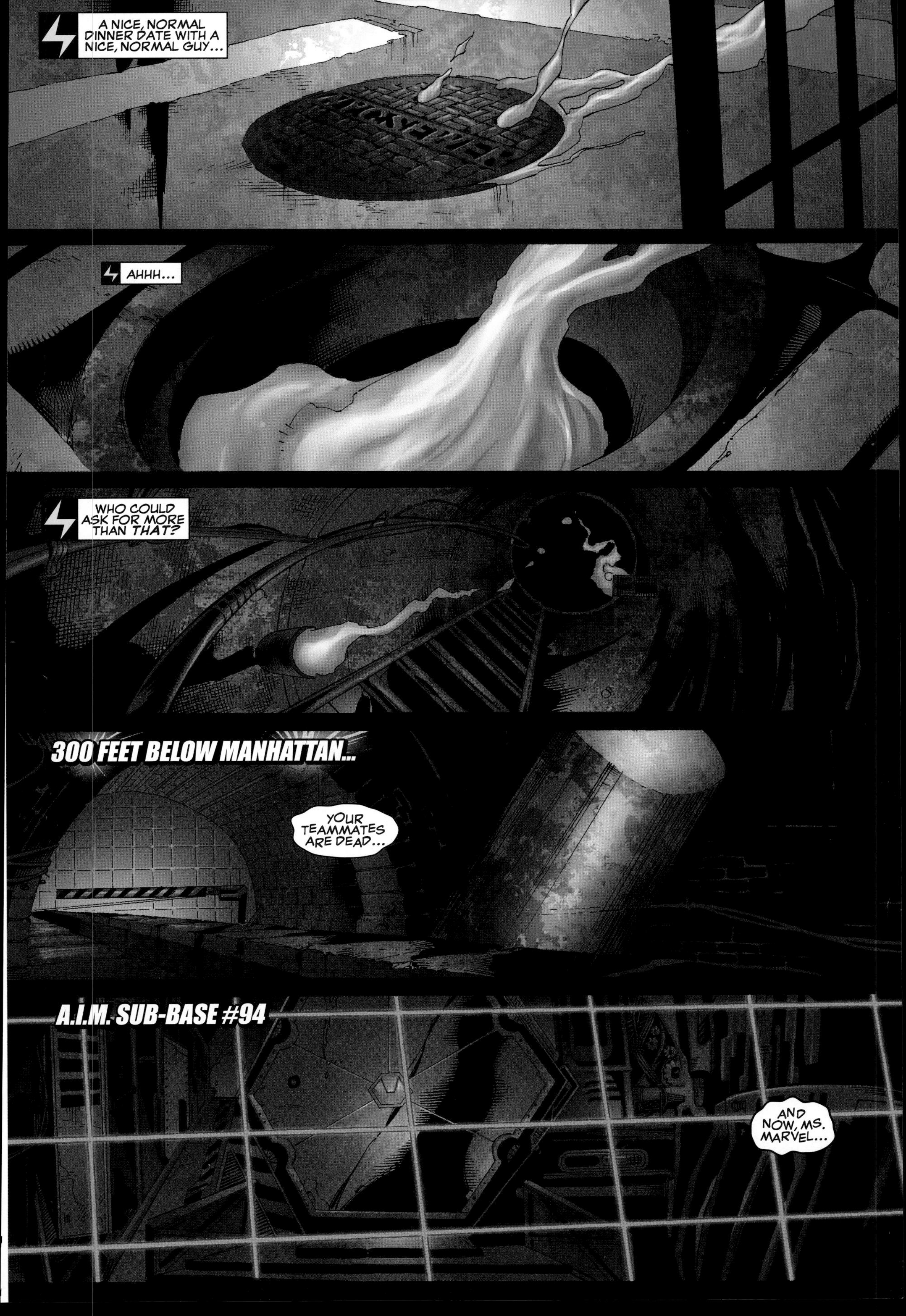
A NICE, NORMAL DINNER DATE WITH A NICE, NORMAL GUY...
AHHH...
WHO COULD ASK FOR MORE THAN THAT?
300 FEET BELOW MANHATTAN...
YOUR TEAMMATES ARE DEAD...
A.I.M. SUB-BASE #94
AND NOW, MS. MARVEL...

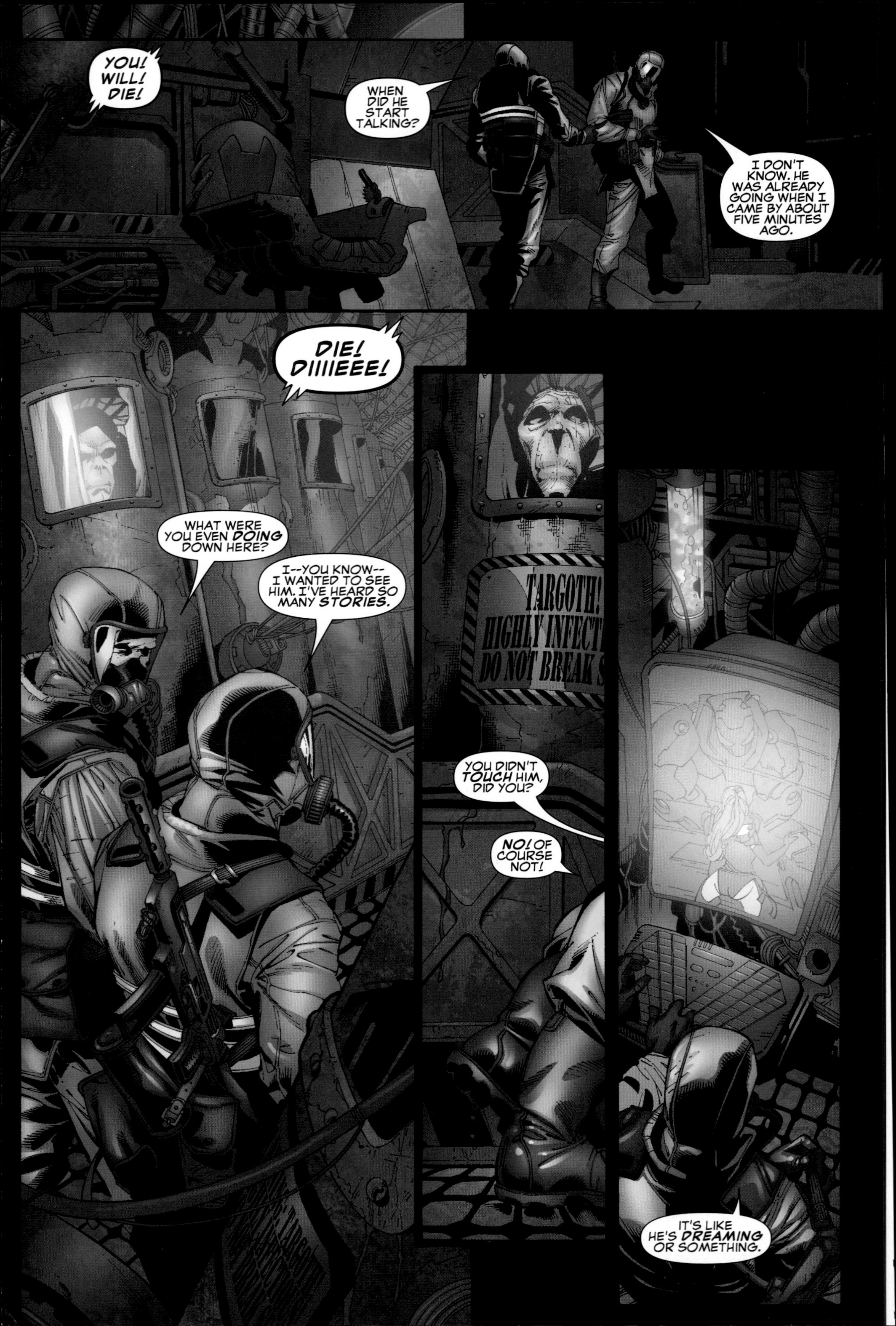
YOU! WILL! DIE!
WHEN DID HE START TALKING?
I DON'T KNOW. HE WAS ALREADY GOING WHEN I CAME BY ABOUT FIVE MINUTES AGO.
DIE! DIIIIEEE!
WHAT WERE YOU EVEN *DOING* DOWN HERE?
I--YOU KNOW-- I WANTED TO SEE HIM. I'VE HEARD SO MANY *STORIES*.
TARGOTH! HIGHLY INFECT DO NOT BREAK
YOU DIDN'T *TOUCH* HIM, DID YOU?
NO! OF COURSE NOT!
IT'S LIKE HE'S *DREAMING* OR SOMETHING.

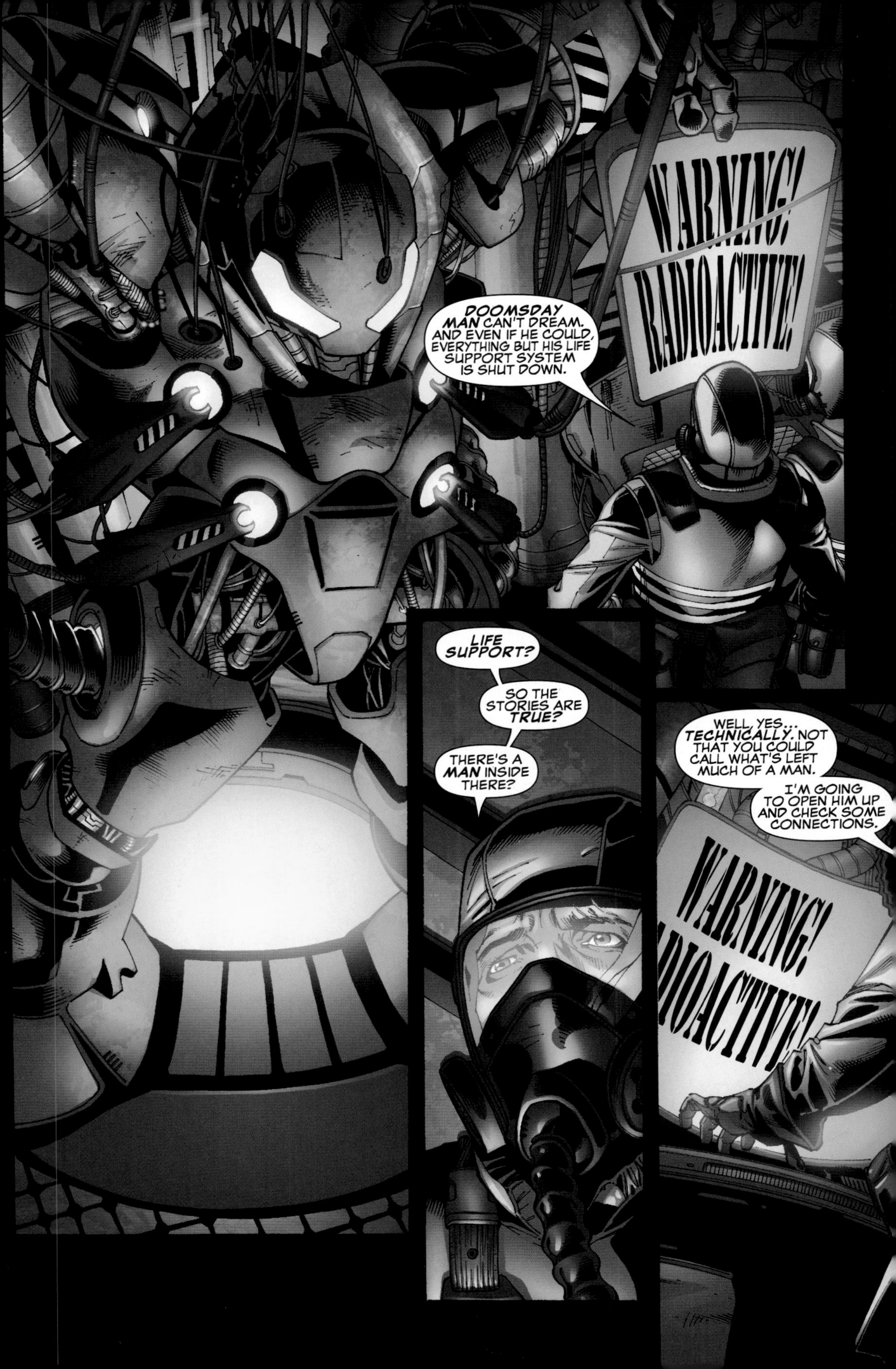
WARNING! RADIOACTIVE!
DOOMSDAY MAN CAN'T DREAM. AND EVEN IF HE COULD, EVERYTHING BUT HIS LIFE SUPPORT SYSTEM IS SHUT DOWN.
LIFE SUPPORT?
SO THE STORIES ARE TRUE?
THERE'S A MAN INSIDE THERE?
WELL, YES... TECHNICALLY. NOT THAT YOU COULD CALL WHAT'S LEFT MUCH OF A MAN.
I'M GOING TO OPEN HIM UP AND CHECK SOME CONNECTIONS.
WARNING! RADIOACTIVE!

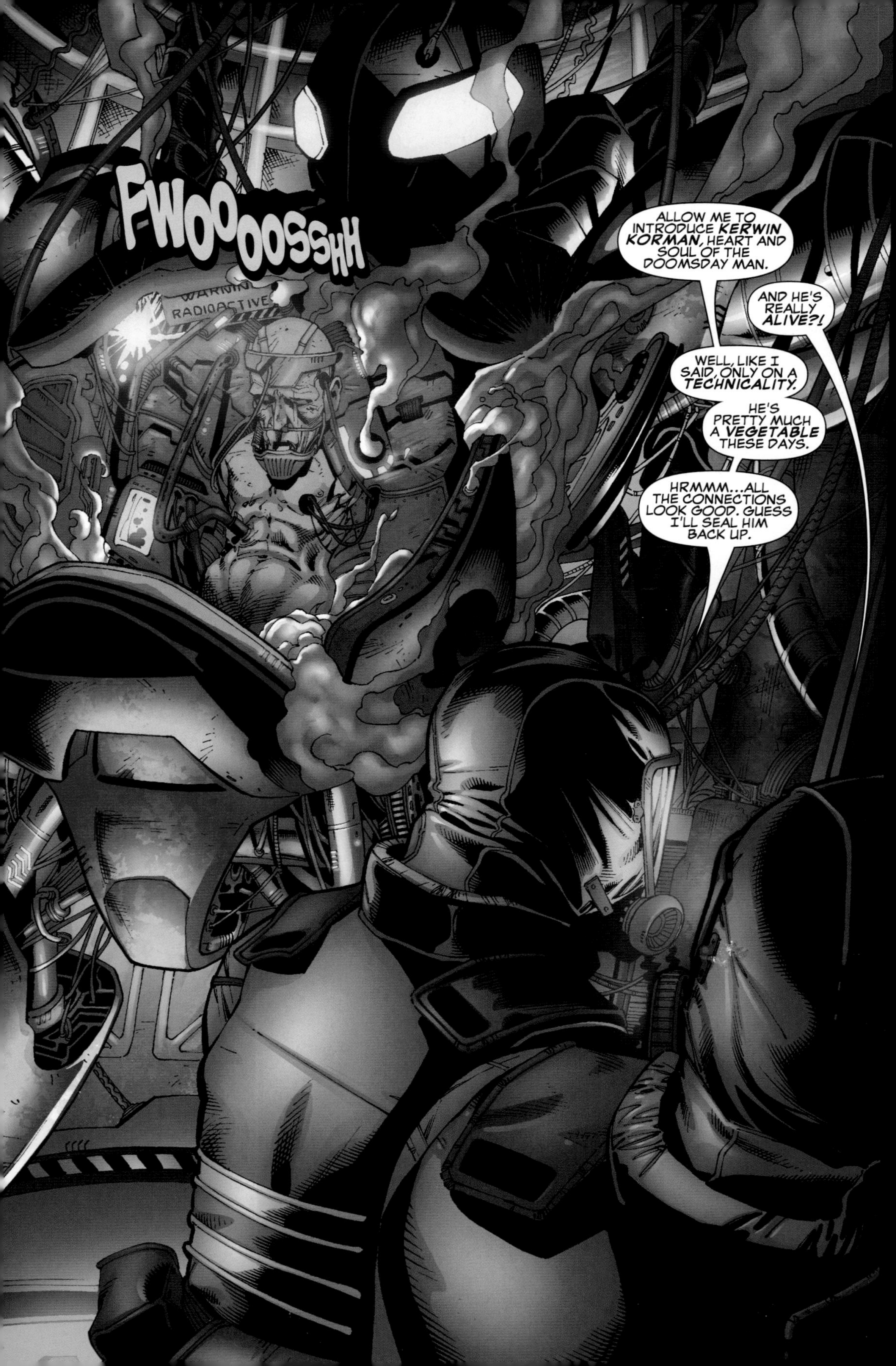
FWOOOOSSHH
WARNING RADIOACTIVE
ALLOW ME TO INTRODUCE KERWIN KORMAN, HEART AND SOUL OF THE DOOMSDAY MAN.
AND HE'S REALLY ALIVE?!
WELL, LIKE I SAID, ONLY ON A TECHNICALITY.
HE'S PRETTY MUCH A VEGETABLE THESE DAYS.
HRMMM...ALL THE CONNECTIONS LOOK GOOD. GUESS I'LL SEAL HIM BACK UP.

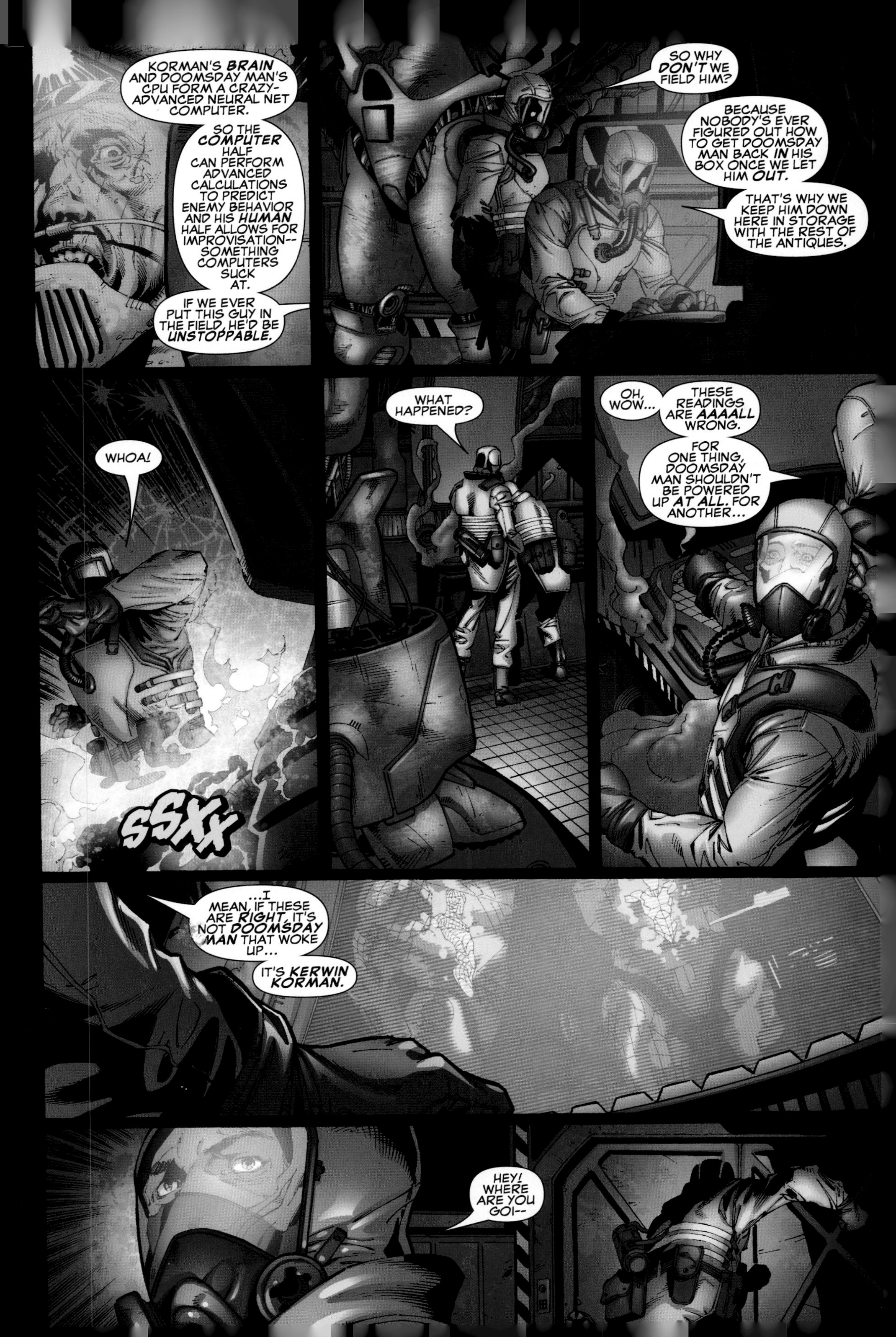
KORMAN'S **BRAIN** AND DOOMSDAY MAN'S CPU FORM A CRAZY-ADVANCED NEURAL NET COMPUTER.
SO THE **COMPUTER** HALF CAN PERFORM ADVANCED CALCULATIONS TO PREDICT ENEMY BEHAVIOR AND HIS **HUMAN** HALF ALLOWS FOR IMPROVISATION--SOMETHING COMPUTERS SUCK AT.
IF WE EVER PUT THIS GUY IN THE FIELD, HE'D BE **UNSTOPPABLE.**
SO WHY **DON'T** WE FIELD HIM?
BECAUSE NOBODY'S EVER FIGURED OUT HOW TO GET DOOMSDAY MAN BACK **IN** HIS BOX ONCE WE LET HIM **OUT.**
THAT'S WHY WE KEEP HIM DOWN HERE IN STORAGE WITH THE REST OF THE ANTIQUES.
WHOA!
SSXX
WHAT HAPPENED?
OH, WOW...
THESE READINGS ARE **AAAALL** WRONG.
FOR ONE THING, DOOMSDAY MAN SHOULDN'T BE POWERED UP **AT ALL.** FOR ANOTHER...
...I MEAN, IF THESE ARE **RIGHT,** IT'S NOT **DOOMSDAY MAN** THAT WOKE UP...
IT'S **KERWIN KORMAN.**
HEY! WHERE ARE YOU GOI--

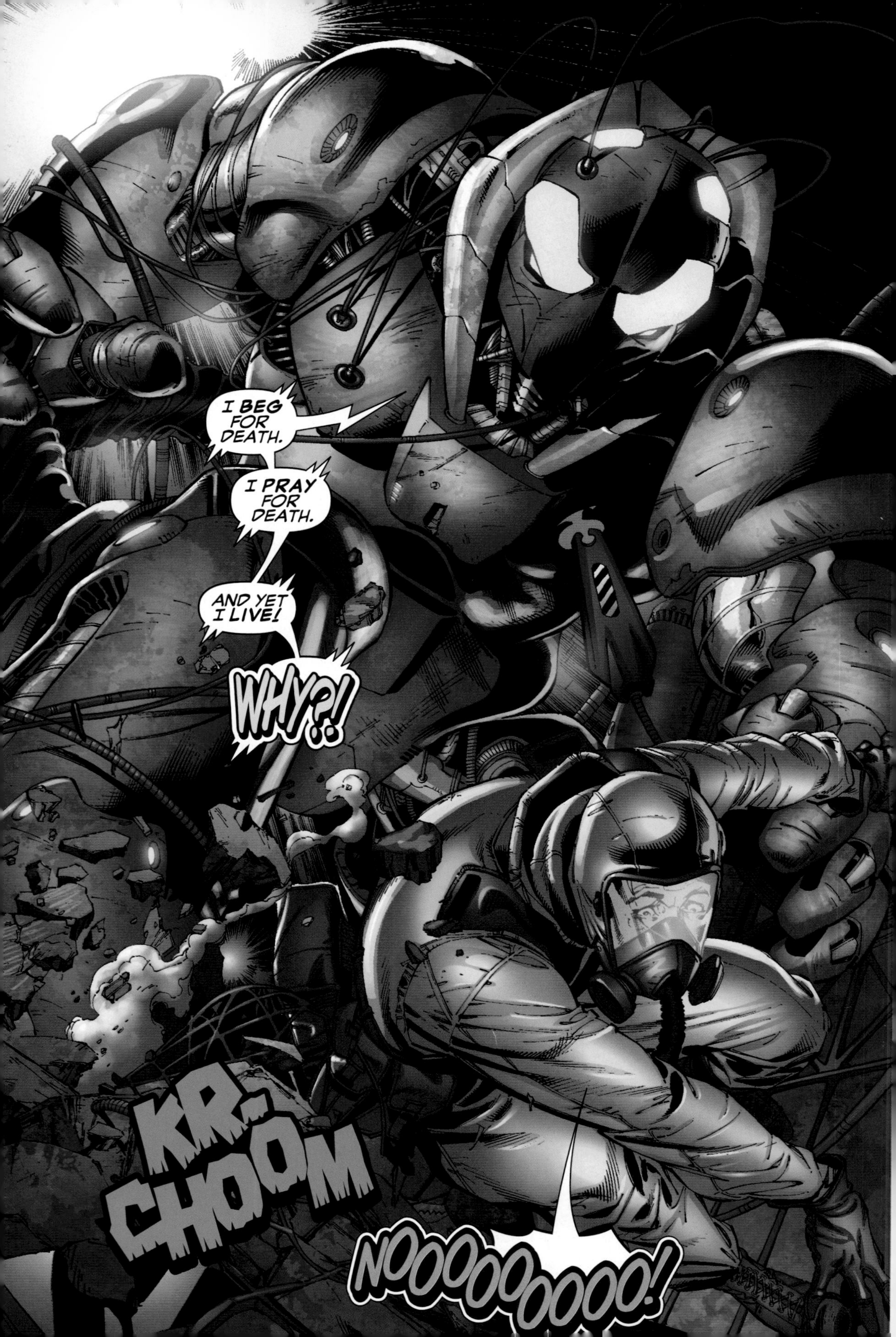
I BEG FOR DEATH.
I PRAY FOR DEATH.
AND YET I LIVE!
WHY?!
KR-CHOOM
NOOOOOOOOO!

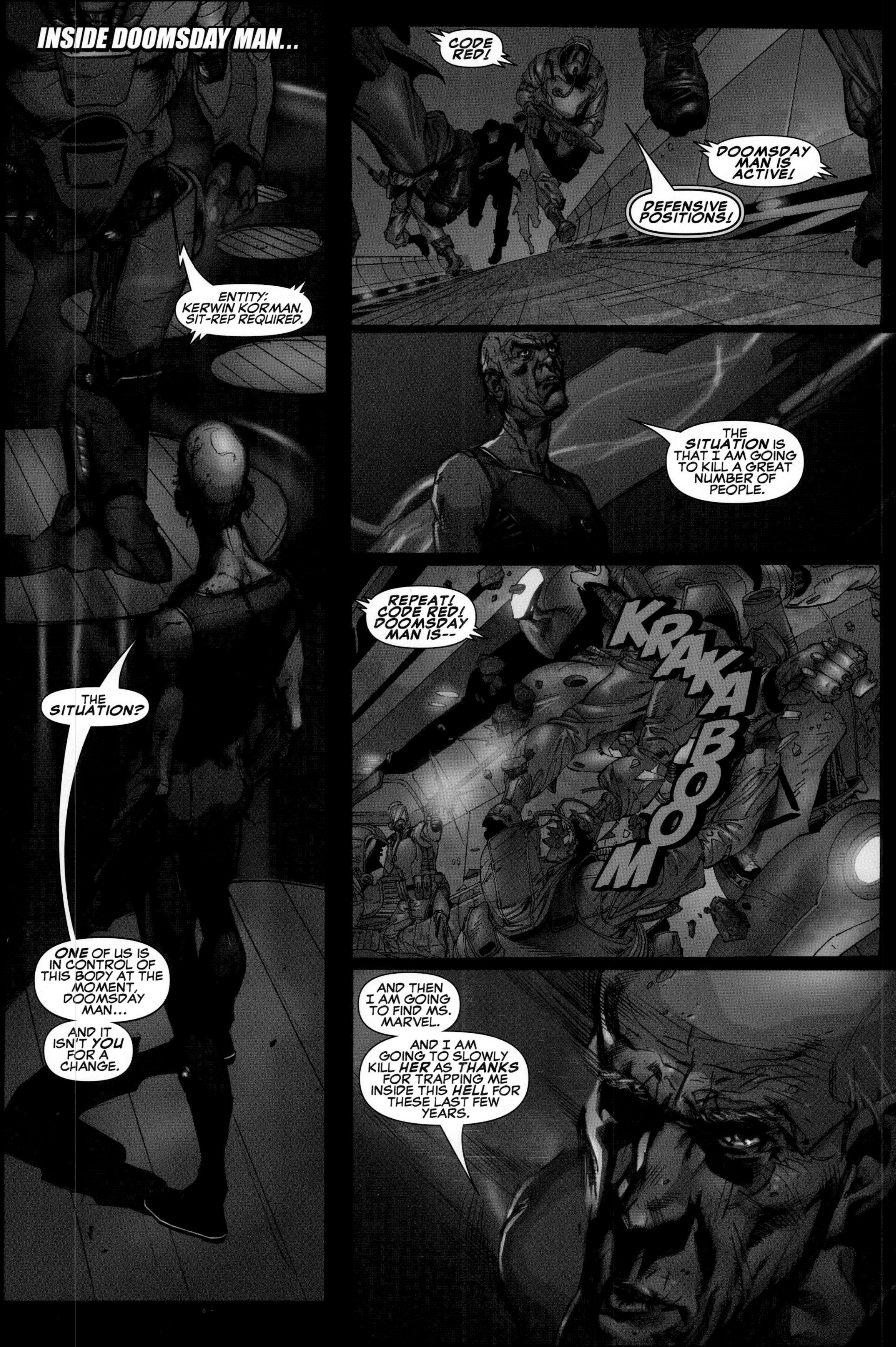
INSIDE DOOMSDAY MAN...
ENTITY: KERWIN KORMAN. SIT-REP REQUIRED.
THE SITUATION?
ONE OF US IS IN CONTROL OF THIS BODY AT THE MOMENT, DOOMSDAY MAN...
AND IT ISN'T YOU FOR A CHANGE.
CODE RED!
DOOMSDAY MAN IS ACTIVE!
DEFENSIVE POSITIONS!
THE SITUATION IS THAT I AM GOING TO KILL A GREAT NUMBER OF PEOPLE.
REPEAT! CODE RED! DOOMSDAY MAN IS--
KRAKABOOOM
AND THEN I AM GOING TO FIND MS. MARVEL.
AND I AM GOING TO SLOWLY KILL HER AS THANKS FOR TRAPPING ME INSIDE THIS HELL FOR THESE LAST FEW YEARS.

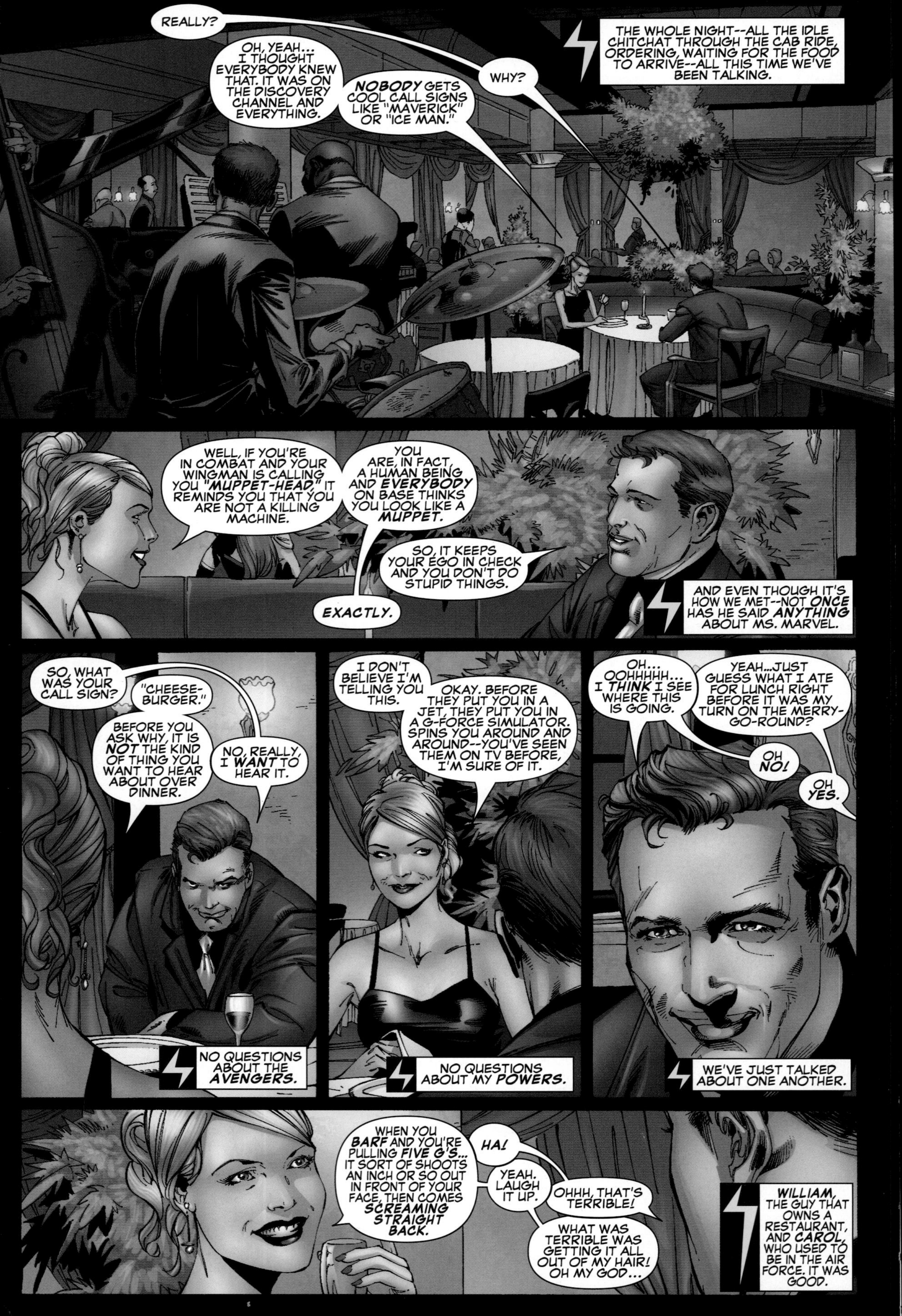
REALLY?
OH, YEAH... I THOUGHT EVERYBODY KNEW THAT. IT WAS ON THE DISCOVERY CHANNEL AND EVERYTHING.
WHY?
NOBODY GETS COOL CALL SIGNS LIKE "MAVERICK" OR "ICE MAN."
THE WHOLE NIGHT--ALL THE IDLE CHITCHAT THROUGH THE CAB RIDE, ORDERING, WAITING FOR THE FOOD TO ARRIVE--ALL THIS TIME WE'VE BEEN TALKING.
WELL, IF YOU'RE IN COMBAT AND YOUR WINGMAN IS CALLING YOU "MUPPET-HEAD," IT REMINDS YOU THAT YOU ARE NOT A KILLING MACHINE.
YOU ARE, IN FACT, A HUMAN BEING AND EVERYBODY ON BASE THINKS YOU LOOK LIKE A MUPPET.
SO, IT KEEPS YOUR EGO IN CHECK AND YOU DON'T DO STUPID THINGS.
EXACTLY.
AND EVEN THOUGH IT'S HOW WE MET--NOT ONCE HAS HE SAID ANYTHING ABOUT MS. MARVEL.
SO, WHAT WAS YOUR CALL SIGN?
"CHEESE-BURGER."
BEFORE YOU ASK WHY, IT IS NOT THE KIND OF THING YOU WANT TO HEAR ABOUT OVER DINNER.
NO, REALLY, I WANT TO HEAR IT.
NO QUESTIONS ABOUT THE AVENGERS.
I DON'T BELIEVE I'M TELLING YOU THIS.
OKAY. BEFORE THEY PUT YOU IN A JET, THEY PUT YOU IN A G-FORCE SIMULATOR. SPINS YOU AROUND AND AROUND--YOU'VE SEEN THEM ON TV BEFORE, I'M SURE OF IT.
NO QUESTIONS ABOUT MY POWERS.
OH... OOHHHHH... I THINK I SEE WHERE THIS IS GOING.
YEAH...JUST GUESS WHAT I ATE FOR LUNCH RIGHT BEFORE IT WAS MY TURN ON THE MERRY-GO-ROUND?
OH NO!
OH YES.
WE'VE JUST TALKED ABOUT ONE ANOTHER.
WHEN YOU BARF AND YOU'RE PULLING FIVE G'S... IT SORT OF SHOOTS AN INCH OR SO OUT IN FRONT OF YOUR FACE, THEN COMES SCREAMING STRAIGHT BACK.
HA!
YEAH. LAUGH IT UP.
OHHH, THAT'S TERRIBLE!
WHAT WAS TERRIBLE WAS GETTING IT ALL OUT OF MY HAIR! OH MY GOD...
WILLIAM, THE GUY THAT OWNS A RESTAURANT, AND CAROL, WHO USED TO BE IN THE AIR FORCE. IT WAS GOOD.

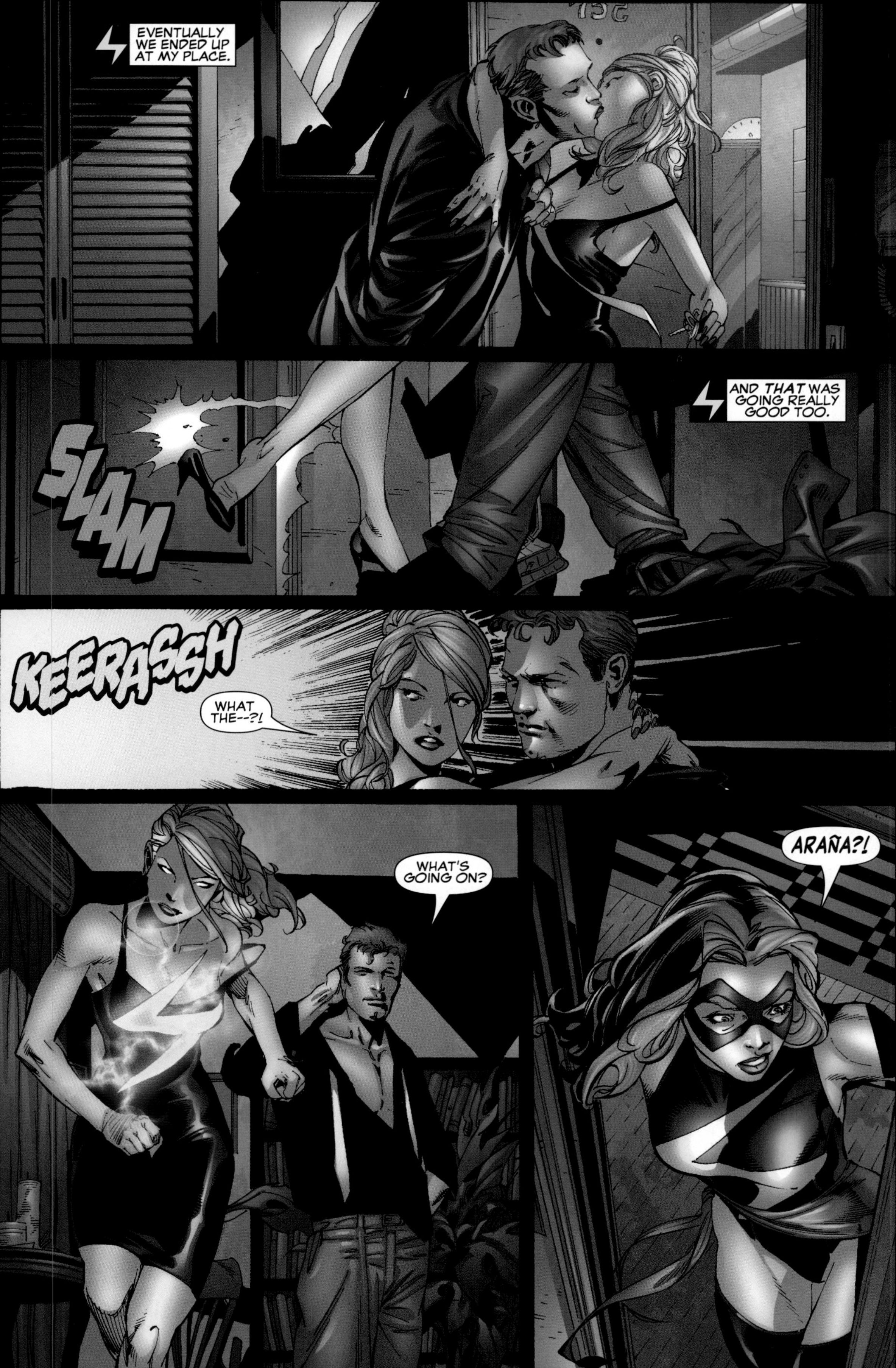
EVENTUALLY WE ENDED UP AT MY PLACE.
SLAM
AND THAT WAS GOING REALLY GOOD TOO.
KEERASSH
WHAT THE--?!
WHAT'S GOING ON?
ARAÑA?!

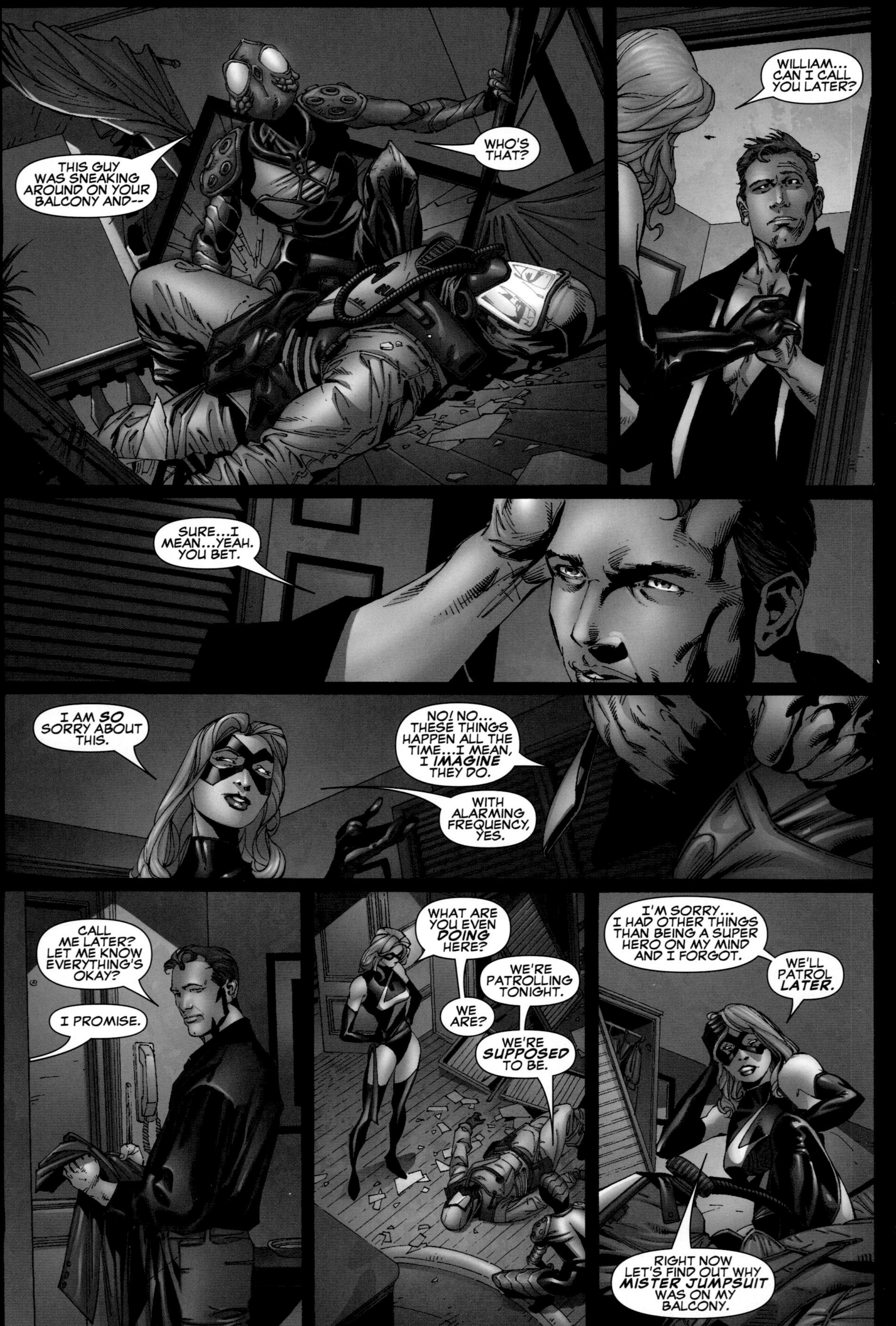
THIS GUY WAS SNEAKING AROUND ON YOUR BALCONY AND--
WHO'S THAT?
WILLIAM... CAN I CALL YOU LATER?
SURE...I MEAN...YEAH. YOU BET.
I AM **SO** SORRY ABOUT THIS.
NO! NO... THESE THINGS HAPPEN ALL THE TIME...I MEAN, I ***IMAGINE*** THEY DO.
WITH ALARMING FREQUENCY, YES.
CALL ME LATER? LET ME KNOW EVERYTHING'S OKAY?
I PROMISE.
WHAT ARE YOU EVEN ***DOING*** HERE?
WE'RE PATROLLING TONIGHT.
WE ARE?
WE'RE ***SUPPOSED*** TO BE.
I'M SORRY... I HAD OTHER THINGS THAN BEING A SUPER HERO ON MY MIND AND I FORGOT.
WE'LL PATROL ***LATER.***
RIGHT NOW LET'S FIND OUT WHY ***MISTER JUMPSUIT*** WAS ON MY BALCONY.

DO YOU KNOW THIS GUY?

I KNOW HIS *TYPE.* HE'S A MEMBER OF *A.I.M.*--ADVANCED *IDEA MECHANICS.* THEY'RE A GROUP OF MAD-SCIENTIST TERRORISTS.

EVIL GEEKS WITH NO FASHION SENSE. GOTCHA.

POKE YOUR HEAD IN THERE AND TAKE A LOOK.

SMELLS LIKE *NERD* SWEAT.

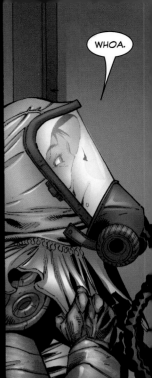

WHOA.

THIS IS COOL!

THE SCREEN IN HERE KNOWS YOUR NAME.

MS. MARVEL--AKA CAROL DANVERS-- POWERS: FLIGHT, PHOTON BEAMS, STRENGTH-- FORMER AVENGER-- ADDRESS: 417 5TH AVE. APT. 108 NEW YORK, NY 10016 Q SCORE: 6

SEAN MADIGAN-- A.I.M. TECHNICIAN 4591

I'M GONNA GET THIS GUY'S UNIFORM OFF AND SEE IF HE HAS ANY WEAPONS--

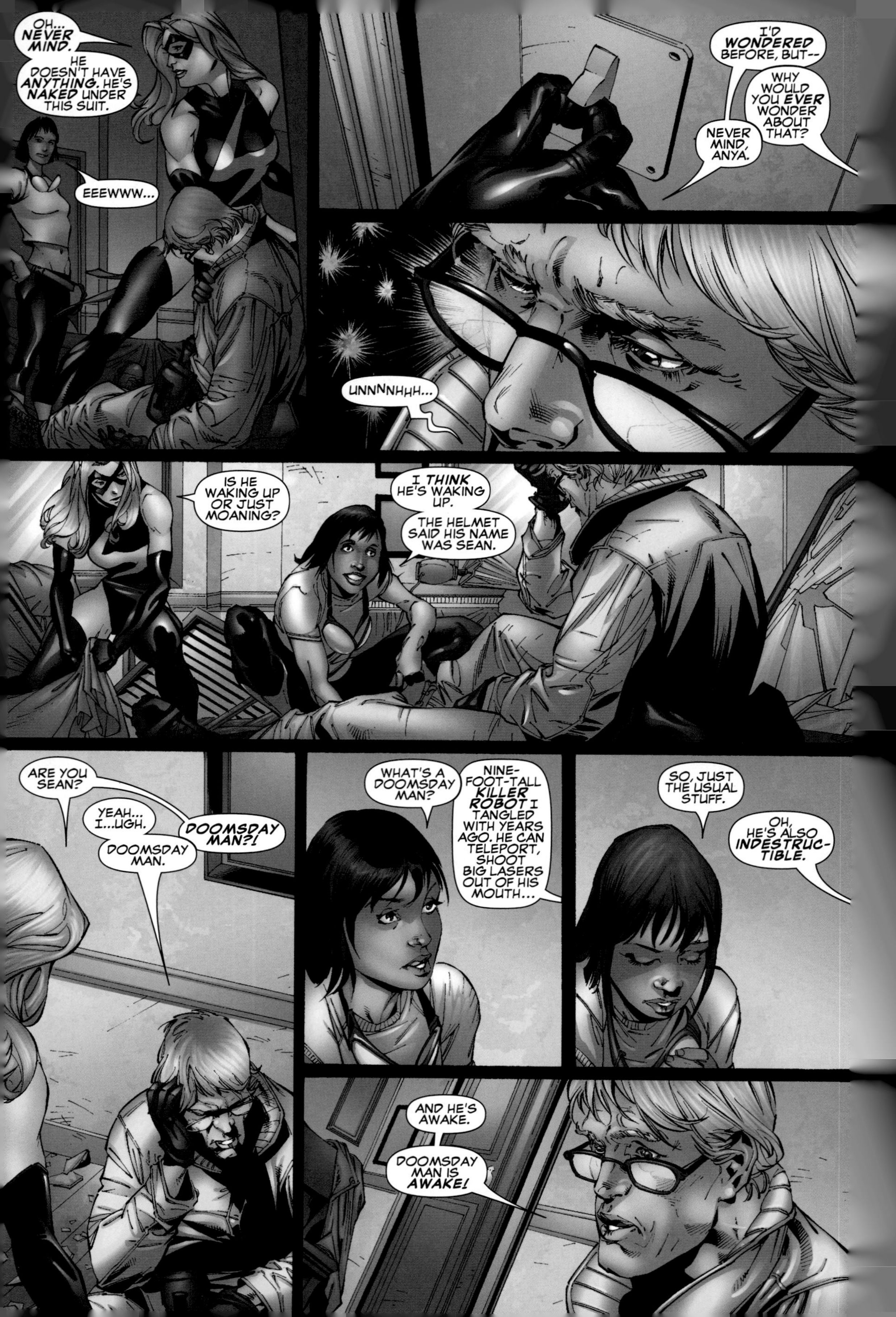
OH... NEVER MIND.
HE DOESN'T HAVE ANYTHING. HE'S NAKED UNDER THIS SUIT.
EEEWWW...
I'D WONDERED BEFORE, BUT--
WHY WOULD YOU EVER WONDER ABOUT THAT?
NEVER MIND, ANYA.
UNNNNHHH...
IS HE WAKING UP OR JUST MOANING?
I THINK HE'S WAKING UP.
THE HELMET SAID HIS NAME WAS SEAN.
ARE YOU SEAN?
YEAH... I...UGH.
DOOMSDAY MAN.
DOOMSDAY MAN?!
WHAT'S A DOOMSDAY MAN?
NINE-FOOT-TALL KILLER ROBOT I TANGLED WITH YEARS AGO. HE CAN TELEPORT, SHOOT BIG LASERS OUT OF HIS MOUTH...
SO, JUST THE USUAL STUFF.
OH, HE'S ALSO INDESTRUC-TIBLE.
AND HE'S AWAKE.
DOOMSDAY MAN IS AWAKE!

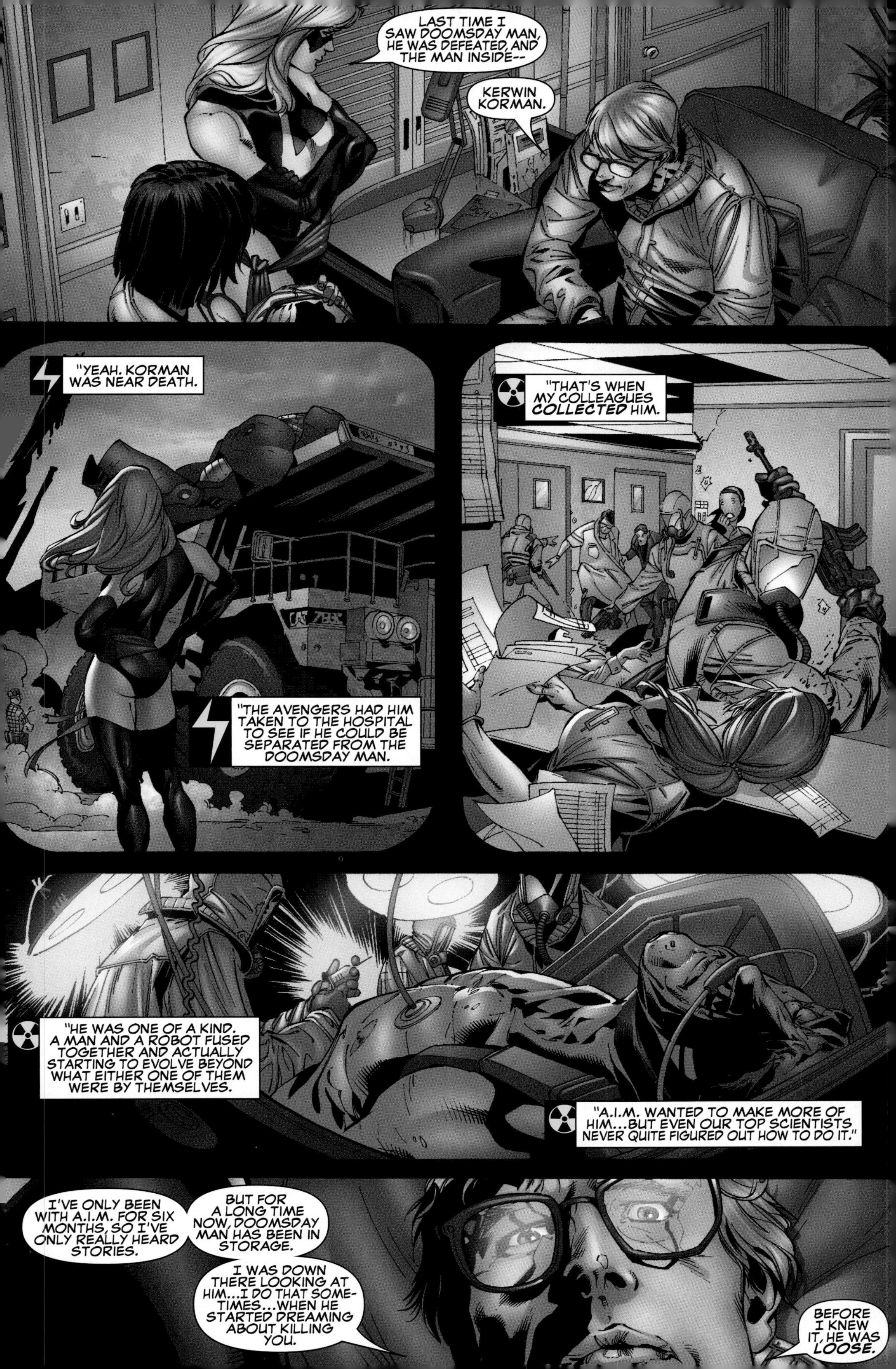

LAST TIME I SAW DOOMSDAY MAN, HE WAS DEFEATED, AND THE MAN INSIDE--
KERWIN KORMAN.
"YEAH. KORMAN WAS NEAR DEATH.
"THE AVENGERS HAD HIM TAKEN TO THE HOSPITAL TO SEE IF HE COULD BE SEPARATED FROM THE DOOMSDAY MAN.
"THAT'S WHEN MY COLLEAGUES COLLECTED HIM.
"HE WAS ONE OF A KIND. A MAN AND A ROBOT FUSED TOGETHER AND ACTUALLY STARTING TO EVOLVE BEYOND WHAT EITHER ONE OF THEM WERE BY THEMSELVES.
"A.I.M. WANTED TO MAKE MORE OF HIM...BUT EVEN OUR TOP SCIENTISTS NEVER QUITE FIGURED OUT HOW TO DO IT."
I'VE ONLY BEEN WITH A.I.M. FOR SIX MONTHS, SO I'VE ONLY REALLY HEARD STORIES.
BUT FOR A LONG TIME NOW, DOOMSDAY MAN HAS BEEN IN STORAGE.
I WAS DOWN THERE LOOKING AT HIM...I DO THAT SOME-TIMES...WHEN HE STARTED DREAMING ABOUT KILLING YOU.
BEFORE I KNEW IT, HE WAS LOOSE.

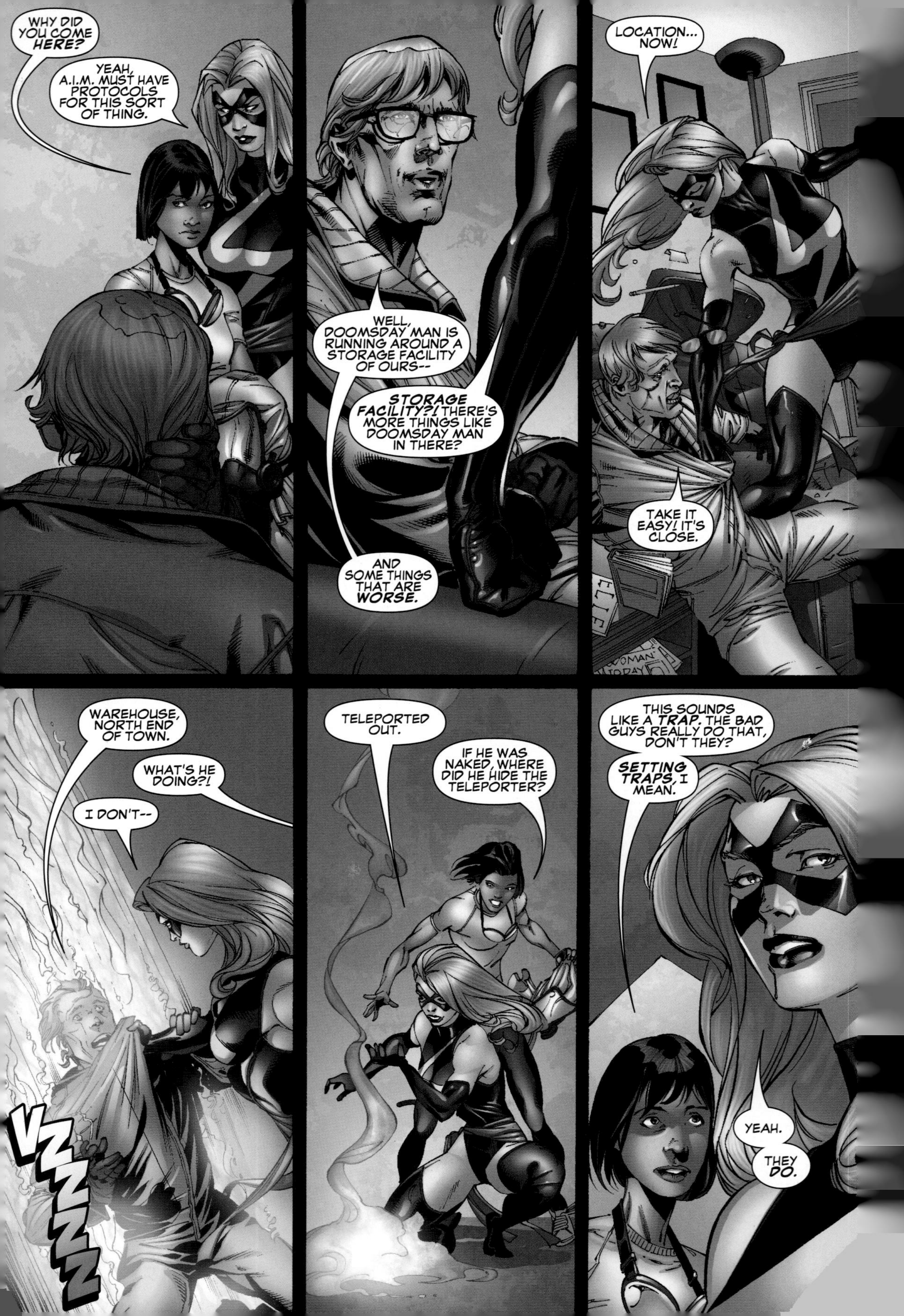
WHY DID YOU COME HERE?
YEAH, A.I.M. MUST HAVE PROTOCOLS FOR THIS SORT OF THING.
WELL, DOOMSDAY MAN IS RUNNING AROUND A STORAGE FACILITY OF OURS--
STORAGE FACILITY?! THERE'S MORE THINGS LIKE DOOMSDAY MAN IN THERE?
AND SOME THINGS THAT ARE WORSE.
LOCATION... NOW!
TAKE IT EASY! IT'S CLOSE.
WAREHOUSE, NORTH END OF TOWN.
WHAT'S HE DOING?!
I DON'T--
VZZZZZ
TELEPORTED OUT.
IF HE WAS NAKED, WHERE DID HE HIDE THE TELEPORTER?
THIS SOUNDS LIKE A TRAP. THE BAD GUYS REALLY DO THAT, DON'T THEY?
SETTING TRAPS, I MEAN.
YEAH.
THEY DO.

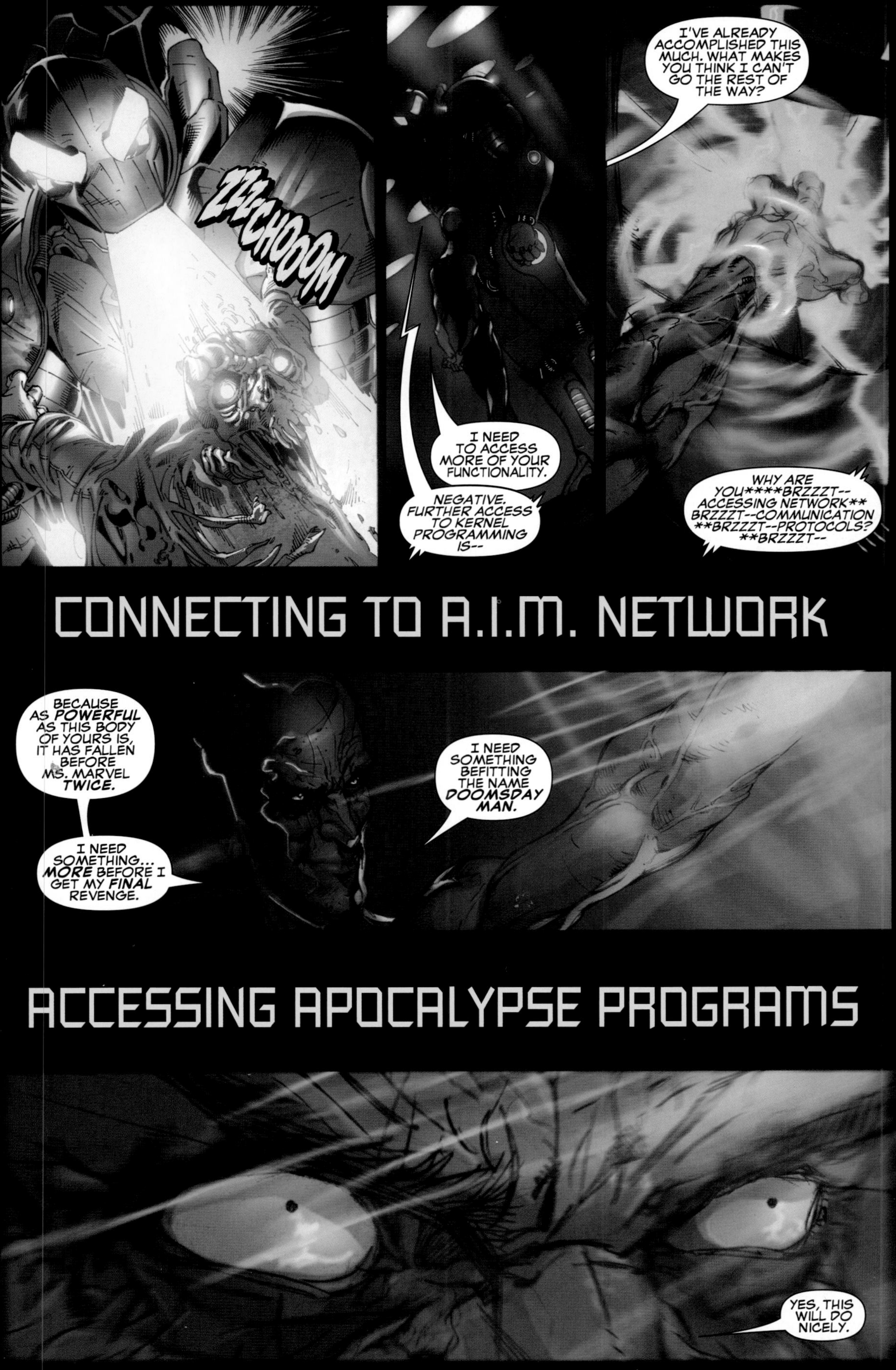
ZZZCHOOOM
I'VE ALREADY ACCOMPLISHED THIS MUCH. WHAT MAKES YOU THINK I CAN'T GO THE REST OF THE WAY?
I NEED TO ACCESS MORE OF YOUR FUNCTIONALITY.
NEGATIVE. FURTHER ACCESS TO KERNEL PROGRAMMING IS--
WHY ARE YOU****BRZZZT--ACCESSING NETWORK**BRZZZT--COMMUNICATION**BRZZZT--PROTOCOLS?**BRZZZT--
CONNECTING TO A.I.M. NETWORK
BECAUSE AS POWERFUL AS THIS BODY OF YOURS IS, IT HAS FALLEN BEFORE MS. MARVEL TWICE.
I NEED SOMETHING... MORE BEFORE I GET MY FINAL REVENGE.
I NEED SOMETHING BEFITTING THE NAME DOOMSDAY MAN.
ACCESSING APOCALYPSE PROGRAMS
YES, THIS WILL DO NICELY.

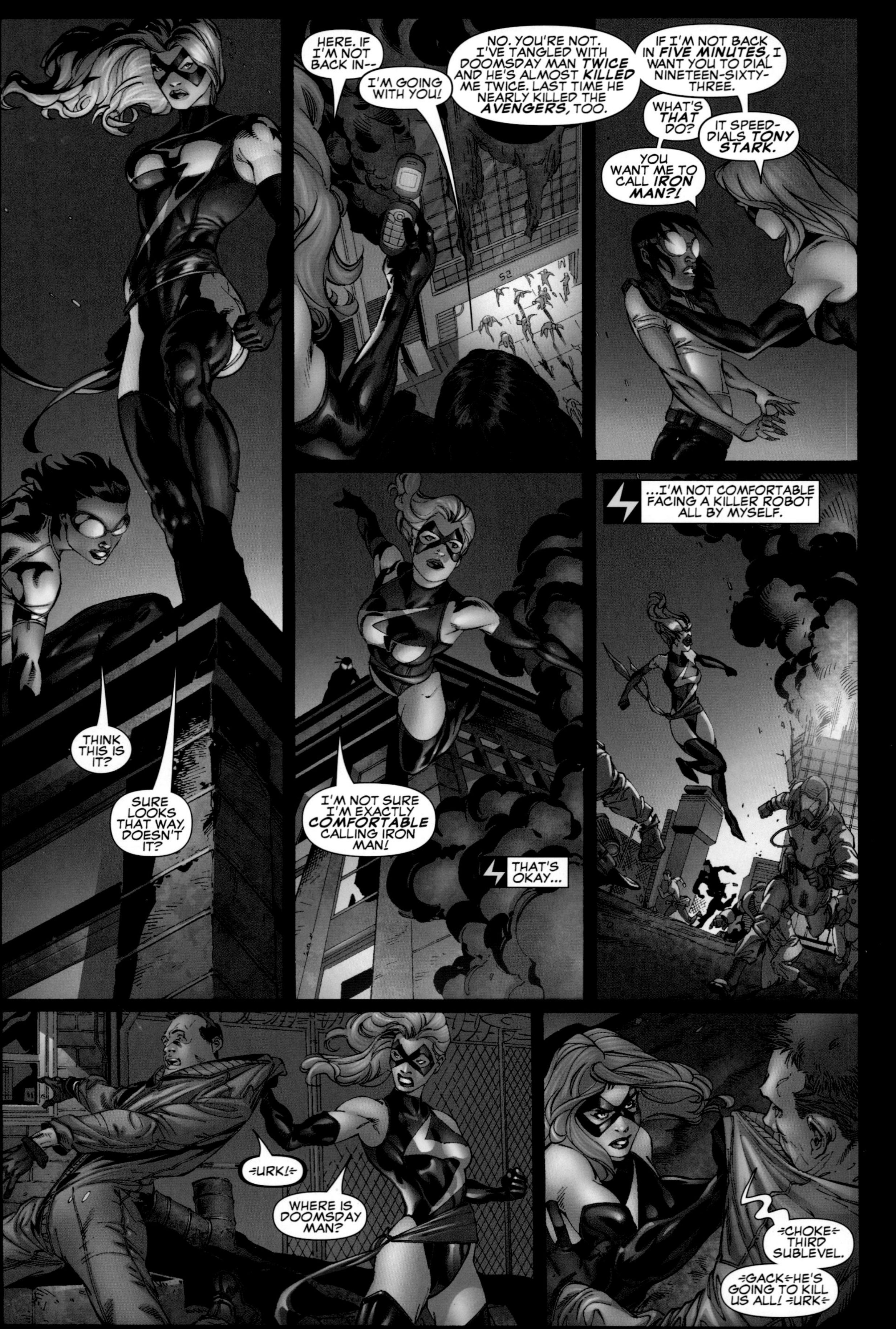
THINK THIS IS IT?
SURE LOOKS THAT WAY, DOESN'T IT?
HERE. IF I'M NOT BACK IN--
I'M GOING WITH YOU!
NO. YOU'RE NOT. I'VE TANGLED WITH DOOMSDAY MAN TWICE AND HE'S ALMOST KILLED ME TWICE. LAST TIME HE NEARLY KILLED THE AVENGERS, TOO.
25
IF I'M NOT BACK IN FIVE MINUTES, I WANT YOU TO DIAL NINETEEN-SIXTY-THREE.
WHAT'S THAT DO?
IT SPEED-DIALS TONY STARK.
YOU WANT ME TO CALL IRON MAN?!
I'M NOT SURE I'M EXACTLY COMFORTABLE CALLING IRON MAN!
THAT'S OKAY...
...I'M NOT COMFORTABLE FACING A KILLER ROBOT ALL BY MYSELF.
=URK!=
WHERE IS DOOMSDAY MAN?
=CHOKE= THIRD SUBLEVEL.
=GACK= HE'S GOING TO KILL US ALL! =URK=

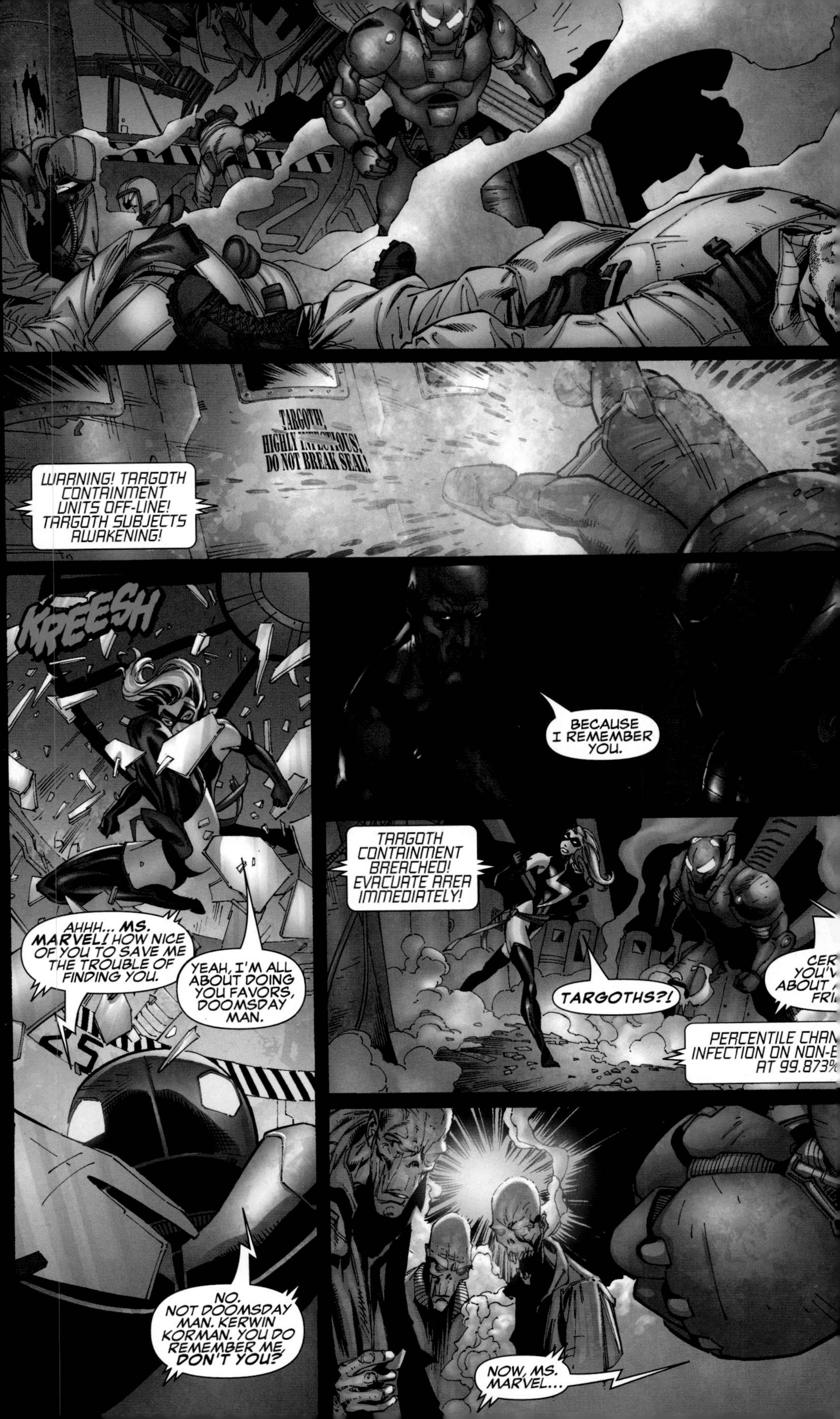
TARGOTH! HIGHLY INFECTIOUS! DO NOT BREAK SEAL!
WARNING! TARGOTH CONTAINMENT UNITS OFF-LINE! TARGOTH SUBJECTS AWAKENING!
KREESH
AHHH... MS. MARVEL! HOW NICE OF YOU TO SAVE ME THE TROUBLE OF FINDING YOU.
YEAH, I'M ALL ABOUT DOING YOU FAVORS, DOOMSDAY MAN.
NO. NOT DOOMSDAY MAN. KERWIN KORMAN. YOU DO REMEMBER ME, DON'T YOU?
BECAUSE I REMEMBER YOU.
TARGOTH CONTAINMENT BREACHED! EVACUATE AREA IMMEDIATELY!
TARGOTHS?!
NOW, MS. MARVEL...

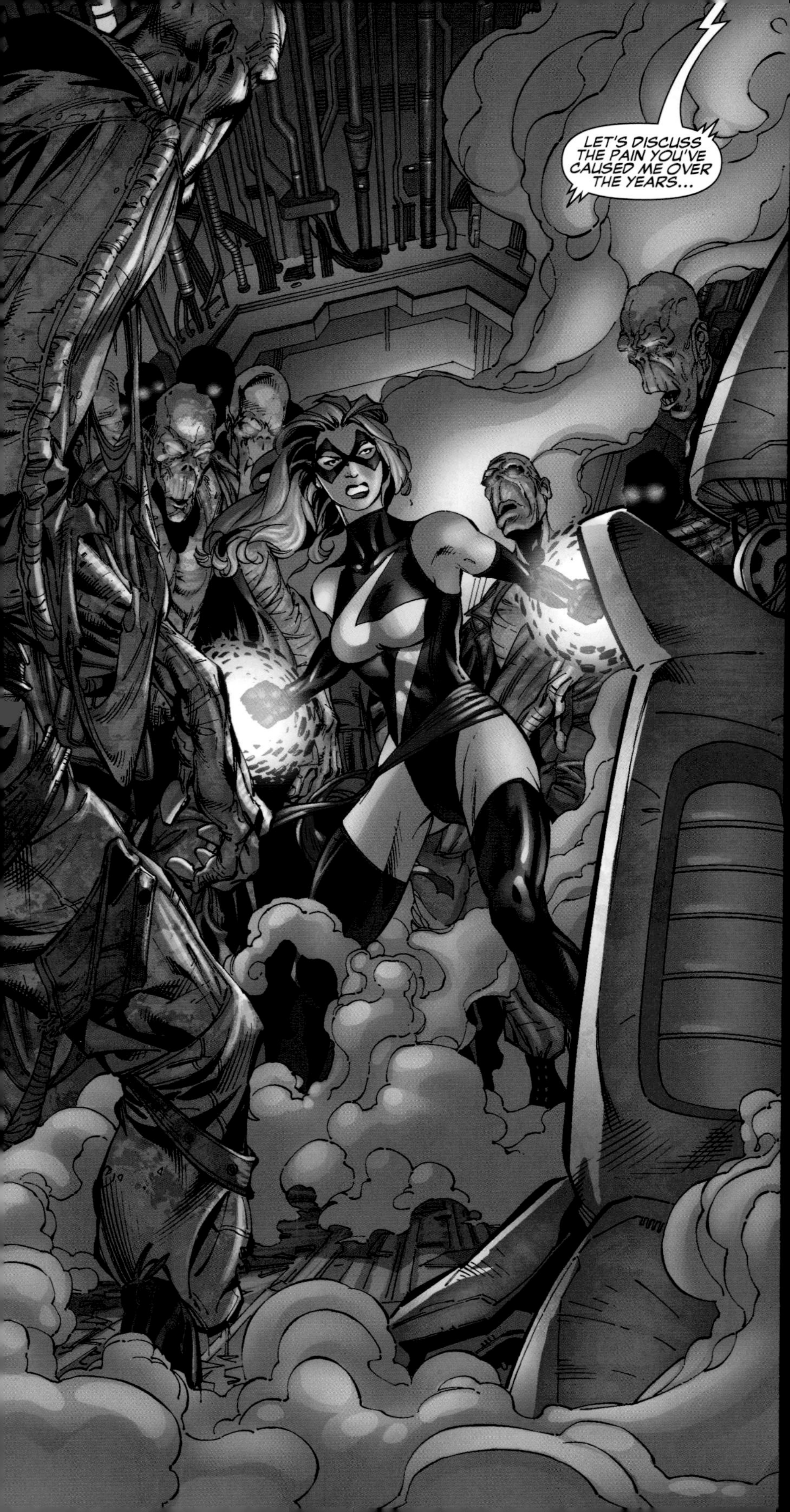
LET'S DISCUSS THE PAIN YOU'VE CAUSED ME OVER THE YEARS...

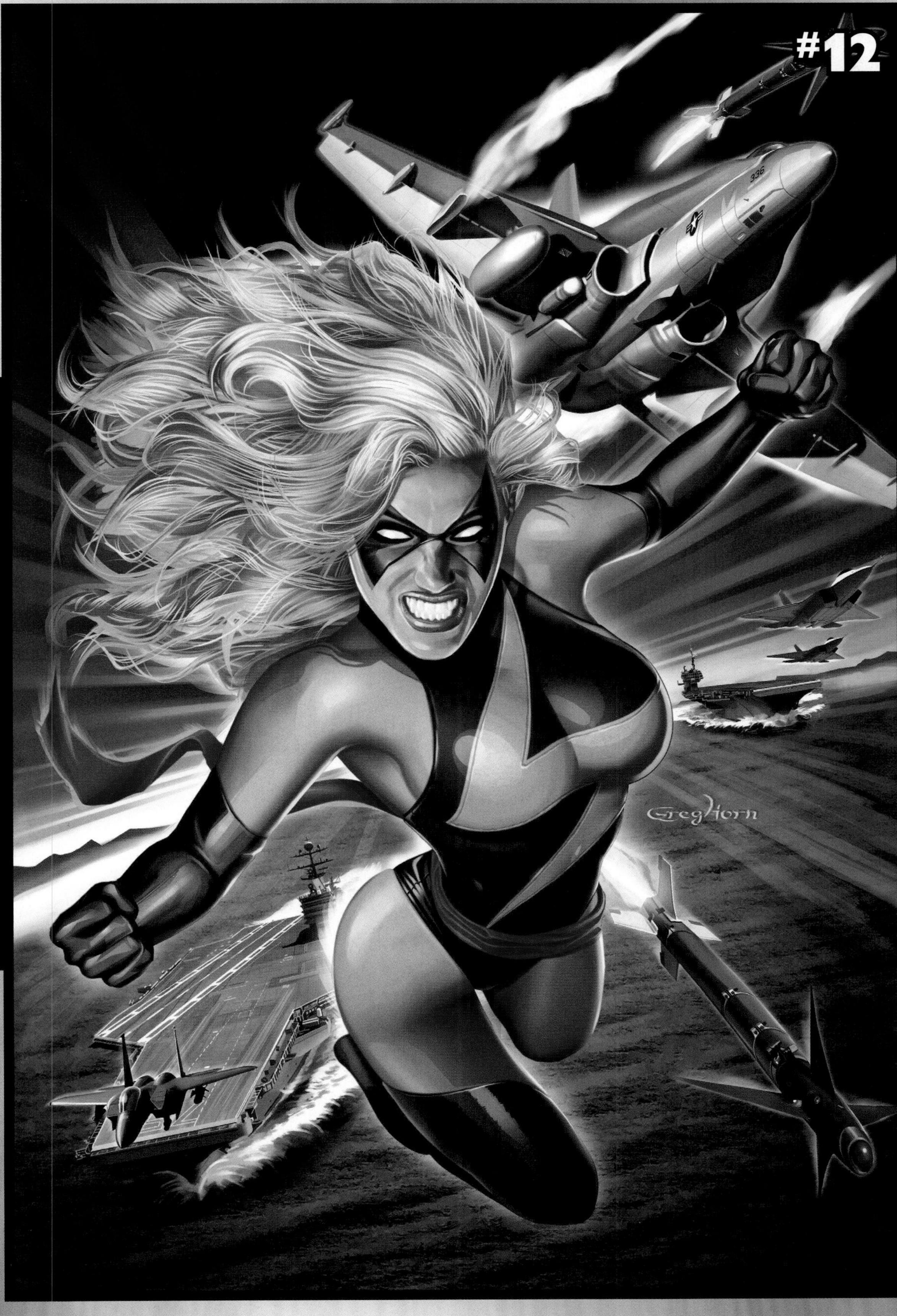
#12
336
Greg Horn

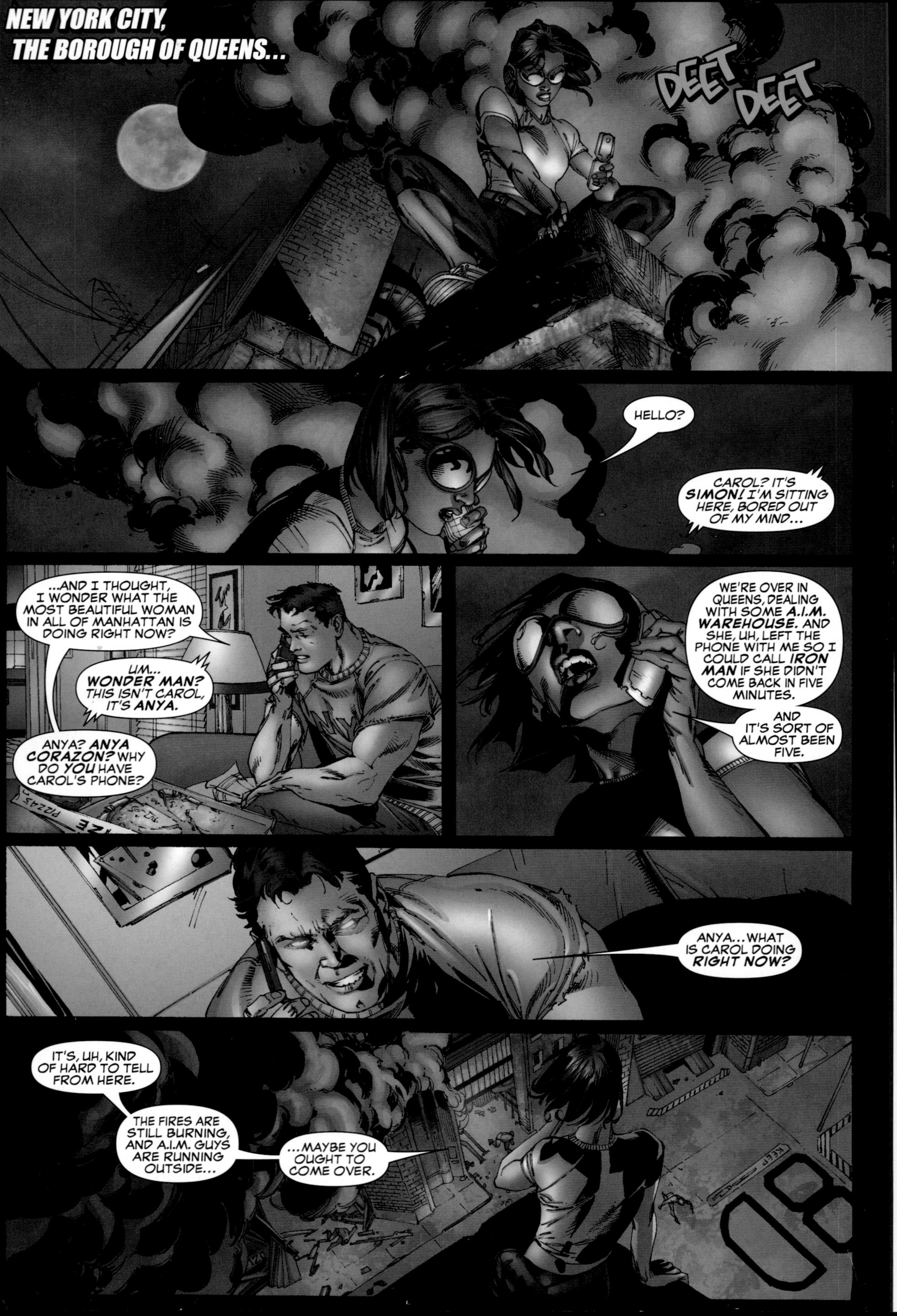

NEW YORK CITY, THE BOROUGH OF QUEENS...
DEET DEET
HELLO?
CAROL? IT'S SIMON! I'M SITTING HERE, BORED OUT OF MY MIND...
...AND I THOUGHT, I WONDER WHAT THE MOST BEAUTIFUL WOMAN IN ALL OF MANHATTAN IS DOING RIGHT NOW?
UM... WONDER MAN? THIS ISN'T CAROL, IT'S ANYA.
ANYA? ANYA CORAZON? WHY DO YOU HAVE CAROL'S PHONE?
WE'RE OVER IN QUEENS, DEALING WITH SOME A.I.M. WAREHOUSE. AND SHE, UH, LEFT THE PHONE WITH ME SO I COULD CALL IRON MAN IF SHE DIDN'T COME BACK IN FIVE MINUTES.
AND IT'S SORT OF ALMOST BEEN FIVE.
ANYA... WHAT IS CAROL DOING RIGHT NOW?
IT'S, UH, KIND OF HARD TO TELL FROM HERE.
THE FIRES ARE STILL BURNING, AND A.I.M. GUYS ARE RUNNING OUTSIDE...
...MAYBE YOU OUGHT TO COME OVER.

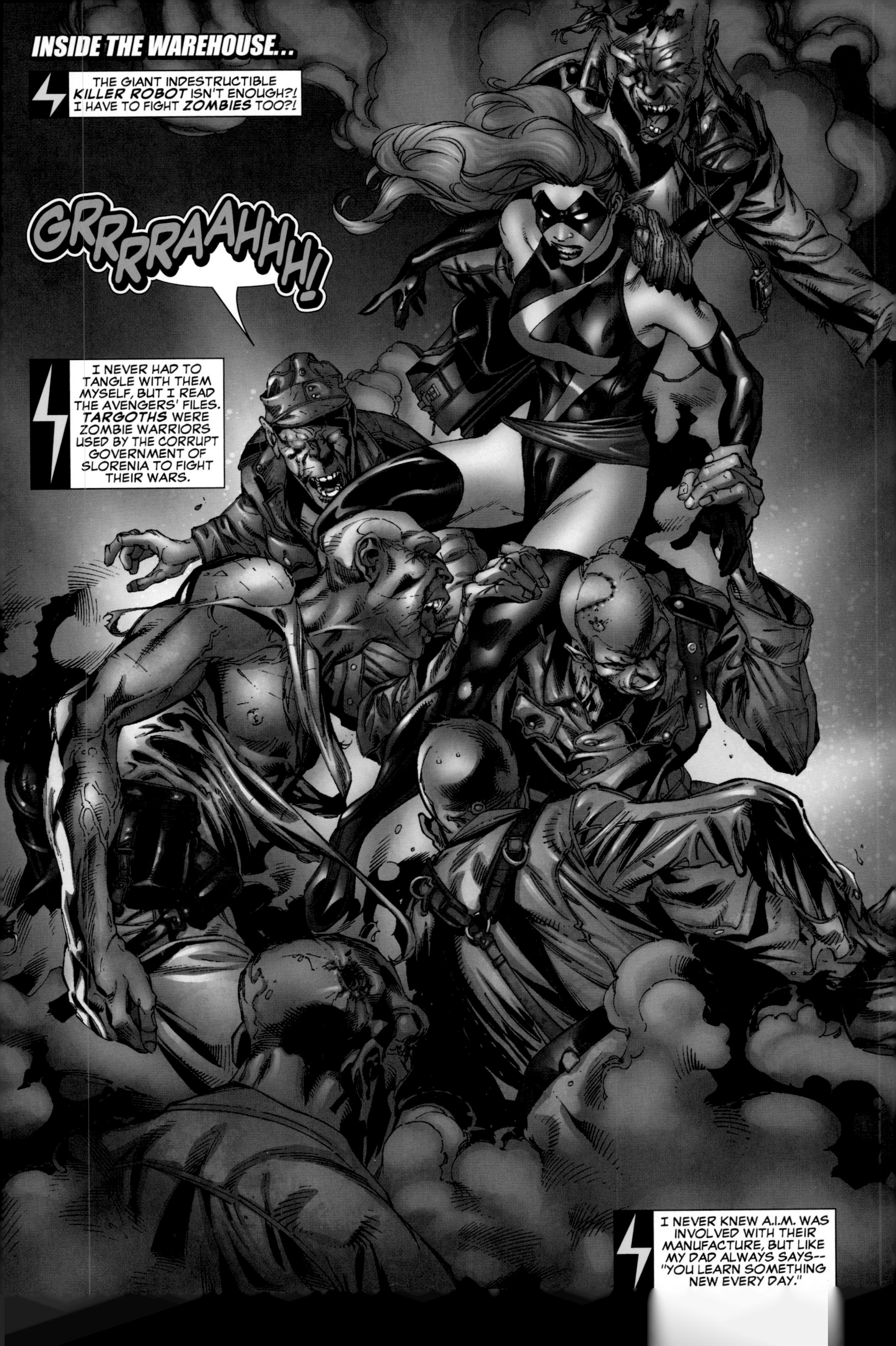
INSIDE THE WAREHOUSE...
THE GIANT INDESTRUCTIBLE KILLER ROBOT ISN'T ENOUGH?! I HAVE TO FIGHT ZOMBIES TOO?!
GRRRRAAHHH!
I NEVER HAD TO TANGLE WITH THEM MYSELF, BUT I READ THE AVENGERS' FILES. TARGOTHS WERE ZOMBIE WARRIORS USED BY THE CORRUPT GOVERNMENT OF SLORENIA TO FIGHT THEIR WARS.
I NEVER KNEW A.I.M. WAS INVOLVED WITH THEIR MANUFACTURE, BUT LIKE MY DAD ALWAYS SAYS-- "YOU LEARN SOMETHING NEW EVERY DAY."

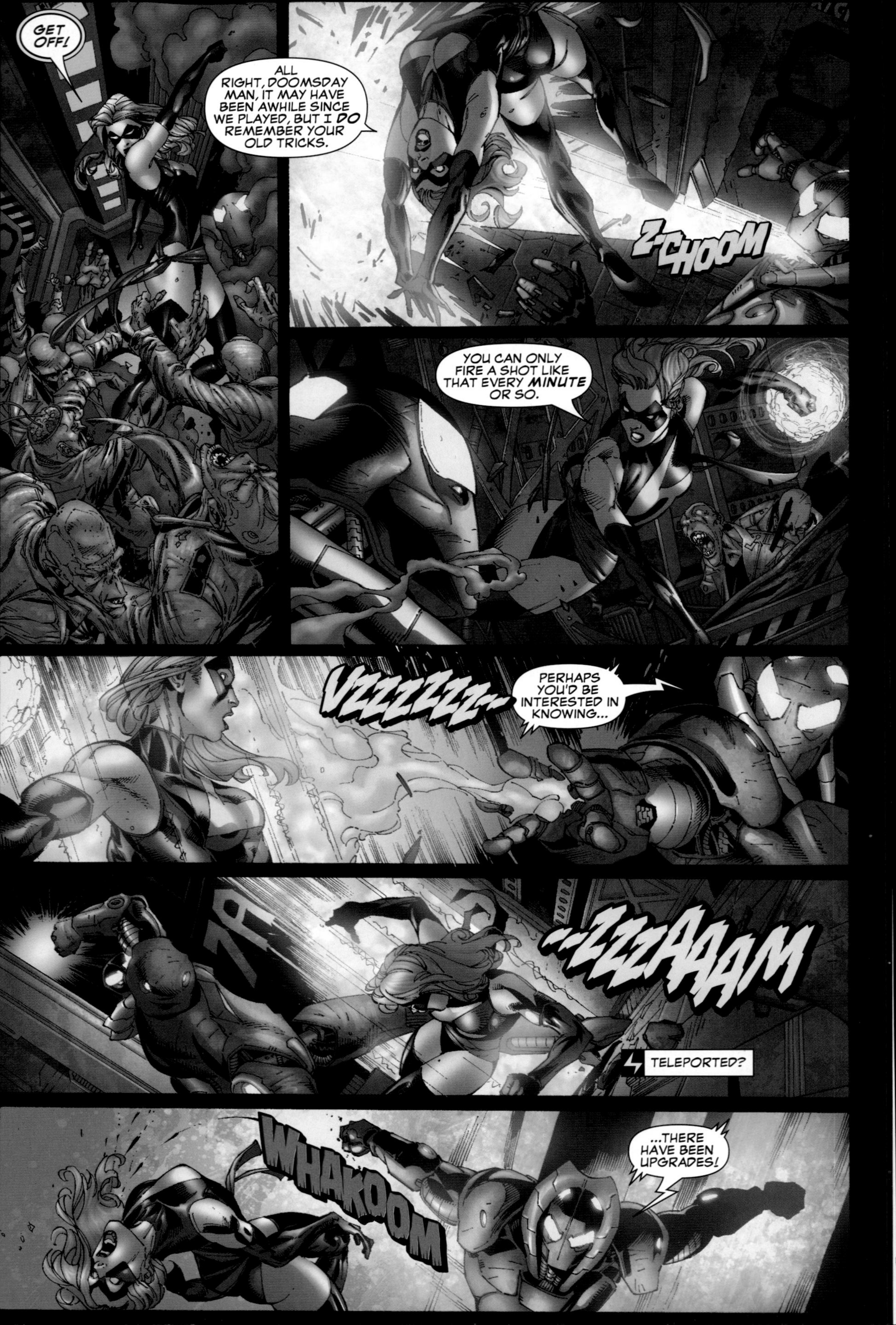
GET OFF!
ALL RIGHT, DOOMSDAY MAN, IT MAY HAVE BEEN AWHILE SINCE WE PLAYED, BUT I DO REMEMBER YOUR OLD TRICKS.
Z-CHOOM
YOU CAN ONLY FIRE A SHOT LIKE THAT EVERY MINUTE OR SO.
VZZZZZZ--
PERHAPS YOU'D BE INTERESTED IN KNOWING...
--ZZZAAAM
TELEPORTED?
WHAKOOM
...THERE HAVE BEEN UPGRADES!

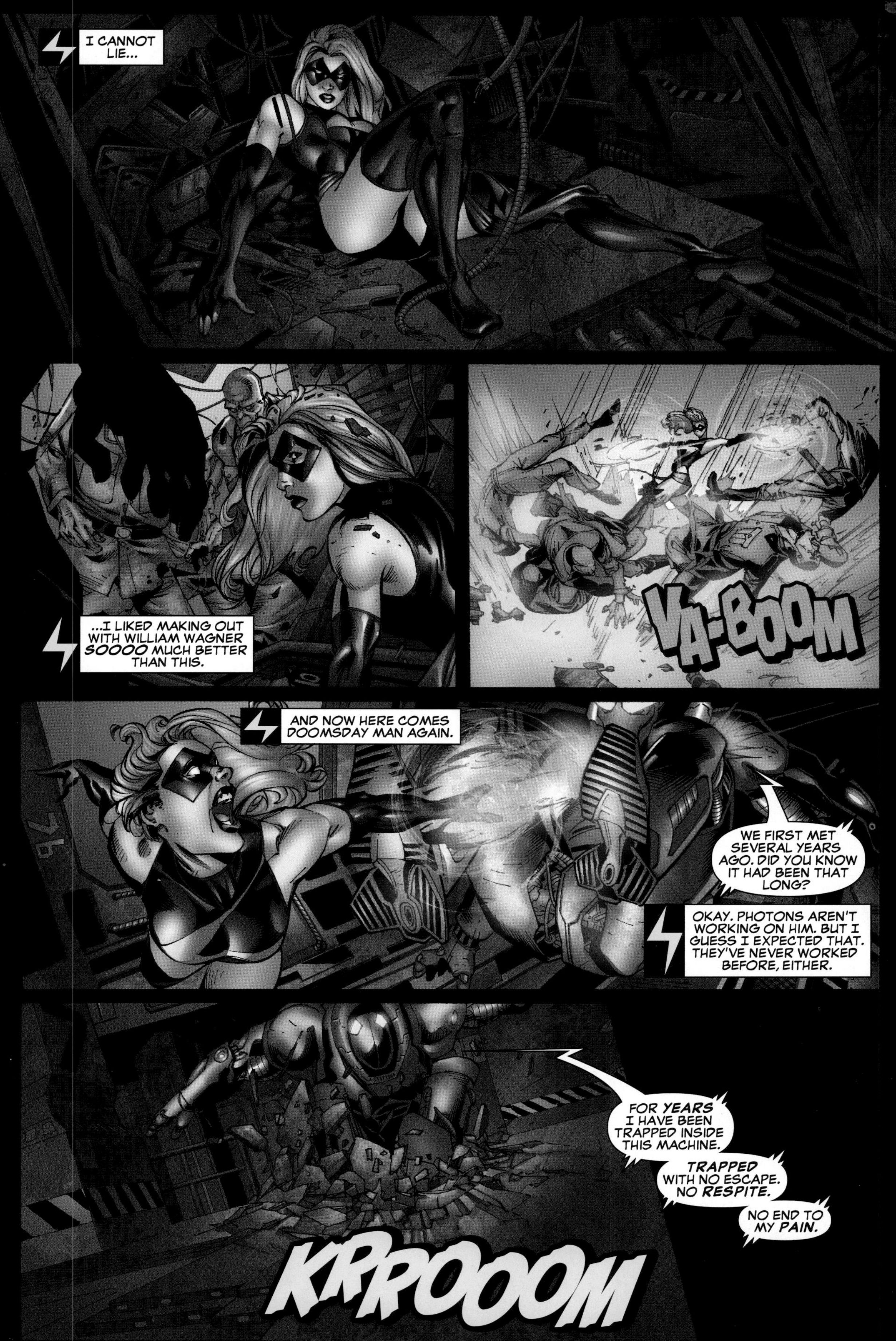

I CANNOT LIE...
...I LIKED MAKING OUT WITH WILLIAM WAGNER SOOOO MUCH BETTER THAN THIS.
VA-BOOM
AND NOW HERE COMES DOOMSDAY MAN AGAIN.
WE FIRST MET SEVERAL YEARS AGO. DID YOU KNOW IT HAD BEEN THAT LONG?
OKAY. PHOTONS AREN'T WORKING ON HIM. BUT I GUESS I EXPECTED THAT. THEY'VE NEVER WORKED BEFORE, EITHER.
FOR YEARS I HAVE BEEN TRAPPED INSIDE THIS MACHINE.
TRAPPED WITH NO ESCAPE. NO RESPITE.
NO END TO MY PAIN.
KRROOOM

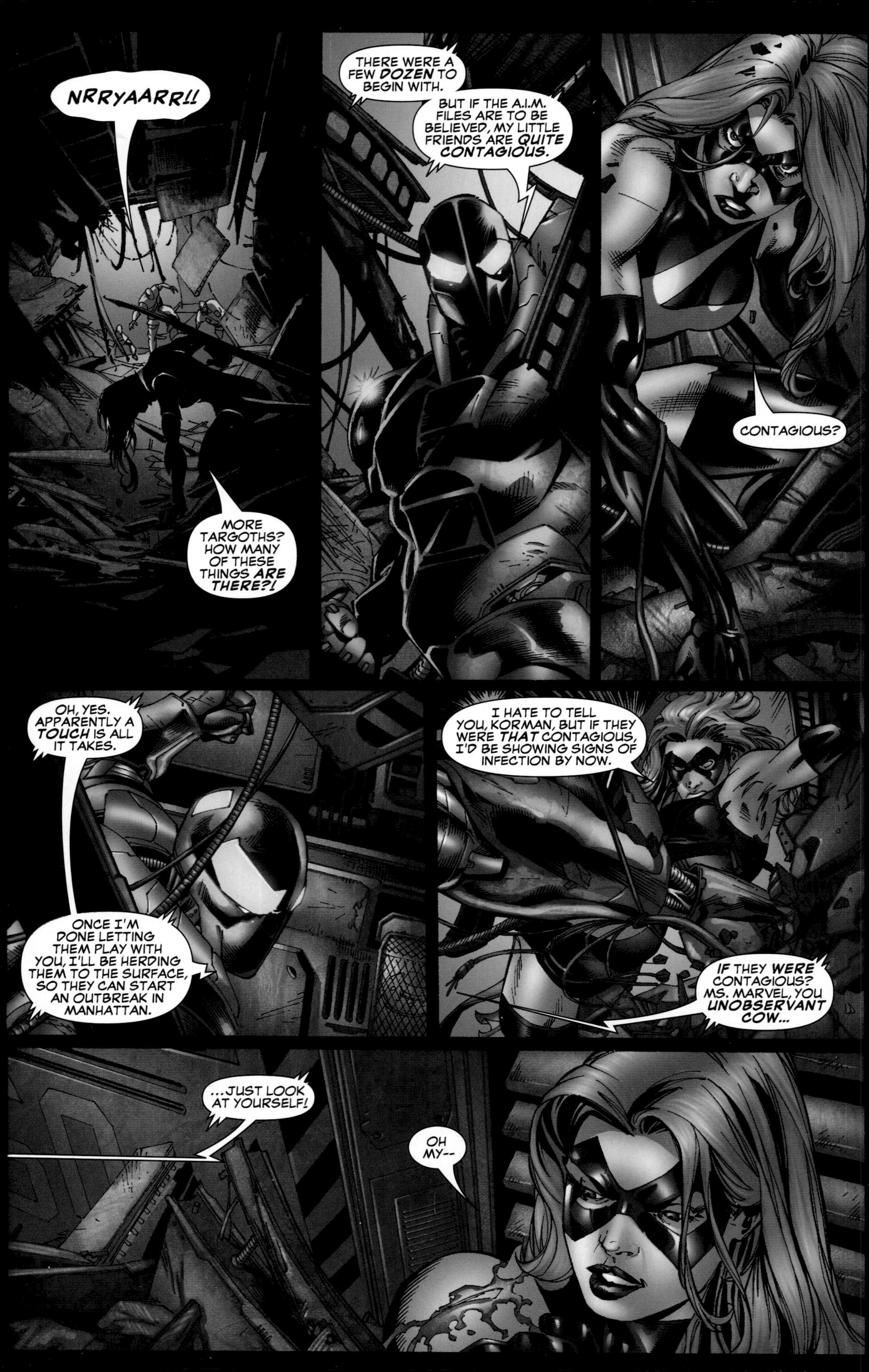
NRRyAARR!!
MORE TARGOTHS? HOW MANY OF THESE THINGS ARE THERE?!
THERE WERE A FEW DOZEN TO BEGIN WITH.
BUT IF THE A.I.M. FILES ARE TO BE BELIEVED, MY LITTLE FRIENDS ARE QUITE CONTAGIOUS.
CONTAGIOUS?
OH, YES. APPARENTLY A TOUCH IS ALL IT TAKES.
ONCE I'M DONE LETTING THEM PLAY WITH YOU, I'LL BE HERDING THEM TO THE SURFACE, SO THEY CAN START AN OUTBREAK IN MANHATTAN.
I HATE TO TELL YOU, KORMAN, BUT IF THEY WERE THAT CONTAGIOUS, I'D BE SHOWING SIGNS OF INFECTION BY NOW.
IF THEY WERE CONTAGIOUS? MS. MARVEL, YOU UNOBSERVANT COW...
...JUST LOOK AT YOURSELF!
OH MY--

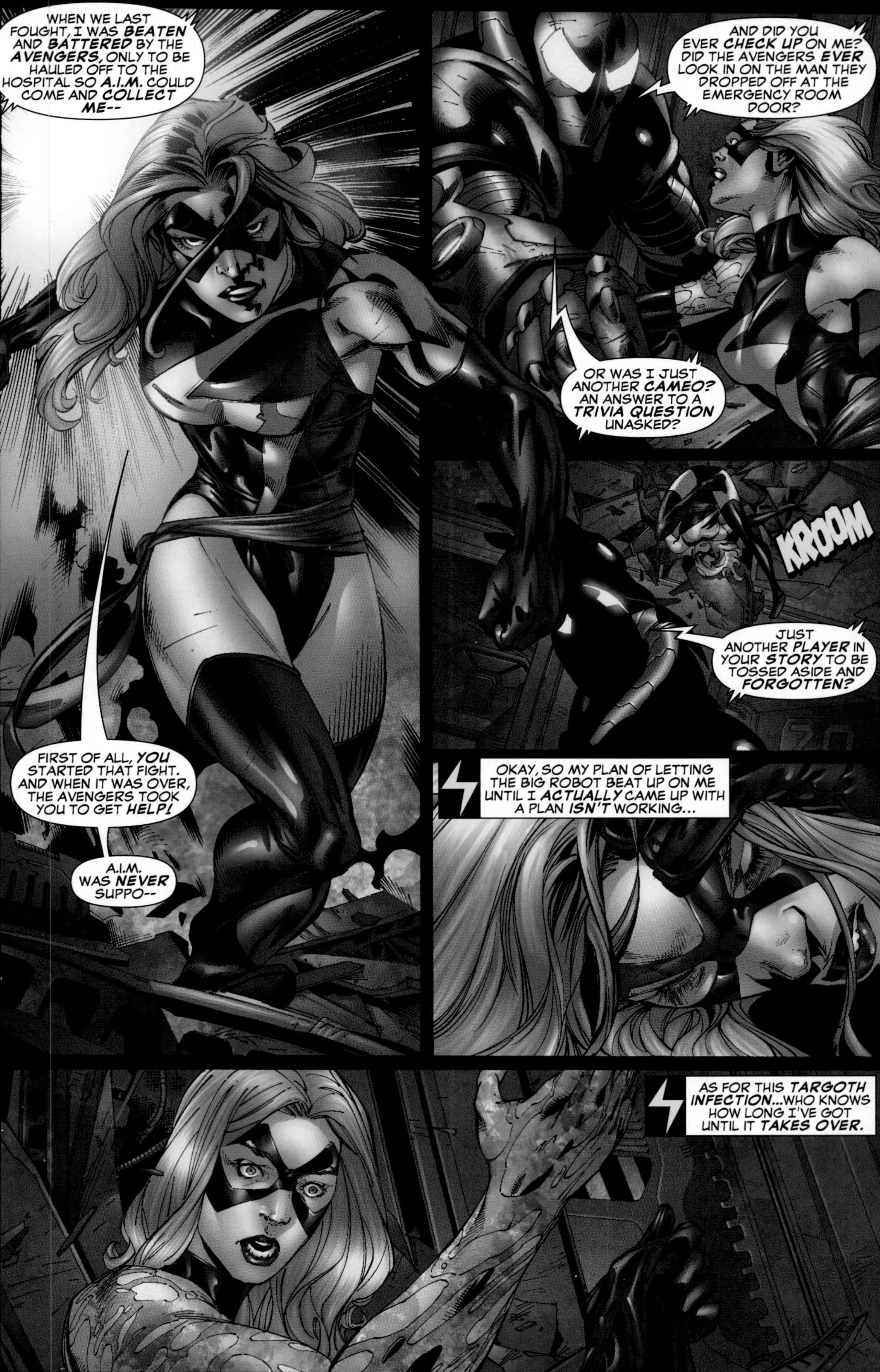
WHEN WE LAST FOUGHT, I WAS BEATEN AND BATTERED BY THE AVENGERS, ONLY TO BE HAULED OFF TO THE HOSPITAL SO A.I.M. COULD COME AND COLLECT ME--
FIRST OF ALL, YOU STARTED THAT FIGHT. AND WHEN IT WAS OVER, THE AVENGERS TOOK YOU TO GET HELP!
A.I.M. WAS NEVER SUPPO--
AND DID YOU EVER CHECK UP ON ME? DID THE AVENGERS EVER LOOK IN ON THE MAN THEY DROPPED OFF AT THE EMERGENCY ROOM DOOR?
OR WAS I JUST ANOTHER CAMEO? AN ANSWER TO A TRIVIA QUESTION UNASKED?
KROOM
JUST ANOTHER PLAYER IN YOUR STORY TO BE TOSSED ASIDE AND FORGOTTEN?
OKAY, SO MY PLAN OF LETTING THE BIG ROBOT BEAT UP ON ME UNTIL I ACTUALLY CAME UP WITH A PLAN ISN'T WORKING...
AS FOR THIS TARGOTH INFECTION...WHO KNOWS HOW LONG I'VE GOT UNTIL IT TAKES OVER.

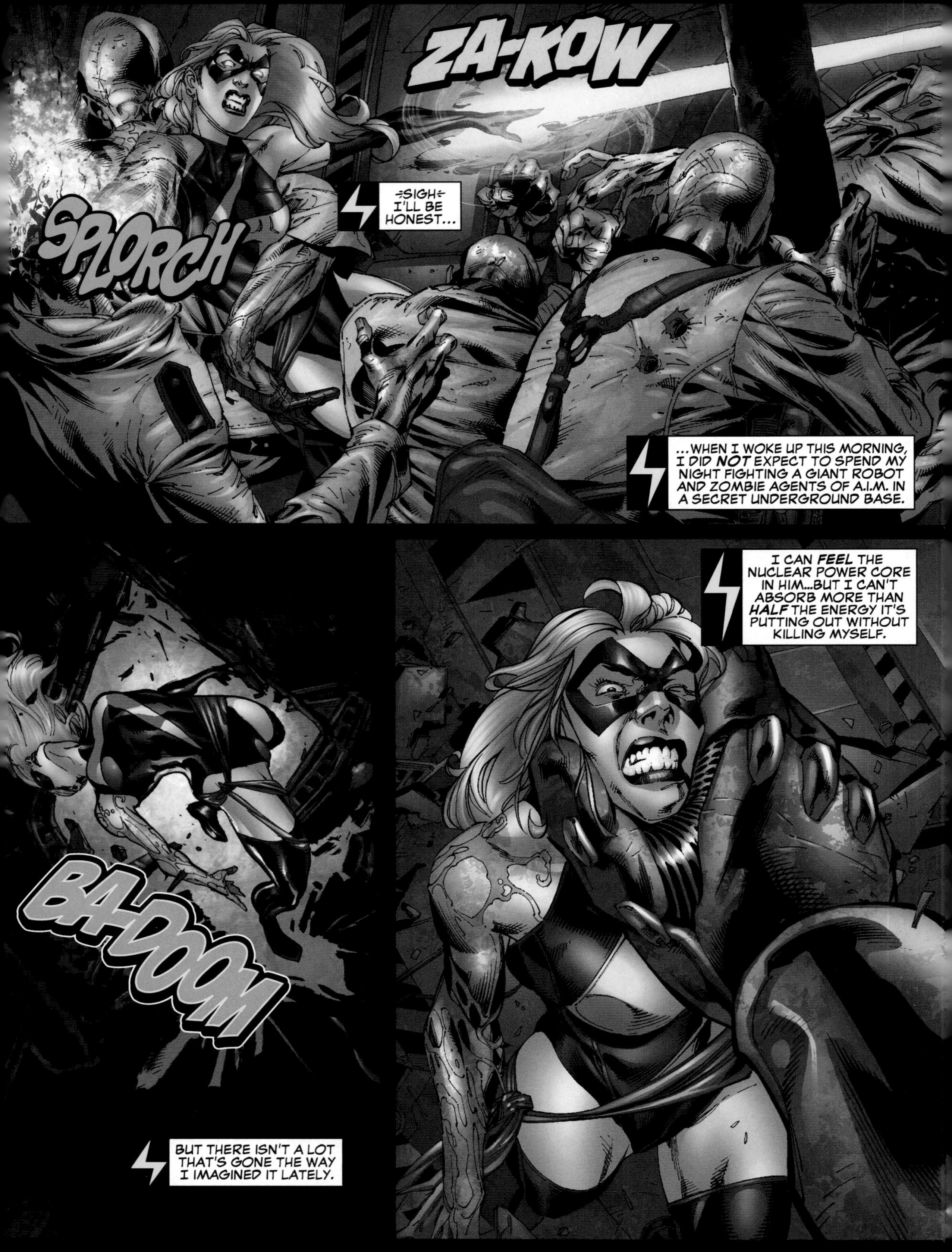

ZA-KOW
SPLORCH
=SIGH= I'LL BE HONEST...
...WHEN I WOKE UP THIS MORNING, I DID NOT EXPECT TO SPEND MY NIGHT FIGHTING A GIANT ROBOT AND ZOMBIE AGENTS OF A.I.M. IN A SECRET UNDERGROUND BASE.
BA-DOOM
BUT THERE ISN'T A LOT THAT'S GONE THE WAY I IMAGINED IT LATELY.
I CAN FEEL THE NUCLEAR POWER CORE IN HIM...BUT I CAN'T ABSORB MORE THAN HALF THE ENERGY IT'S PUTTING OUT WITHOUT KILLING MYSELF.

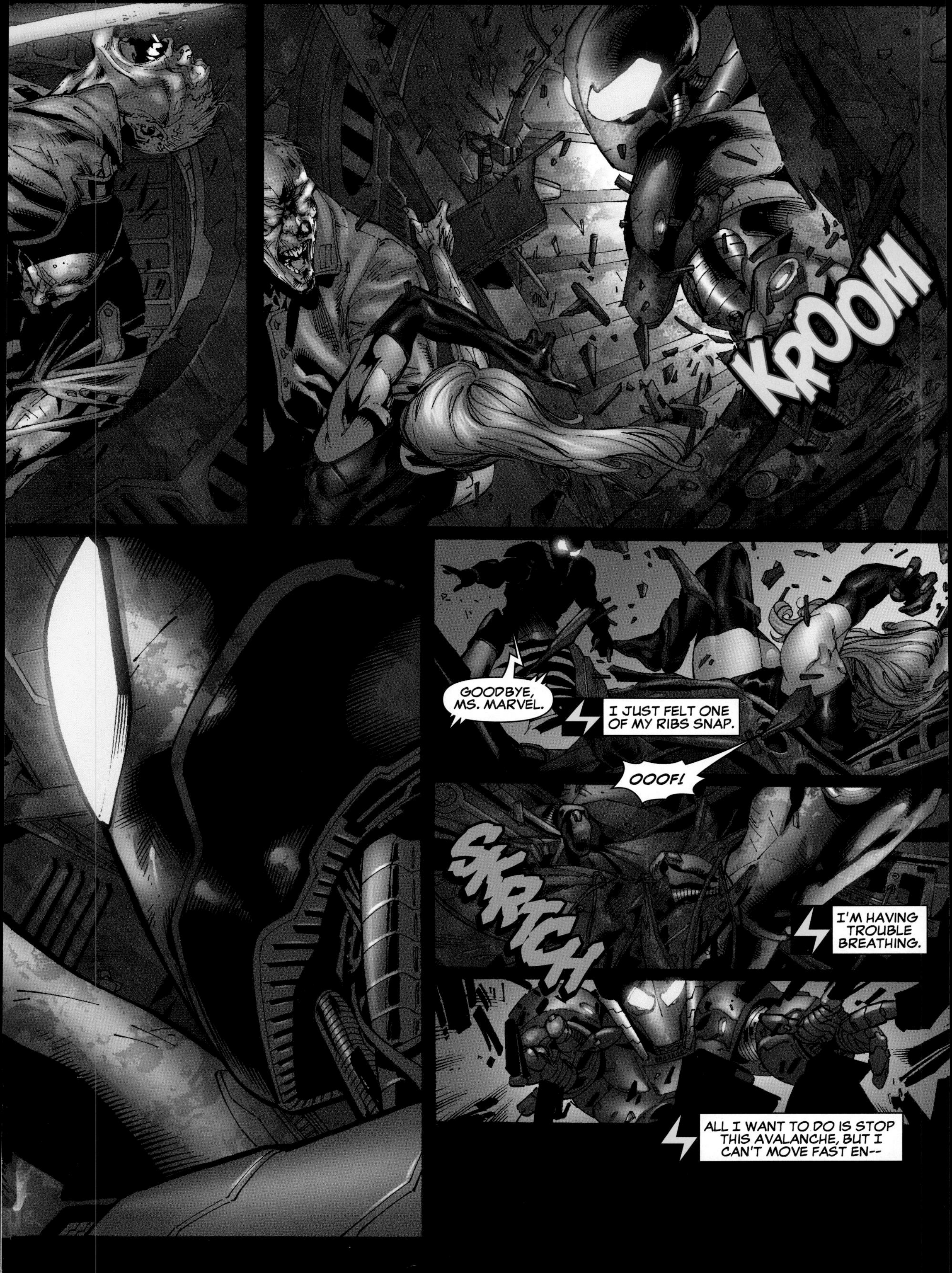
KROOM
GOODBYE, MS. MARVEL.
I JUST FELT ONE OF MY RIBS SNAP.
OOOF!
SKRTCH
I'M HAVING TROUBLE BREATHING.
ALL I WANT TO DO IS STOP THIS AVALANCHE, BUT I CAN'T MOVE FAST EN--

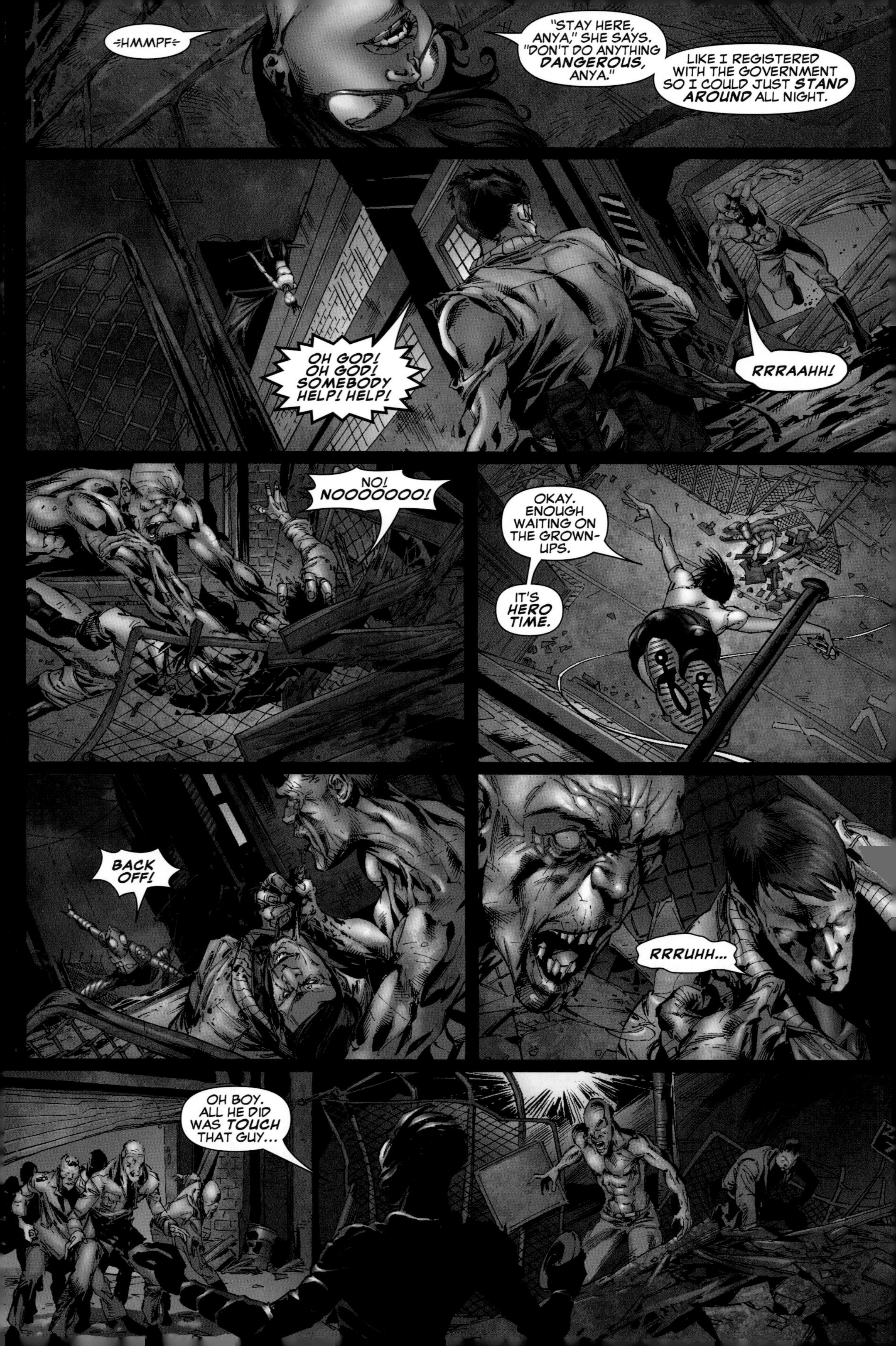
=HMMPF=
"STAY HERE, ANYA," SHE SAYS. "DON'T DO ANYTHING DANGEROUS, ANYA."
LIKE I REGISTERED WITH THE GOVERNMENT SO I COULD JUST STAND AROUND ALL NIGHT.
OH GOD! OH GOD! SOMEBODY HELP! HELP!
RRRAAHH!
NO! NOOOOOOO!
OKAY. ENOUGH WAITING ON THE GROWN-UPS.
IT'S HERO TIME.
BACK OFF!
RRRUHH...
OH BOY. ALL HE DID WAS TOUCH THAT GUY...

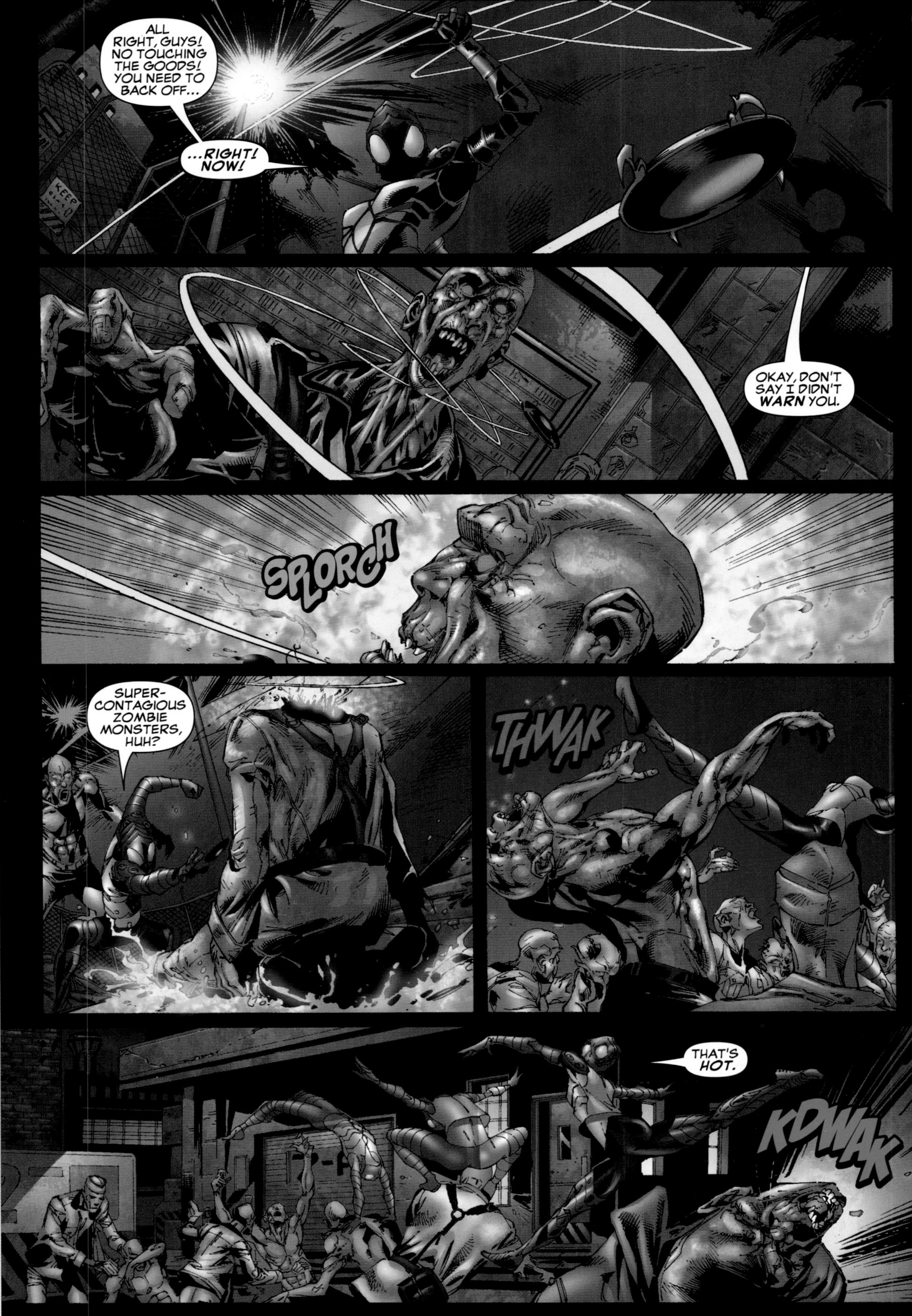
ALL RIGHT, GUYS! NO TOUCHING THE GOODS! YOU NEED TO BACK OFF...
...RIGHT! NOW!
OKAY, DON'T SAY I DIDN'T WARN YOU.
SPLORCH
SUPER-CONTAGIOUS ZOMBIE MONSTERS, HUH?
THWAK
THAT'S HOT.
KDWAK

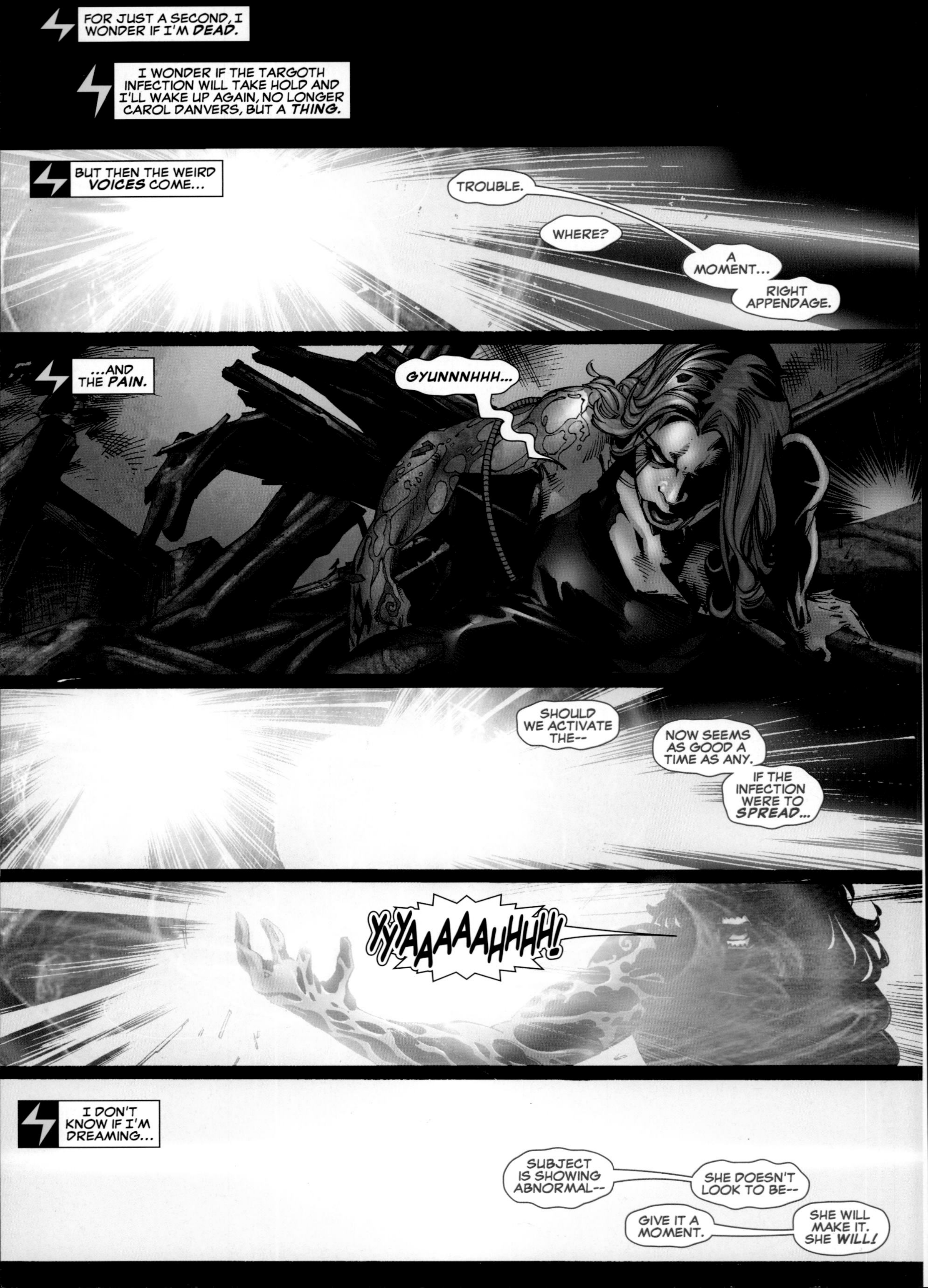
FOR JUST A SECOND, I WONDER IF I'M *DEAD.*
I WONDER IF THE TARGOTH INFECTION WILL TAKE HOLD AND I'LL WAKE UP AGAIN, NO LONGER CAROL DANVERS, BUT A *THING.*
BUT THEN THE WEIRD *VOICES* COME...
TROUBLE.
WHERE?
A MOMENT...
RIGHT APPENDAGE.
...AND THE *PAIN.*
GYUNNNHHH...
SHOULD WE ACTIVATE THE--
NOW SEEMS AS GOOD A TIME AS ANY.
IF THE INFECTION WERE TO *SPREAD...*
YYYAAAAAHHHH!
I DON'T KNOW IF I'M DREAMING...
SUBJECT IS SHOWING ABNORMAL--
SHE DOESN'T LOOK TO BE--
GIVE IT A MOMENT.
SHE WILL MAKE IT. SHE *WILL!*

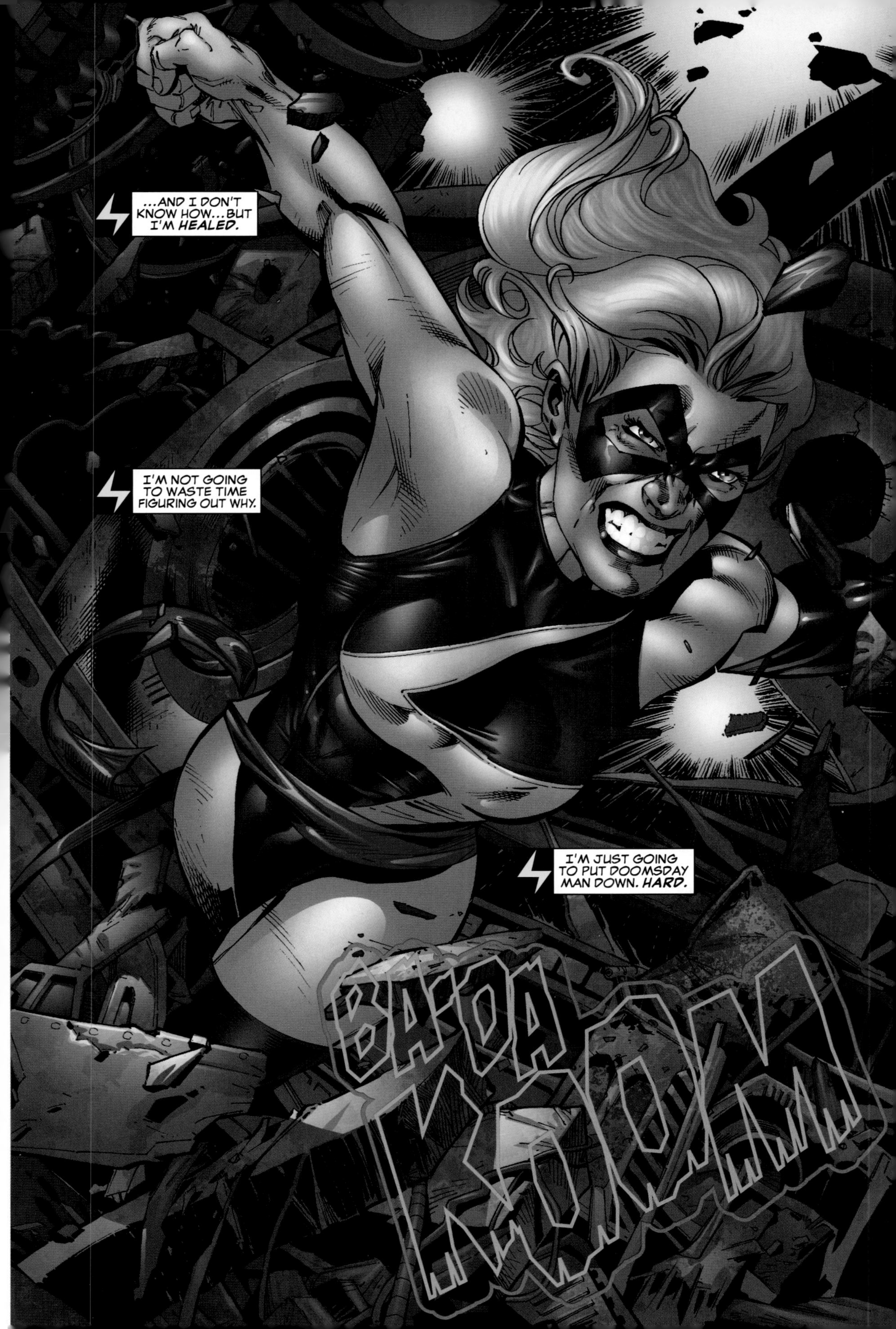
...AND I DON'T KNOW HOW...BUT I'M HEALED.
I'M NOT GOING TO WASTE TIME FIGURING OUT WHY.
I'M JUST GOING TO PUT DOOMSDAY MAN DOWN. HARD.
BA-OOA KOOOM

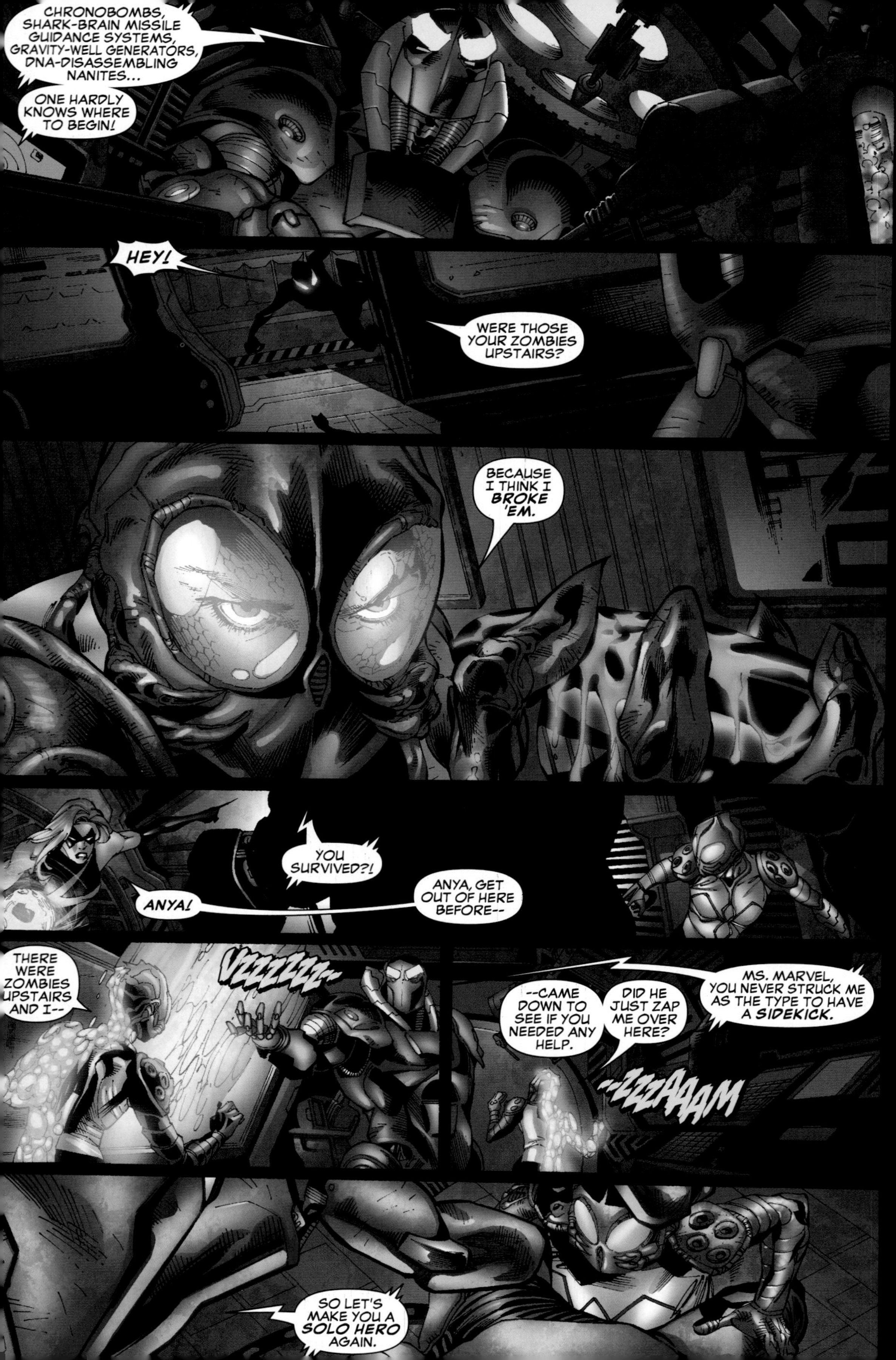
CHRONOBOMBS, SHARK-BRAIN MISSILE GUIDANCE SYSTEMS, GRAVITY-WELL GENERATORS, DNA-DISASSEMBLING NANITES...
ONE HARDLY KNOWS WHERE TO BEGIN!
HEY!
WERE THOSE YOUR ZOMBIES UPSTAIRS?
BECAUSE I THINK I BROKE 'EM.
YOU SURVIVED?!
ANYA!
ANYA, GET OUT OF HERE BEFORE--
THERE WERE ZOMBIES UPSTAIRS AND I--
VZZZZZZZ--
--CAME DOWN TO SEE IF YOU NEEDED ANY HELP.
DID HE JUST ZAP ME OVER HERE?
MS. MARVEL, YOU NEVER STRUCK ME AS THE TYPE TO HAVE A SIDEKICK.
--ZZZAAAM
SO LET'S MAKE YOU A SOLO HERO AGAIN.

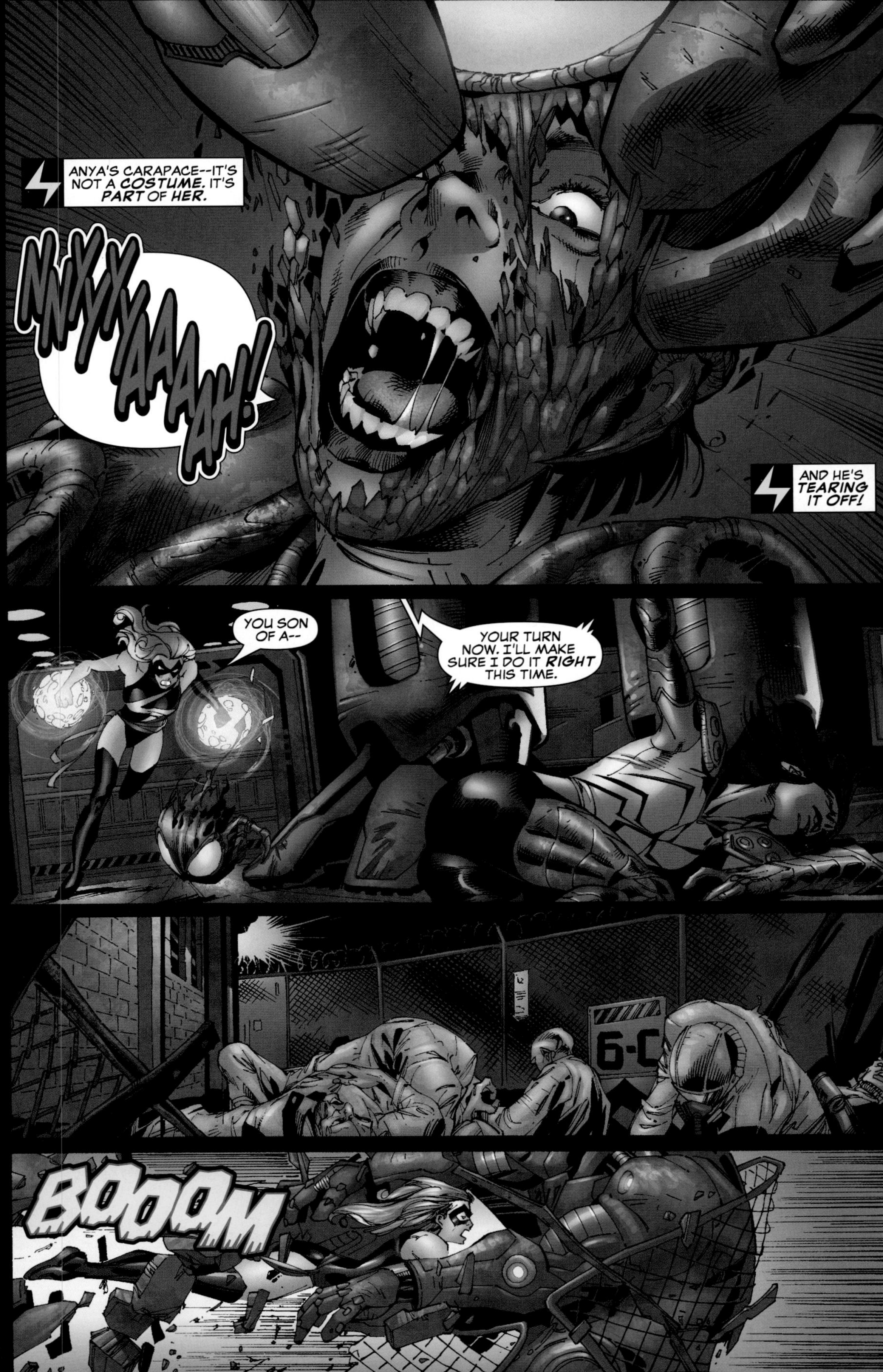
ANYA'S CARAPACE--IT'S NOT A COSTUME. IT'S PART OF HER.
NNYYYAAAAH!
AND HE'S TEARING IT OFF!
YOU SON OF A--
YOUR TURN NOW. I'LL MAKE SURE I DO IT RIGHT THIS TIME.
6-C
BOOOM

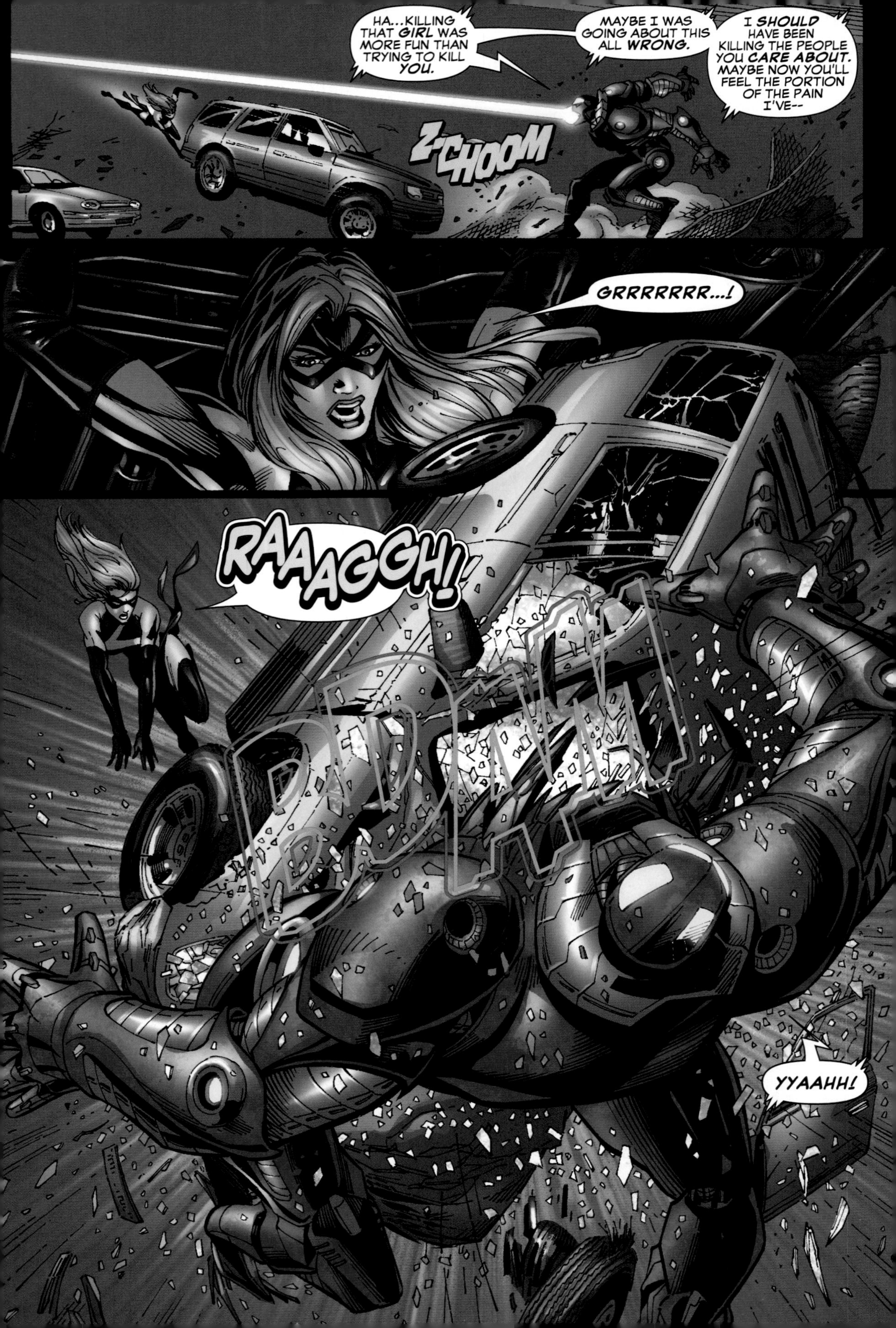

HA...KILLING THAT GIRL WAS MORE FUN THAN TRYING TO KILL YOU.
MAYBE I WAS GOING ABOUT THIS ALL WRONG.
I SHOULD HAVE BEEN KILLING THE PEOPLE YOU CARE ABOUT. MAYBE NOW YOU'LL FEEL THE PORTION OF THE PAIN I'VE--
Z-CHOOM
GRRRRRRR...!
RAAAGGH!
YYAAHH!

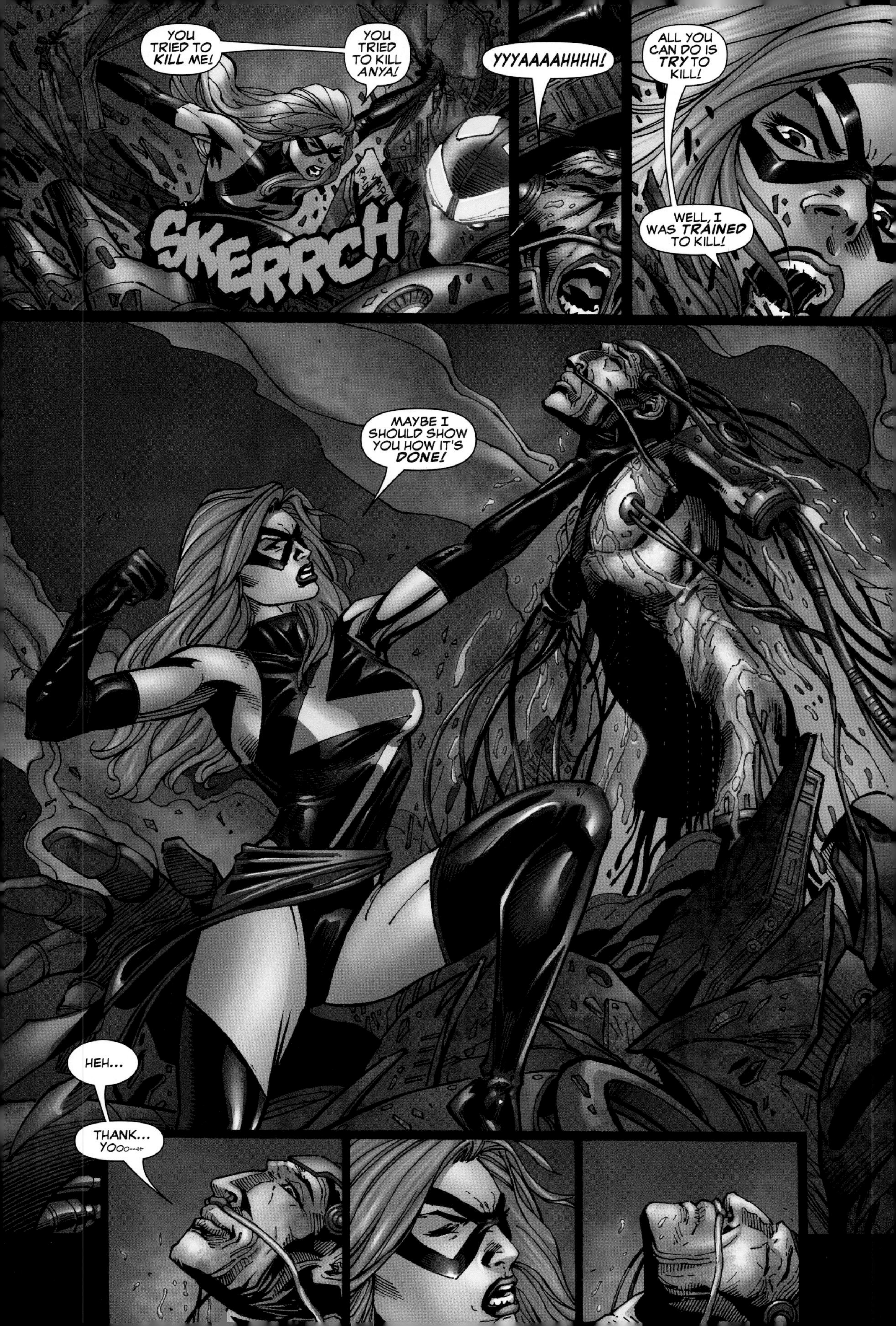
YOU TRIED TO KILL ME!
YOU TRIED TO KILL ANYA!
SKERRCH
YYYAAAAHHHH!
ALL YOU CAN DO IS TRY TO KILL!
WELL, I WAS TRAINED TO KILL!
MAYBE I SHOULD SHOW YOU HOW IT'S DONE!
HEH...
THANK... YOOo---

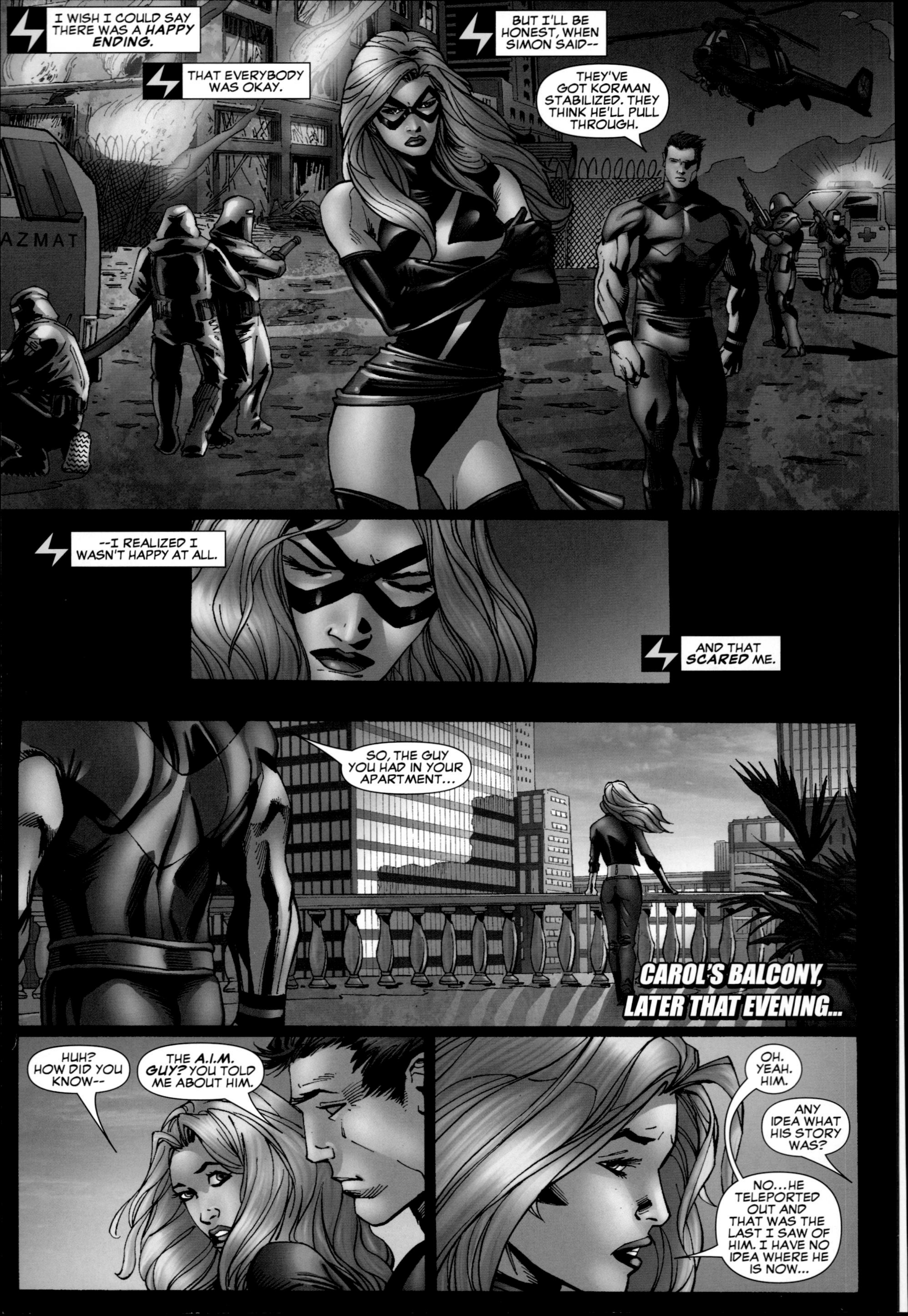

I WISH I COULD SAY THERE WAS A HAPPY ENDING.
THAT EVERYBODY WAS OKAY.
BUT I'LL BE HONEST, WHEN SIMON SAID--
THEY'VE GOT KORMAN STABILIZED. THEY THINK HE'LL PULL THROUGH.
AZMAT
--I REALIZED I WASN'T HAPPY AT ALL.
AND THAT SCARED ME.
CAROL'S BALCONY, LATER THAT EVENING...
SO, THE GUY YOU HAD IN YOUR APARTMENT...
HUH? HOW DID YOU KNOW--
THE A.I.M. GUY? YOU TOLD ME ABOUT HIM.
OH. YEAH. HIM.
ANY IDEA WHAT HIS STORY WAS?
NO...HE TELEPORTED OUT AND THAT WAS THE LAST I SAW OF HIM. I HAVE NO IDEA WHERE HE IS NOW...

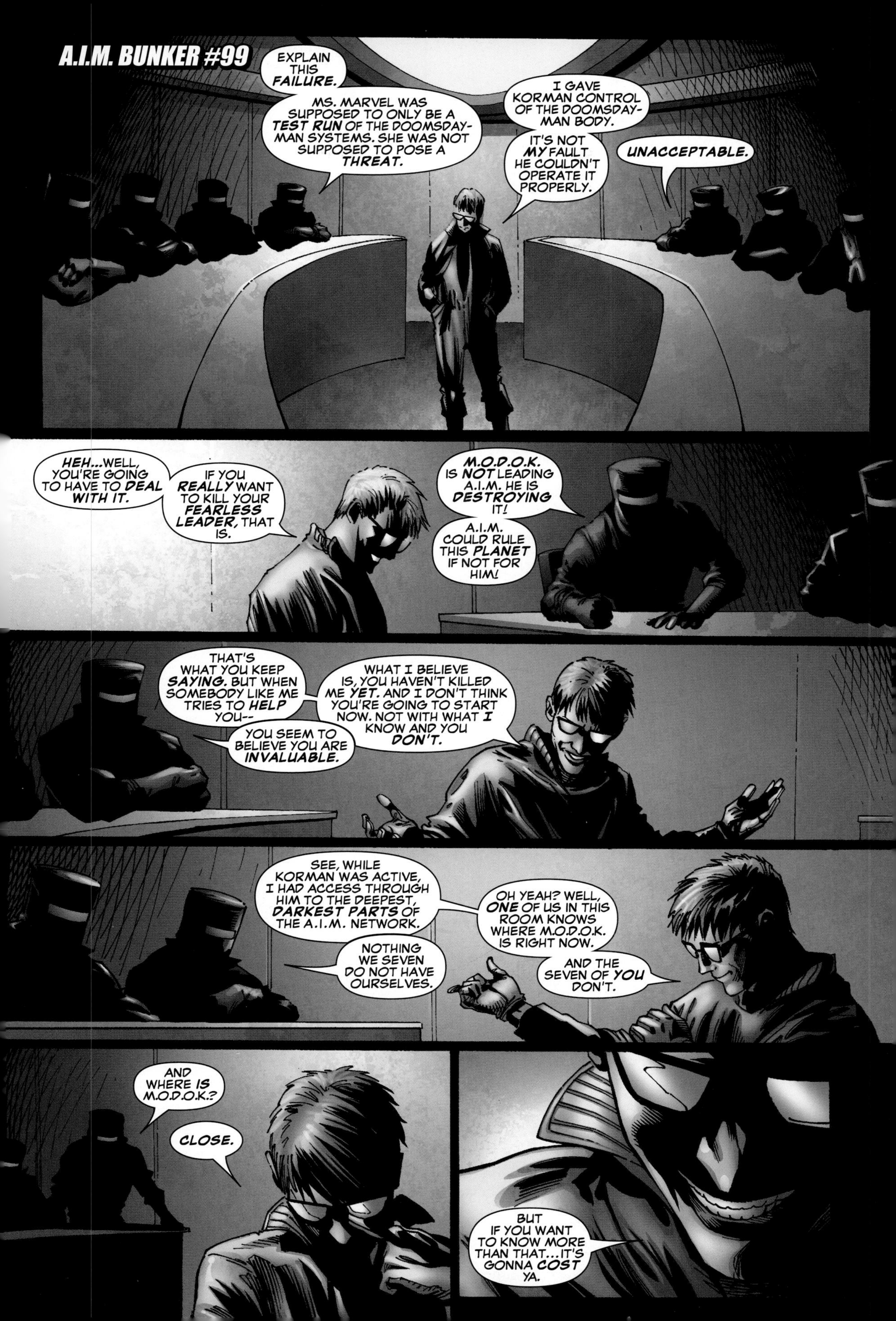
A.I.M. BUNKER #99
EXPLAIN THIS FAILURE.
MS. MARVEL WAS SUPPOSED TO ONLY BE A TEST RUN OF THE DOOMSDAY-MAN SYSTEMS. SHE WAS NOT SUPPOSED TO POSE A THREAT.
I GAVE KORMAN CONTROL OF THE DOOMSDAY-MAN BODY.
IT'S NOT MY FAULT HE COULDN'T OPERATE IT PROPERLY.
UNACCEPTABLE.
HEH...WELL, YOU'RE GOING TO HAVE TO DEAL WITH IT.
IF YOU REALLY WANT TO KILL YOUR FEARLESS LEADER, THAT IS.
M.O.D.O.K. IS NOT LEADING A.I.M. HE IS DESTROYING IT!
A.I.M. COULD RULE THIS PLANET IF NOT FOR HIM!
THAT'S WHAT YOU KEEP SAYING. BUT WHEN SOMEBODY LIKE ME TRIES TO HELP YOU--
YOU SEEM TO BELIEVE YOU ARE INVALUABLE.
WHAT I BELIEVE IS, YOU HAVEN'T KILLED ME YET. AND I DON'T THINK YOU'RE GOING TO START NOW. NOT WITH WHAT I KNOW AND YOU DON'T.
SEE, WHILE KORMAN WAS ACTIVE, I HAD ACCESS THROUGH HIM TO THE DEEPEST, DARKEST PARTS OF THE A.I.M. NETWORK.
NOTHING WE SEVEN DO NOT HAVE OURSELVES.
OH YEAH? WELL, ONE OF US IN THIS ROOM KNOWS WHERE M.O.D.O.K. IS RIGHT NOW.
AND THE SEVEN OF YOU DON'T.
AND WHERE IS M.O.D.O.K.?
CLOSE.
BUT IF YOU WANT TO KNOW MORE THAN THAT...IT'S GONNA COST YA.

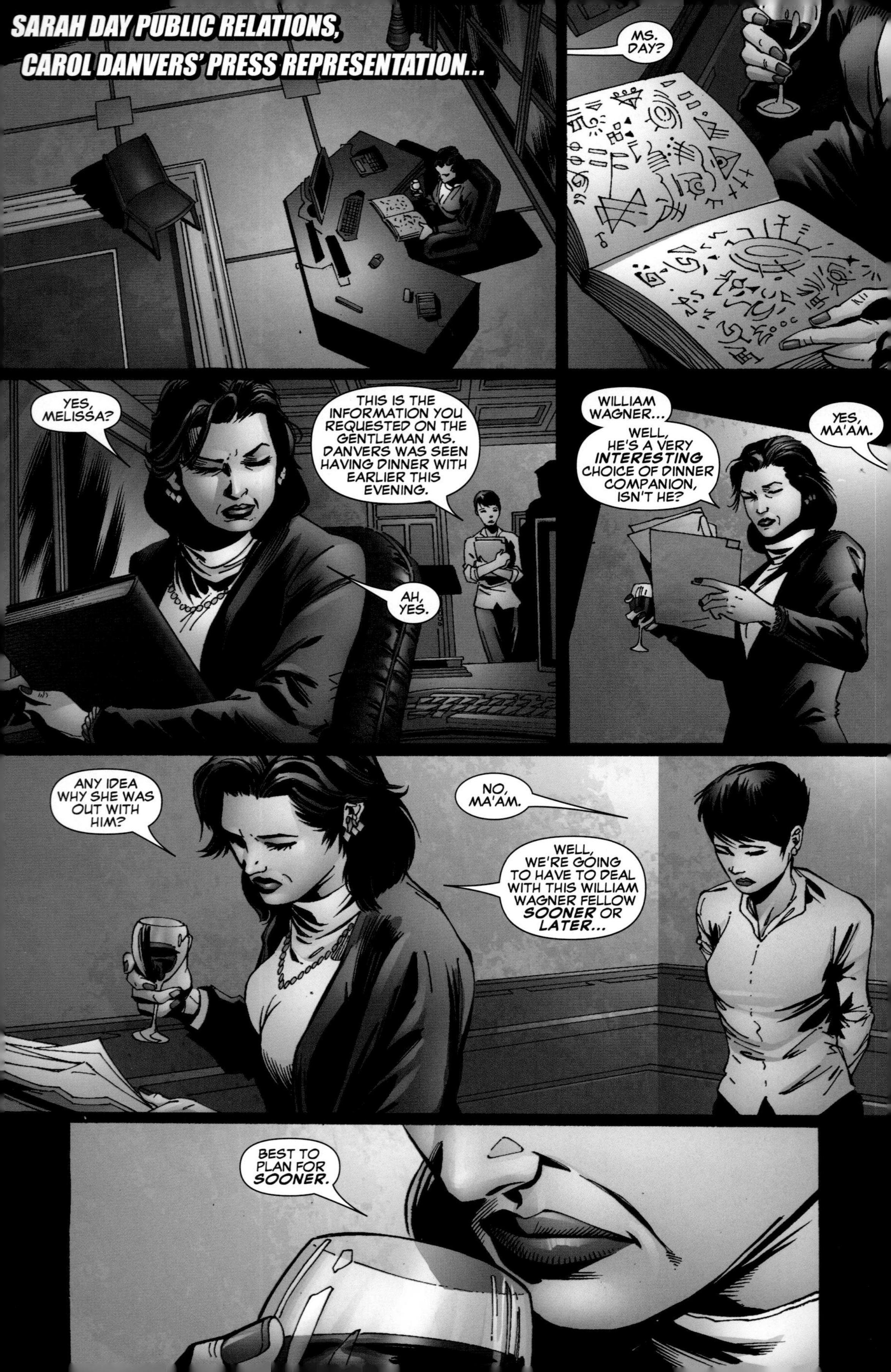
SARAH DAY PUBLIC RELATIONS, CAROL DANVERS' PRESS REPRESENTATION...
MS. DAY?
YES, MELISSA?
THIS IS THE INFORMATION YOU REQUESTED ON THE GENTLEMAN MS. DANVERS WAS SEEN HAVING DINNER WITH EARLIER THIS EVENING.
AH, YES.
WILLIAM WAGNER...
WELL, HE'S A VERY INTERESTING CHOICE OF DINNER COMPANION, ISN'T HE?
YES, MA'AM.
ANY IDEA WHY SHE WAS OUT WITH HIM?
NO, MA'AM.
WELL, WE'RE GOING TO HAVE TO DEAL WITH THIS WILLIAM WAGNER FELLOW SOONER OR LATER...
BEST TO PLAN FOR SOONER.

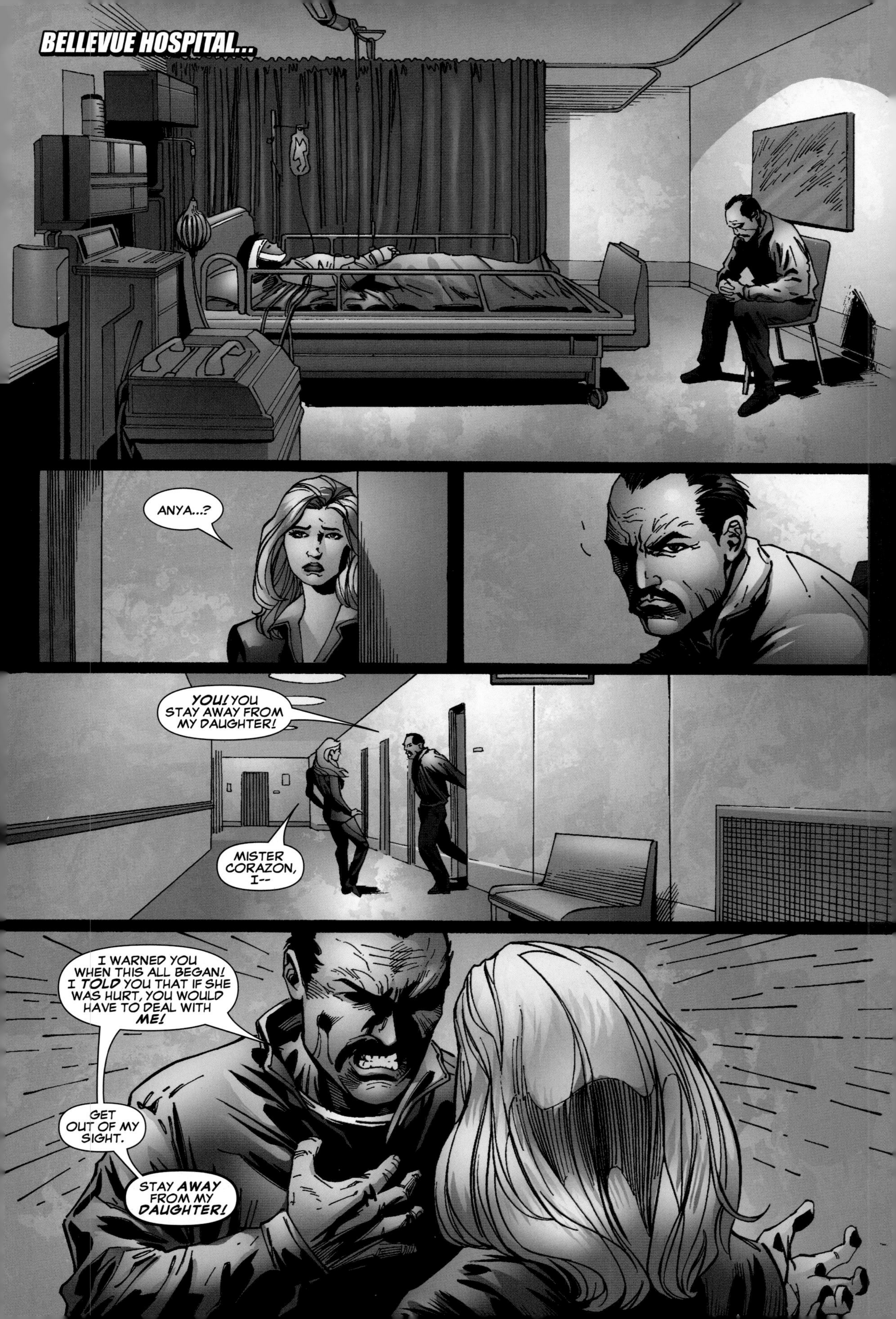
BELLEVUE HOSPITAL...
ANYA...?
YOU! YOU STAY AWAY FROM MY DAUGHTER!
MISTER CORAZON, I--
I WARNED YOU WHEN THIS ALL BEGAN! I TOLD YOU THAT IF SHE WAS HURT, YOU WOULD HAVE TO DEAL WITH ME!
GET OUT OF MY SIGHT.
STAY AWAY FROM MY DAUGHTER!

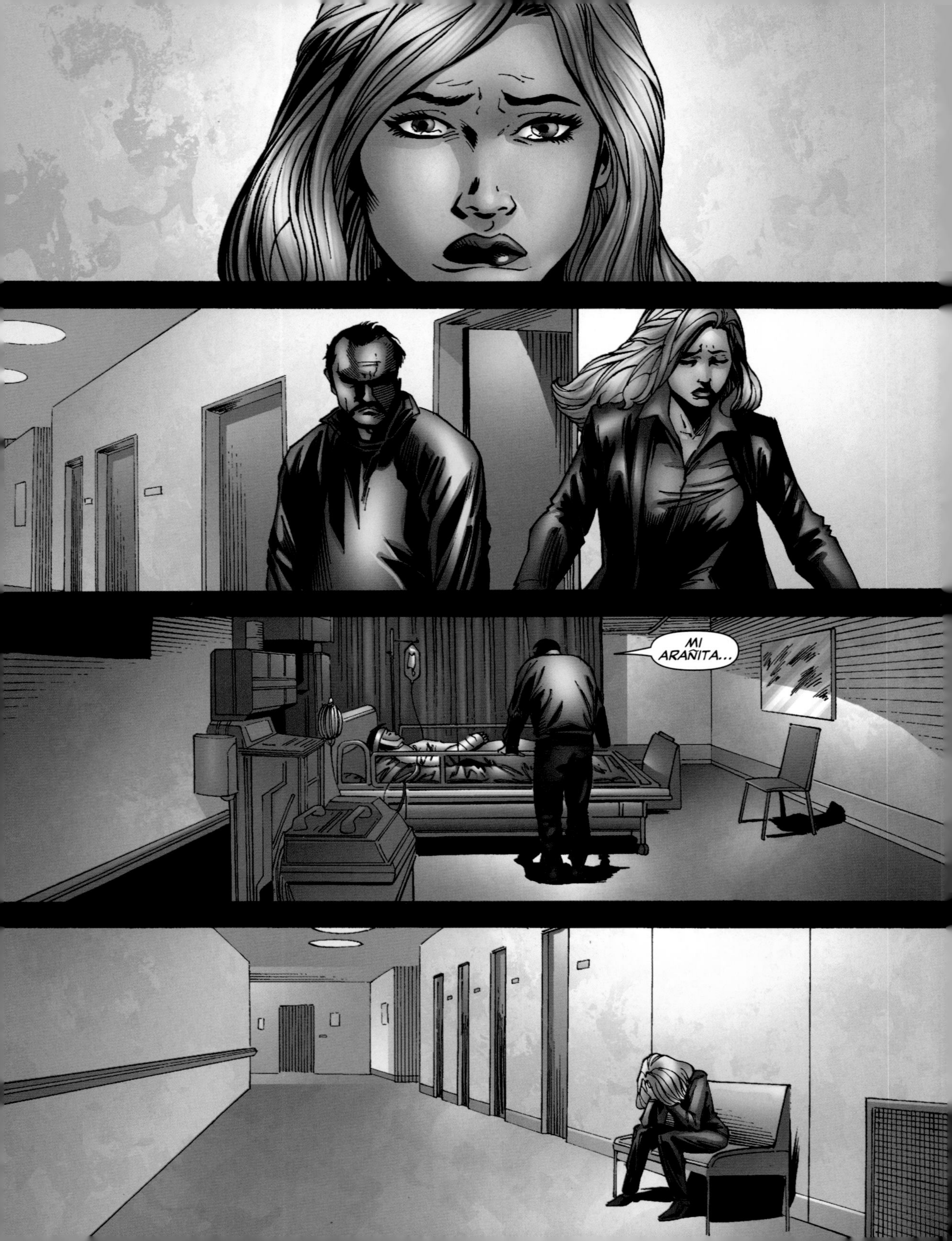
MI ARAÑITA...

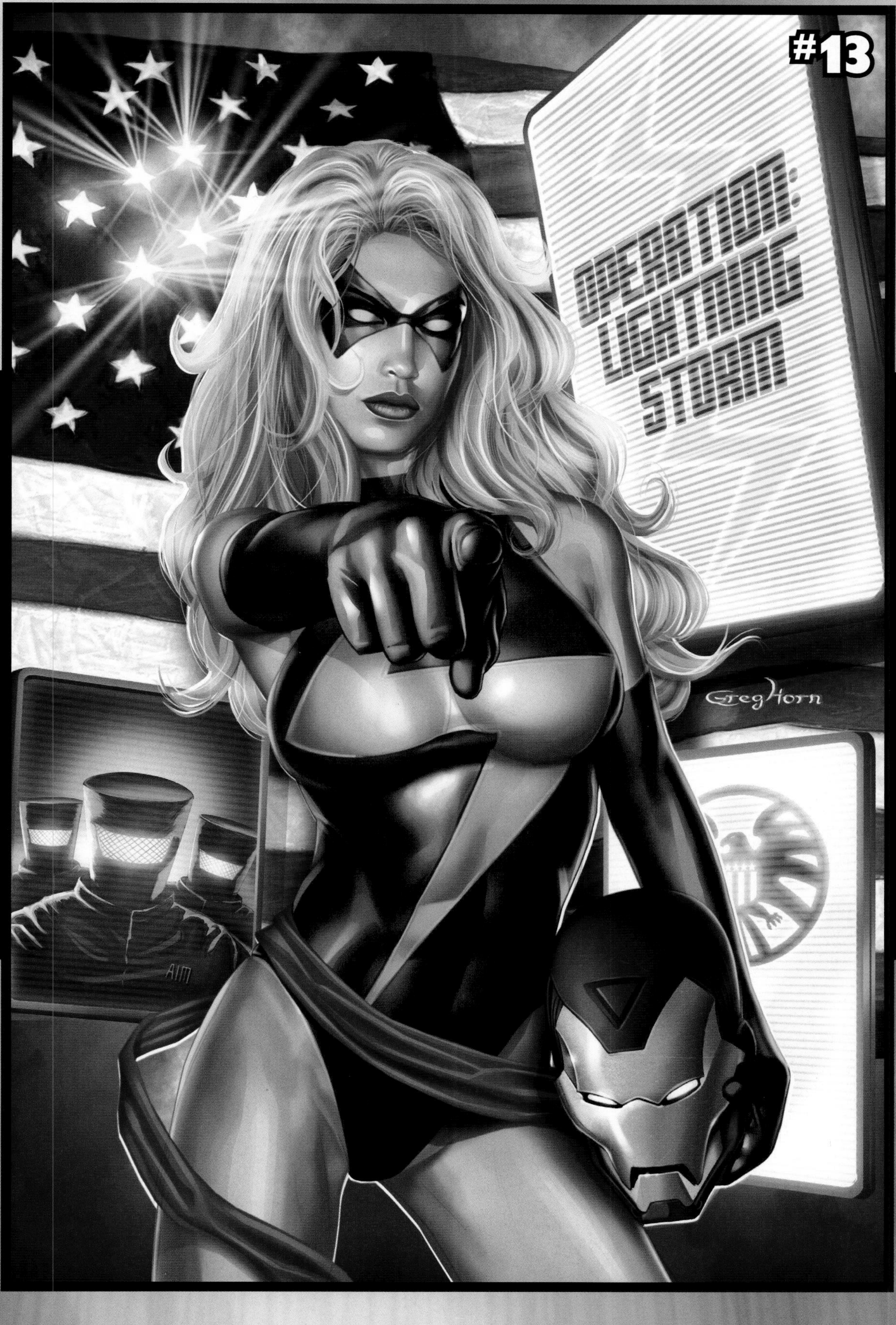
#13
OPERATION: LIGHTNING STORM
Greg Horn
AIM

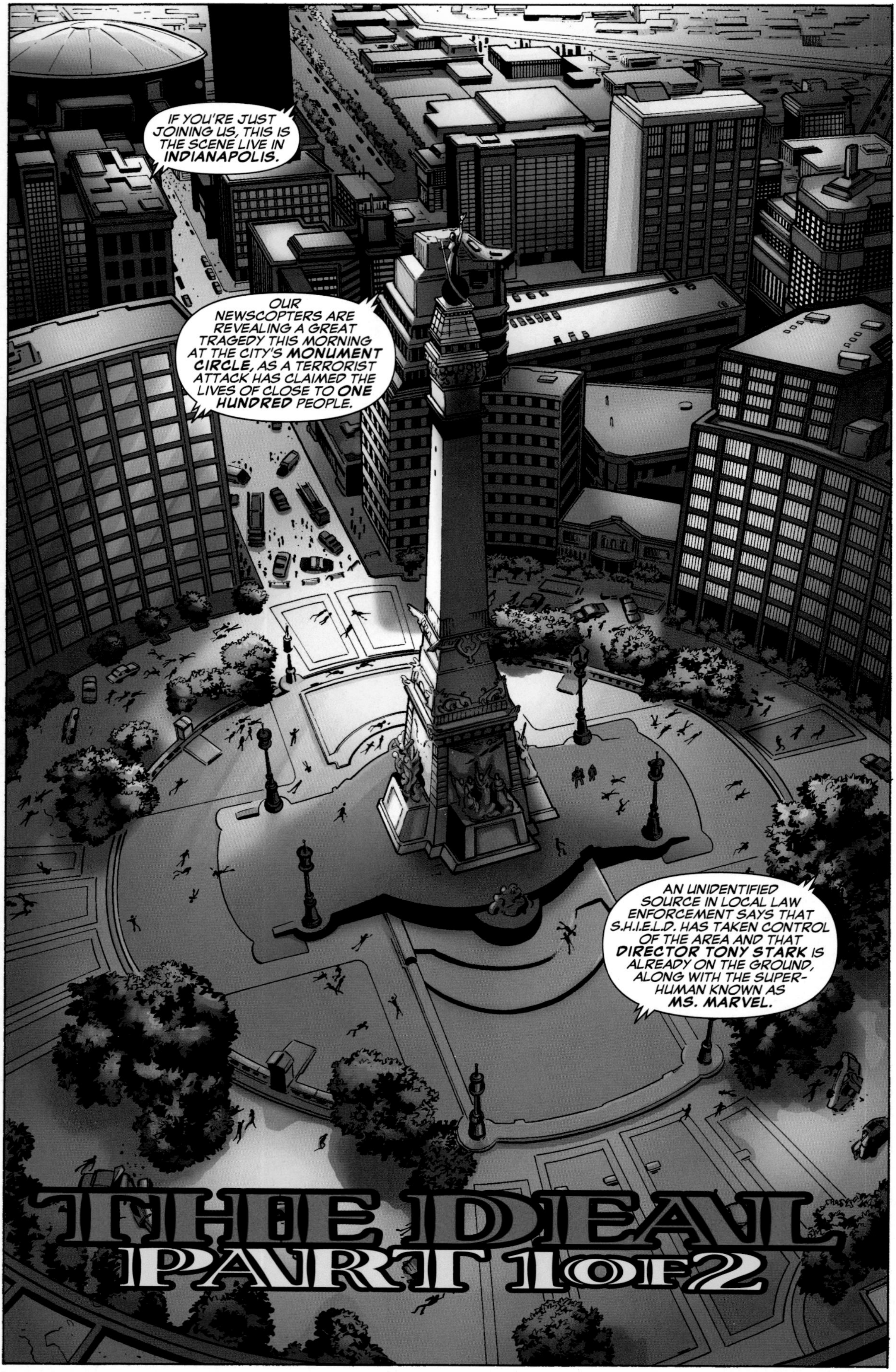
IF YOU'RE JUST JOINING US, THIS IS THE SCENE LIVE IN INDIANAPOLIS.
OUR NEWSCOPTERS ARE REVEALING A GREAT TRAGEDY THIS MORNING AT THE CITY'S MONUMENT CIRCLE, AS A TERRORIST ATTACK HAS CLAIMED THE LIVES OF CLOSE TO ONE HUNDRED PEOPLE.
AN UNIDENTIFIED SOURCE IN LOCAL LAW ENFORCEMENT SAYS THAT S.H.I.E.L.D. HAS TAKEN CONTROL OF THE AREA AND THAT DIRECTOR TONY STARK IS ALREADY ON THE GROUND, ALONG WITH THE SUPER-HUMAN KNOWN AS MS. MARVEL.
THE DEAL
PART 1 OF 2

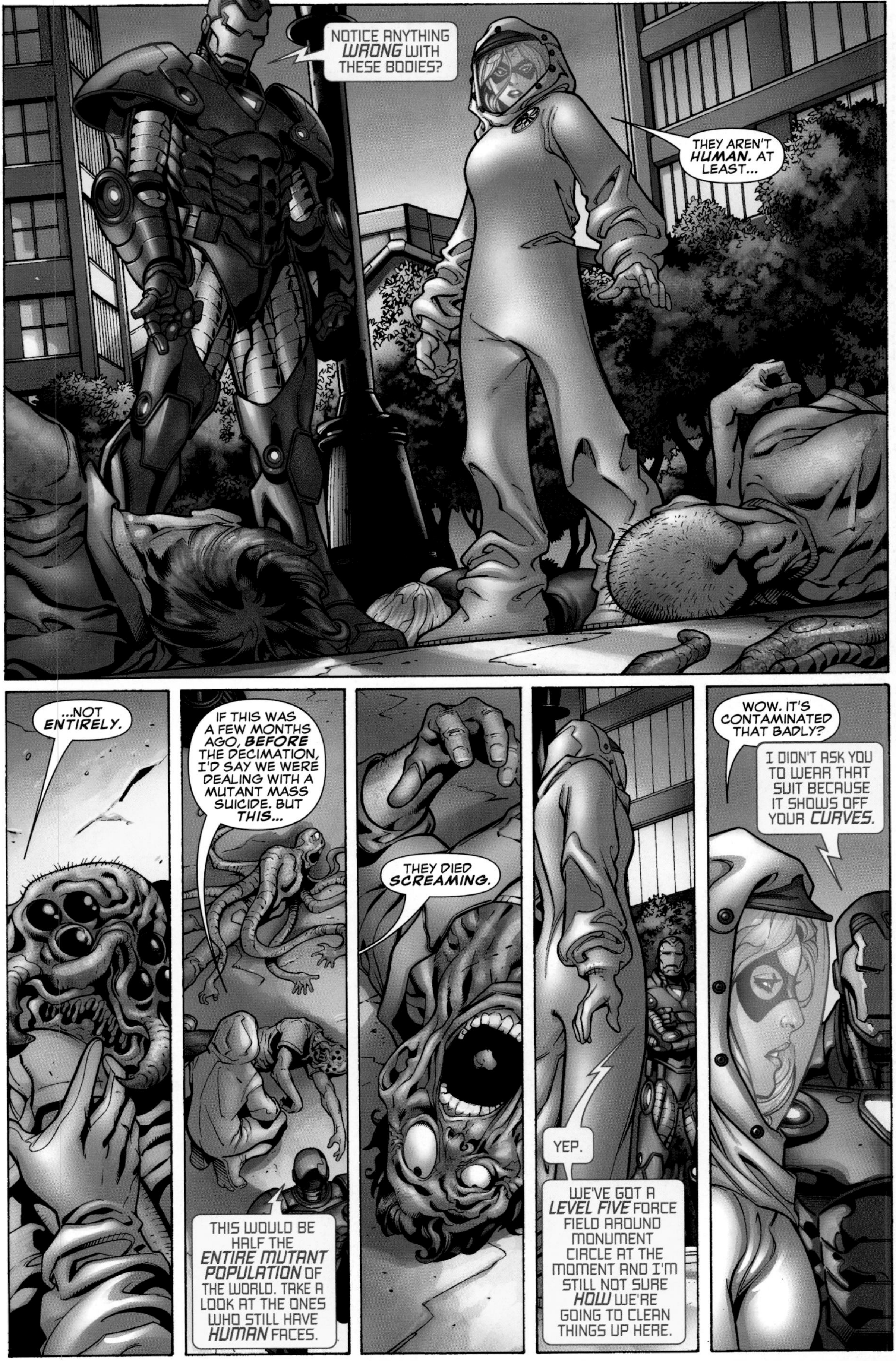
NOTICE ANYTHING WRONG WITH THESE BODIES?
THEY AREN'T HUMAN. AT LEAST...
...NOT ENTIRELY.
IF THIS WAS A FEW MONTHS AGO, BEFORE THE DECIMATION, I'D SAY WE WERE DEALING WITH A MUTANT MASS SUICIDE. BUT THIS...
THIS WOULD BE HALF THE ENTIRE MUTANT POPULATION OF THE WORLD. TAKE A LOOK AT THE ONES WHO STILL HAVE HUMAN FACES.
THEY DIED SCREAMING.
YEP.
WE'VE GOT A LEVEL FIVE FORCE FIELD AROUND MONUMENT CIRCLE AT THE MOMENT AND I'M STILL NOT SURE HOW WE'RE GOING TO CLEAN THINGS UP HERE.
WOW. IT'S CONTAMINATED THAT BADLY?
I DIDN'T ASK YOU TO WEAR THAT SUIT BECAUSE IT SHOWS OFF YOUR CURVES.

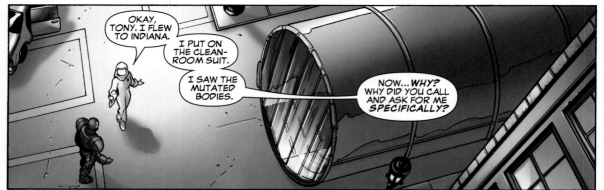

OKAY, TONY. I FLEW TO INDIANA.

I PUT ON THE CLEAN-ROOM SUIT.

I SAW THE MUTATED BODIES.

NOW... *WHY?* WHY DID YOU CALL AND ASK FOR ME *SPECIFICALLY?*

CAROL, THIS WAS AN ATTACK WITH A BOMB DESIGNED TO CAUSE RANDOM FLUCTUATIONS IN THE *ADENINE, GUANINE, CYTOSINE* AND *THYMINE* MAKEUPS OF THE VICTIMS.

IF YOU TWO WILL PLEASE STAND IN THE MIDDLE OF THE ROOM, WITH YOUR ARMS OUTSTRETCHED, I'LL ACTIVATE THE CLEANSING SOLUTION.

A DNA BOMB? WHO ON EARTH COULD EVEN FATHOM--

A.I.M.

GOT IT IN ONE.

S.H.I.E.L.D. HAS BEEN CHASING AFTER A.I.M. FOR SEVERAL MONTHS AND--

PLEASE PAUSE IN THE NEXT ROOM FOR A FEW MOMENTS. LET THE ULTRAVIOLETS DO THEIR WORK.

I DON'T GET IT. HOW HARD IS IT FOR THE WORLD'S TOP *ESPIONAGE ORGANIZATION* TO FIND A BUNCH OF GUYS IN *BEEKEEPER* COSTUMES?

CAROL, WE *HAVE* BEEN LOOKING FOR THEM.

AND DON'T UNDERESTIMATE A.I.M. EVEN THEIR MOST LOWLY OPERATIVE IS A SCIENTIFIC GENIUS.

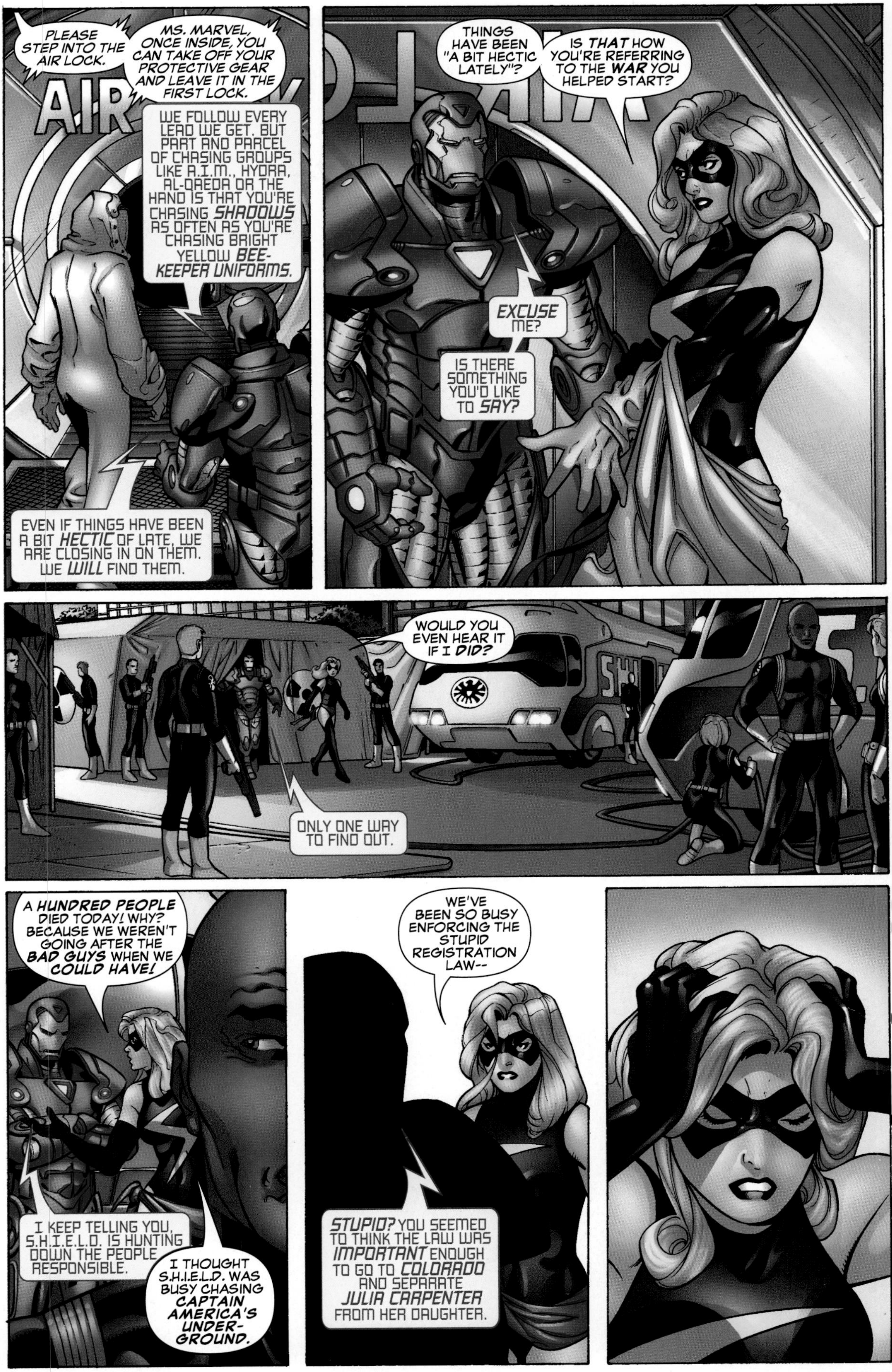
PLEASE STEP INTO THE AIR LOCK.
MS. MARVEL, ONCE INSIDE, YOU CAN TAKE OFF YOUR PROTECTIVE GEAR AND LEAVE IT IN THE FIRST LOCK.
AIR
WE FOLLOW EVERY LEAD WE GET. BUT PART AND PARCEL OF CHASING GROUPS LIKE A.I.M., HYDRA, AL-QAEDA OR THE HAND IS THAT YOU'RE CHASING SHADOWS AS OFTEN AS YOU'RE CHASING BRIGHT YELLOW BEE-KEEPER UNIFORMS.
EVEN IF THINGS HAVE BEEN A BIT HECTIC OF LATE, WE ARE CLOSING IN ON THEM. WE WILL FIND THEM.
THINGS HAVE BEEN "A BIT HECTIC LATELY"?
IS THAT HOW YOU'RE REFERRING TO THE WAR YOU HELPED START?
EXCUSE ME?
IS THERE SOMETHING YOU'D LIKE TO SAY?
WOULD YOU EVEN HEAR IT IF I DID?
ONLY ONE WAY TO FIND OUT.
A HUNDRED PEOPLE DIED TODAY! WHY? BECAUSE WE WEREN'T GOING AFTER THE BAD GUYS WHEN WE COULD HAVE!
I KEEP TELLING YOU, S.H.I.E.L.D. IS HUNTING DOWN THE PEOPLE RESPONSIBLE.
I THOUGHT S.H.I.E.L.D. WAS BUSY CHASING CAPTAIN AMERICA'S UNDER-GROUND.
WE'VE BEEN SO BUSY ENFORCING THE STUPID REGISTRATION LAW--
STUPID? YOU SEEMED TO THINK THE LAW WAS IMPORTANT ENOUGH TO GO TO COLORADO AND SEPARATE JULIA CARPENTER FROM HER DAUGHTER.

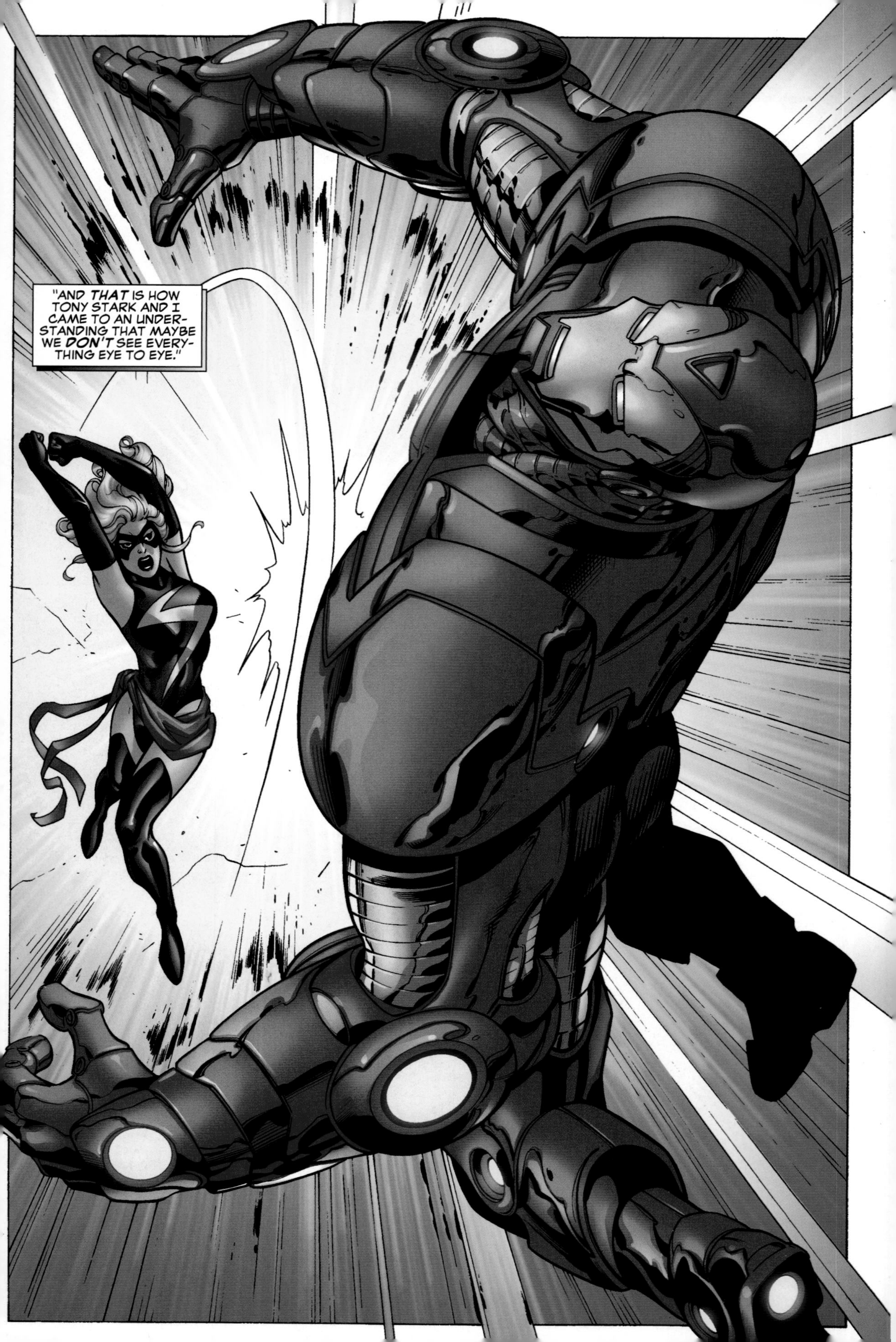
"AND THAT IS HOW TONY STARK AND I CAME TO AN UNDER-STANDING THAT MAYBE WE DON'T SEE EVERY-THING EYE TO EYE."

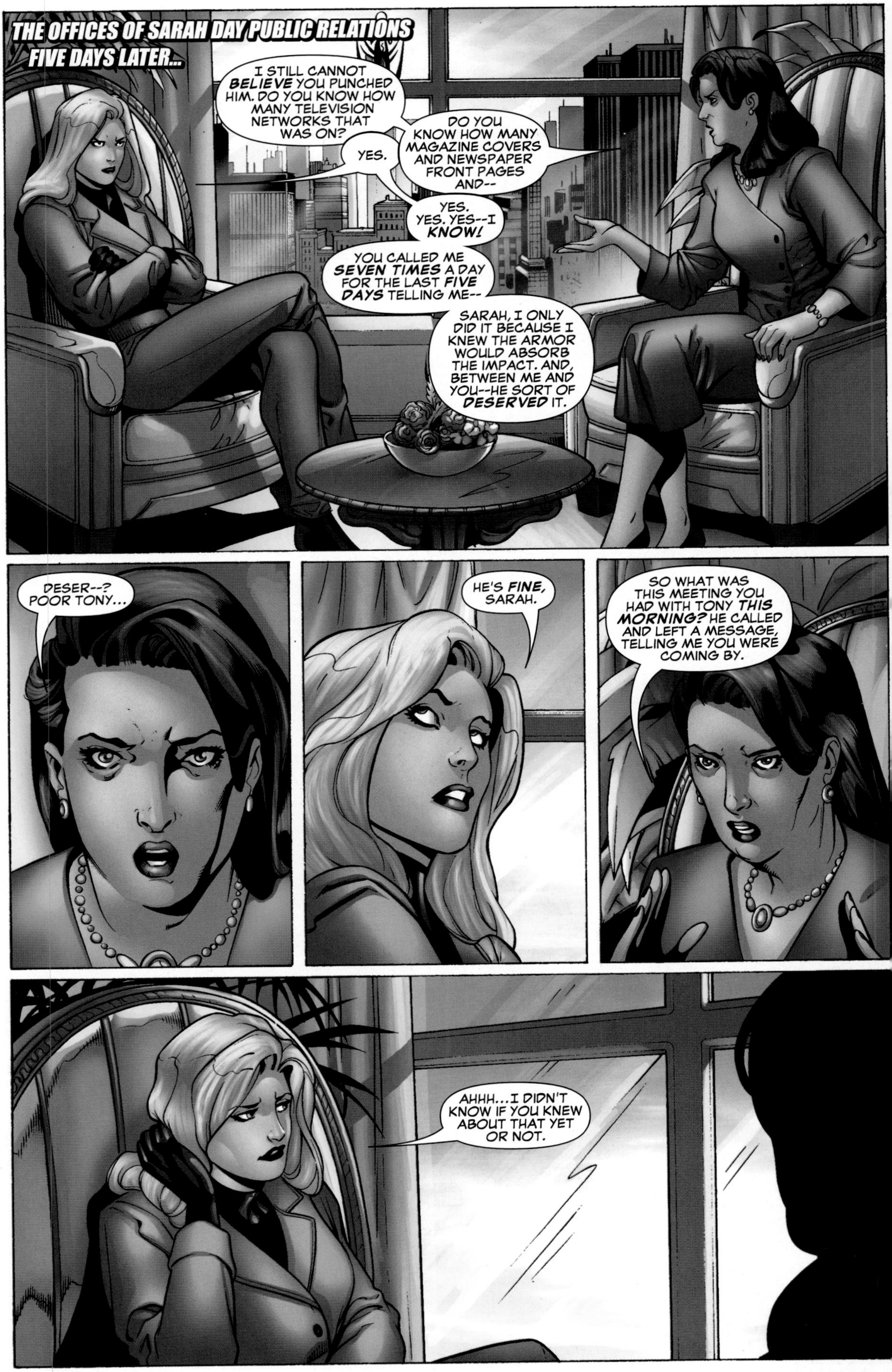
THE OFFICES OF SARAH DAY PUBLIC RELATIONS
FIVE DAYS LATER...
I STILL CANNOT BELIEVE YOU PUNCHED HIM. DO YOU KNOW HOW MANY TELEVISION NETWORKS THAT WAS ON?
YES.
DO YOU KNOW HOW MANY MAGAZINE COVERS AND NEWSPAPER FRONT PAGES AND--
YES. YES. YES--I KNOW!
YOU CALLED ME SEVEN TIMES A DAY FOR THE LAST FIVE DAYS TELLING ME--
SARAH, I ONLY DID IT BECAUSE I KNEW THE ARMOR WOULD ABSORB THE IMPACT. AND, BETWEEN ME AND YOU--HE SORT OF DESERVED IT.
DESER--? POOR TONY...
HE'S FINE, SARAH.
SO WHAT WAS THIS MEETING YOU HAD WITH TONY THIS MORNING? HE CALLED AND LEFT A MESSAGE, TELLING ME YOU WERE COMING BY.
AHHH...I DIDN'T KNOW IF YOU KNEW ABOUT THAT YET OR NOT.

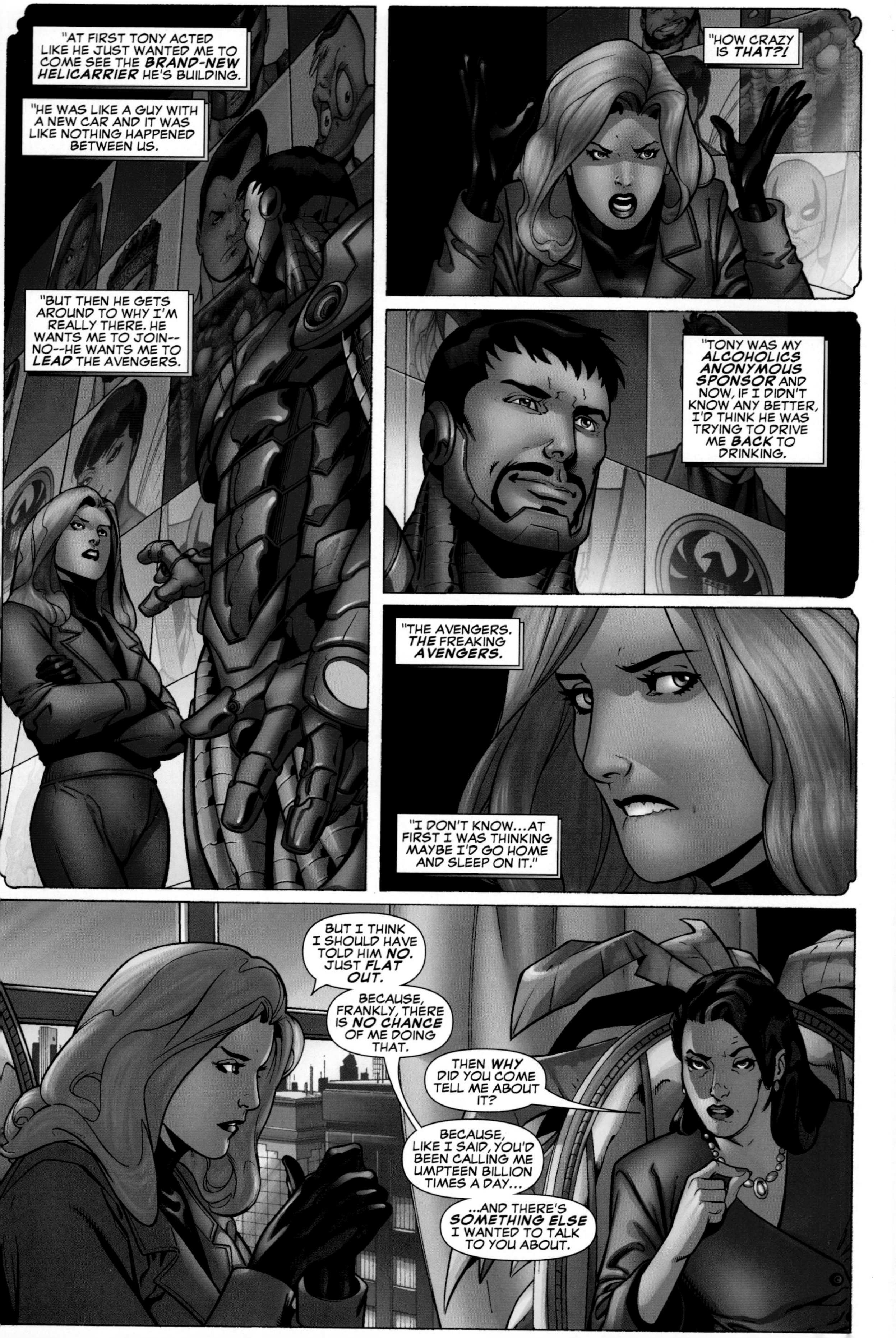
"AT FIRST TONY ACTED LIKE HE JUST WANTED ME TO COME SEE THE BRAND-NEW HELICARRIER HE'S BUILDING.
"HE WAS LIKE A GUY WITH A NEW CAR AND IT WAS LIKE NOTHING HAPPENED BETWEEN US.
"BUT THEN HE GETS AROUND TO WHY I'M REALLY THERE. HE WANTS ME TO JOIN--NO--HE WANTS ME TO LEAD THE AVENGERS.
"HOW CRAZY IS THAT?!
"TONY WAS MY ALCOHOLICS ANONYMOUS SPONSOR AND NOW, IF I DIDN'T KNOW ANY BETTER, I'D THINK HE WAS TRYING TO DRIVE ME BACK TO DRINKING.
"THE AVENGERS. THE FREAKING AVENGERS.
"I DON'T KNOW...AT FIRST I WAS THINKING MAYBE I'D GO HOME AND SLEEP ON IT."
BUT I THINK I SHOULD HAVE TOLD HIM NO. JUST FLAT OUT.
BECAUSE, FRANKLY, THERE IS NO CHANCE OF ME DOING THAT.
THEN WHY DID YOU COME TELL ME ABOUT IT?
BECAUSE, LIKE I SAID, YOU'D BEEN CALLING ME UMPTEEN BILLION TIMES A DAY...
...AND THERE'S SOMETHING ELSE I WANTED TO TALK TO YOU ABOUT.

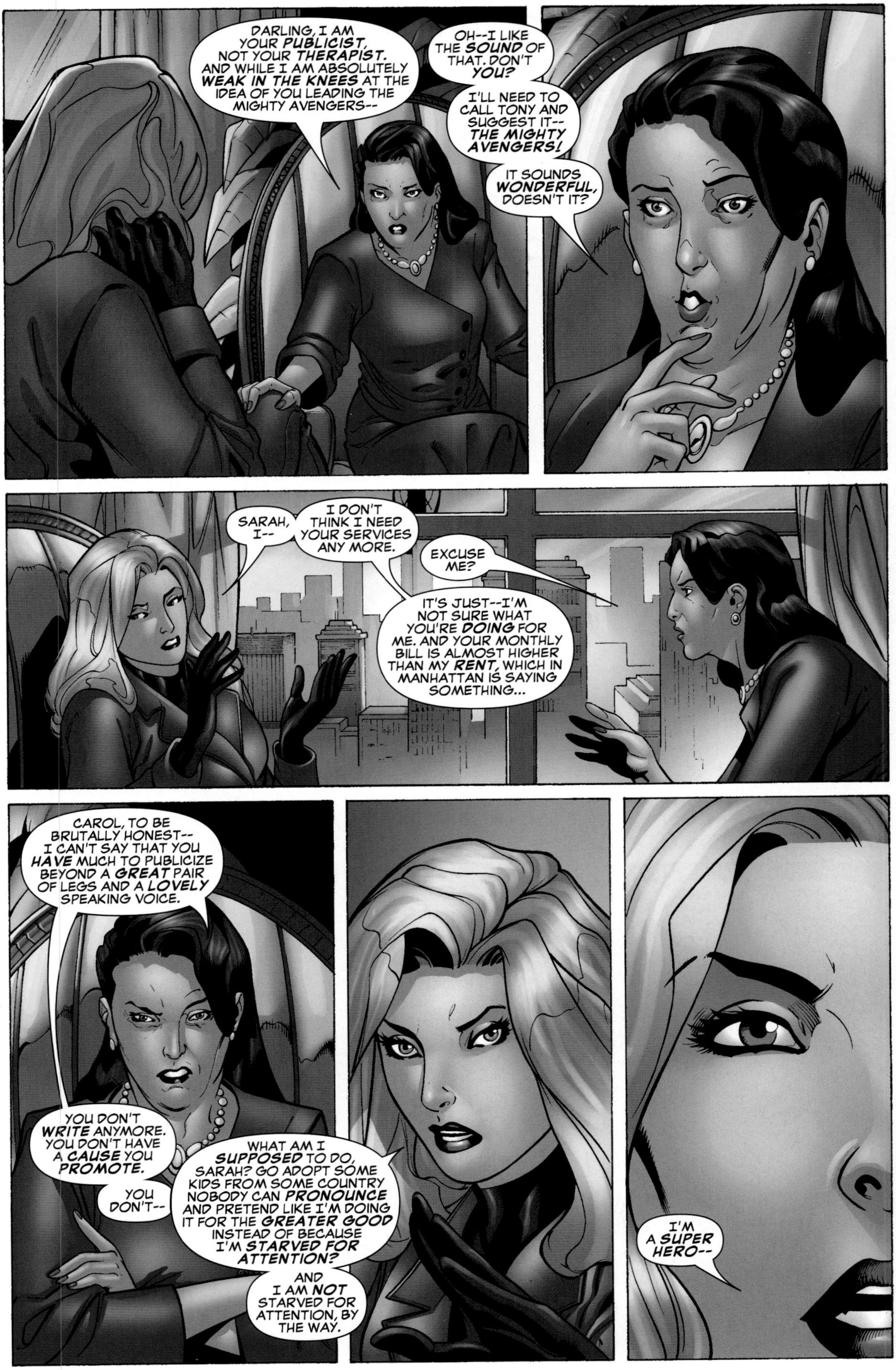
DARLING, I AM YOUR PUBLICIST, NOT YOUR THERAPIST. AND WHILE I AM ABSOLUTELY WEAK IN THE KNEES AT THE IDEA OF YOU LEADING THE MIGHTY AVENGERS--
OH--I LIKE THE SOUND OF THAT. DON'T YOU?
I'LL NEED TO CALL TONY AND SUGGEST IT-- THE MIGHTY AVENGERS!
IT SOUNDS WONDERFUL, DOESN'T IT?
SARAH, I--
I DON'T THINK I NEED YOUR SERVICES ANY MORE.
EXCUSE ME?
IT'S JUST--I'M NOT SURE WHAT YOU'RE DOING FOR ME. AND YOUR MONTHLY BILL IS ALMOST HIGHER THAN MY RENT, WHICH IN MANHATTAN IS SAYING SOMETHING...
CAROL, TO BE BRUTALLY HONEST-- I CAN'T SAY THAT YOU HAVE MUCH TO PUBLICIZE BEYOND A GREAT PAIR OF LEGS AND A LOVELY SPEAKING VOICE.
YOU DON'T WRITE ANYMORE. YOU DON'T HAVE A CAUSE YOU PROMOTE.
YOU DON'T--
WHAT AM I SUPPOSED TO DO, SARAH? GO ADOPT SOME KIDS FROM SOME COUNTRY NOBODY CAN PRONOUNCE AND PRETEND LIKE I'M DOING IT FOR THE GREATER GOOD INSTEAD OF BECAUSE I'M STARVED FOR ATTENTION?
AND I AM NOT STARVED FOR ATTENTION, BY THE WAY.
I'M A SUPER HERO--

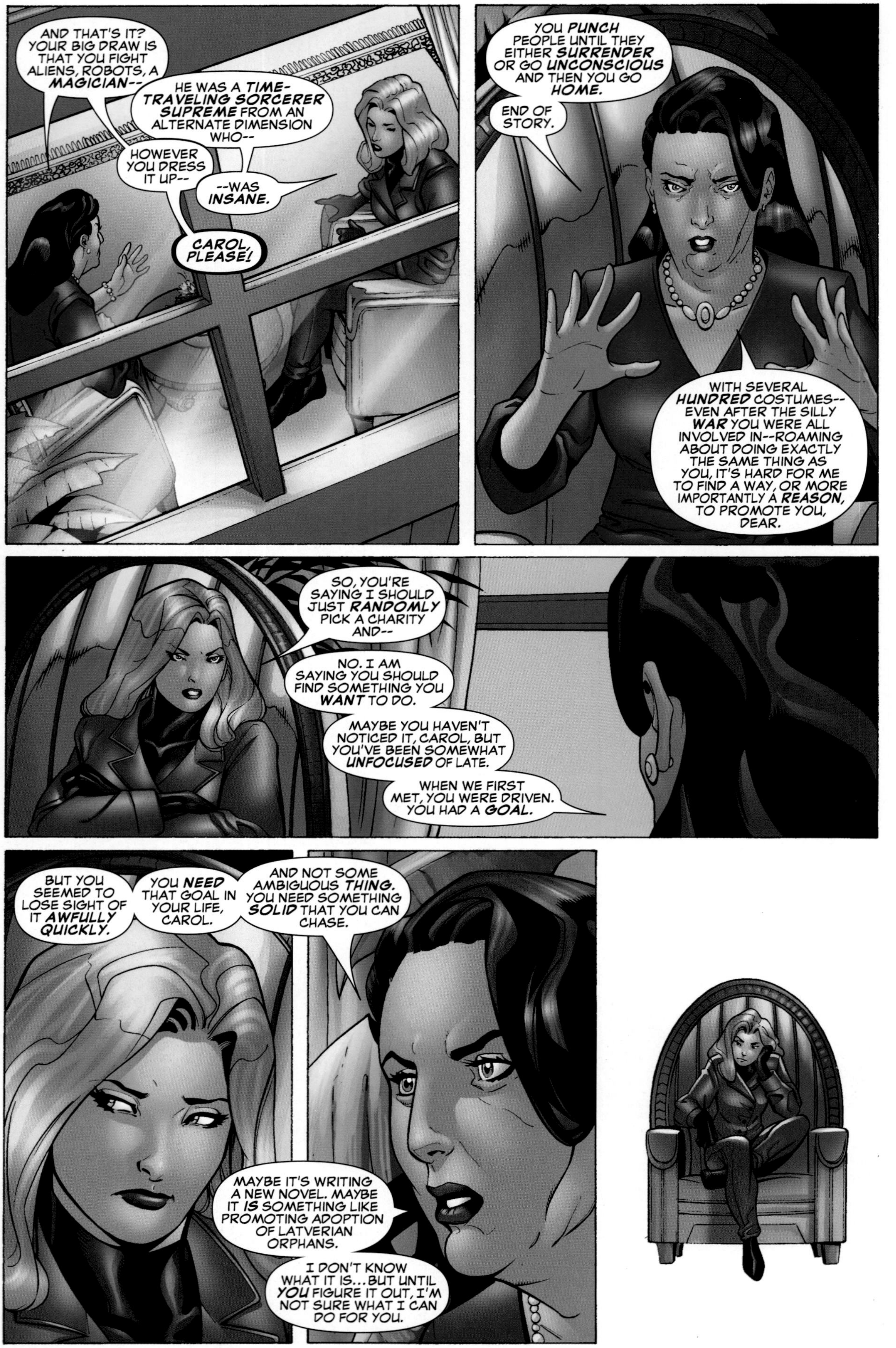

AND THAT'S IT? YOUR BIG DRAW IS THAT YOU FIGHT ALIENS, ROBOTS, A MAGICIAN--
HE WAS A TIME-TRAVELING SORCERER SUPREME FROM AN ALTERNATE DIMENSION WHO--
HOWEVER YOU DRESS IT UP--
--WAS INSANE.
CAROL, PLEASE!
YOU PUNCH PEOPLE UNTIL THEY EITHER SURRENDER OR GO UNCONSCIOUS AND THEN YOU GO HOME.
END OF STORY.
WITH SEVERAL HUNDRED COSTUMES--EVEN AFTER THE SILLY WAR YOU WERE ALL INVOLVED IN--ROAMING ABOUT DOING EXACTLY THE SAME THING AS YOU, IT'S HARD FOR ME TO FIND A WAY, OR MORE IMPORTANTLY A REASON, TO PROMOTE YOU, DEAR.
SO, YOU'RE SAYING I SHOULD JUST RANDOMLY PICK A CHARITY AND--
NO. I AM SAYING YOU SHOULD FIND SOMETHING YOU WANT TO DO.
MAYBE YOU HAVEN'T NOTICED IT, CAROL, BUT YOU'VE BEEN SOMEWHAT UNFOCUSED OF LATE.
WHEN WE FIRST MET, YOU WERE DRIVEN. YOU HAD A GOAL.
BUT YOU SEEMED TO LOSE SIGHT OF IT AWFULLY QUICKLY.
YOU NEED THAT GOAL IN YOUR LIFE, CAROL.
AND NOT SOME AMBIGUOUS THING. YOU NEED SOMETHING SOLID THAT YOU CAN CHASE.
MAYBE IT'S WRITING A NEW NOVEL. MAYBE IT IS SOMETHING LIKE PROMOTING ADOPTION OF LATVERIAN ORPHANS.
I DON'T KNOW WHAT IT IS... BUT UNTIL YOU FIGURE IT OUT, I'M NOT SURE WHAT I CAN DO FOR YOU.

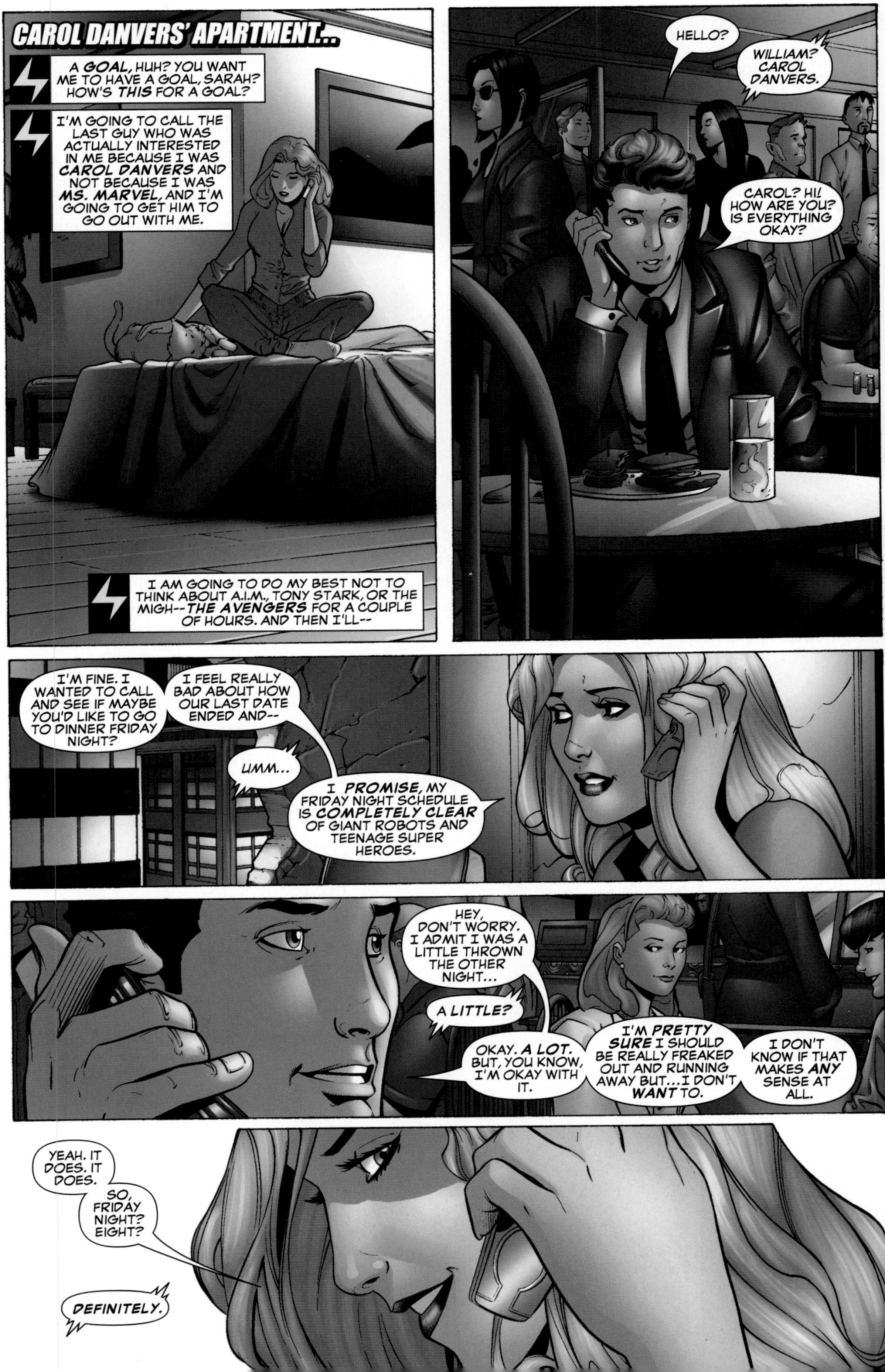
CAROL DANVERS' APARTMENT...
A GOAL, HUH? YOU WANT ME TO HAVE A GOAL, SARAH? HOW'S THIS FOR A GOAL?
I'M GOING TO CALL THE LAST GUY WHO WAS ACTUALLY INTERESTED IN ME BECAUSE I WAS CAROL DANVERS AND NOT BECAUSE I WAS MS. MARVEL, AND I'M GOING TO GET HIM TO GO OUT WITH ME.
I AM GOING TO DO MY BEST NOT TO THINK ABOUT A.I.M., TONY STARK, OR THE MIGH--THE AVENGERS FOR A COUPLE OF HOURS. AND THEN I'LL--
HELLO?
WILLIAM? CAROL DANVERS.
CAROL? HI! HOW ARE YOU? IS EVERYTHING OKAY?
I'M FINE. I WANTED TO CALL AND SEE IF MAYBE YOU'D LIKE TO GO TO DINNER FRIDAY NIGHT?
I FEEL REALLY BAD ABOUT HOW OUR LAST DATE ENDED AND--
UMM...
I PROMISE, MY FRIDAY NIGHT SCHEDULE IS COMPLETELY CLEAR OF GIANT ROBOTS AND TEENAGE SUPER HEROES.
HEY, DON'T WORRY. I ADMIT I WAS A LITTLE THROWN THE OTHER NIGHT...
A LITTLE?
OKAY. A LOT. BUT, YOU KNOW, I'M OKAY WITH IT.
I'M PRETTY SURE I SHOULD BE REALLY FREAKED OUT AND RUNNING AWAY BUT...I DON'T WANT TO.
I DON'T KNOW IF THAT MAKES ANY SENSE AT ALL.
YEAH. IT DOES. IT DOES.
SO, FRIDAY NIGHT? EIGHT?
DEFINITELY.

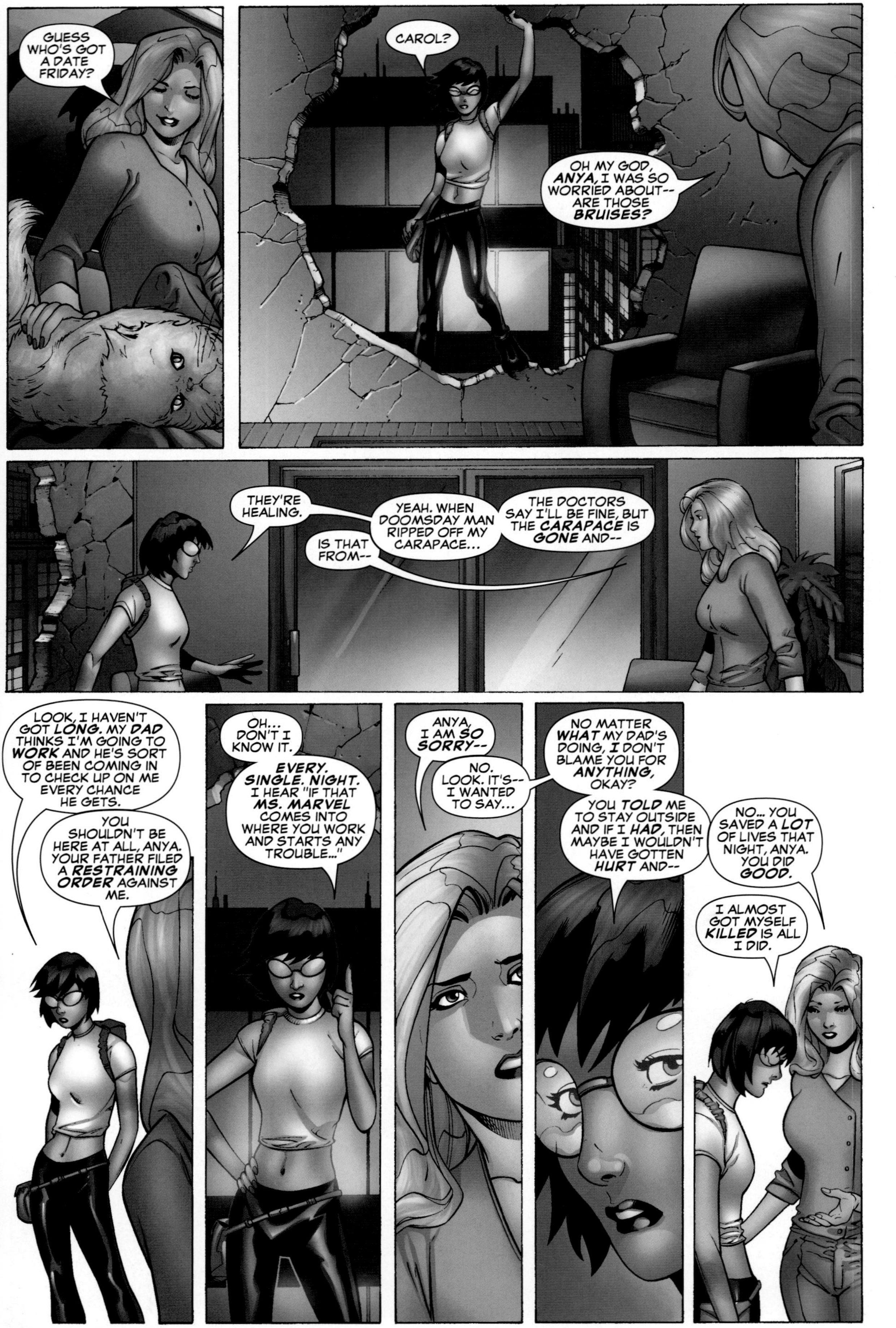
GUESS WHO'S GOT A DATE FRIDAY?
CAROL?
OH MY GOD, ANYA, I WAS SO WORRIED ABOUT-- ARE THOSE BRUISES?
THEY'RE HEALING.
YEAH. WHEN DOOMSDAY MAN RIPPED OFF MY CARAPACE...
IS THAT FROM--
THE DOCTORS SAY I'LL BE FINE, BUT THE CARAPACE IS GONE AND--
LOOK, I HAVEN'T GOT LONG. MY DAD THINKS I'M GOING TO WORK AND HE'S SORT OF BEEN COMING IN TO CHECK UP ON ME EVERY CHANCE HE GETS.
YOU SHOULDN'T BE HERE AT ALL, ANYA. YOUR FATHER FILED A RESTRAINING ORDER AGAINST ME.
OH... DON'T I KNOW IT.
EVERY. SINGLE. NIGHT. I HEAR "IF THAT MS. MARVEL COMES INTO WHERE YOU WORK AND STARTS ANY TROUBLE..."
ANYA, I AM SO SORRY--
NO. LOOK. IT'S-- I WANTED TO SAY...
NO MATTER WHAT MY DAD'S DOING, I DON'T BLAME YOU FOR ANYTHING, OKAY?
YOU TOLD ME TO STAY OUTSIDE AND IF I HAD, THEN MAYBE I WOULDN'T HAVE GOTTEN HURT AND--
NO... YOU SAVED A LOT OF LIVES THAT NIGHT, ANYA. YOU DID GOOD.
I ALMOST GOT MYSELF KILLED IS ALL I DID.

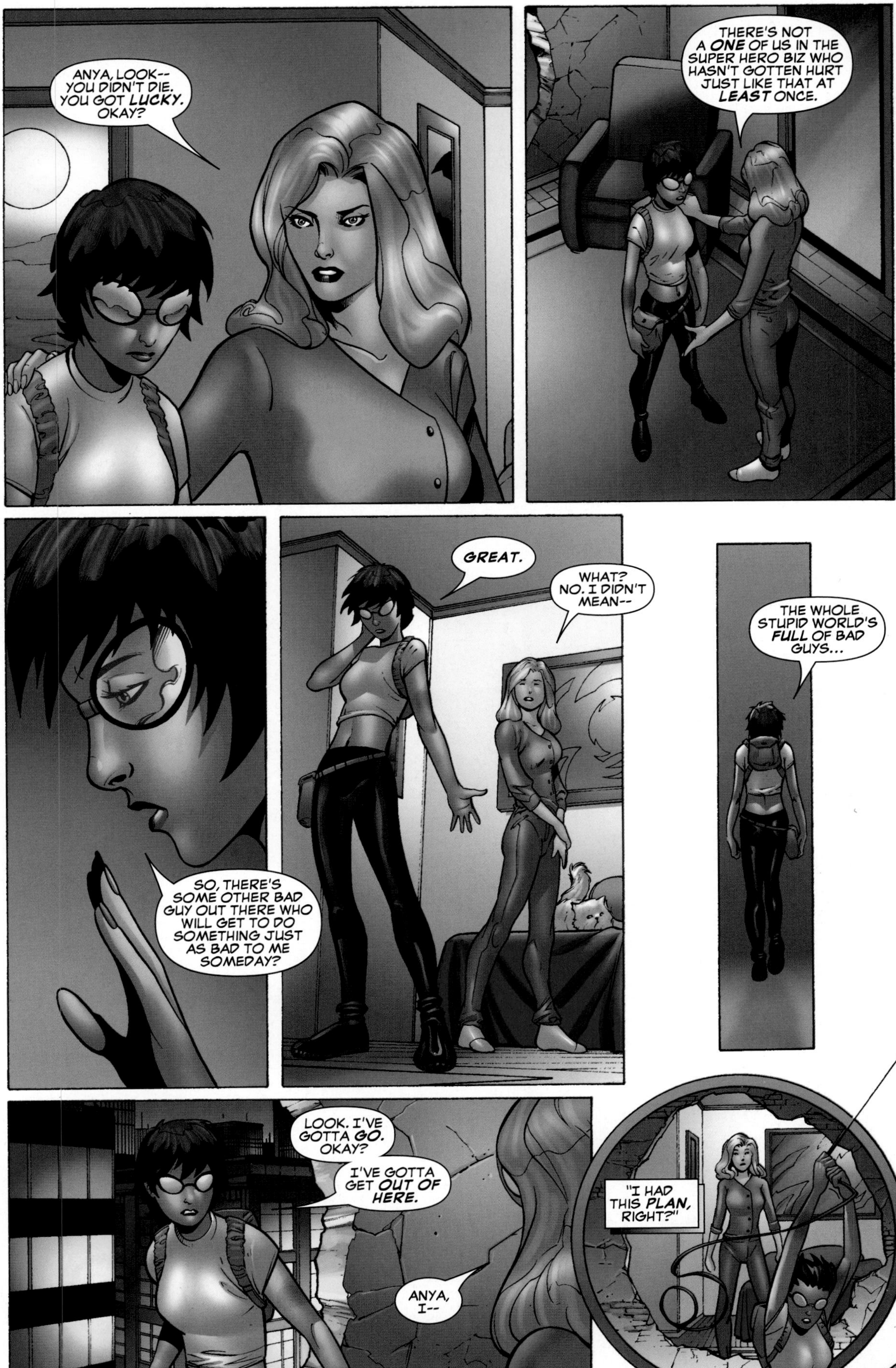
ANYA, LOOK-- YOU DIDN'T DIE. YOU GOT LUCKY. OKAY?
THERE'S NOT A ONE OF US IN THE SUPER HERO BIZ WHO HASN'T GOTTEN HURT JUST LIKE THAT AT LEAST ONCE.
SO, THERE'S SOME OTHER BAD GUY OUT THERE WHO WILL GET TO DO SOMETHING JUST AS BAD TO ME SOMEDAY?
GREAT.
WHAT? NO. I DIDN'T MEAN--
THE WHOLE STUPID WORLD'S FULL OF BAD GUYS...
LOOK. I'VE GOTTA GO. OKAY?
I'VE GOTTA GET OUT OF HERE.
ANYA, I--
"I HAD THIS PLAN, RIGHT?"

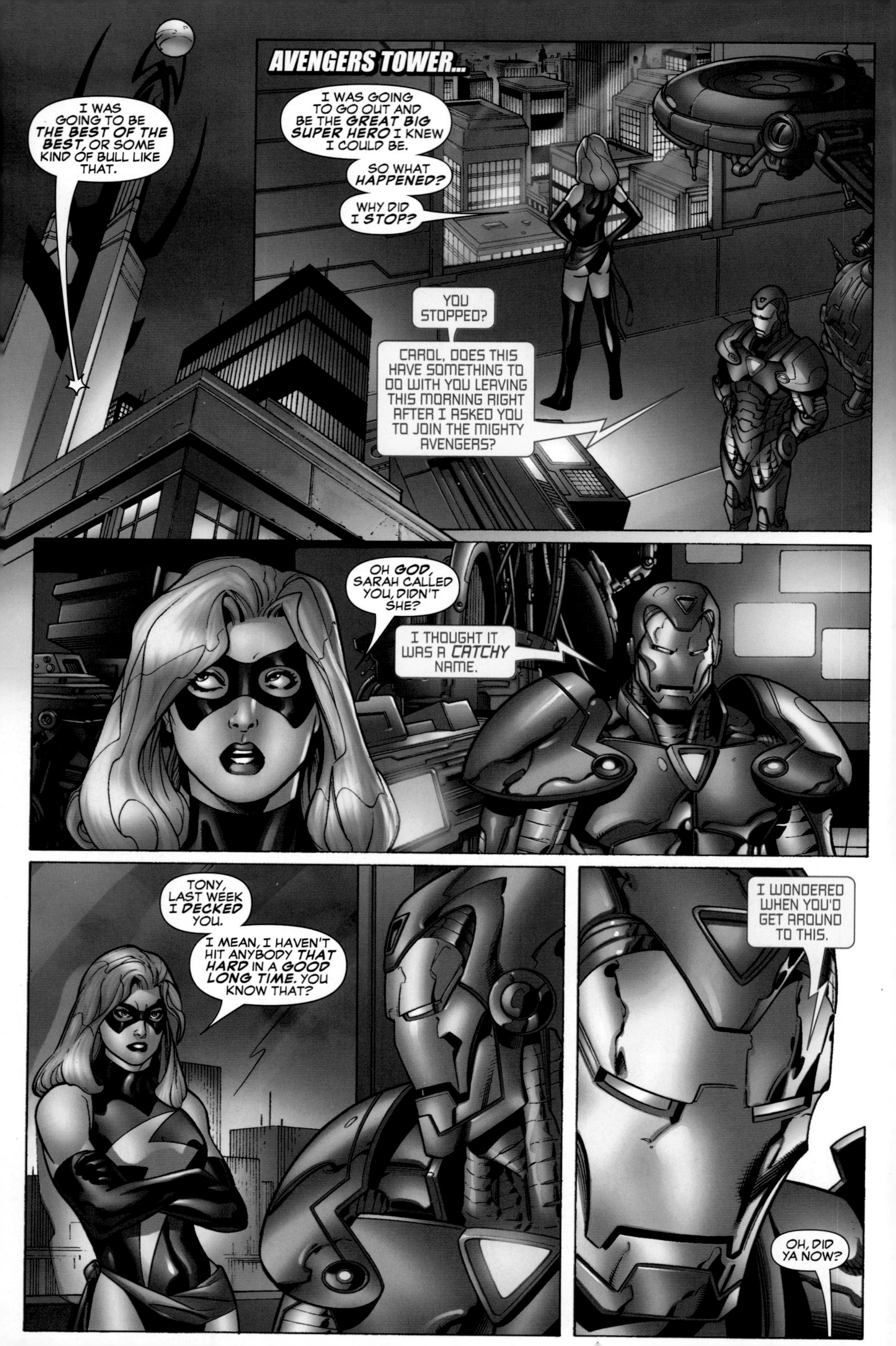
AVENGERS TOWER...
I WAS GOING TO BE THE BEST OF THE BEST, OR SOME KIND OF BULL LIKE THAT.
I WAS GOING TO GO OUT AND BE THE GREAT BIG SUPER HERO I KNEW I COULD BE.
SO WHAT HAPPENED?
WHY DID I STOP?
YOU STOPPED?
CAROL, DOES THIS HAVE SOMETHING TO DO WITH YOU LEAVING THIS MORNING RIGHT AFTER I ASKED YOU TO JOIN THE MIGHTY AVENGERS?
OH GOD, SARAH CALLED YOU, DIDN'T SHE?
I THOUGHT IT WAS A CATCHY NAME.
TONY, LAST WEEK I DECKED YOU.
I MEAN, I HAVEN'T HIT ANYBODY THAT HARD IN A GOOD LONG TIME. YOU KNOW THAT?
I WONDERED WHEN YOU'D GET AROUND TO THIS.
OH, DID YA NOW?

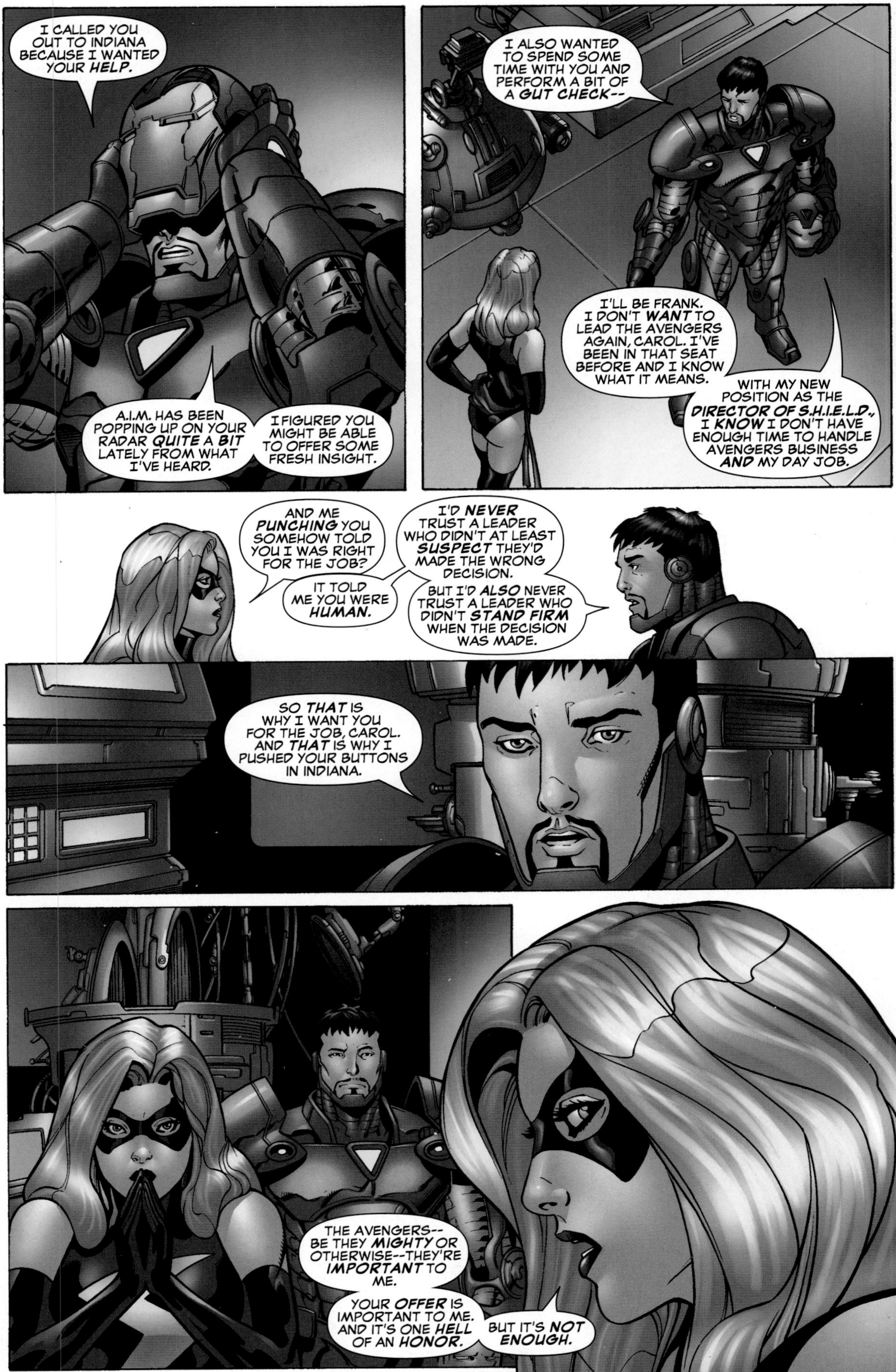
I CALLED YOU OUT TO INDIANA BECAUSE I WANTED YOUR HELP.
A.I.M. HAS BEEN POPPING UP ON YOUR RADAR QUITE A BIT LATELY FROM WHAT I'VE HEARD.
I FIGURED YOU MIGHT BE ABLE TO OFFER SOME FRESH INSIGHT.
I ALSO WANTED TO SPEND SOME TIME WITH YOU AND PERFORM A BIT OF A GUT CHECK--
I'LL BE FRANK. I DON'T WANT TO LEAD THE AVENGERS AGAIN, CAROL. I'VE BEEN IN THAT SEAT BEFORE AND I KNOW WHAT IT MEANS.
WITH MY NEW POSITION AS THE DIRECTOR OF S.H.I.E.L.D., I KNOW I DON'T HAVE ENOUGH TIME TO HANDLE AVENGERS BUSINESS AND MY DAY JOB.
AND ME PUNCHING YOU SOMEHOW TOLD YOU I WAS RIGHT FOR THE JOB?
IT TOLD ME YOU WERE HUMAN.
I'D NEVER TRUST A LEADER WHO DIDN'T AT LEAST SUSPECT THEY'D MADE THE WRONG DECISION.
BUT I'D ALSO NEVER TRUST A LEADER WHO DIDN'T STAND FIRM WHEN THE DECISION WAS MADE.
SO THAT IS WHY I WANT YOU FOR THE JOB, CAROL. AND THAT IS WHY I PUSHED YOUR BUTTONS IN INDIANA.
THE AVENGERS-- BE THEY MIGHTY OR OTHERWISE--THEY'RE IMPORTANT TO ME.
YOUR OFFER IS IMPORTANT TO ME. AND IT'S ONE HELL OF AN HONOR.
BUT IT'S NOT ENOUGH.

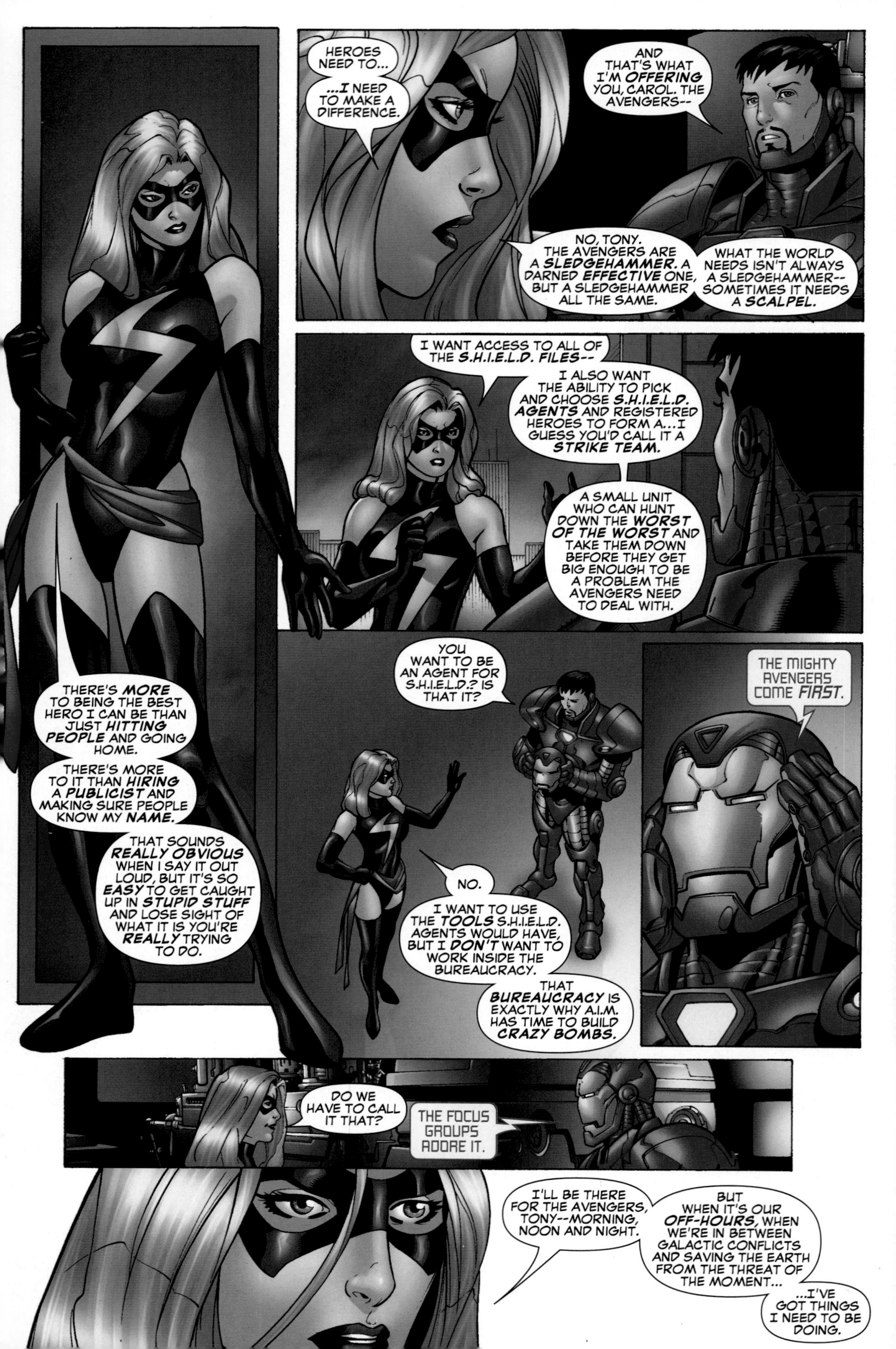
HEROES NEED TO...
...I NEED TO MAKE A DIFFERENCE.
AND THAT'S WHAT I'M OFFERING YOU, CAROL. THE AVENGERS--
NO, TONY. THE AVENGERS ARE A SLEDGEHAMMER. A DARNED EFFECTIVE ONE, BUT A SLEDGEHAMMER ALL THE SAME.
WHAT THE WORLD NEEDS ISN'T ALWAYS A SLEDGEHAMMER--SOMETIMES IT NEEDS A SCALPEL.
THERE'S MORE TO BEING THE BEST HERO I CAN BE THAN JUST HITTING PEOPLE AND GOING HOME.
THERE'S MORE TO IT THAN HIRING A PUBLICIST AND MAKING SURE PEOPLE KNOW MY NAME.
THAT SOUNDS REALLY OBVIOUS WHEN I SAY IT OUT LOUD, BUT IT'S SO EASY TO GET CAUGHT UP IN STUPID STUFF AND LOSE SIGHT OF WHAT IT IS YOU'RE REALLY TRYING TO DO.
I WANT ACCESS TO ALL OF THE S.H.I.E.L.D. FILES--
I ALSO WANT THE ABILITY TO PICK AND CHOOSE S.H.I.E.L.D. AGENTS AND REGISTERED HEROES TO FORM A...I GUESS YOU'D CALL IT A STRIKE TEAM.
A SMALL UNIT WHO CAN HUNT DOWN THE WORST OF THE WORST AND TAKE THEM DOWN BEFORE THEY GET BIG ENOUGH TO BE A PROBLEM THE AVENGERS NEED TO DEAL WITH.
YOU WANT TO BE AN AGENT FOR S.H.I.E.L.D.? IS THAT IT?
NO.
I WANT TO USE THE TOOLS S.H.I.E.L.D. AGENTS WOULD HAVE, BUT I DON'T WANT TO WORK INSIDE THE BUREAUCRACY.
THAT BUREAUCRACY IS EXACTLY WHY A.I.M. HAS TIME TO BUILD CRAZY BOMBS.
THE MIGHTY AVENGERS COME FIRST.
DO WE HAVE TO CALL IT THAT?
THE FOCUS GROUPS ADORE IT.
I'LL BE THERE FOR THE AVENGERS, TONY--MORNING, NOON AND NIGHT.
BUT WHEN IT'S OUR OFF-HOURS, WHEN WE'RE IN BETWEEN GALACTIC CONFLICTS AND SAVING THE EARTH FROM THE THREAT OF THE MOMENT...
...I'VE GOT THINGS I NEED TO BE DOING.

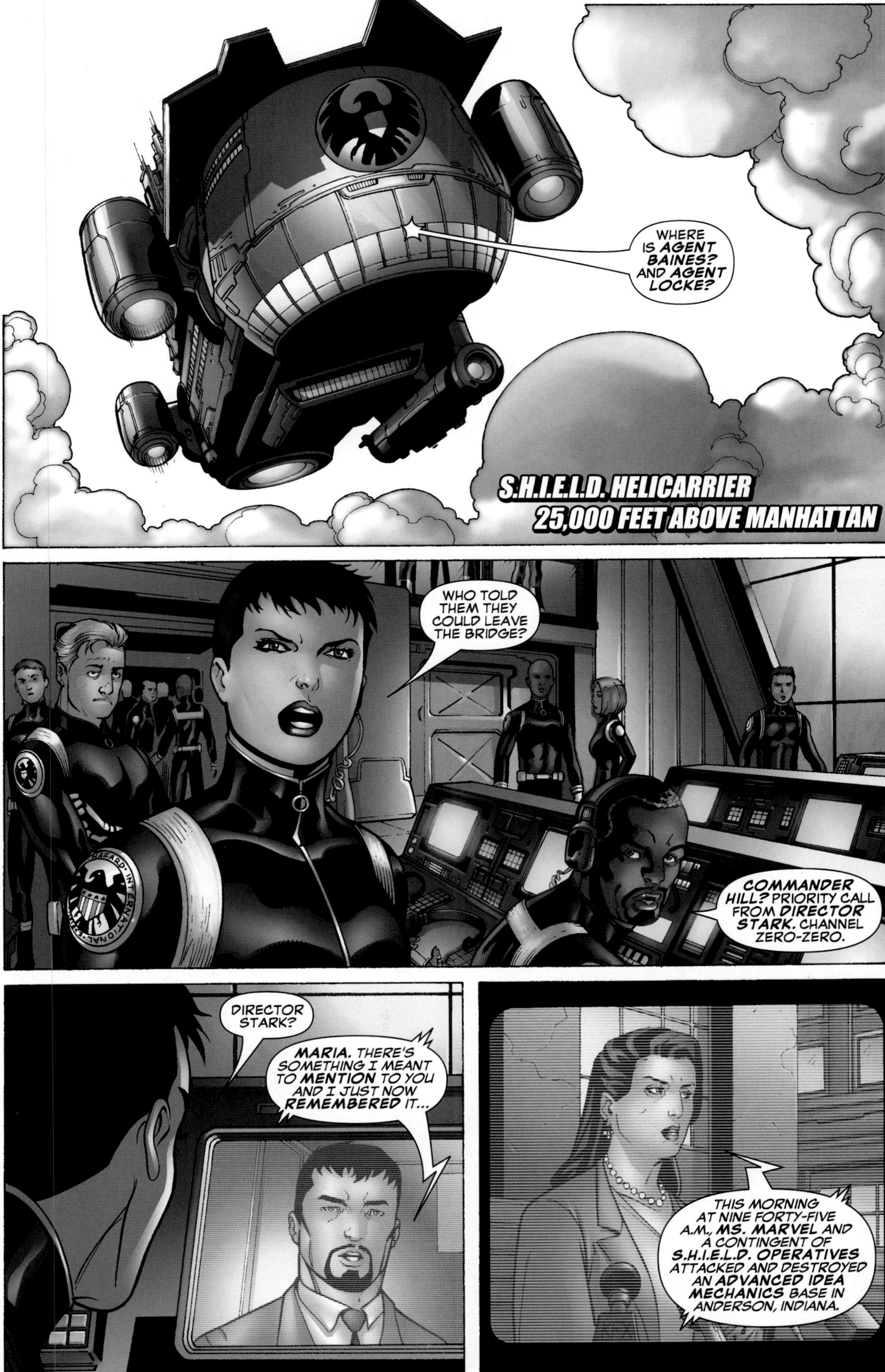
WHERE IS AGENT BAINES? AND AGENT LOCKE?
S.H.I.E.L.D. HELICARRIER
25,000 FEET ABOVE MANHATTAN
WHO TOLD THEM THEY COULD LEAVE THE BRIDGE?
COMMANDER HILL? PRIORITY CALL FROM DIRECTOR STARK. CHANNEL ZERO-ZERO.
DIRECTOR STARK?
MARIA. THERE'S SOMETHING I MEANT TO MENTION TO YOU AND I JUST NOW REMEMBERED IT...
THIS MORNING AT NINE FORTY-FIVE A.M., MS. MARVEL AND A CONTINGENT OF S.H.I.E.L.D. OPERATIVES ATTACKED AND DESTROYED AN ADVANCED IDEA MECHANICS BASE IN ANDERSON, INDIANA.

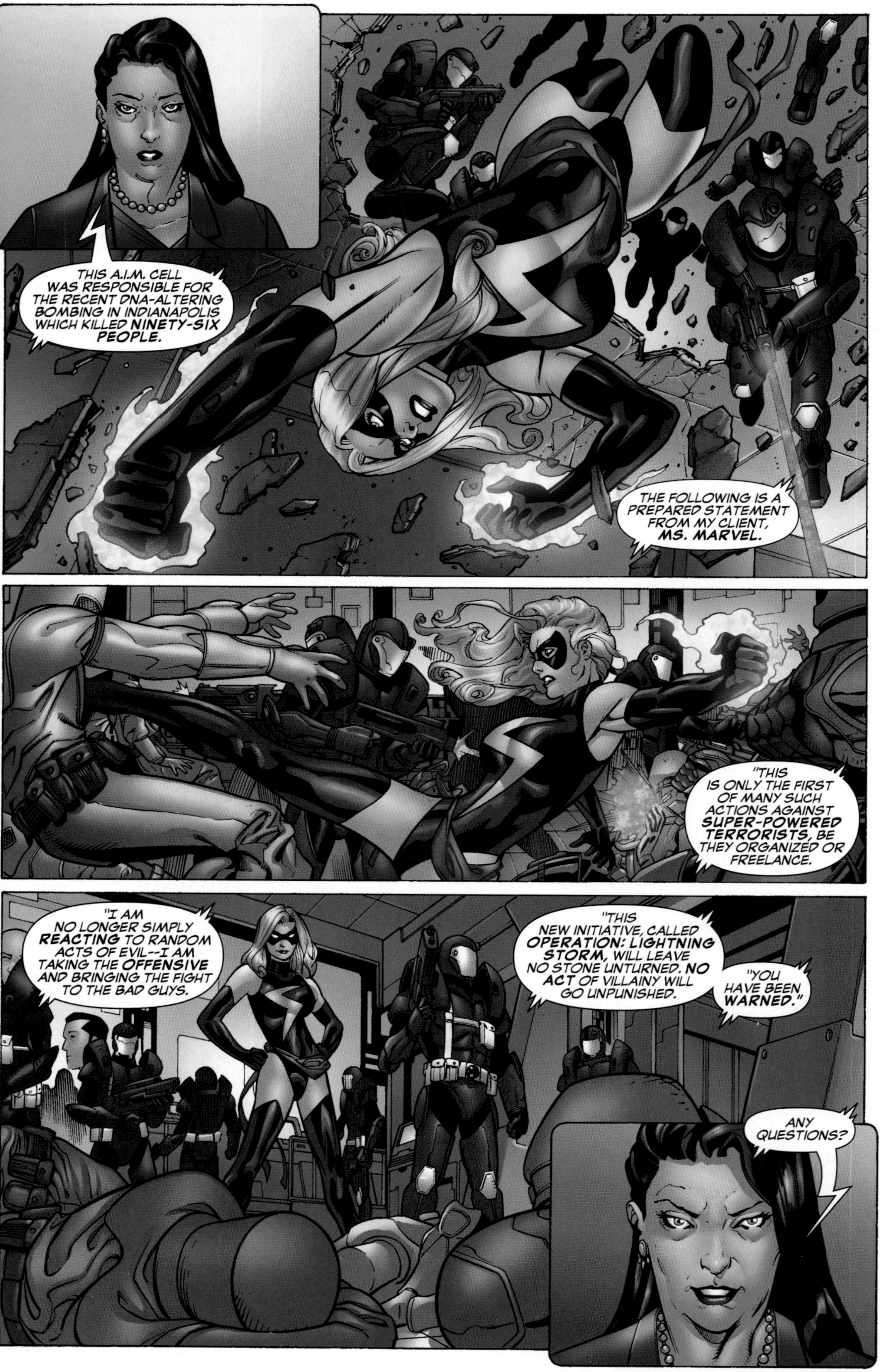
THIS A.I.M. CELL WAS RESPONSIBLE FOR THE RECENT DNA-ALTERING BOMBING IN INDIANAPOLIS WHICH KILLED NINETY-SIX PEOPLE.
THE FOLLOWING IS A PREPARED STATEMENT FROM MY CLIENT, MS. MARVEL.
"THIS IS ONLY THE FIRST OF MANY SUCH ACTIONS AGAINST SUPER-POWERED TERRORISTS, BE THEY ORGANIZED OR FREELANCE.
"I AM NO LONGER SIMPLY REACTING TO RANDOM ACTS OF EVIL--I AM TAKING THE OFFENSIVE AND BRINGING THE FIGHT TO THE BAD GUYS.
"THIS NEW INITIATIVE, CALLED OPERATION: LIGHTNING STORM, WILL LEAVE NO STONE UNTURNED. NO ACT OF VILLAINY WILL GO UNPUNISHED.
"YOU HAVE BEEN WARNED."
ANY QUESTIONS?

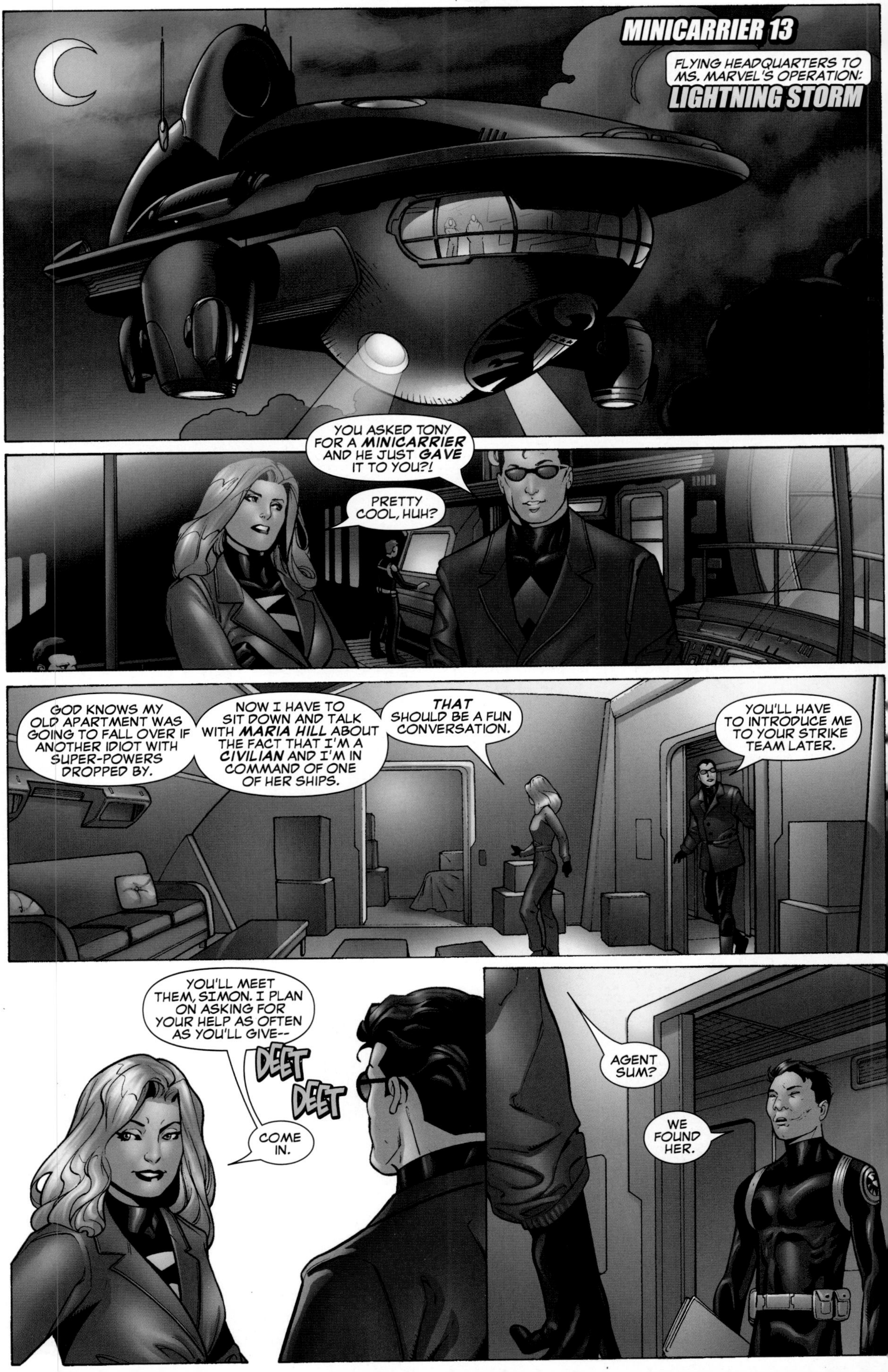
MINICARRIER 13
FLYING HEADQUARTERS TO MS. MARVEL'S OPERATION: LIGHTNING STORM
YOU ASKED TONY FOR A MINICARRIER AND HE JUST GAVE IT TO YOU?!
PRETTY COOL, HUH?
GOD KNOWS MY OLD APARTMENT WAS GOING TO FALL OVER IF ANOTHER IDIOT WITH SUPER-POWERS DROPPED BY.
NOW I HAVE TO SIT DOWN AND TALK WITH MARIA HILL ABOUT THE FACT THAT I'M A CIVILIAN AND I'M IN COMMAND OF ONE OF HER SHIPS.
THAT SHOULD BE A FUN CONVERSATION.
YOU'LL HAVE TO INTRODUCE ME TO YOUR STRIKE TEAM LATER.
YOU'LL MEET THEM, SIMON. I PLAN ON ASKING FOR YOUR HELP AS OFTEN AS YOU'LL GIVE--
DEET DEET
COME IN.
AGENT SUM?
WE FOUND HER.

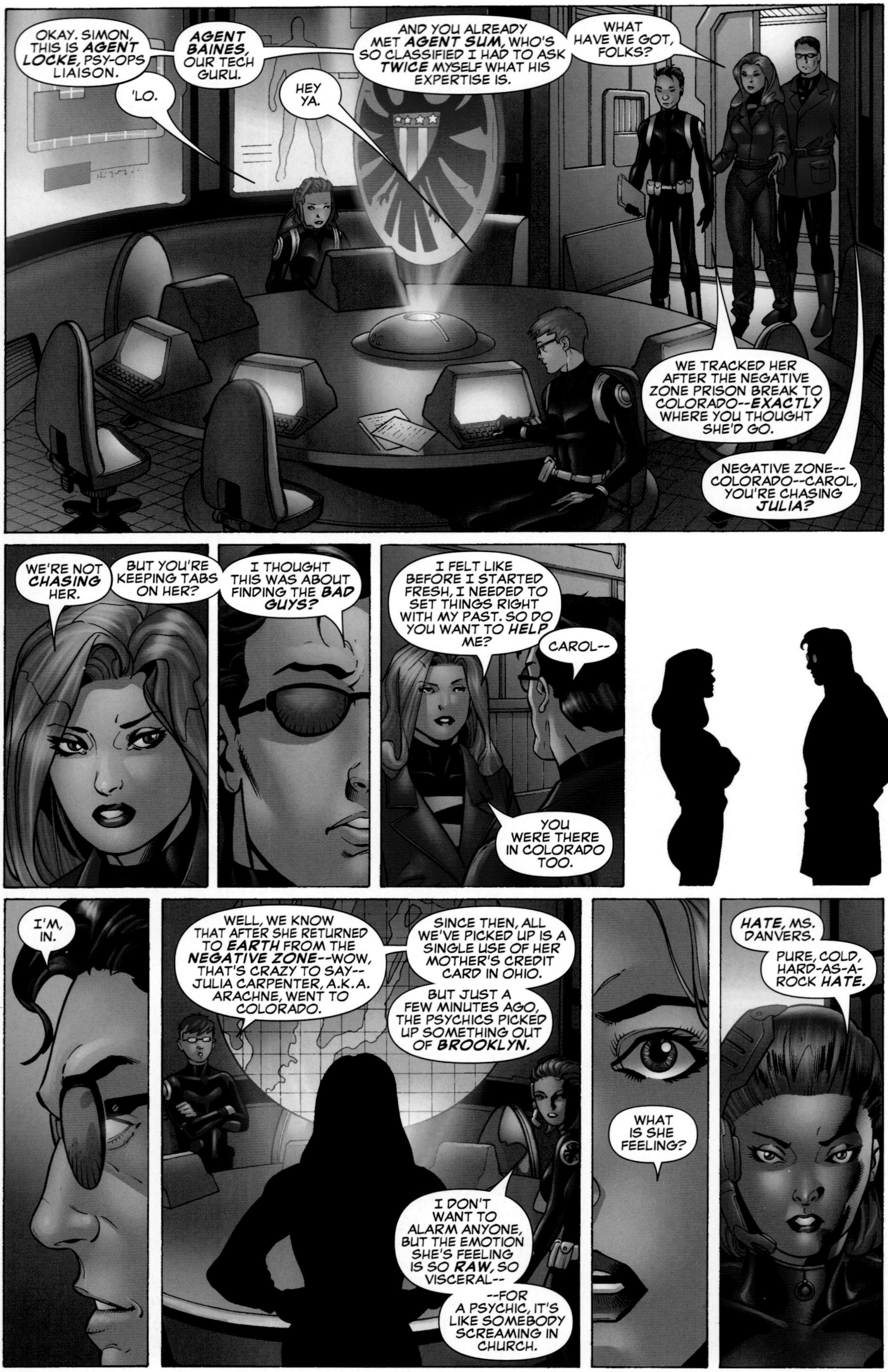

OKAY. SIMON, THIS IS AGENT LOCKE, PSY-OPS LIAISON.
AGENT BAINES, OUR TECH GURU.
AND YOU ALREADY MET AGENT SUM, WHO'S SO CLASSIFIED I HAD TO ASK TWICE MYSELF WHAT HIS EXPERTISE IS.
WHAT HAVE WE GOT, FOLKS?
'LO.
HEY YA.
WE TRACKED HER AFTER THE NEGATIVE ZONE PRISON BREAK TO COLORADO--EXACTLY WHERE YOU THOUGHT SHE'D GO.
NEGATIVE ZONE--COLORADO--CAROL, YOU'RE CHASING JULIA?
WE'RE NOT CHASING HER.
BUT YOU'RE KEEPING TABS ON HER?
I THOUGHT THIS WAS ABOUT FINDING THE BAD GUYS?
I FELT LIKE BEFORE I STARTED FRESH, I NEEDED TO SET THINGS RIGHT WITH MY PAST. SO DO YOU WANT TO HELP ME?
CAROL--
YOU WERE THERE IN COLORADO TOO.
I'M, IN.
WELL, WE KNOW THAT AFTER SHE RETURNED TO EARTH FROM THE NEGATIVE ZONE--WOW, THAT'S CRAZY TO SAY--JULIA CARPENTER, A.K.A. ARACHNE, WENT TO COLORADO.
SINCE THEN, ALL WE'VE PICKED UP IS A SINGLE USE OF HER MOTHER'S CREDIT CARD IN OHIO.
BUT JUST A FEW MINUTES AGO, THE PSYCHICS PICKED UP SOMETHING OUT OF BROOKLYN.
I DON'T WANT TO ALARM ANYONE, BUT THE EMOTION SHE'S FEELING IS SO RAW, SO VISCERAL--
--FOR A PSYCHIC, IT'S LIKE SOMEBODY SCREAMING IN CHURCH.
WHAT IS SHE FEELING?
HATE, MS. DANVERS.
PURE, COLD, HARD-AS-A-ROCK HATE.

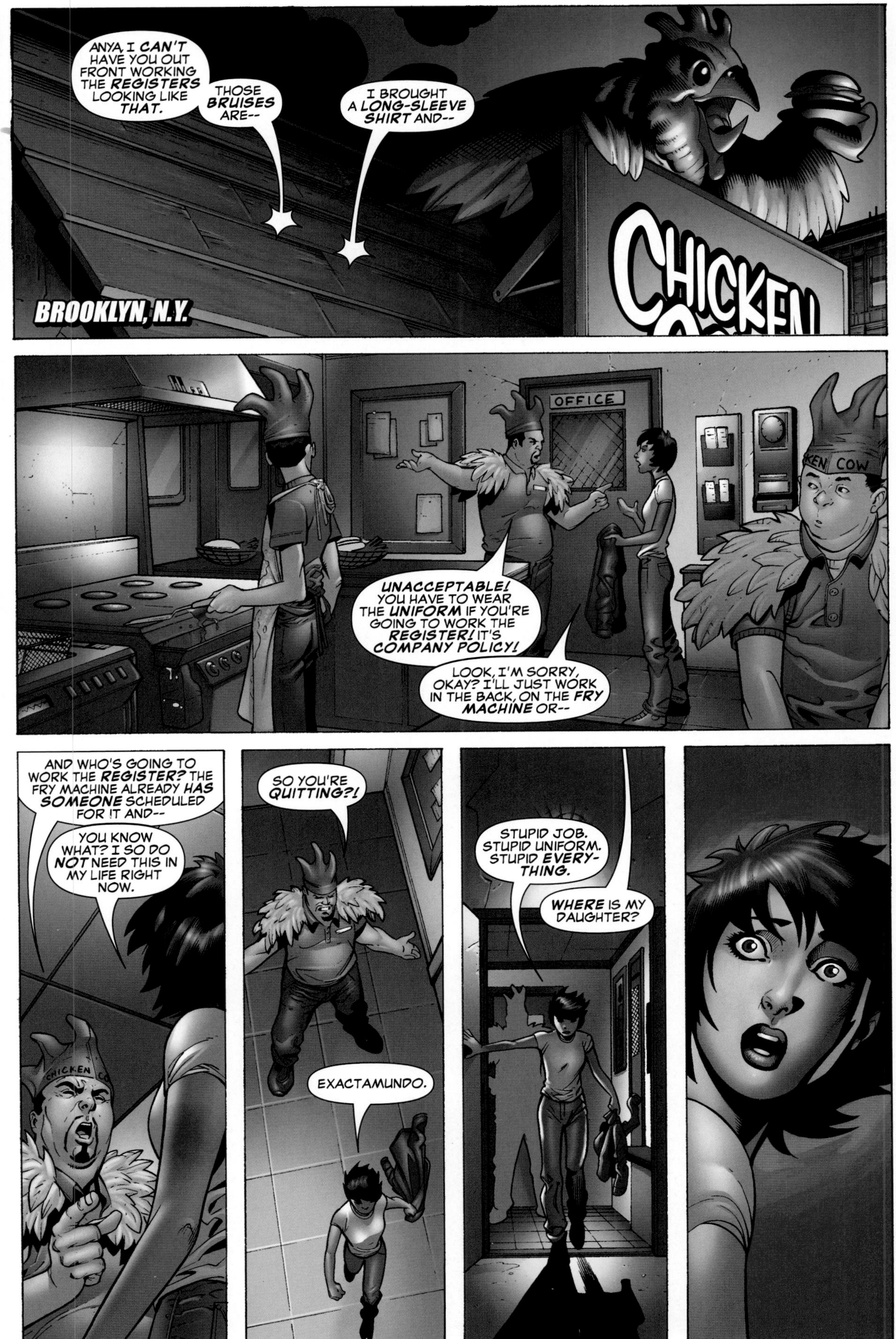
ANYA, I CAN'T HAVE YOU OUT FRONT WORKING THE REGISTERS LOOKING LIKE THAT.
THOSE BRUISES ARE--
I BROUGHT A LONG-SLEEVE SHIRT AND--
BROOKLYN, N.Y.
CHICKEN
OFFICE
KEN COW
UNACCEPTABLE! YOU HAVE TO WEAR THE UNIFORM IF YOU'RE GOING TO WORK THE REGISTER! IT'S COMPANY POLICY!
LOOK, I'M SORRY, OKAY? I'LL JUST WORK IN THE BACK, ON THE FRY MACHINE OR--
AND WHO'S GOING TO WORK THE REGISTER? THE FRY MACHINE ALREADY HAS SOMEONE SCHEDULED FOR IT AND--
YOU KNOW WHAT? I SO DO NOT NEED THIS IN MY LIFE RIGHT NOW.
CHICKEN CO
SO YOU'RE QUITTING?!
EXACTAMUNDO.
STUPID JOB. STUPID UNIFORM. STUPID EVERYTHING.
WHERE IS MY DAUGHTER?

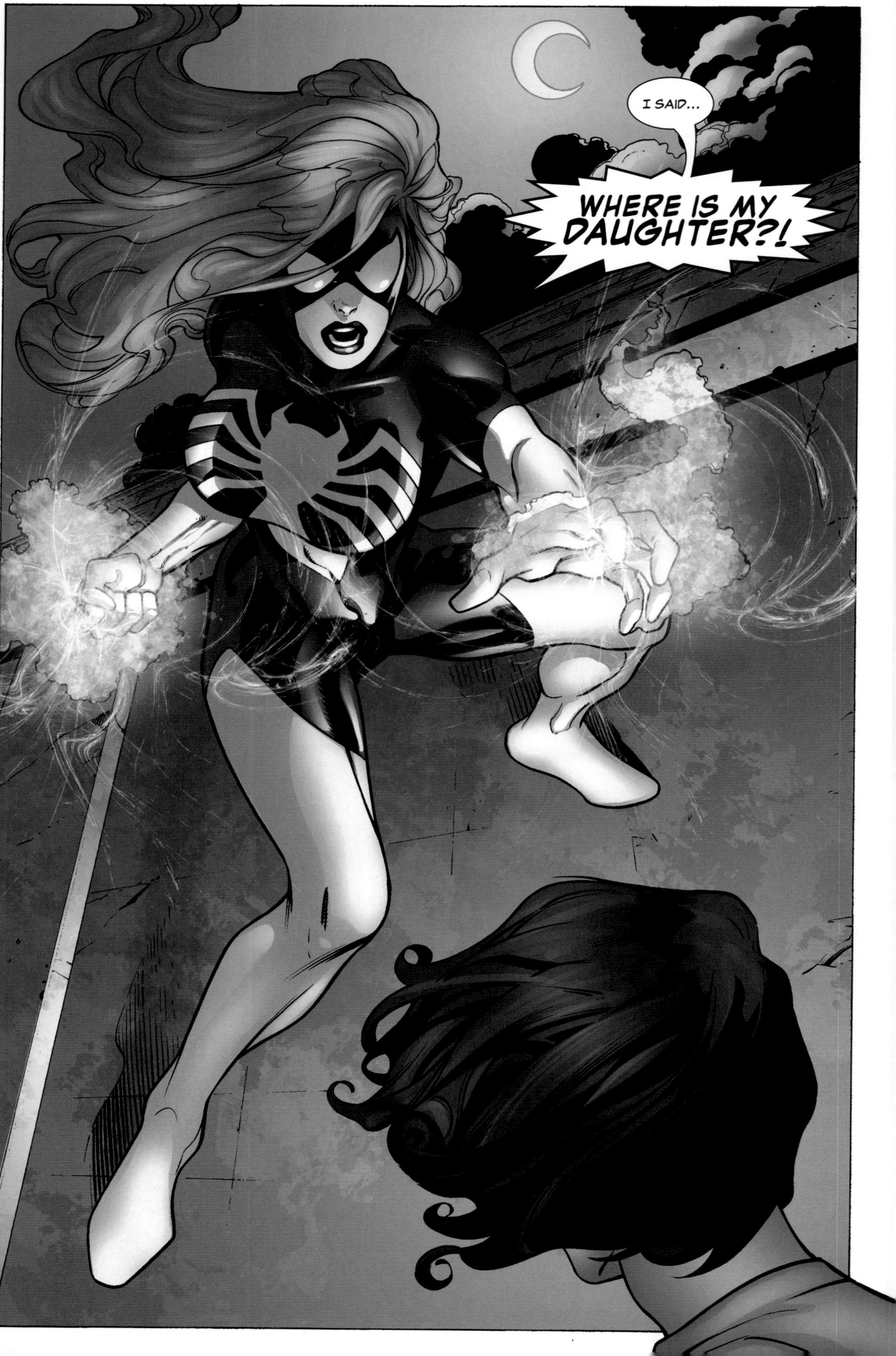
I SAID...
WHERE IS MY DAUGHTER?!

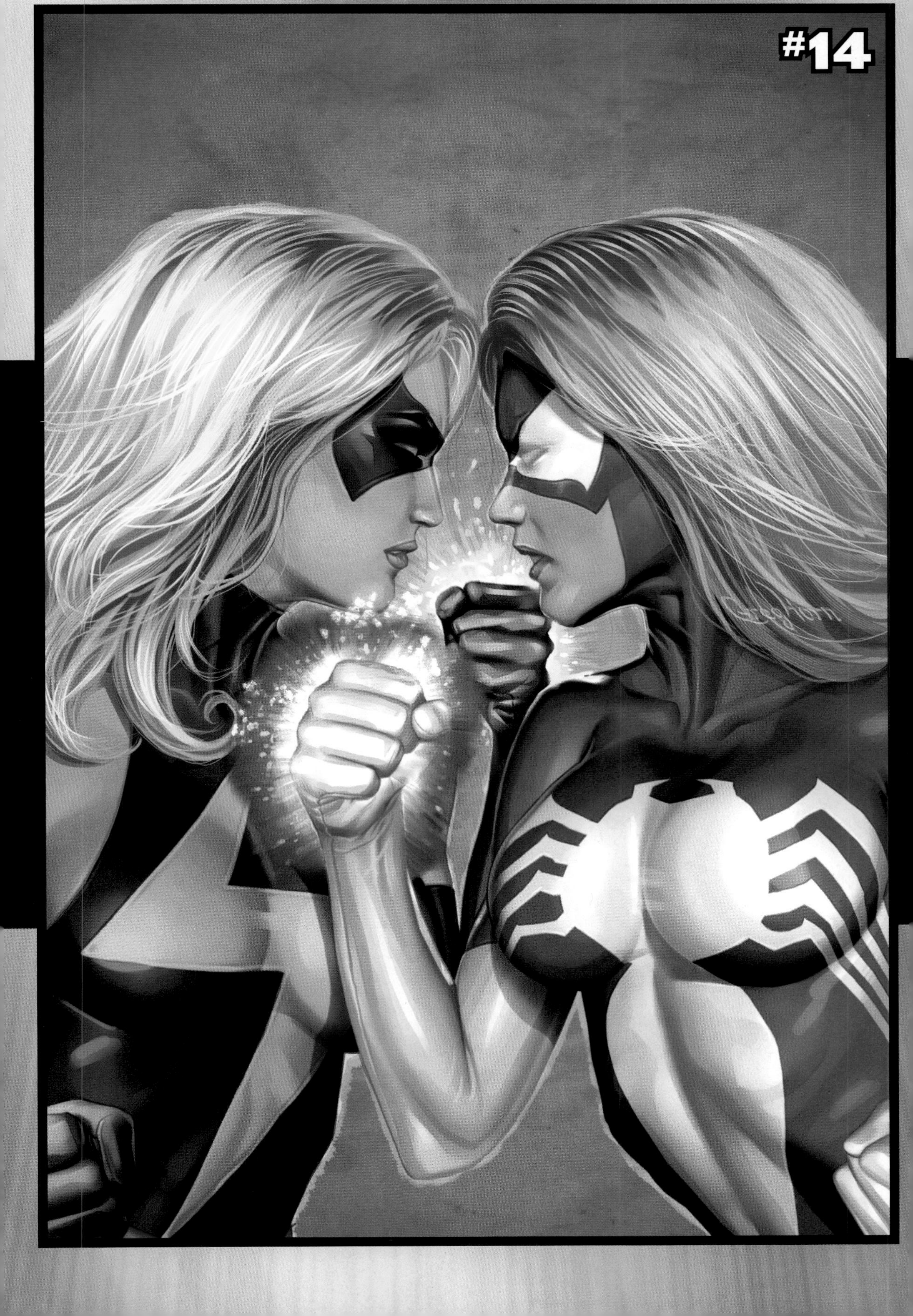
#14

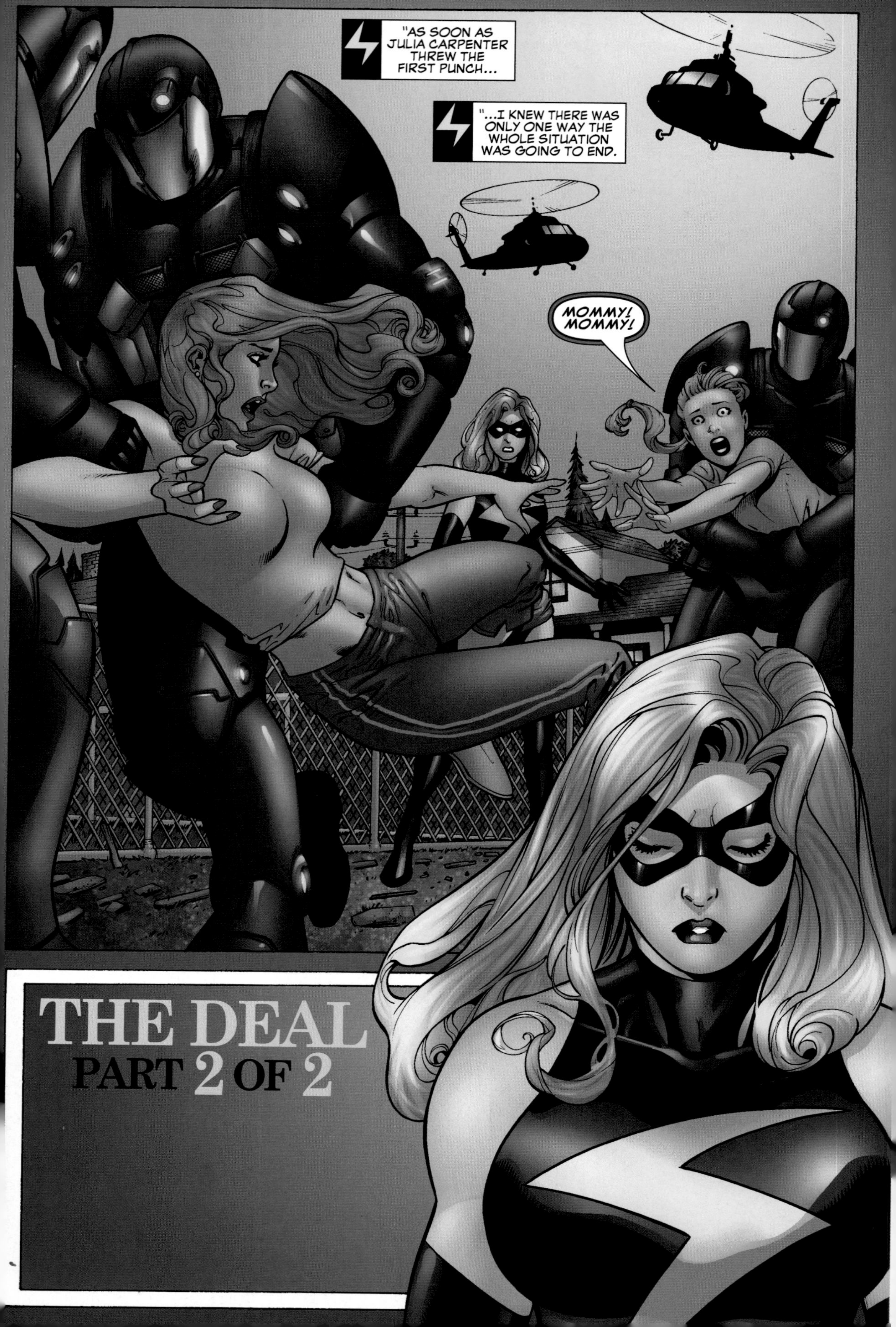

"AS SOON AS JULIA CARPENTER THREW THE FIRST PUNCH...
"...I KNEW THERE WAS ONLY ONE WAY THE WHOLE SITUATION WAS GOING TO END.
MOMMY! MOMMY!
THE DEAL
PART 2 OF 2

"I'M NOT SAYING SHE DIDN'T NEED TO BE TAKEN IN, TONY. SHE DID.

"SHE BROKE *MULTIPLE* LAWS--

WONDER MAN? WONDER MAN, WHAT ARE THEY DOING?

WHAT THEY HAVE TO, ANYA.

"JUST OFF THE TOP OF MY HEAD, SHE WAS RESPONSIBLE FOR PETTY THEFT, GRAND THEFT, AIDING AND ABETTING UNREGISTERED COMBATANTS, ATTACKING OFFICERS OF THE LAW, *AND* TREASON."

ELIZABETH! *NO!*

THAT'S OUR DAUGHTER THEY'RE ATTACKING!

AND THAT'S THE *UNITED STATES GOVERNMENT* SHE JUST PICKED A FIGHT WITH!

EVEN WITH ALL HER POWERS, THEY STILL PUT HER DOWN! WHAT CAN YOU DO TO HELP HER?

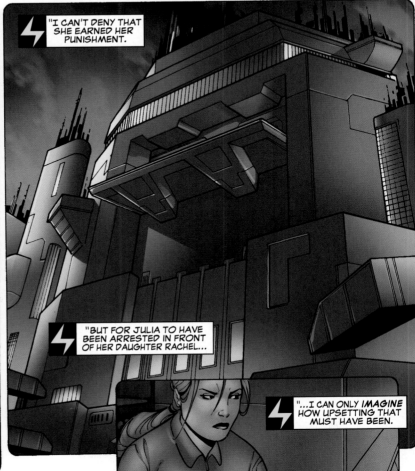

"I CAN'T DENY THAT SHE EARNED HER PUNISHMENT.

"BUT FOR JULIA TO HAVE BEEN ARRESTED IN FRONT OF HER DAUGHTER RACHEL...

"...I CAN ONLY *IMAGINE* HOW UPSETTING THAT MUST HAVE BEEN.

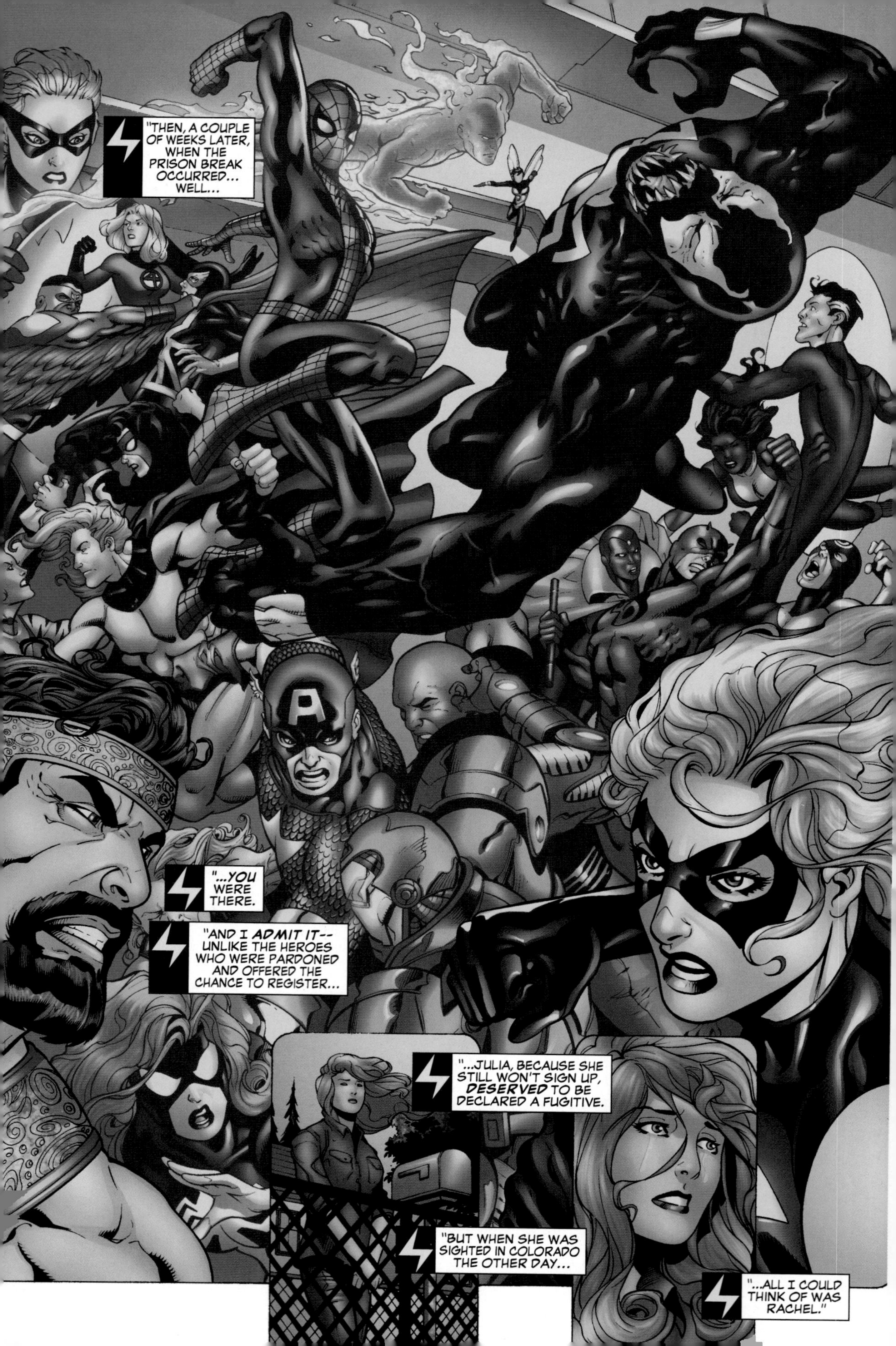
"THEN, A COUPLE OF WEEKS LATER, WHEN THE PRISON BREAK OCCURRED... WELL...
"...YOU WERE THERE.
"AND I ADMIT IT-- UNLIKE THE HEROES WHO WERE PARDONED AND OFFERED THE CHANCE TO REGISTER...
"...JULIA, BECAUSE SHE STILL WON'T SIGN UP, DESERVED TO BE DECLARED A FUGITIVE.
"BUT WHEN SHE WAS SIGHTED IN COLORADO THE OTHER DAY...
"...ALL I COULD THINK OF WAS RACHEL."

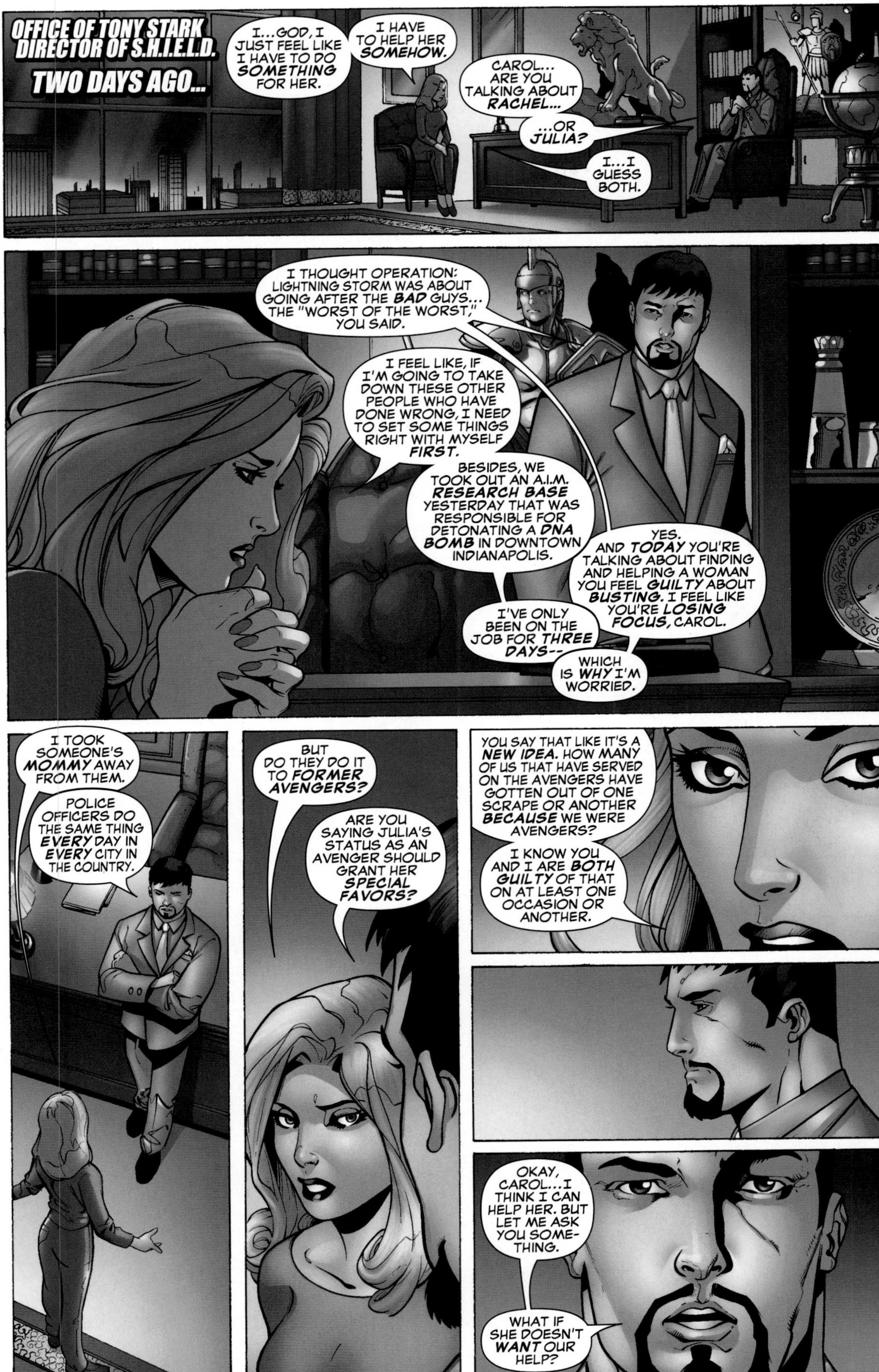

OFFICE OF TONY STARK DIRECTOR OF S.H.I.E.L.D.
TWO DAYS AGO...
I...GOD, I JUST FEEL LIKE I HAVE TO DO SOMETHING FOR HER.
I HAVE TO HELP HER SOMEHOW.
CAROL... ARE YOU TALKING ABOUT RACHEL...
...OR JULIA?
I...I GUESS BOTH.
I THOUGHT OPERATION: LIGHTNING STORM WAS ABOUT GOING AFTER THE BAD GUYS... THE "WORST OF THE WORST," YOU SAID.
I FEEL LIKE, IF I'M GOING TO TAKE DOWN THESE OTHER PEOPLE WHO HAVE DONE WRONG, I NEED TO SET SOME THINGS RIGHT WITH MYSELF FIRST.
BESIDES, WE TOOK OUT AN A.I.M. RESEARCH BASE YESTERDAY THAT WAS RESPONSIBLE FOR DETONATING A DNA BOMB IN DOWNTOWN INDIANAPOLIS.
YES. AND TODAY YOU'RE TALKING ABOUT FINDING AND HELPING A WOMAN YOU FEEL GUILTY ABOUT BUSTING. I FEEL LIKE YOU'RE LOSING FOCUS, CAROL.
I'VE ONLY BEEN ON THE JOB FOR THREE DAYS--
WHICH IS WHY I'M WORRIED.
I TOOK SOMEONE'S MOMMY AWAY FROM THEM.
POLICE OFFICERS DO THE SAME THING EVERY DAY IN EVERY CITY IN THE COUNTRY.
BUT DO THEY DO IT TO FORMER AVENGERS?
ARE YOU SAYING JULIA'S STATUS AS AN AVENGER SHOULD GRANT HER SPECIAL FAVORS?
YOU SAY THAT LIKE IT'S A NEW IDEA. HOW MANY OF US THAT HAVE SERVED ON THE AVENGERS HAVE GOTTEN OUT OF ONE SCRAPE OR ANOTHER BECAUSE WE WERE AVENGERS?
I KNOW YOU AND I ARE BOTH GUILTY OF THAT ON AT LEAST ONE OCCASION OR ANOTHER.
OKAY, CAROL...I THINK I CAN HELP HER. BUT LET ME ASK YOU SOME-THING.
WHAT IF SHE DOESN'T WANT OUR HELP?

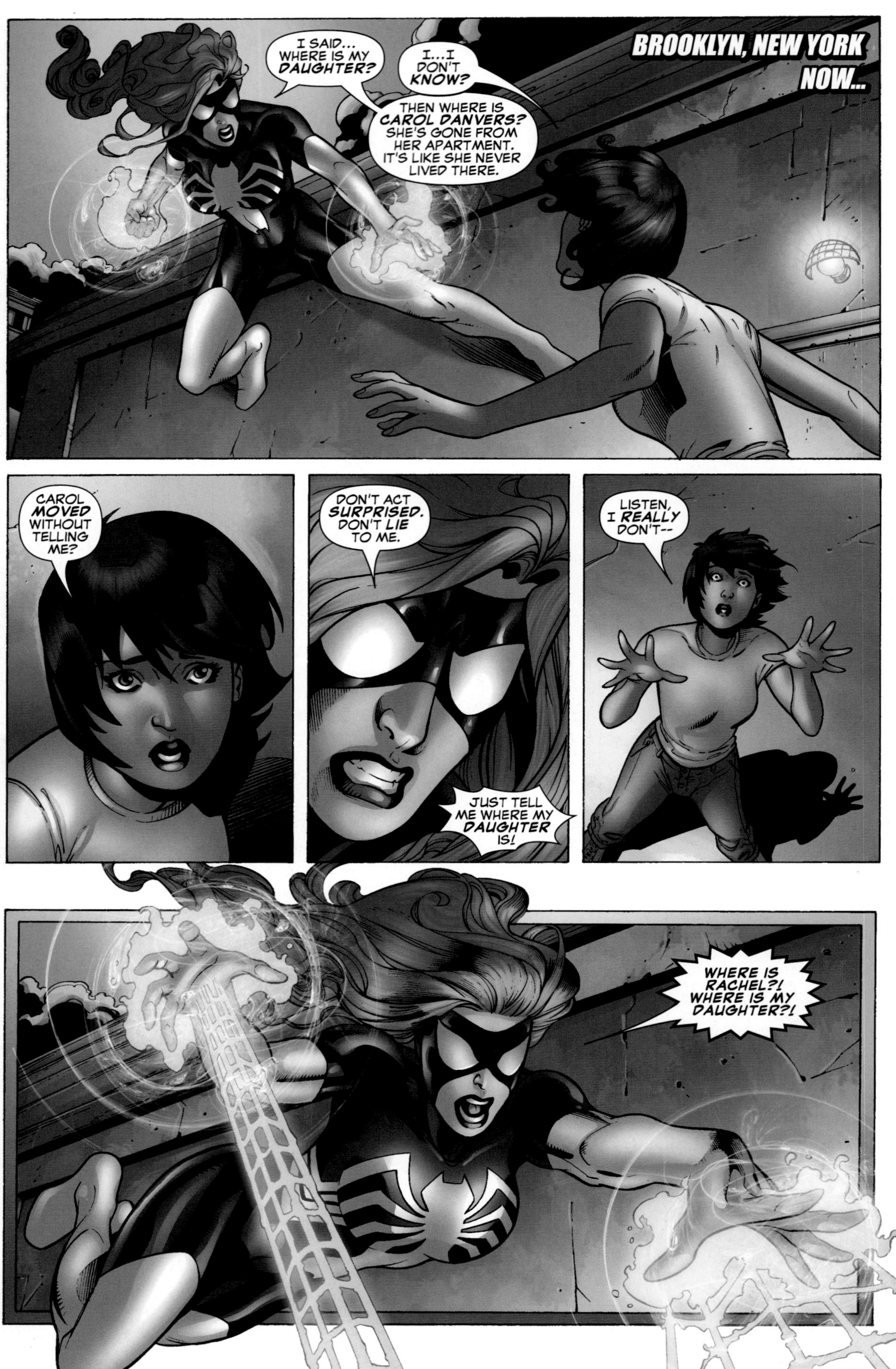
BROOKLYN, NEW YORK NOW...
I SAID... WHERE IS MY DAUGHTER?
I...I DON'T KNOW?
THEN WHERE IS CAROL DANVERS? SHE'S GONE FROM HER APARTMENT. IT'S LIKE SHE NEVER LIVED THERE.
CAROL MOVED WITHOUT TELLING ME?
DON'T ACT SURPRISED. DON'T LIE TO ME.
JUST TELL ME WHERE MY DAUGHTER IS!
LISTEN, I REALLY DON'T--
WHERE IS RACHEL?! WHERE IS MY DAUGHTER?!

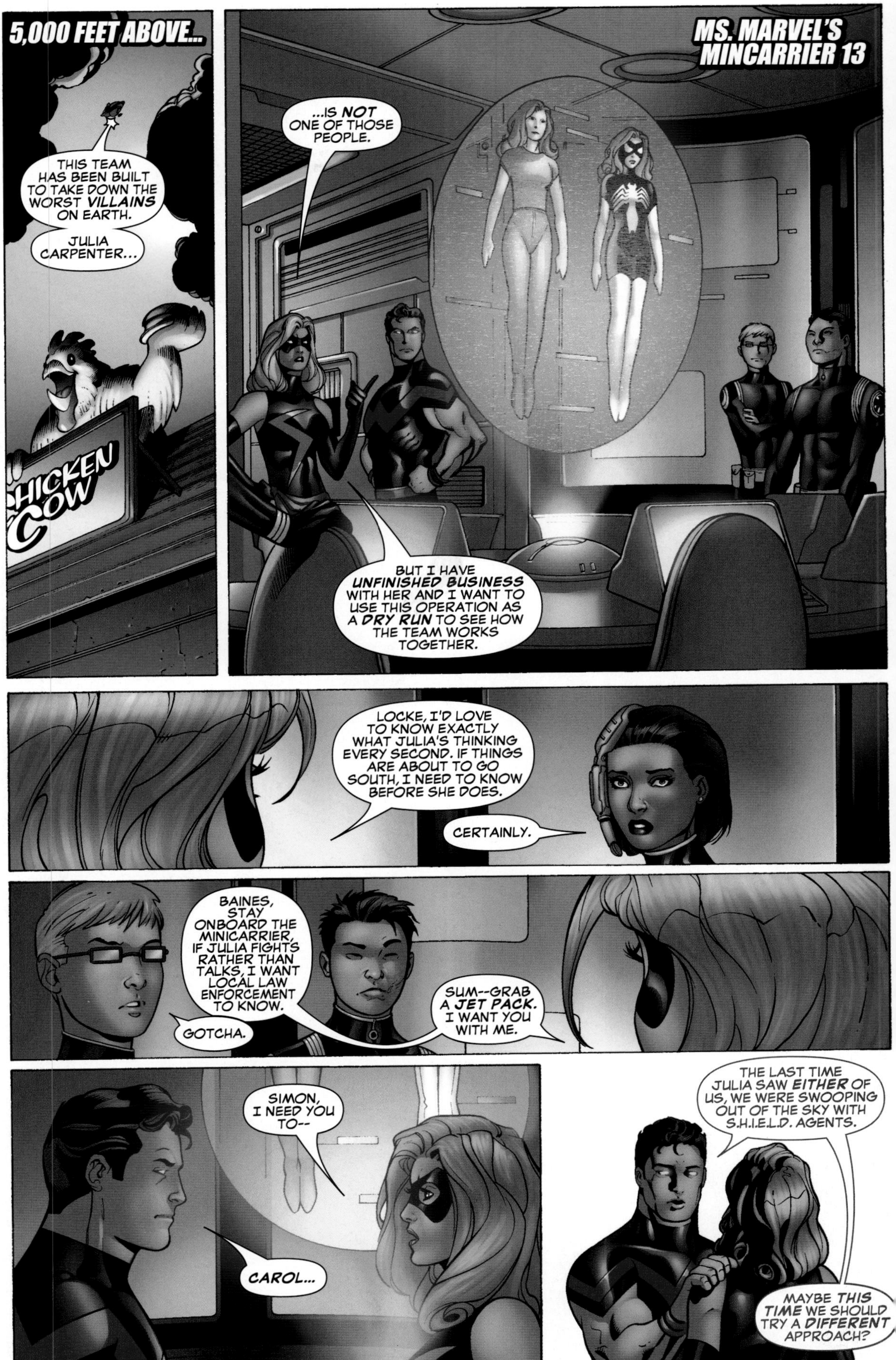

5,000 FEET ABOVE...
THIS TEAM HAS BEEN BUILT TO TAKE DOWN THE WORST VILLAINS ON EARTH.
JULIA CARPENTER...
CHICKEN COW
MS. MARVEL'S MINCARRIER 13
...IS NOT ONE OF THOSE PEOPLE.
BUT I HAVE UNFINISHED BUSINESS WITH HER AND I WANT TO USE THIS OPERATION AS A DRY RUN TO SEE HOW THE TEAM WORKS TOGETHER.
LOCKE, I'D LOVE TO KNOW EXACTLY WHAT JULIA'S THINKING EVERY SECOND. IF THINGS ARE ABOUT TO GO SOUTH, I NEED TO KNOW BEFORE SHE DOES.
CERTAINLY.
BAINES, STAY ONBOARD THE MINICARRIER, IF JULIA FIGHTS RATHER THAN TALKS, I WANT LOCAL LAW ENFORCEMENT TO KNOW.
GOTCHA.
SUM--GRAB A JET PACK. I WANT YOU WITH ME.
SIMON, I NEED YOU TO--
CAROL...
THE LAST TIME JULIA SAW EITHER OF US, WE WERE SWOOPING OUT OF THE SKY WITH S.H.I.E.L.D. AGENTS.
MAYBE THIS TIME WE SHOULD TRY A DIFFERENT APPROACH?

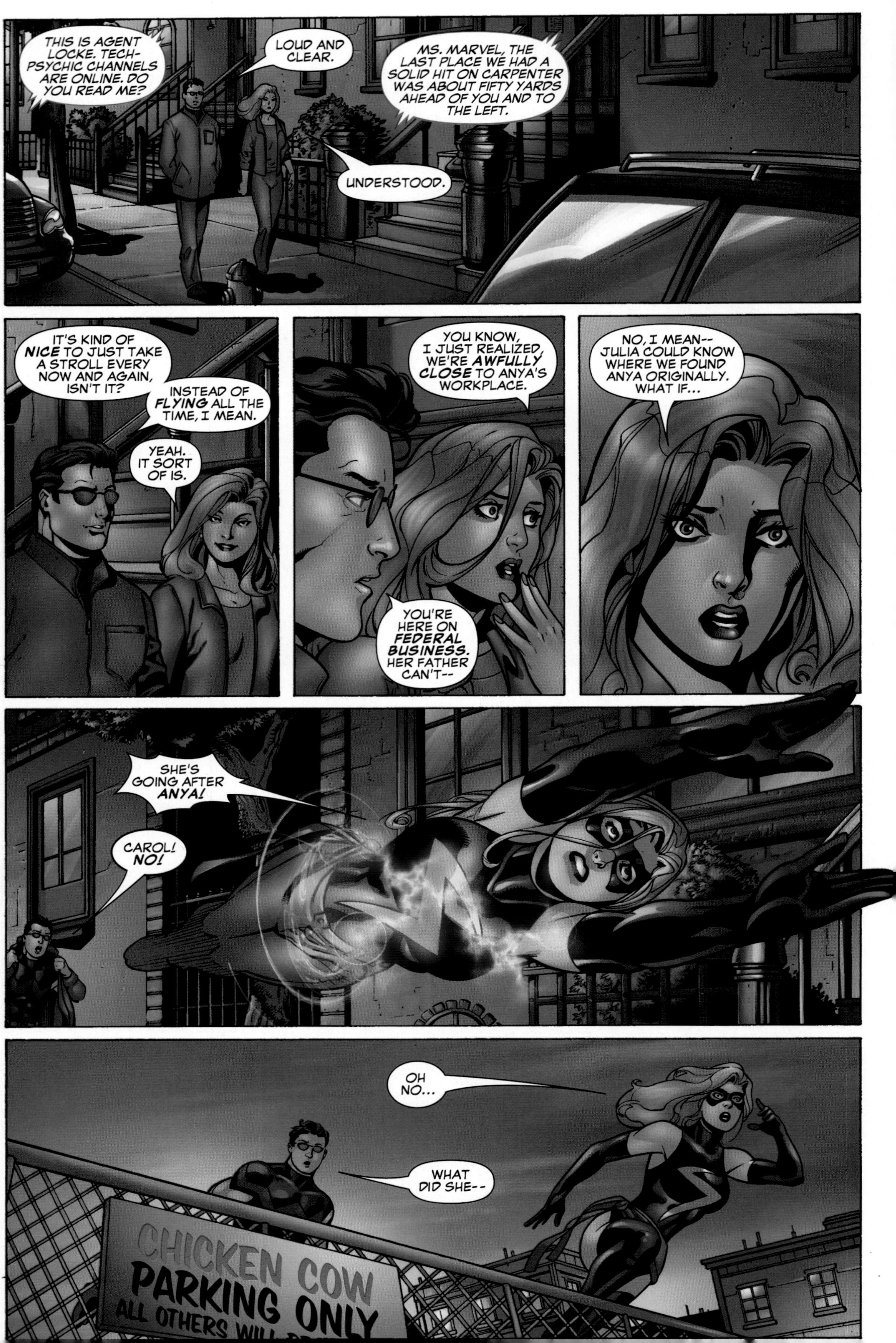
THIS IS AGENT LOCKE. TECH-PSYCHIC CHANNELS ARE ONLINE. DO YOU READ ME?
LOUD AND CLEAR.
MS. MARVEL, THE LAST PLACE WE HAD A SOLID HIT ON CARPENTER WAS ABOUT FIFTY YARDS AHEAD OF YOU AND TO THE LEFT.
UNDERSTOOD.
IT'S KIND OF NICE TO JUST TAKE A STROLL EVERY NOW AND AGAIN, ISN'T IT?
INSTEAD OF FLYING ALL THE TIME, I MEAN.
YEAH. IT SORT OF IS.
YOU KNOW, I JUST REALIZED, WE'RE AWFULLY CLOSE TO ANYA'S WORKPLACE.
YOU'RE HERE ON FEDERAL BUSINESS. HER FATHER CAN'T--
NO, I MEAN-- JULIA COULD KNOW WHERE WE FOUND ANYA ORIGINALLY. WHAT IF...
SHE'S GOING AFTER ANYA!
CAROL! NO!
OH NO...
WHAT DID SHE--
CHICKEN COW
PARKING ONLY
ALL OTHERS WILL

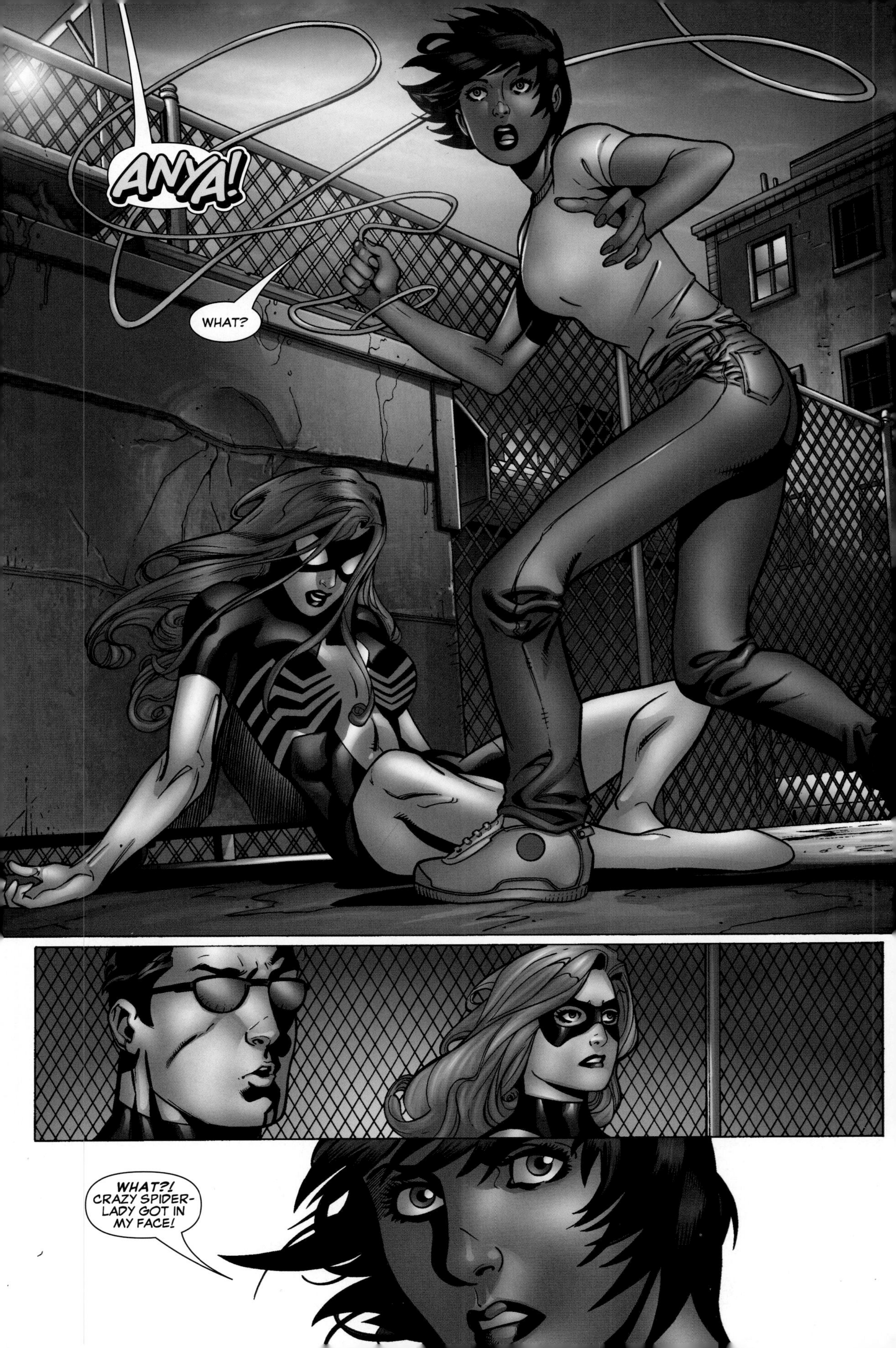
ANYA!
WHAT?
WHAT?! CRAZY SPIDER-LADY GOT IN MY FACE!

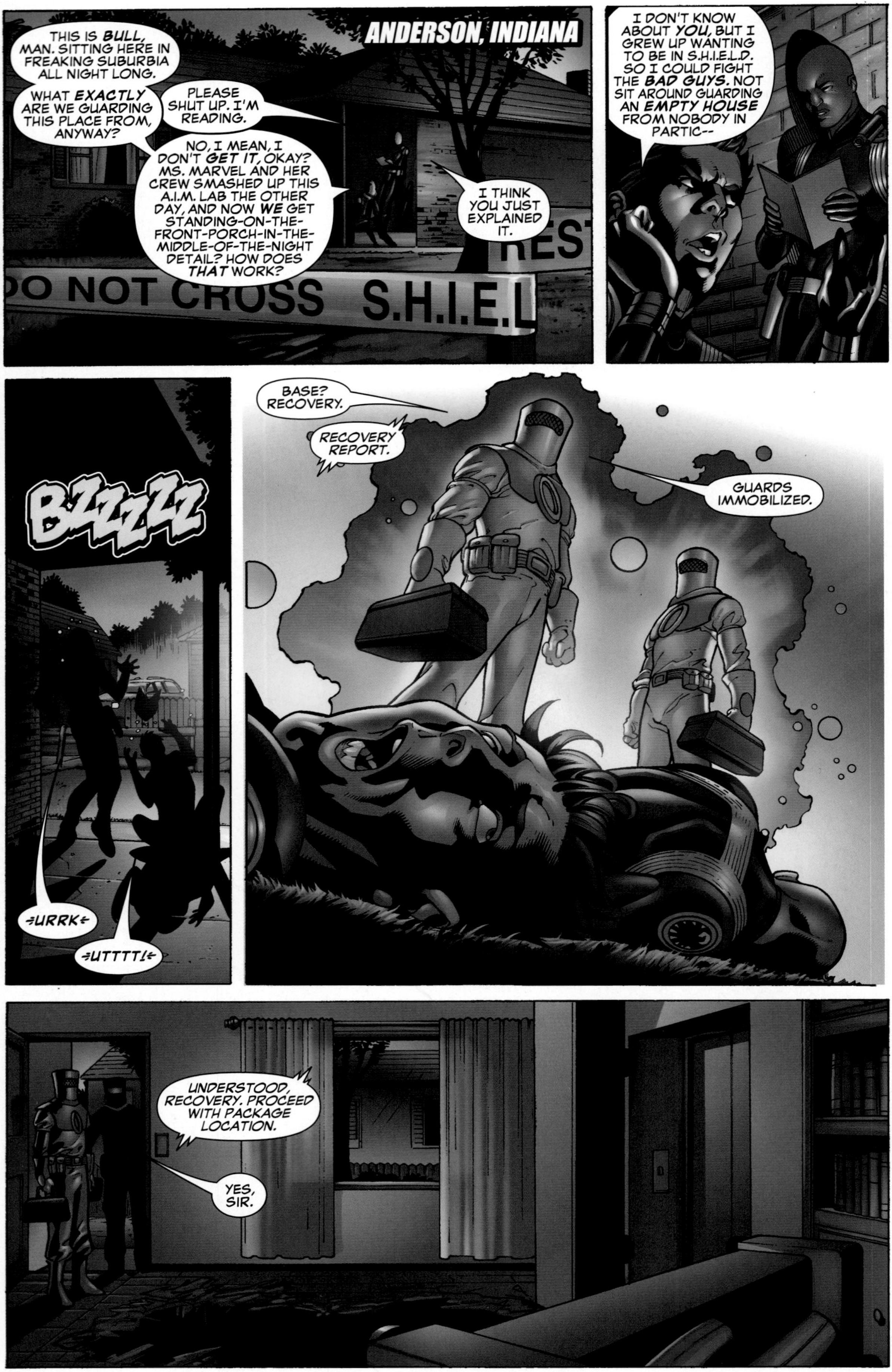
ANDERSON, INDIANA
THIS IS BULL, MAN. SITTING HERE IN FREAKING SUBURBIA ALL NIGHT LONG.
WHAT EXACTLY ARE WE GUARDING THIS PLACE FROM, ANYWAY?
PLEASE SHUT UP. I'M READING.
NO, I MEAN, I DON'T GET IT, OKAY? MS. MARVEL AND HER CREW SMASHED UP THIS A.I.M. LAB THE OTHER DAY, AND NOW WE GET STANDING-ON-THE-FRONT-PORCH-IN-THE-MIDDLE-OF-THE-NIGHT DETAIL? HOW DOES THAT WORK?
I THINK YOU JUST EXPLAINED IT.
DO NOT CROSS S.H.I.E.L
REST
I DON'T KNOW ABOUT YOU, BUT I GREW UP WANTING TO BE IN S.H.I.E.L.D. SO I COULD FIGHT THE BAD GUYS. NOT SIT AROUND GUARDING AN EMPTY HOUSE FROM NOBODY IN PARTIC--
BZZZZZ
URRK
UTTTT!
BASE? RECOVERY.
RECOVERY REPORT.
GUARDS IMMOBILIZED.
UNDERSTOOD, RECOVERY. PROCEED WITH PACKAGE LOCATION.
YES, SIR.

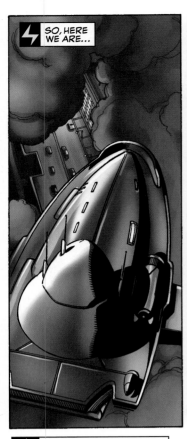

SO, HERE WE ARE...

...JUST ME AND JULIA CARPENTER.

SIMON SHOULD BE HERE. THEY WERE AT LEAST FRIENDS BEFORE THIS WHOLE MESS.

BUT SOMEBODY HAD TO TAKE ANYA HOME, AND WITH HER FATHER'S RESTRAINING ORDER AGAINST ME...

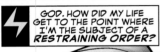

GOD. HOW DID MY LIFE GET TO THE POINT WHERE I'M THE SUBJECT OF A RESTRAINING ORDER?

WHERE...?

JULIA? IT'S ME.

IT'S CAROL DANVERS.

BEDROOM

YOU...

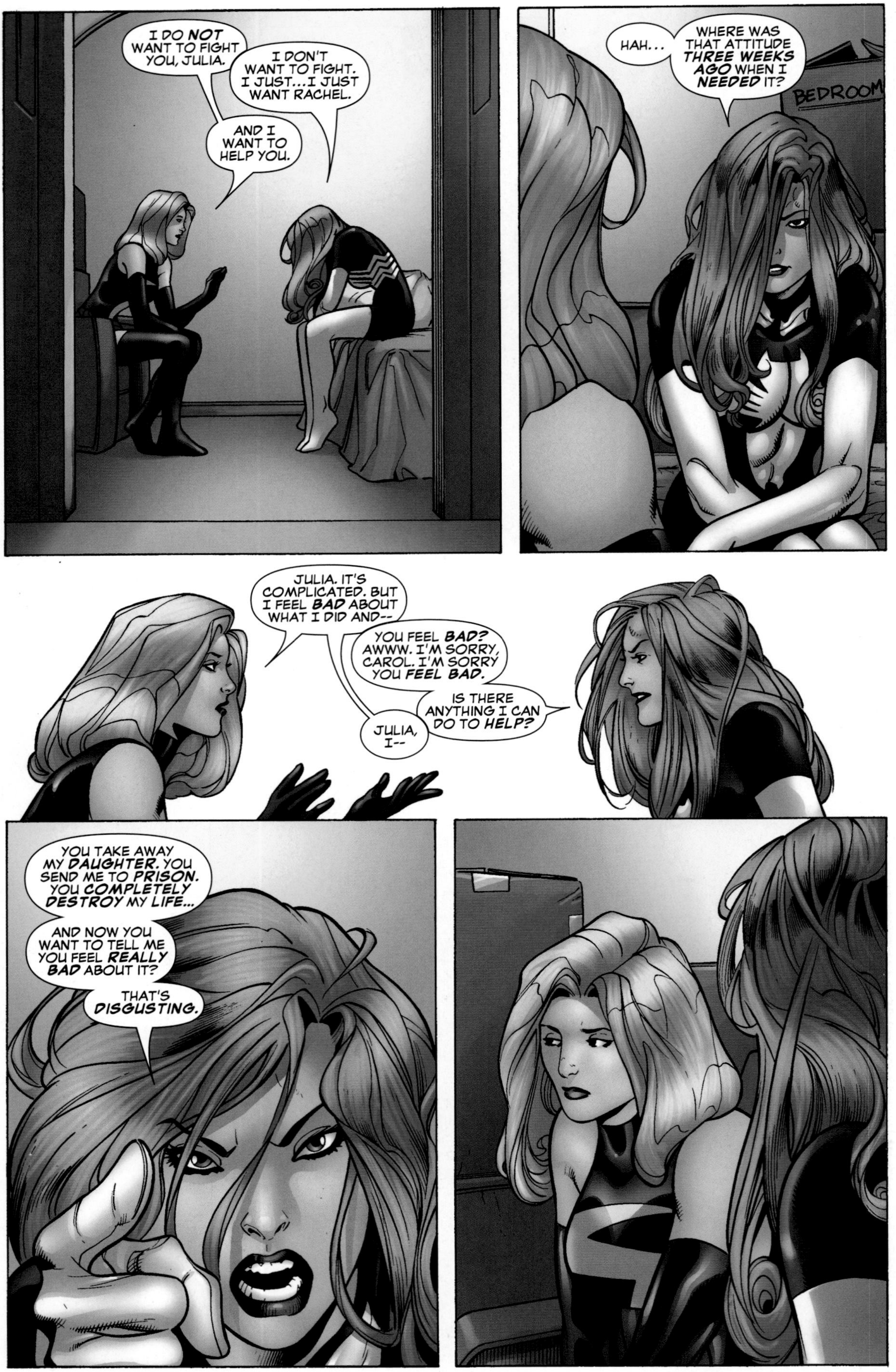
I DO NOT WANT TO FIGHT YOU, JULIA.
I DON'T WANT TO FIGHT. I JUST...I JUST WANT RACHEL.
AND I WANT TO HELP YOU.
HAH...
WHERE WAS THAT ATTITUDE THREE WEEKS AGO WHEN I NEEDED IT?
BEDROOM
JULIA. IT'S COMPLICATED. BUT I FEEL BAD ABOUT WHAT I DID AND--
YOU FEEL BAD? AWWW. I'M SORRY, CAROL. I'M SORRY YOU FEEL BAD.
IS THERE ANYTHING I CAN DO TO HELP?
JULIA, I--
YOU TAKE AWAY MY DAUGHTER. YOU SEND ME TO PRISON. YOU COMPLETELY DESTROY MY LIFE...
AND NOW YOU WANT TO TELL ME YOU FEEL REALLY BAD ABOUT IT?
THAT'S DISGUSTING.

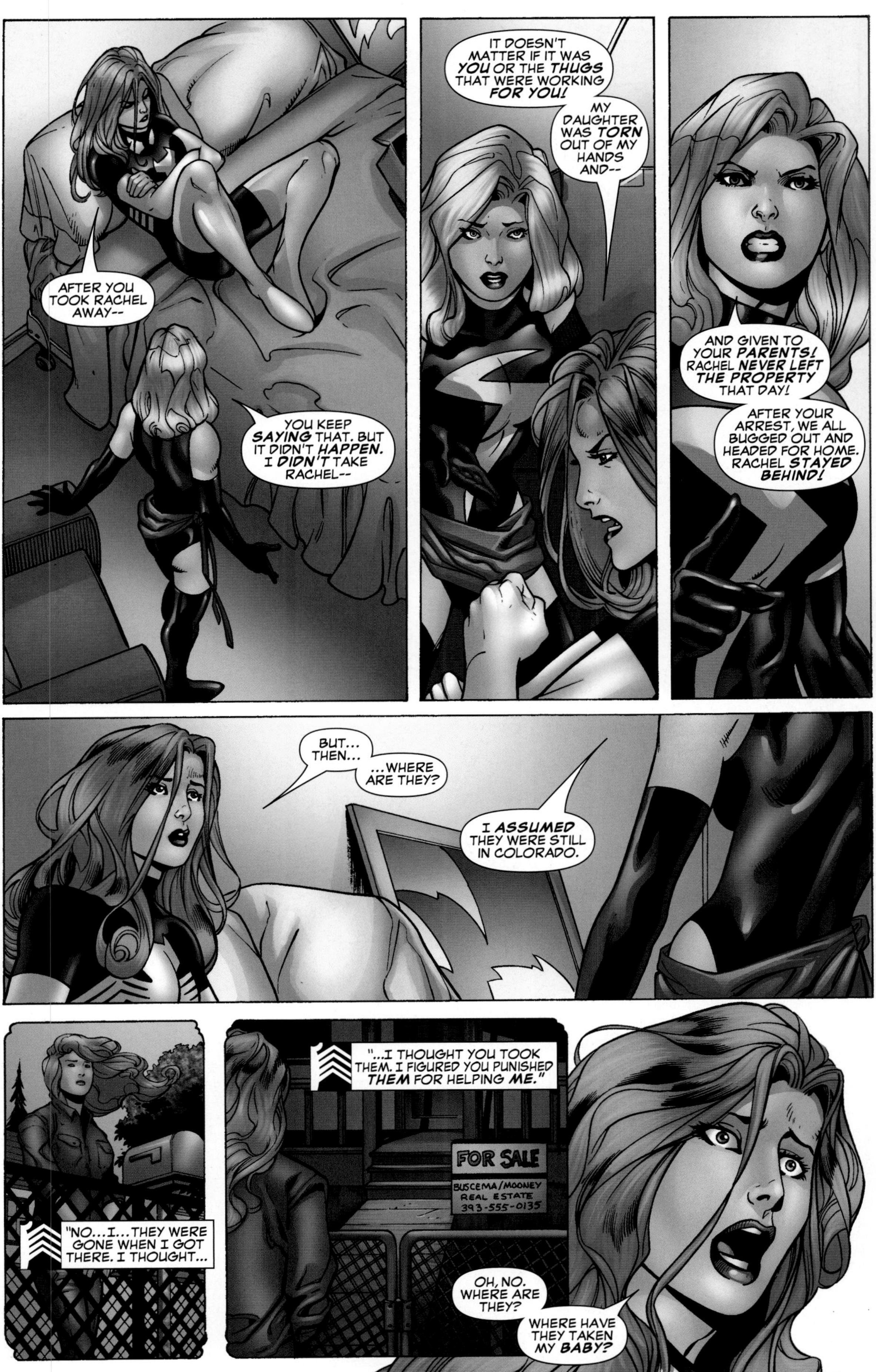
AFTER YOU TOOK RACHEL AWAY--
YOU KEEP SAYING THAT. BUT IT DIDN'T HAPPEN. I DIDN'T TAKE RACHEL--
IT DOESN'T MATTER IF IT WAS YOU OR THE THUGS THAT WERE WORKING FOR YOU!
MY DAUGHTER WAS TORN OUT OF MY HANDS AND--
AND GIVEN TO YOUR PARENTS! RACHEL NEVER LEFT THE PROPERTY THAT DAY!
AFTER YOUR ARREST, WE ALL BUGGED OUT AND HEADED FOR HOME. RACHEL STAYED BEHIND!
BUT... THEN...
...WHERE ARE THEY?
I ASSUMED THEY WERE STILL IN COLORADO.
"NO...I...THEY WERE GONE WHEN I GOT THERE. I THOUGHT...
"...I THOUGHT YOU TOOK THEM. I FIGURED YOU PUNISHED THEM FOR HELPING ME."
FOR SALE
BUSCEMA/MOONEY REAL ESTATE 393-555-0135
OH, NO. WHERE ARE THEY?
WHERE HAVE THEY TAKEN MY BABY?

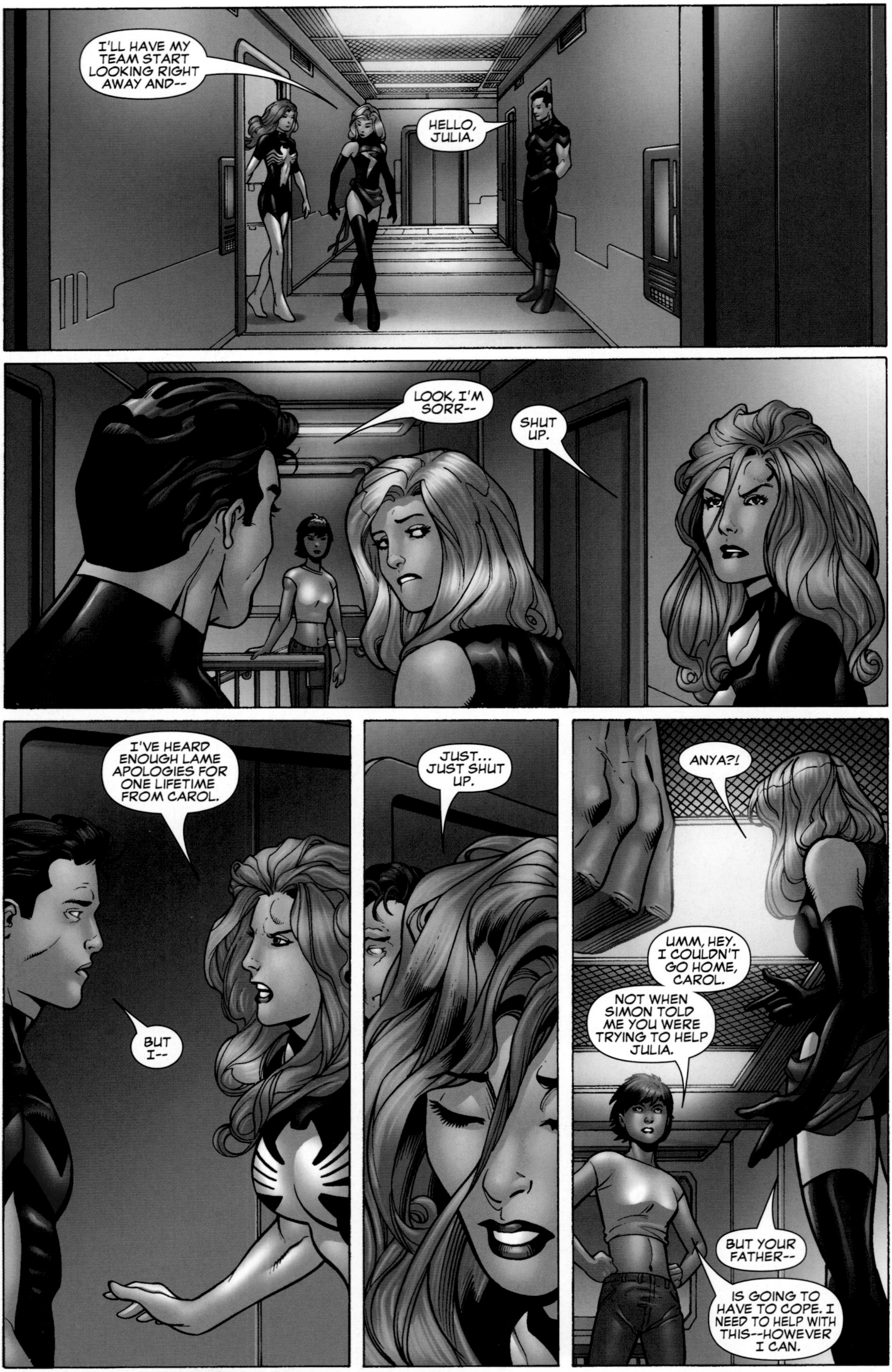
I'LL HAVE MY TEAM START LOOKING RIGHT AWAY AND--
HELLO, JULIA.
LOOK, I'M SORR--
SHUT UP.
I'VE HEARD ENOUGH LAME APOLOGIES FOR ONE LIFETIME FROM CAROL.
BUT I--
JUST... JUST SHUT UP.
ANYA?!
UMM, HEY. I COULDN'T GO HOME, CAROL.
NOT WHEN SIMON TOLD ME YOU WERE TRYING TO HELP JULIA.
BUT YOUR FATHER--
IS GOING TO HAVE TO COPE. I NEED TO HELP WITH THIS--HOWEVER I CAN.

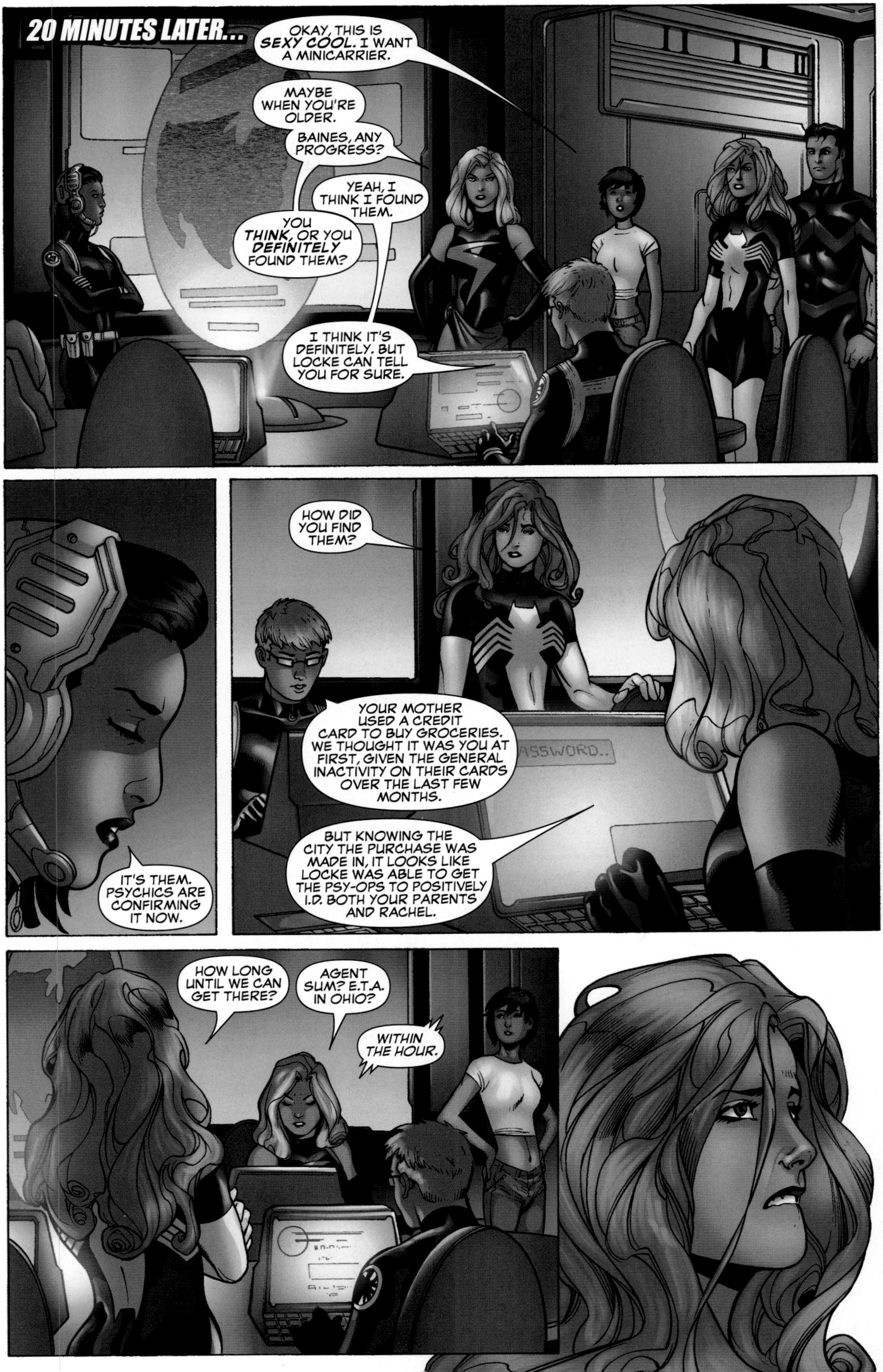
20 MINUTES LATER...
OKAY, THIS IS SEXY COOL. I WANT A MINICARRIER.
MAYBE WHEN YOU'RE OLDER.
BAINES, ANY PROGRESS?
YEAH, I THINK I FOUND THEM.
YOU THINK, OR YOU DEFINITELY FOUND THEM?
I THINK IT'S DEFINITELY. BUT LOCKE CAN TELL YOU FOR SURE.
IT'S THEM. PSYCHICS ARE CONFIRMING IT NOW.
HOW DID YOU FIND THEM?
YOUR MOTHER USED A CREDIT CARD TO BUY GROCERIES. WE THOUGHT IT WAS YOU AT FIRST, GIVEN THE GENERAL INACTIVITY ON THEIR CARDS OVER THE LAST FEW MONTHS.
BUT KNOWING THE CITY THE PURCHASE WAS MADE IN, IT LOOKS LIKE LOCKE WAS ABLE TO GET THE PSY-OPS TO POSITIVELY I.D. BOTH YOUR PARENTS AND RACHEL.
HOW LONG UNTIL WE CAN GET THERE?
AGENT SUM? E.T.A. IN OHIO?
WITHIN THE HOUR.

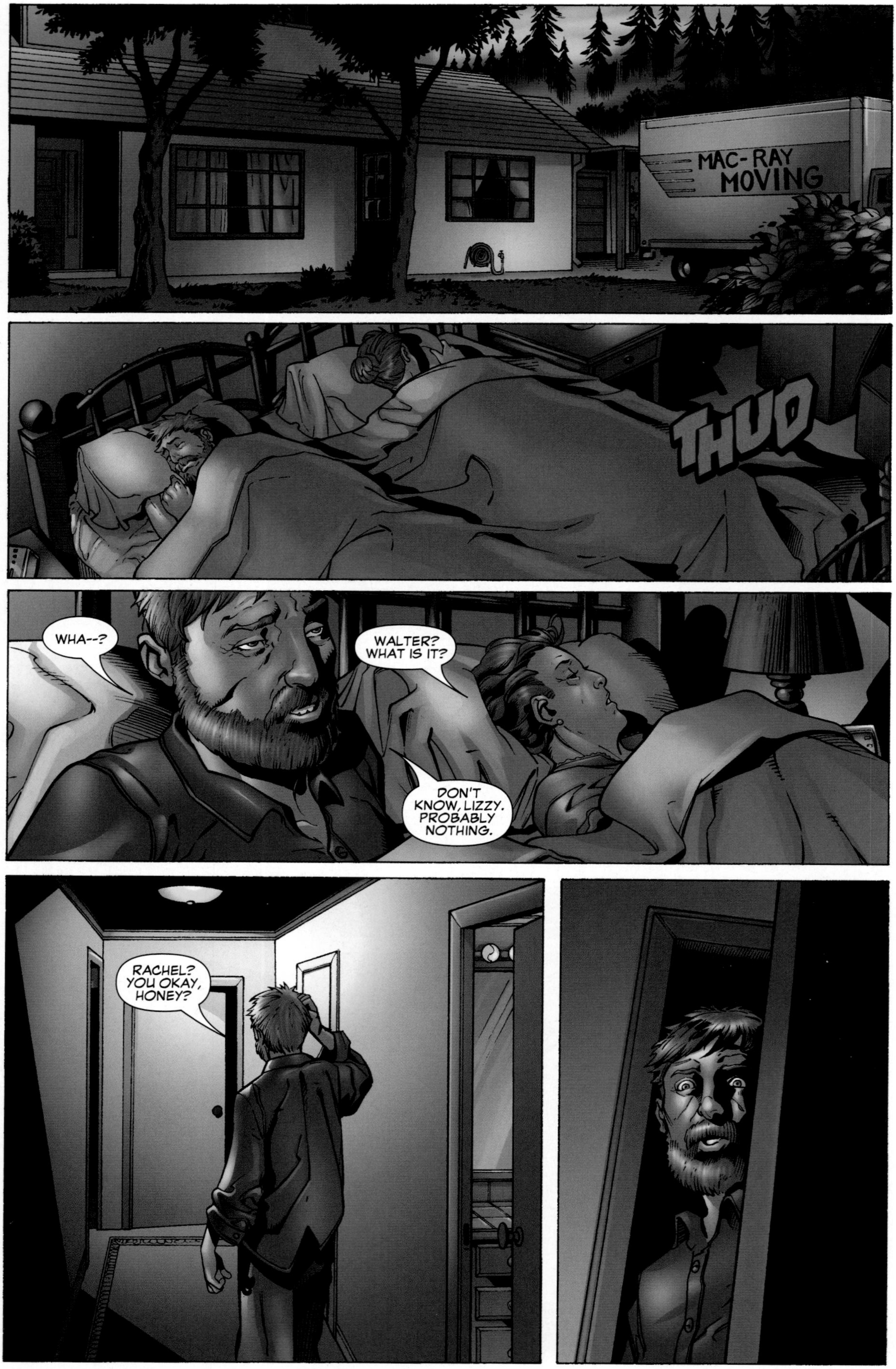
MAC-RAY
MOVING
THUD
WHA--?
WALTER? WHAT IS IT?
DON'T KNOW, LIZZY. PROBABLY NOTHING.
RACHEL? YOU OKAY, HONEY?

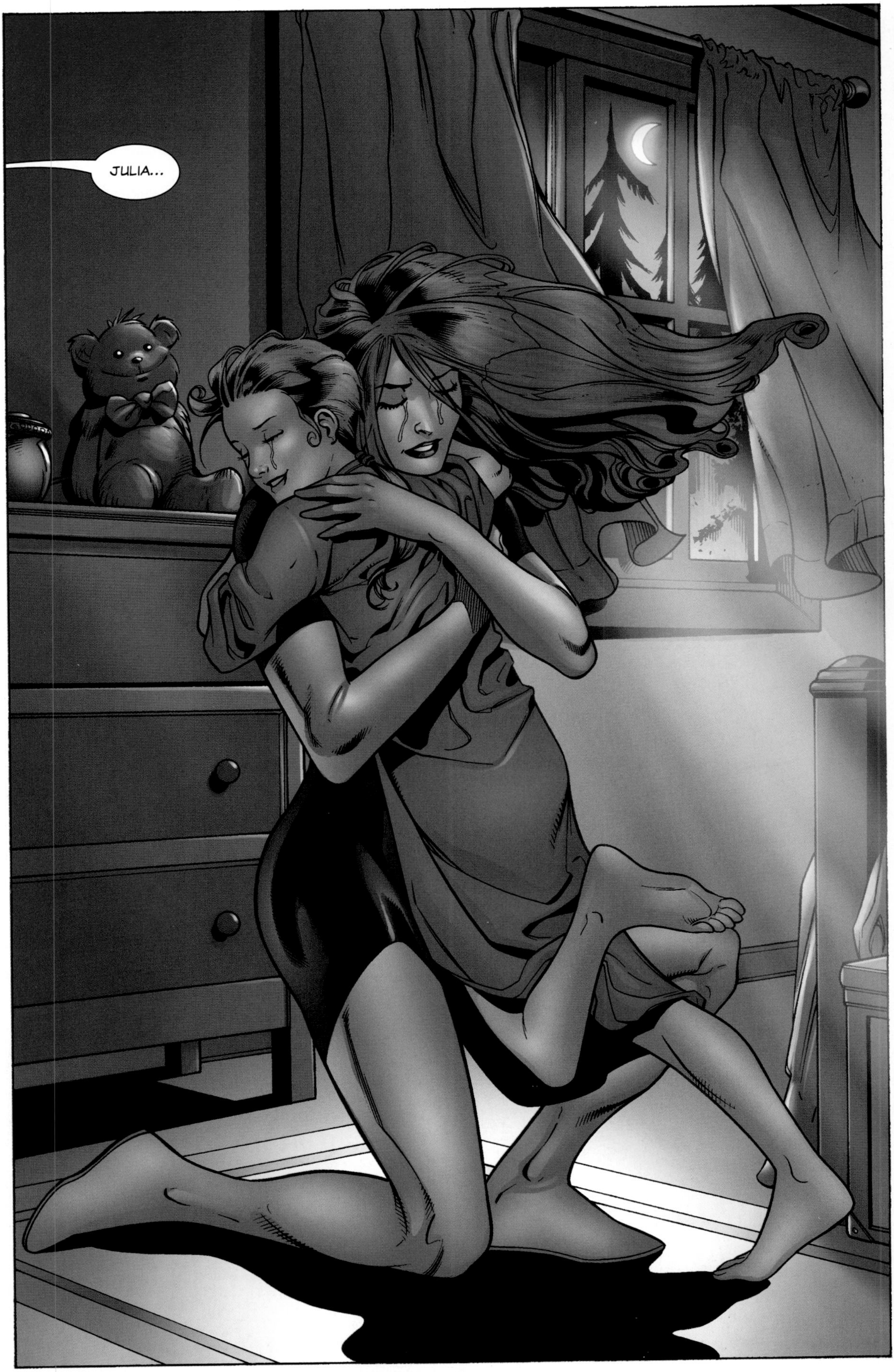
JULIA...

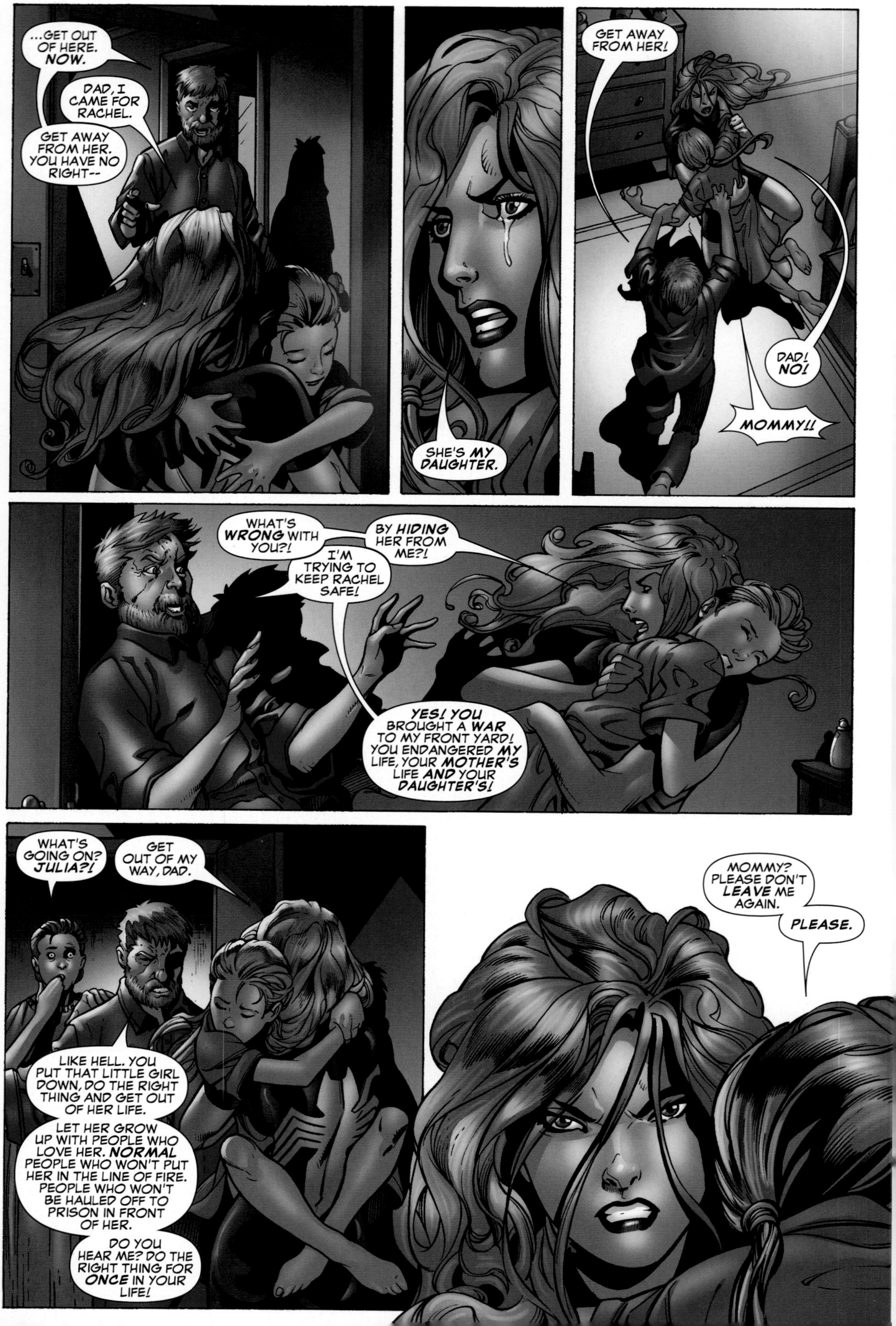
...GET OUT OF HERE. **NOW.**
DAD, I CAME FOR RACHEL.
GET AWAY FROM HER. YOU HAVE NO RIGHT--
SHE'S **MY DAUGHTER.**
GET AWAY FROM HER!
DAD! **NO!**
MOMMY!!
WHAT'S **WRONG** WITH YOU?!
BY **HIDING** HER FROM ME?!
I'M TRYING TO KEEP RACHEL SAFE!
YES! YOU BROUGHT A **WAR** TO MY FRONT YARD! YOU ENDANGERED **MY** LIFE, YOUR **MOTHER'S** LIFE **AND** YOUR **DAUGHTER'S!**
WHAT'S GOING ON? **JULIA?!**
GET OUT OF MY WAY, DAD.
LIKE HELL. YOU PUT THAT LITTLE GIRL DOWN, DO THE RIGHT THING AND GET OUT OF HER LIFE.
LET HER GROW UP WITH PEOPLE WHO LOVE HER. **NORMAL** PEOPLE WHO WON'T PUT HER IN THE LINE OF FIRE. PEOPLE WHO WON'T BE HAULED OFF TO PRISON IN FRONT OF HER.
DO YOU HEAR ME? DO THE RIGHT THING FOR **ONCE** IN YOUR LIFE!
MOMMY? PLEASE DON'T **LEAVE** ME AGAIN.
PLEASE.

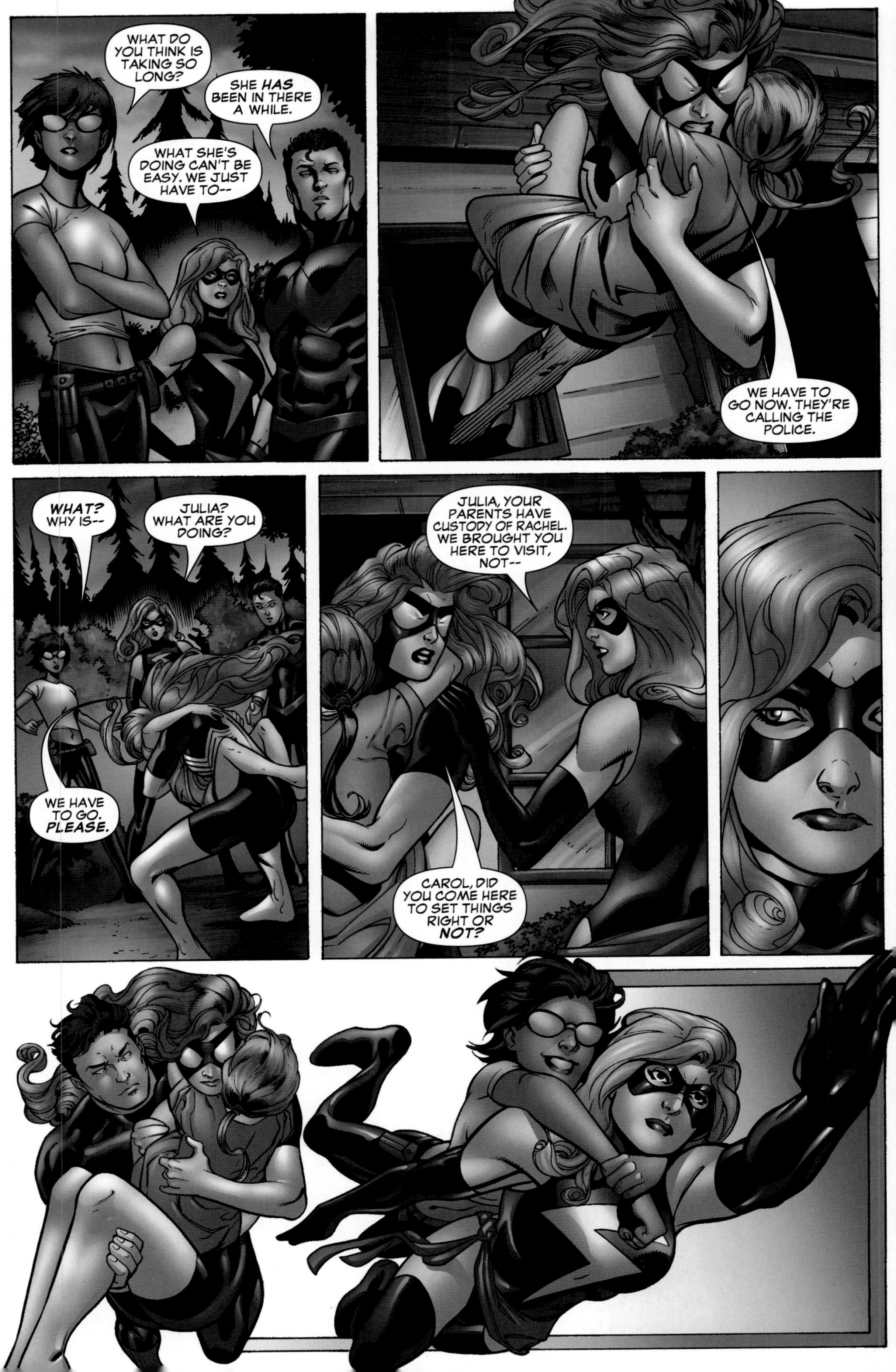

WHAT DO YOU THINK IS TAKING SO LONG?
SHE *HAS* BEEN IN THERE A WHILE.
WHAT SHE'S DOING CAN'T BE EASY. WE JUST HAVE TO--
WE HAVE TO GO NOW. THEY'RE CALLING THE POLICE.
WHAT? WHY IS--
JULIA? WHAT ARE YOU DOING?
WE HAVE TO GO. *PLEASE.*
JULIA, YOUR PARENTS HAVE CUSTODY OF RACHEL. WE BROUGHT YOU HERE TO VISIT, NOT--
CAROL, DID YOU COME HERE TO SET THINGS RIGHT OR *NOT?*

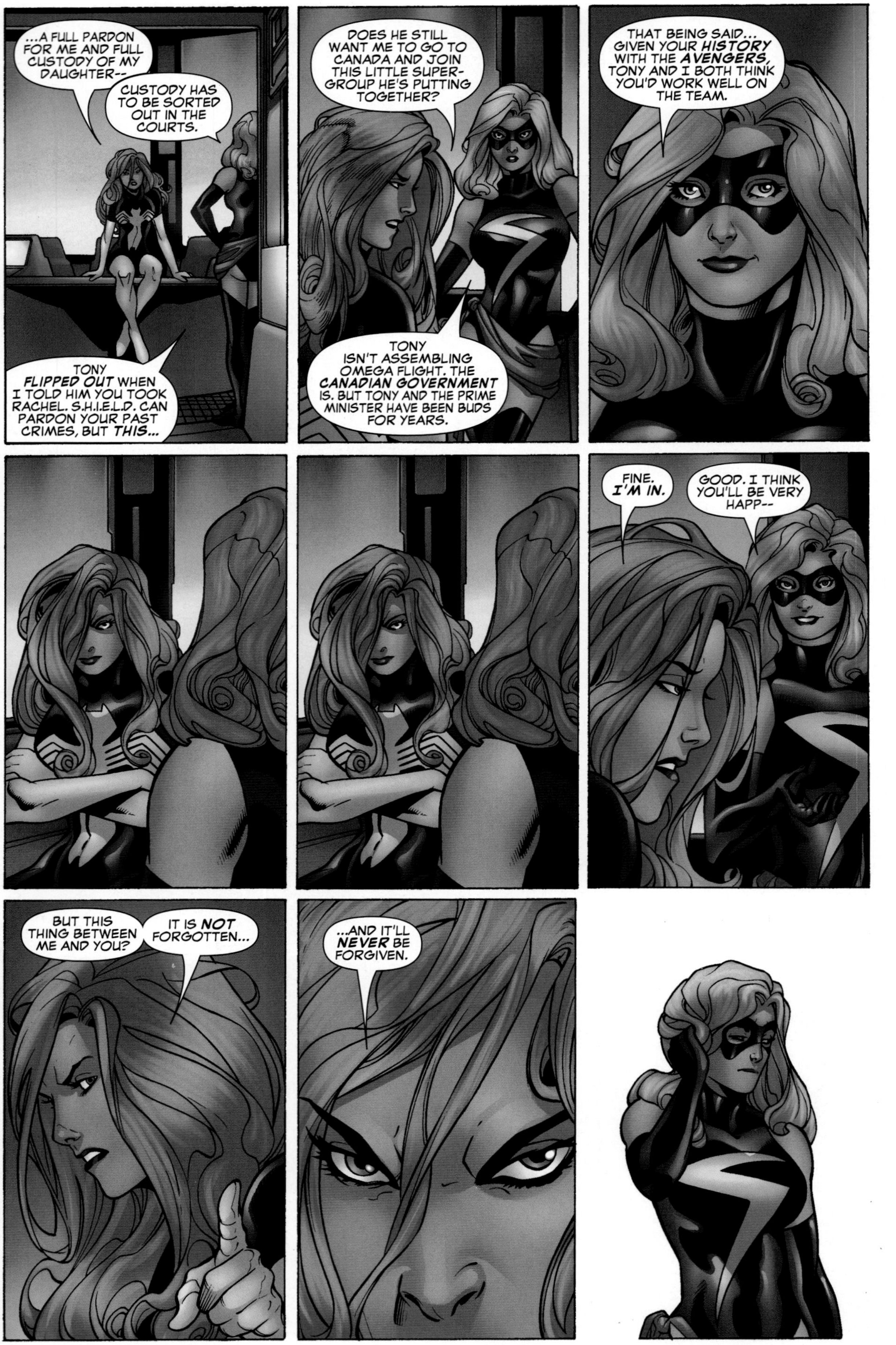
...A FULL PARDON FOR ME AND FULL CUSTODY OF MY DAUGHTER--
CUSTODY HAS TO BE SORTED OUT IN THE COURTS.
TONY **FLIPPED OUT** WHEN I TOLD HIM YOU TOOK RACHEL. S.H.I.E.L.D. CAN PARDON YOUR PAST CRIMES, BUT **THIS...**
DOES HE STILL WANT ME TO GO TO CANADA AND JOIN THIS LITTLE SUPER-GROUP HE'S PUTTING TOGETHER?
TONY ISN'T ASSEMBLING OMEGA FLIGHT. THE **CANADIAN GOVERNMENT** IS. BUT TONY AND THE PRIME MINISTER HAVE BEEN BUDS FOR YEARS.
THAT BEING SAID... GIVEN YOUR **HISTORY** WITH THE **AVENGERS,** TONY AND I BOTH THINK YOU'D WORK WELL ON THE TEAM.
FINE. **I'M IN.**
GOOD. I THINK YOU'LL BE VERY HAPP--
BUT THIS THING BETWEEN ME AND YOU?
IT IS **NOT** FORGOTTEN...
...AND IT'LL **NEVER** BE FORGIVEN.

I'M NOT GETTING ANYTHING. ARE YOU SURE WE HAVE THE CORRECT FREQ--

HEY. NEVER MIND.

ANDERSON, INDIANA

FOUND IT.

HIDING THINGS IN *EXTRA DIMENSIONS*... MAN, THIS KIND OF STUFF ALWAYS GIVES ME THE WILLIES.

YEAH, BUT IF WE DIDN'T HAVE A FAIL-SAFE LIKE THIS, THEN S.H.I.E.L.D. WOULD HAVE ALL OUR BEST TOYS.

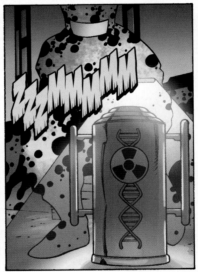

ZZZMMMMMM

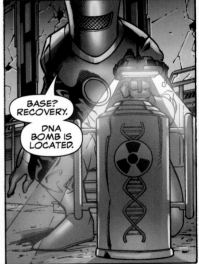

BASE? RECOVERY.

DNA BOMB IS LOCATED.

EXCELLENT WORK, RECOVERY.

NOW, BRING IT TO ME...

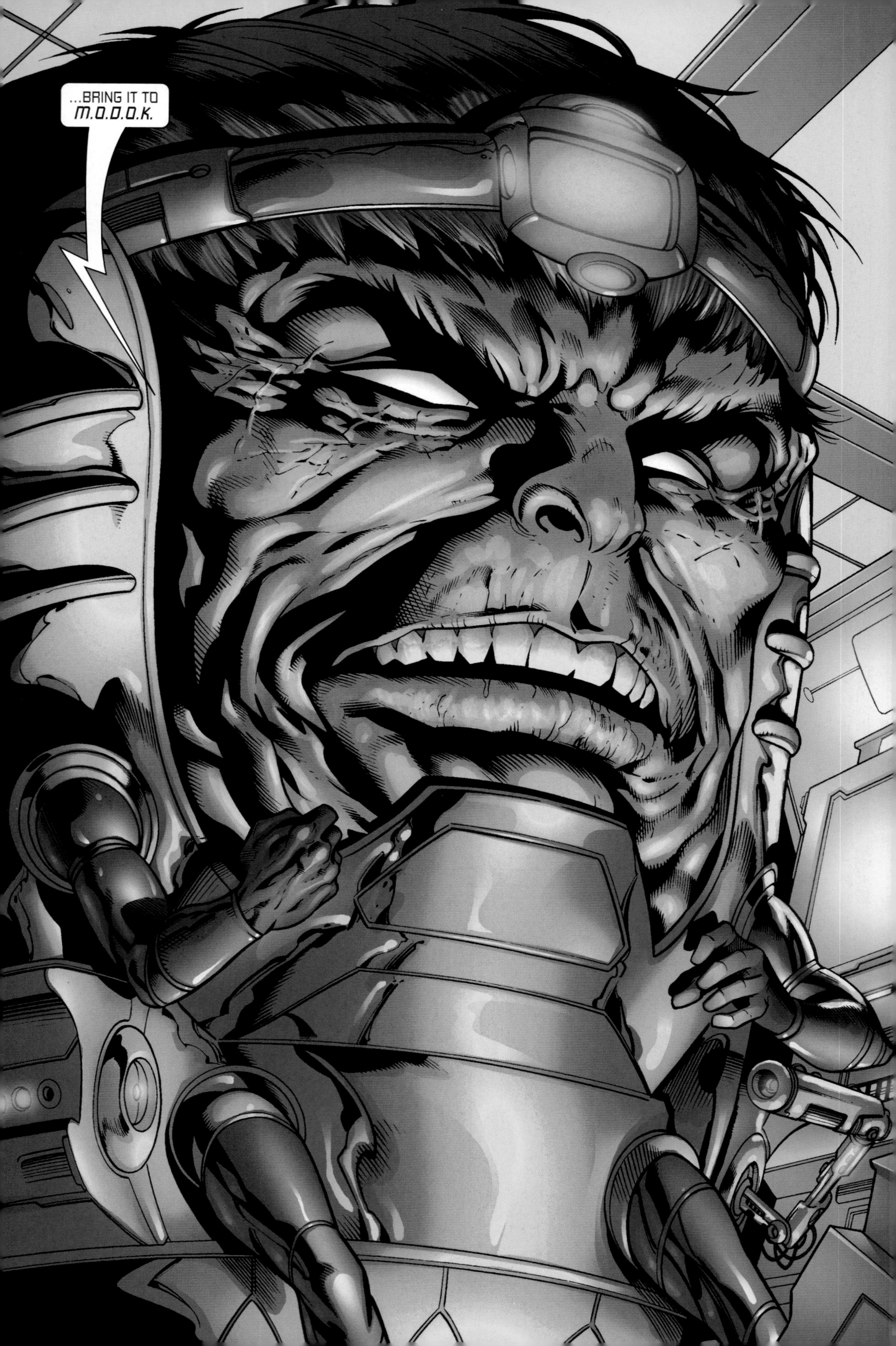
...BRING IT TO M.O.D.O.K.

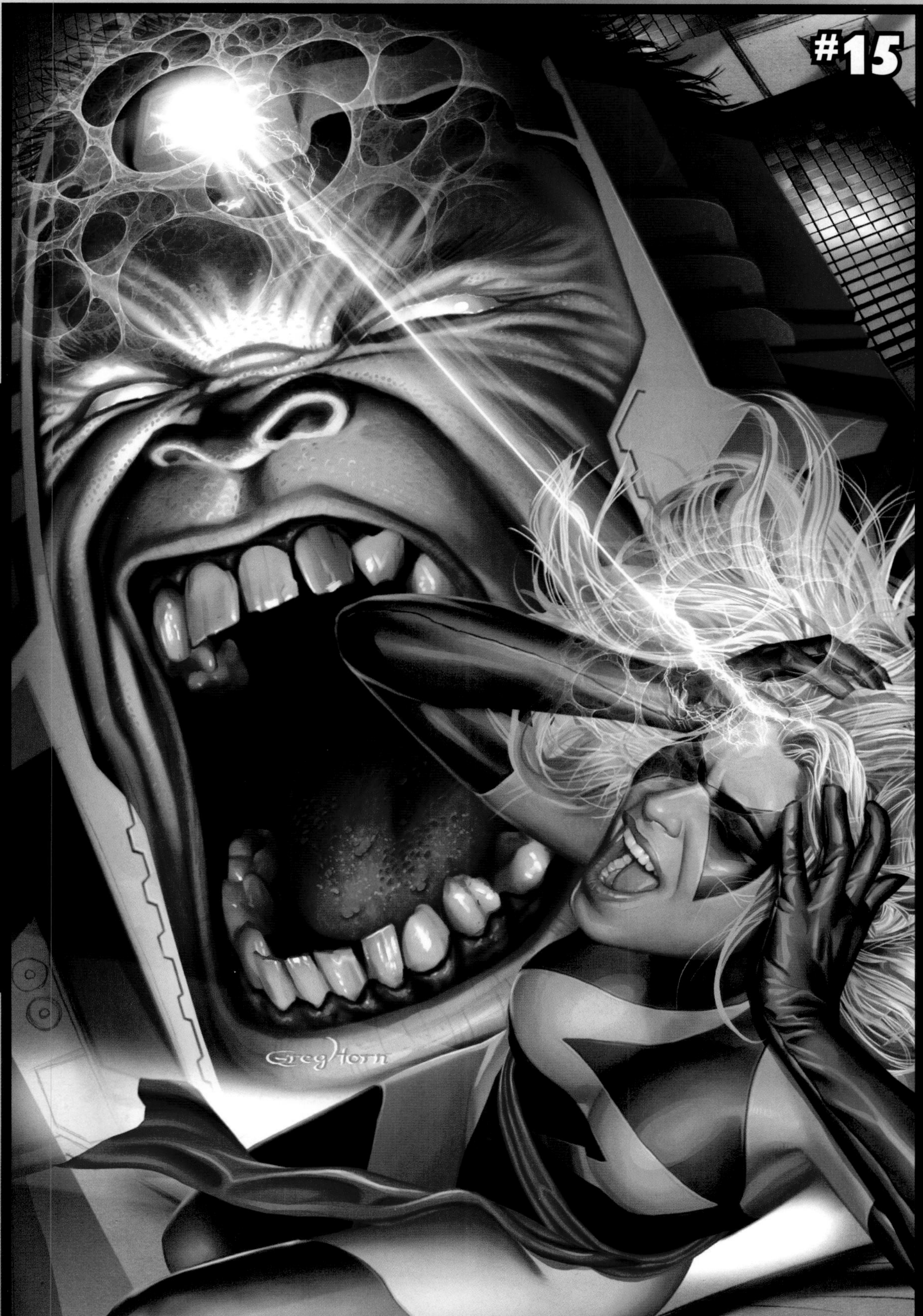
#15
Greg Horn

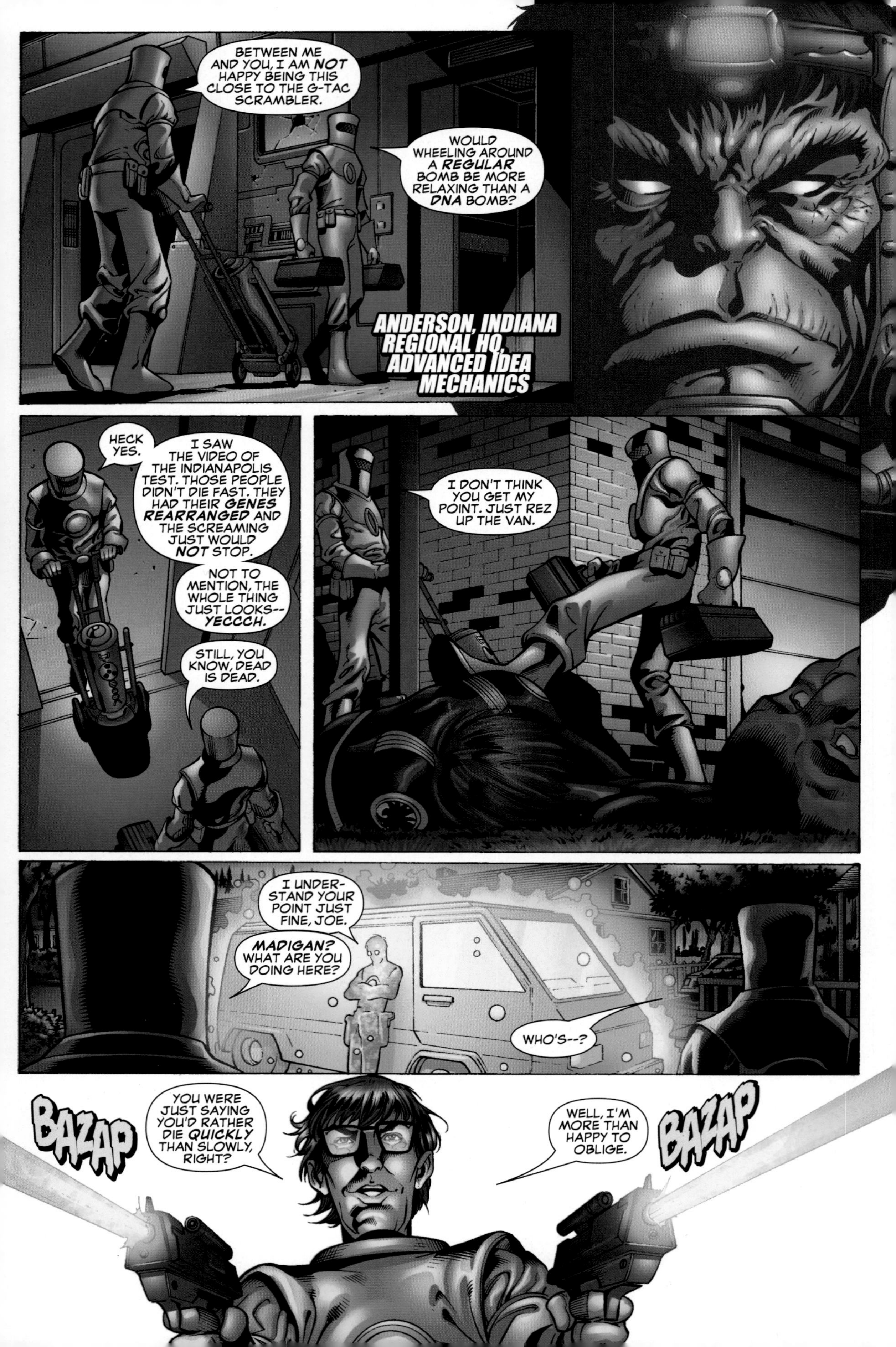
ANDERSON, INDIANA
REGIONAL HQ,
ADVANCED IDEA
MECHANICS
BETWEEN ME AND YOU, I AM NOT HAPPY BEING THIS CLOSE TO THE G-TAC SCRAMBLER.
WOULD WHEELING AROUND A REGULAR BOMB BE MORE RELAXING THAN A DNA BOMB?
HECK YES.
I SAW THE VIDEO OF THE INDIANAPOLIS TEST. THOSE PEOPLE DIDN'T DIE FAST. THEY HAD THEIR GENES REARRANGED AND THE SCREAMING JUST WOULD NOT STOP.
NOT TO MENTION, THE WHOLE THING JUST LOOKS--YECCCH.
STILL, YOU KNOW, DEAD IS DEAD.
I DON'T THINK YOU GET MY POINT. JUST REZ UP THE VAN.
I UNDERSTAND YOUR POINT JUST FINE, JOE.
MADIGAN? WHAT ARE YOU DOING HERE?
WHO'S--?
BAZAP
YOU WERE JUST SAYING YOU'D RATHER DIE QUICKLY THAN SLOWLY, RIGHT?
WELL, I'M MORE THAN HAPPY TO OBLIGE.
BAZAP

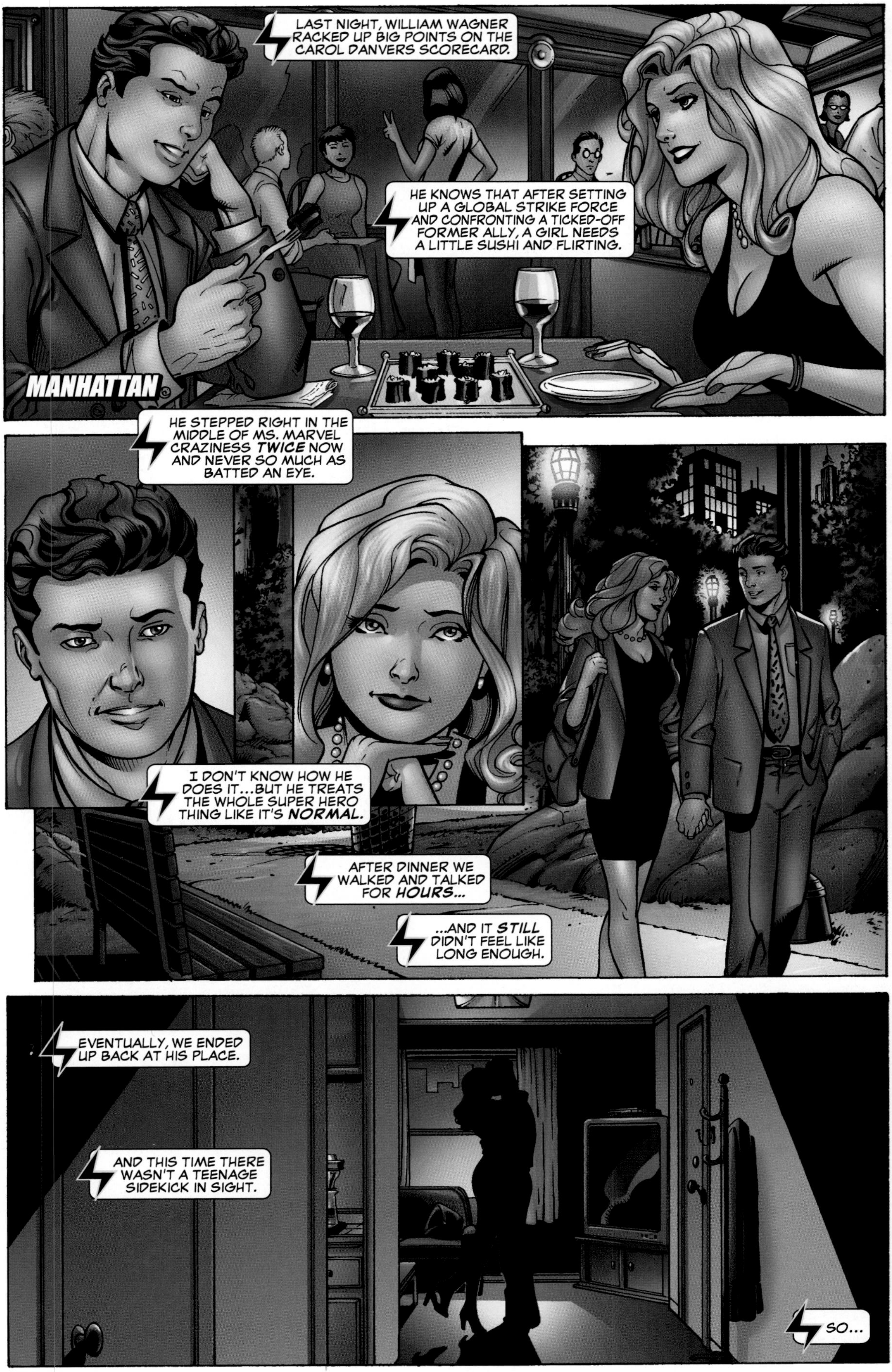
LAST NIGHT, WILLIAM WAGNER RACKED UP BIG POINTS ON THE CAROL DANVERS SCORECARD.
HE KNOWS THAT AFTER SETTING UP A GLOBAL STRIKE FORCE AND CONFRONTING A TICKED-OFF FORMER ALLY, A GIRL NEEDS A LITTLE SUSHI AND FLIRTING.
MANHATTAN
HE STEPPED RIGHT IN THE MIDDLE OF MS. MARVEL CRAZINESS TWICE NOW AND NEVER SO MUCH AS BATTED AN EYE.
I DON'T KNOW HOW HE DOES IT...BUT HE TREATS THE WHOLE SUPER HERO THING LIKE IT'S NORMAL.
AFTER DINNER WE WALKED AND TALKED FOR HOURS...
...AND IT STILL DIDN'T FEEL LIKE LONG ENOUGH.
EVENTUALLY, WE ENDED UP BACK AT HIS PLACE.
AND THIS TIME THERE WASN'T A TEENAGE SIDEKICK IN SIGHT.
SO...

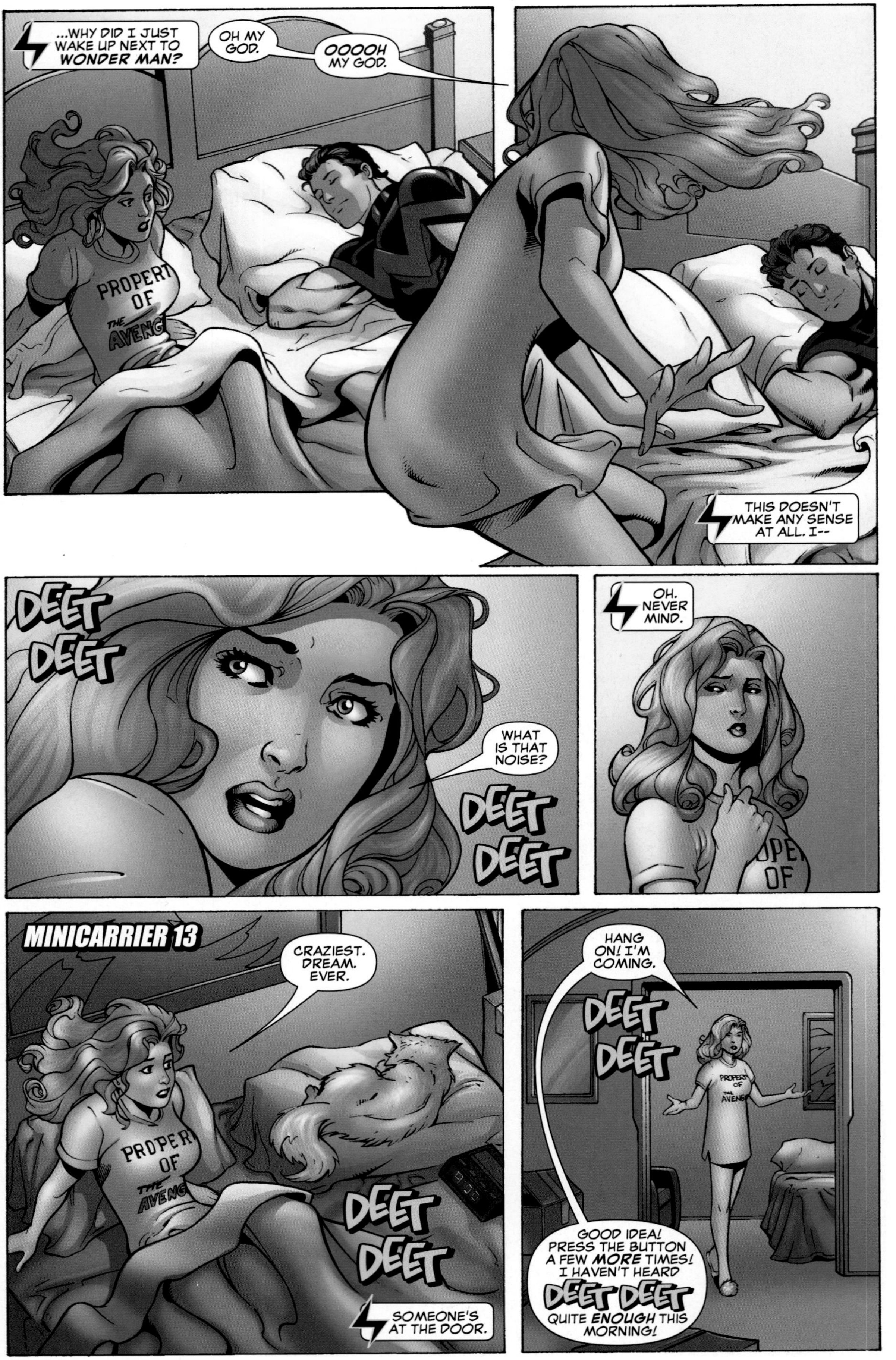
...WHY DID I JUST WAKE UP NEXT TO WONDER MAN?
OH MY GOD.
OOOOH MY GOD.
PROPERT OF THE AVENG
THIS DOESN'T MAKE ANY SENSE AT ALL. I--
DEET DEET
WHAT IS THAT NOISE?
DEET DEET
OH. NEVER MIND.
MINICARRIER 13
CRAZIEST. DREAM. EVER.
PROPERT OF THE AVENG
DEET DEET
SOMEONE'S AT THE DOOR.
HANG ON! I'M COMING.
DEET DEET
GOOD IDEA! PRESS THE BUTTON A FEW MORE TIMES! I HAVEN'T HEARD DEET DEET QUITE ENOUGH THIS MORNING!

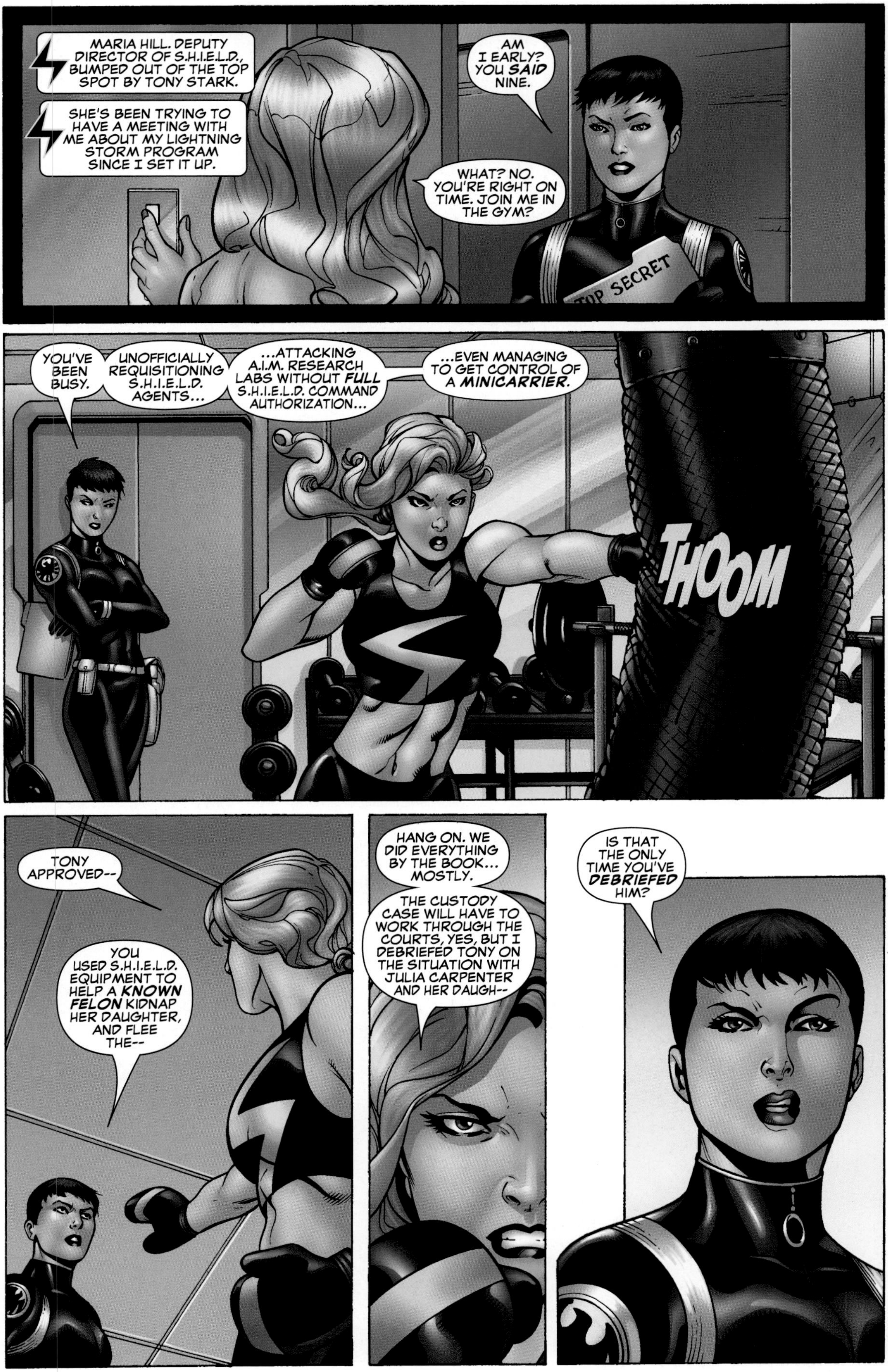
MARIA HILL. DEPUTY DIRECTOR OF S.H.I.E.L.D., BUMPED OUT OF THE TOP SPOT BY TONY STARK.
SHE'S BEEN TRYING TO HAVE A MEETING WITH ME ABOUT MY LIGHTNING STORM PROGRAM SINCE I SET IT UP.
AM I EARLY? YOU SAID NINE.
WHAT? NO. YOU'RE RIGHT ON TIME. JOIN ME IN THE GYM?
TOP SECRET
YOU'VE BEEN BUSY.
UNOFFICIALLY REQUISITIONING S.H.I.E.L.D. AGENTS...
...ATTACKING A.I.M. RESEARCH LABS WITHOUT FULL S.H.I.E.L.D. COMMAND AUTHORIZATION...
...EVEN MANAGING TO GET CONTROL OF A MINICARRIER.
THOOM
TONY APPROVED--
YOU USED S.H.I.E.L.D. EQUIPMENT TO HELP A KNOWN FELON KIDNAP HER DAUGHTER, AND FLEE THE--
HANG ON. WE DID EVERYTHING BY THE BOOK... MOSTLY.
THE CUSTODY CASE WILL HAVE TO WORK THROUGH THE COURTS, YES, BUT I DEBRIEFED TONY ON THE SITUATION WITH JULIA CARPENTER AND HER DAUGH--
IS THAT THE ONLY TIME YOU'VE DEBRIEFED HIM?

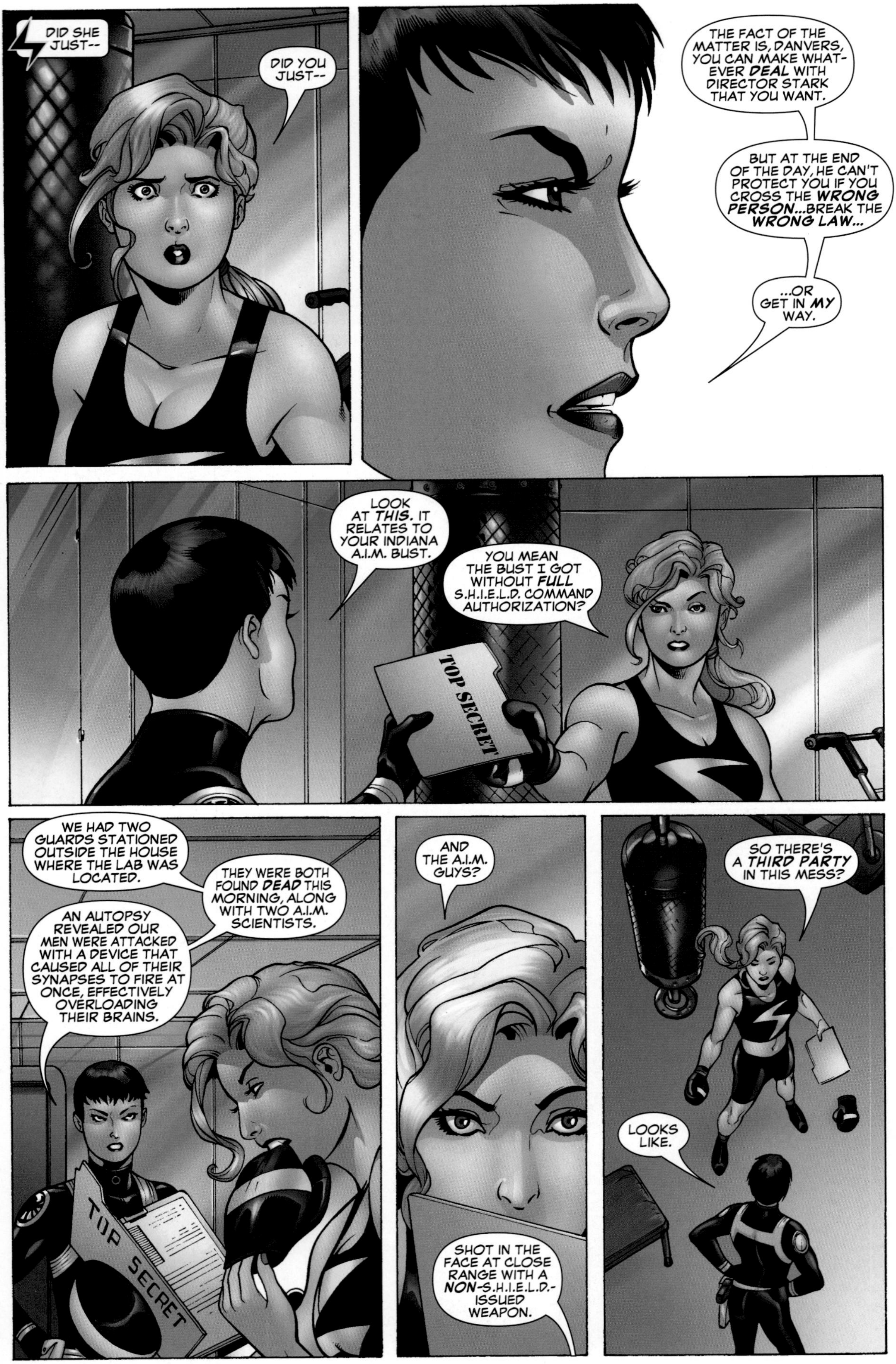
DID SHE JUST--
DID YOU JUST--
THE FACT OF THE MATTER IS, DANVERS, YOU CAN MAKE WHATEVER DEAL WITH DIRECTOR STARK THAT YOU WANT.
BUT AT THE END OF THE DAY, HE CAN'T PROTECT YOU IF YOU CROSS THE WRONG PERSON...BREAK THE WRONG LAW...
...OR GET IN MY WAY.
LOOK AT THIS. IT RELATES TO YOUR INDIANA A.I.M. BUST.
YOU MEAN THE BUST I GOT WITHOUT FULL S.H.I.E.L.D. COMMAND AUTHORIZATION?
TOP SECRET
WE HAD TWO GUARDS STATIONED OUTSIDE THE HOUSE WHERE THE LAB WAS LOCATED.
THEY WERE BOTH FOUND DEAD THIS MORNING, ALONG WITH TWO A.I.M. SCIENTISTS.
AN AUTOPSY REVEALED OUR MEN WERE ATTACKED WITH A DEVICE THAT CAUSED ALL OF THEIR SYNAPSES TO FIRE AT ONCE, EFFECTIVELY OVERLOADING THEIR BRAINS.
TOP SECRET
AND THE A.I.M. GUYS?
SHOT IN THE FACE AT CLOSE RANGE WITH A NON-S.H.I.E.L.D.-ISSUED WEAPON.
SO THERE'S A THIRD PARTY IN THIS MESS?
LOOKS LIKE.

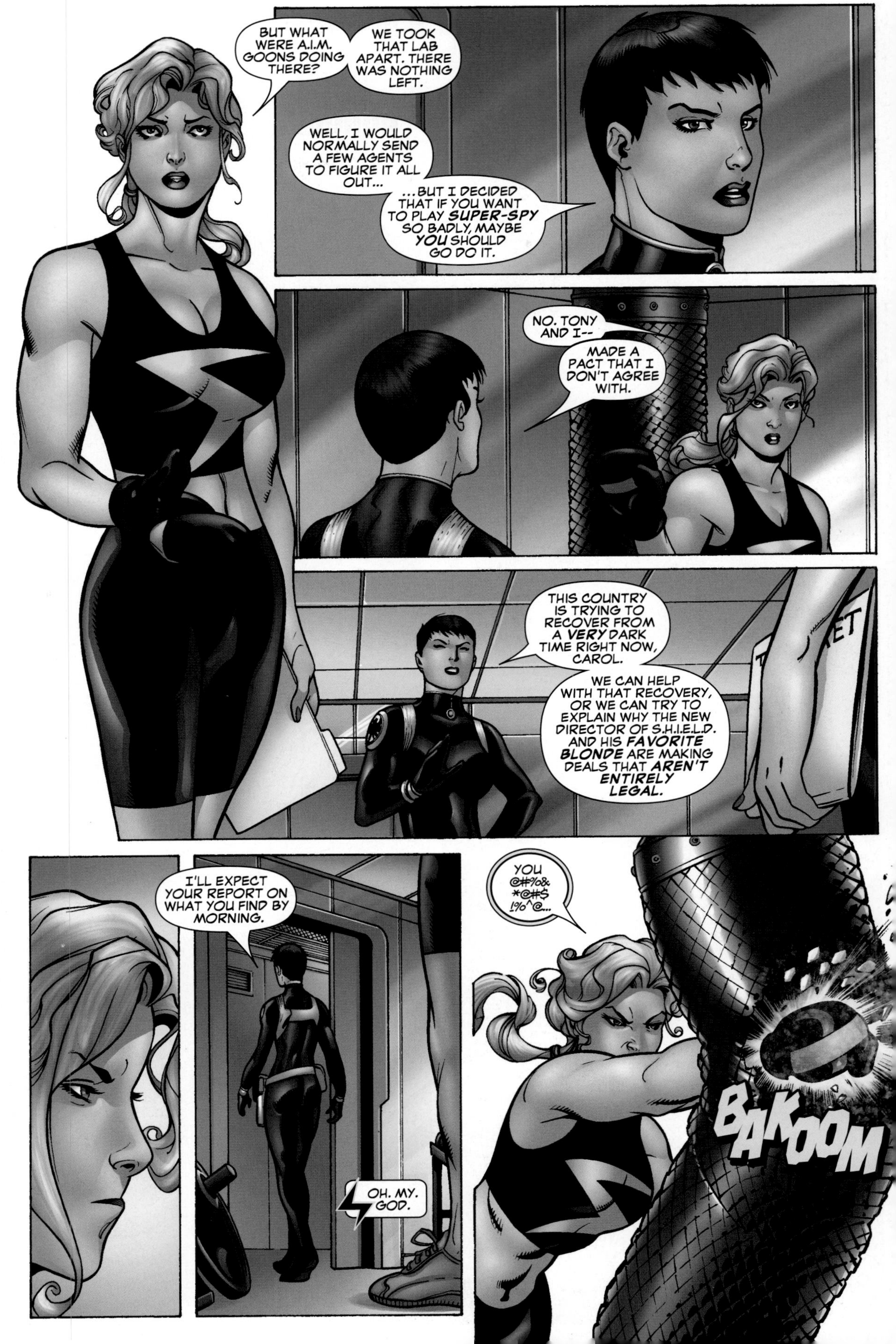
BUT WHAT WERE A.I.M. GOONS DOING THERE?
WE TOOK THAT LAB APART. THERE WAS NOTHING LEFT.
WELL, I WOULD NORMALLY SEND A FEW AGENTS TO FIGURE IT ALL OUT...
...BUT I DECIDED THAT IF YOU WANT TO PLAY SUPER-SPY SO BADLY, MAYBE YOU SHOULD GO DO IT.
NO. TONY AND I--
MADE A PACT THAT I DON'T AGREE WITH.
THIS COUNTRY IS TRYING TO RECOVER FROM A VERY DARK TIME RIGHT NOW, CAROL.
WE CAN HELP WITH THAT RECOVERY, OR WE CAN TRY TO EXPLAIN WHY THE NEW DIRECTOR OF S.H.I.E.L.D. AND HIS FAVORITE BLONDE ARE MAKING DEALS THAT AREN'T ENTIRELY LEGAL.
I'LL EXPECT YOUR REPORT ON WHAT YOU FIND BY MORNING.
OH. MY. GOD.
YOU @#%& *@#$!%^@...
BAKOOM

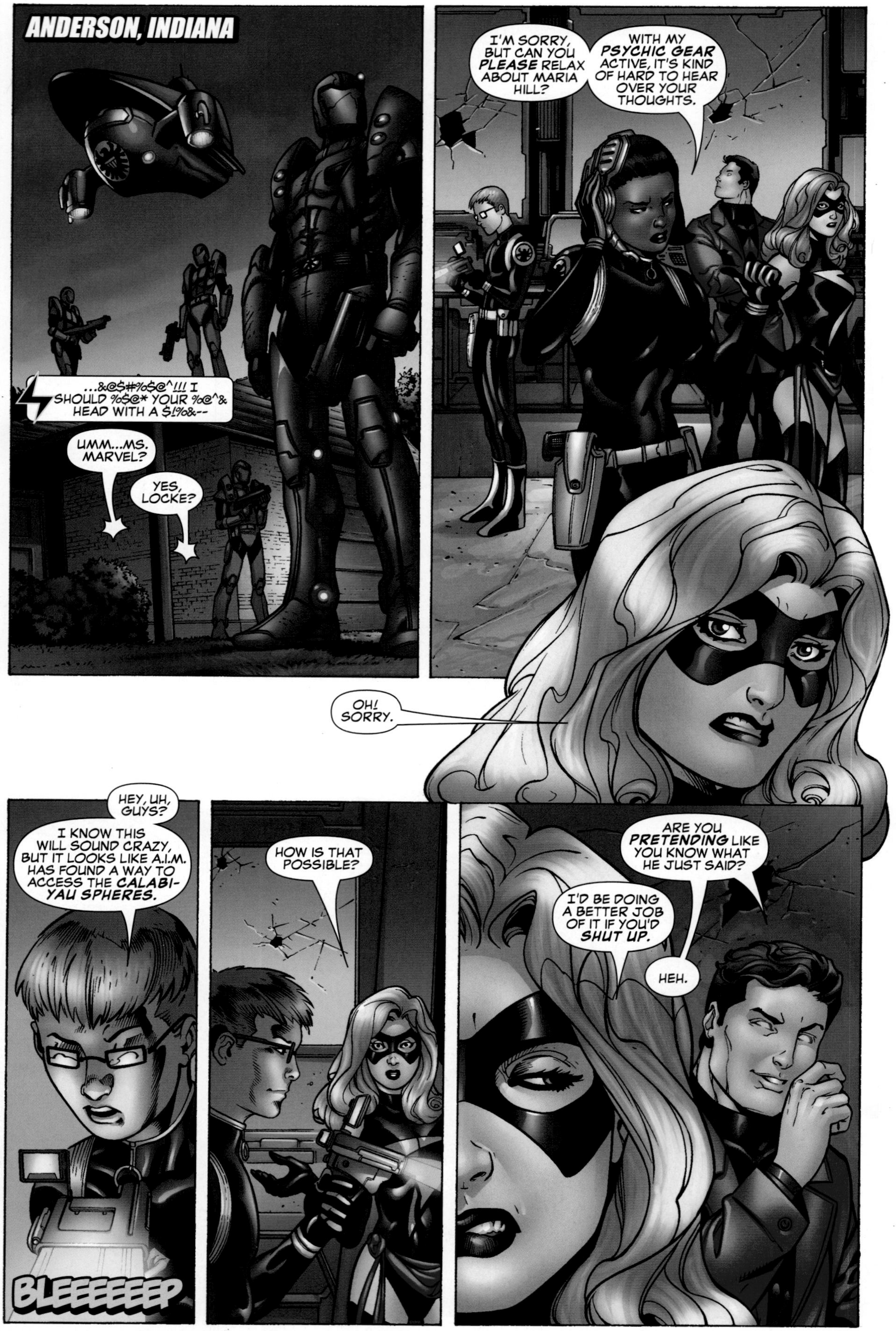
ANDERSON, INDIANA
...&@$#%$@^!!! I SHOULD %$@* YOUR %@^& HEAD WITH A $!%&--
UMM...MS. MARVEL?
YES, LOCKE?
I'M SORRY, BUT CAN YOU PLEASE RELAX ABOUT MARIA HILL?
WITH MY PSYCHIC GEAR ACTIVE, IT'S KIND OF HARD TO HEAR OVER YOUR THOUGHTS.
OH! SORRY.
HEY, UH, GUYS?
I KNOW THIS WILL SOUND CRAZY, BUT IT LOOKS LIKE A.I.M. HAS FOUND A WAY TO ACCESS THE CALABI-YAU SPHERES.
BLEEEEEEP
HOW IS THAT POSSIBLE?
ARE YOU PRETENDING LIKE YOU KNOW WHAT HE JUST SAID?
I'D BE DOING A BETTER JOB OF IT IF YOU'D SHUT UP.
HEH.

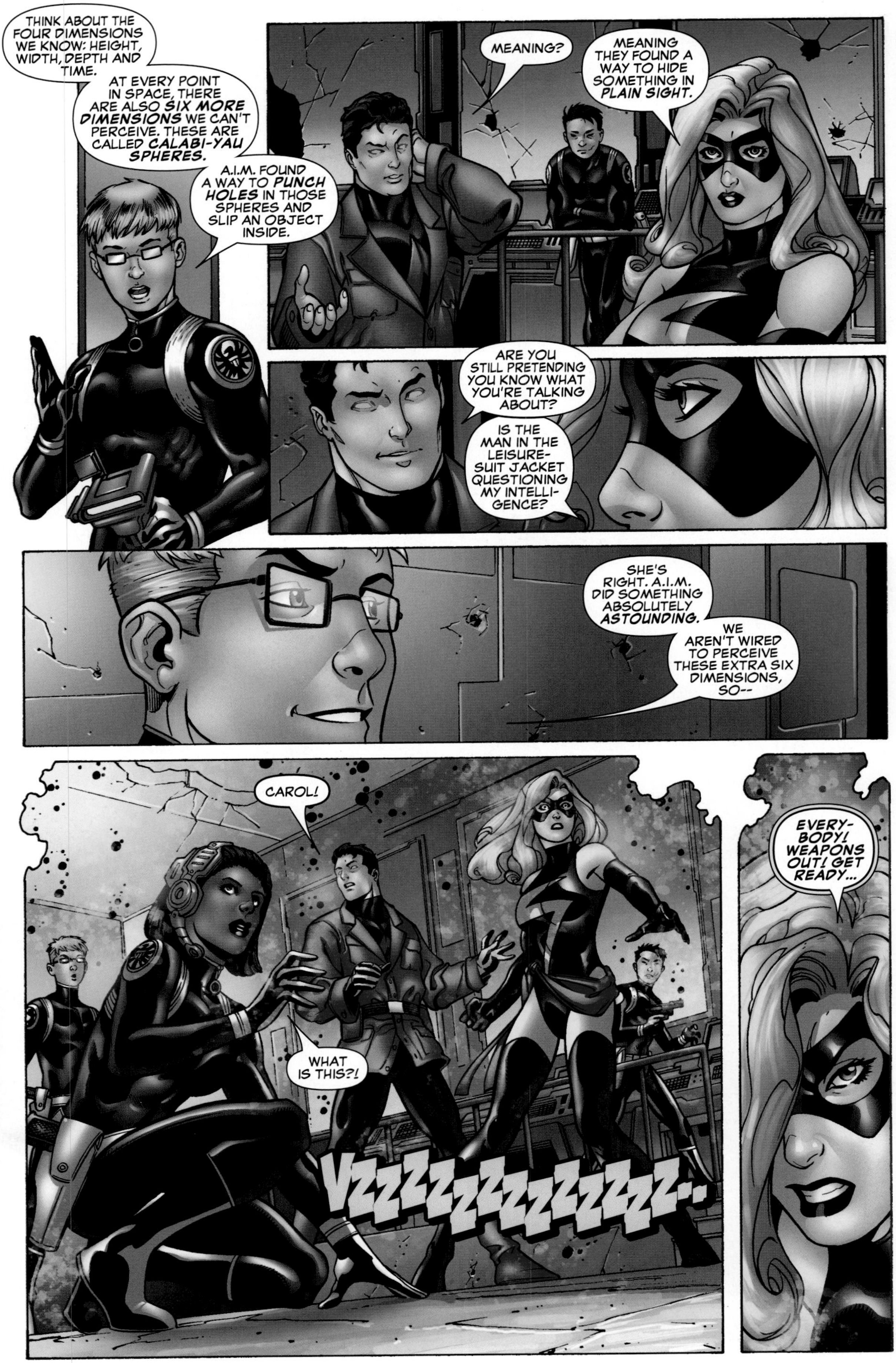
THINK ABOUT THE FOUR DIMENSIONS WE KNOW: HEIGHT, WIDTH, DEPTH AND TIME.
AT EVERY POINT IN SPACE, THERE ARE ALSO SIX MORE DIMENSIONS WE CAN'T PERCEIVE. THESE ARE CALLED CALABI-YAU SPHERES.
A.I.M. FOUND A WAY TO PUNCH HOLES IN THOSE SPHERES AND SLIP AN OBJECT INSIDE.
MEANING?
MEANING THEY FOUND A WAY TO HIDE SOMETHING IN PLAIN SIGHT.
ARE YOU STILL PRETENDING YOU KNOW WHAT YOU'RE TALKING ABOUT?
IS THE MAN IN THE LEISURE-SUIT JACKET QUESTIONING MY INTELLI-GENCE?
SHE'S RIGHT. A.I.M. DID SOMETHING ABSOLUTELY ASTOUNDING.
WE AREN'T WIRED TO PERCEIVE THESE EXTRA SIX DIMENSIONS, SO--
CAROL!
WHAT IS THIS?!
VZZZZZZZZZZZZZZZ..
EVERY-BODY! WEAPONS OUT! GET READY...

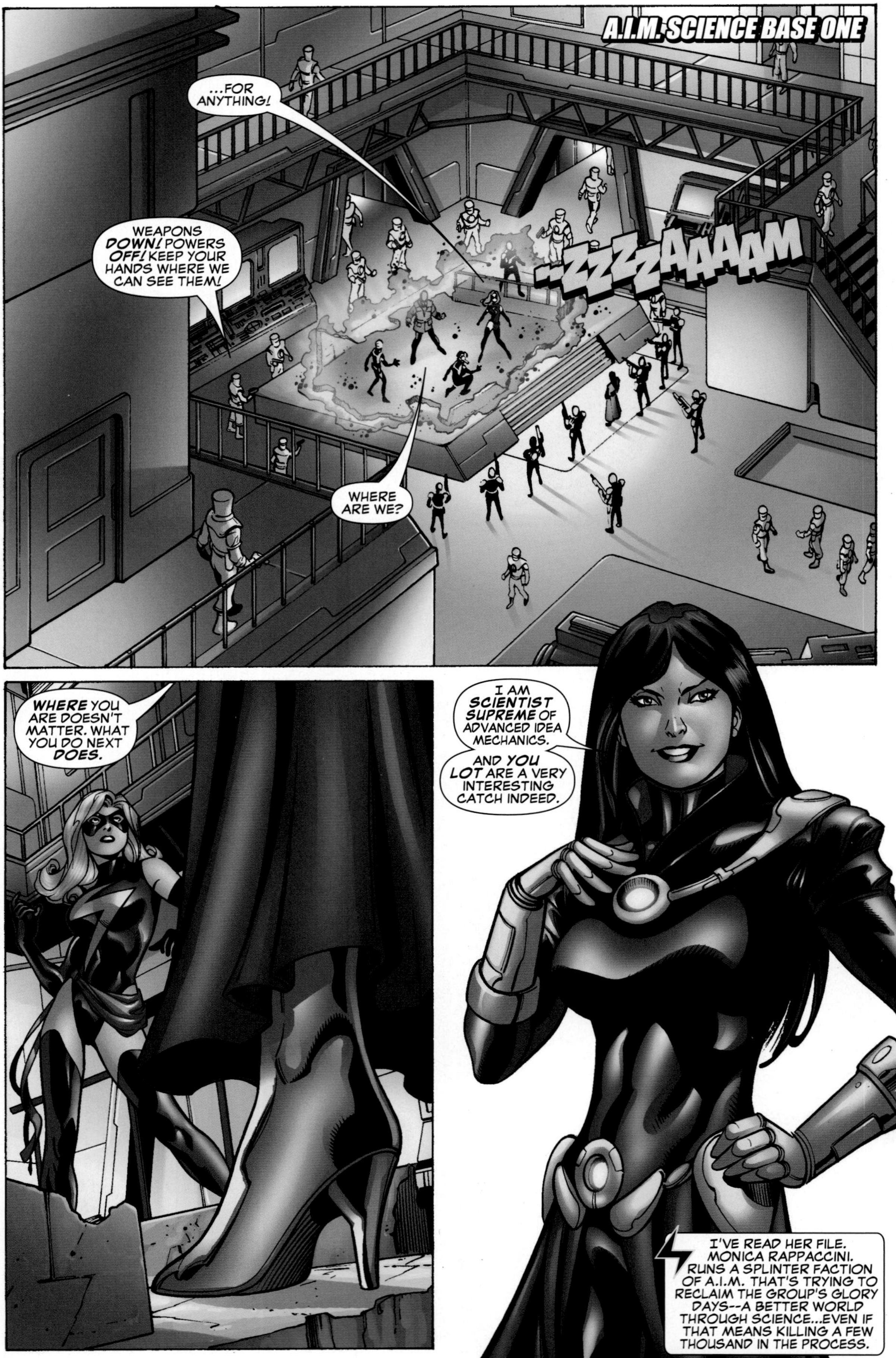
A.I.M. SCIENCE BASE ONE
...FOR ANYTHING!
WEAPONS DOWN! POWERS OFF! KEEP YOUR HANDS WHERE WE CAN SEE THEM!
--ZZZZAAAAM
WHERE ARE WE?
WHERE YOU ARE DOESN'T MATTER. WHAT YOU DO NEXT DOES.
I AM SCIENTIST SUPREME OF ADVANCED IDEA MECHANICS.
AND YOU LOT ARE A VERY INTERESTING CATCH INDEED.
I'VE READ HER FILE. MONICA RAPPACCINI. RUNS A SPLINTER FACTION OF A.I.M. THAT'S TRYING TO RECLAIM THE GROUP'S GLORY DAYS--A BETTER WORLD THROUGH SCIENCE...EVEN IF THAT MEANS KILLING A FEW THOUSAND IN THE PROCESS.

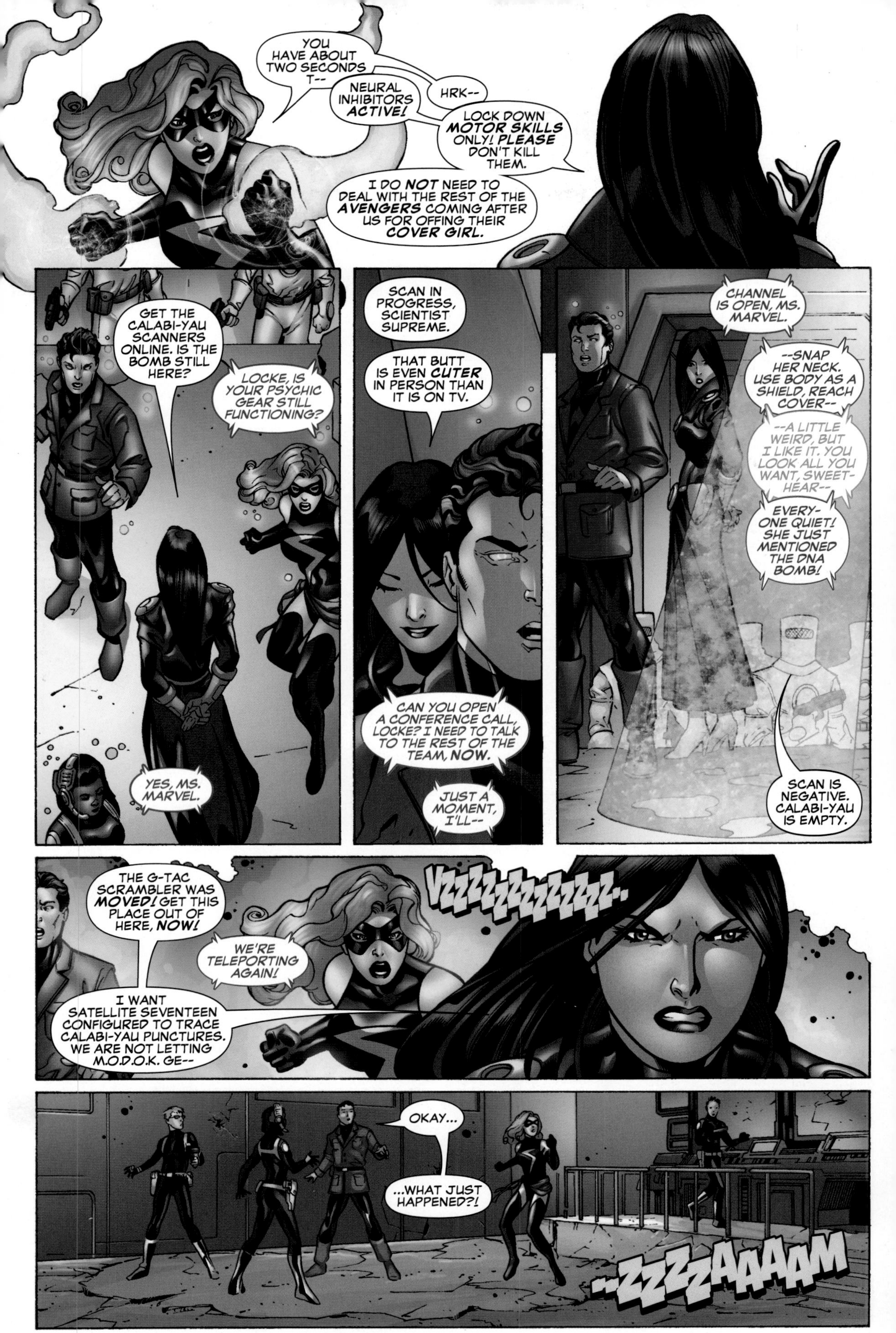
YOU HAVE ABOUT TWO SECONDS T--
HRK--
NEURAL INHIBITORS ACTIVE!
LOCK DOWN MOTOR SKILLS ONLY! PLEASE DON'T KILL THEM.
I DO NOT NEED TO DEAL WITH THE REST OF THE AVENGERS COMING AFTER US FOR OFFING THEIR COVER GIRL.
GET THE CALABI-YAU SCANNERS ONLINE. IS THE BOMB STILL HERE?
LOCKE, IS YOUR PSYCHIC GEAR STILL FUNCTIONING?
YES, MS. MARVEL.
SCAN IN PROGRESS, SCIENTIST SUPREME.
THAT BUTT IS EVEN CUTER IN PERSON THAN IT IS ON TV.
CAN YOU OPEN A CONFERENCE CALL, LOCKE? I NEED TO TALK TO THE REST OF THE TEAM, NOW.
JUST A MOMENT, I'LL--
CHANNEL IS OPEN, MS. MARVEL.
--SNAP HER NECK. USE BODY AS A SHIELD, REACH COVER--
--A LITTLE WEIRD, BUT I LIKE IT. YOU LOOK ALL YOU WANT, SWEET-HEAR--
EVERY-ONE QUIET! SHE JUST MENTIONED THE DNA BOMB!
SCAN IS NEGATIVE. CALABI-YAU IS EMPTY.
THE G-TAC SCRAMBLER WAS MOVED! GET THIS PLACE OUT OF HERE, NOW!
WE'RE TELEPORTING AGAIN!
VZZZZZZZZZZZZZ..
I WANT SATELLITE SEVENTEEN CONFIGURED TO TRACE CALABI-YAU PUNCTURES. WE ARE NOT LETTING M.O.D.O.K. GE--
OKAY...
...WHAT JUST HAPPENED?!
--ZZZZAAAAM

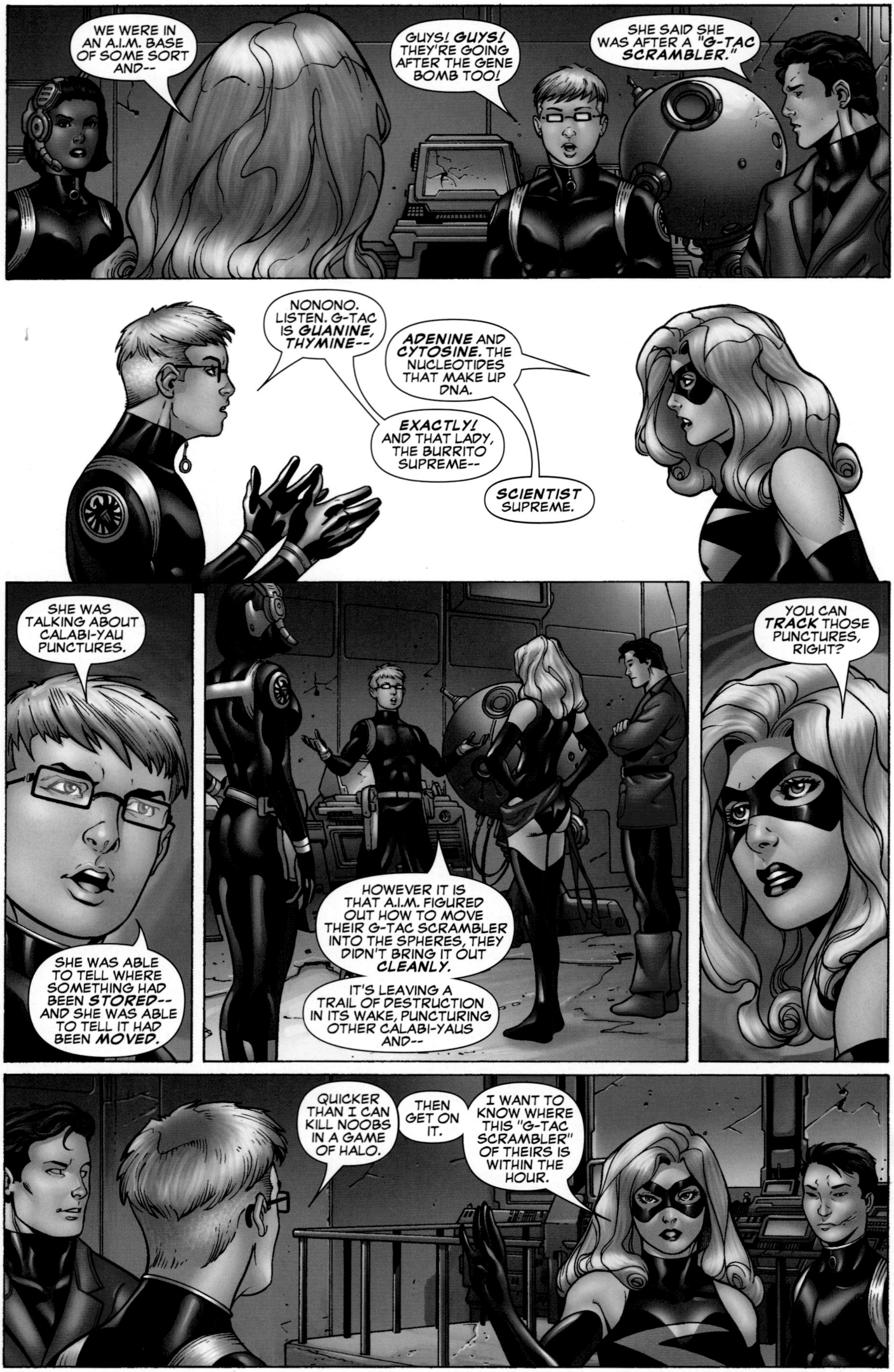
WE WERE IN AN A.I.M. BASE OF SOME SORT AND--
GUYS! GUYS! THEY'RE GOING AFTER THE GENE BOMB TOO!
SHE SAID SHE WAS AFTER A "G-TAC SCRAMBLER."
NONONO. LISTEN. G-TAC IS GUANINE, THYMINE--
ADENINE AND CYTOSINE. THE NUCLEOTIDES THAT MAKE UP DNA.
EXACTLY! AND THAT LADY, THE BURRITO SUPREME--
SCIENTIST SUPREME.
SHE WAS TALKING ABOUT CALABI-YAU PUNCTURES.
SHE WAS ABLE TO TELL WHERE SOMETHING HAD BEEN STORED-- AND SHE WAS ABLE TO TELL IT HAD BEEN MOVED.
HOWEVER IT IS THAT A.I.M. FIGURED OUT HOW TO MOVE THEIR G-TAC SCRAMBLER INTO THE SPHERES, THEY DIDN'T BRING IT OUT CLEANLY.
IT'S LEAVING A TRAIL OF DESTRUCTION IN ITS WAKE, PUNCTURING OTHER CALABI-YAUS AND--
YOU CAN TRACK THOSE PUNCTURES, RIGHT?
QUICKER THAN I CAN KILL NOOBS IN A GAME OF HALO.
THEN GET ON IT.
I WANT TO KNOW WHERE THIS "G-TAC SCRAMBLER" OF THEIRS IS WITHIN THE HOUR.

A.I.M. RESEARCH BASE ALPHA

OUR GENE MANIPULATION HAS BECOME MORE RELIABLE AND THE *GNASHERS* ARE SURVIVING LONGER AFTER REMOVAL FROM THE ARTIFICIAL WOMB.

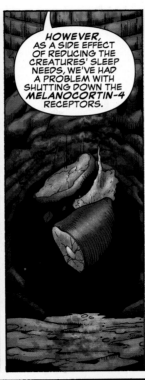

HOWEVER, AS A SIDE EFFECT OF REDUCING THE CREATURES' SLEEP NEEDS, WE'VE HAD A PROBLEM WITH SHUTTING DOWN THE *MELANOCORTIN-4* RECEPTORS.

ONCE WE GET *THAT* DEALT WITH, THE GNASHERS WILL BE *INCAPABLE* OF FEELING FULL AND WILL *CONTINUOUSLY* HUNT AND FEED.

SRLAK

AND, UM, SIR... SOMETIMES THE GNASHERS ONLY WANT *LIVE* MEAT.

IS THAT SO?

YES, WE'RE TRYING TO ACQUIRE SOME VOLUN--

--TEEEEEERS! NOOOOO!!!!

THUD

OH...OH, GOD.

PLEASE... GET ME OUT OF HERE.

PLEASE!

GRRRAAAAGGHHH!

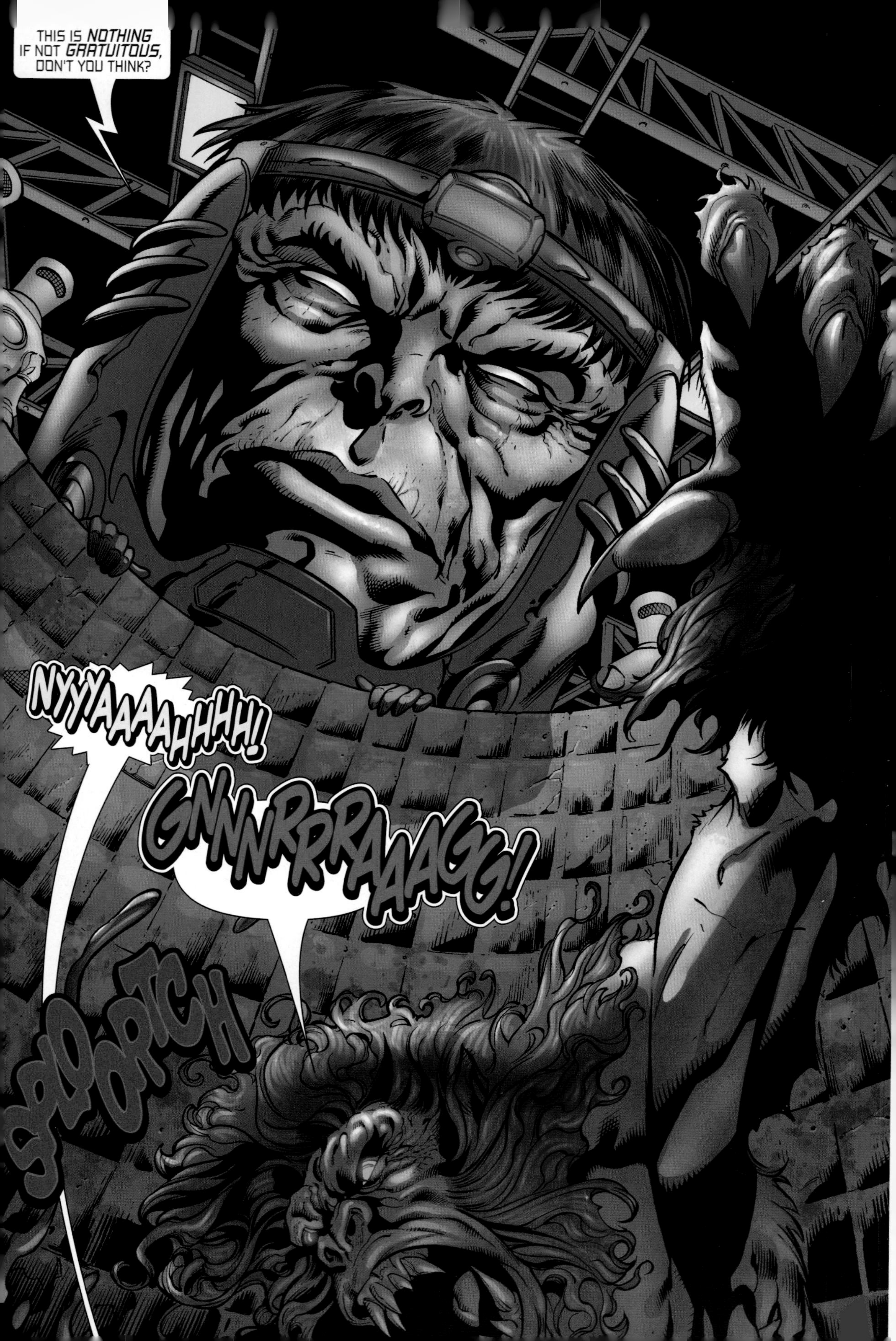

THIS IS NOTHING IF NOT GRATUITOUS, DON'T YOU THINK?
NYYYAAAAHHHH!
GNNNRRRAAAGG!
SQQORTCH

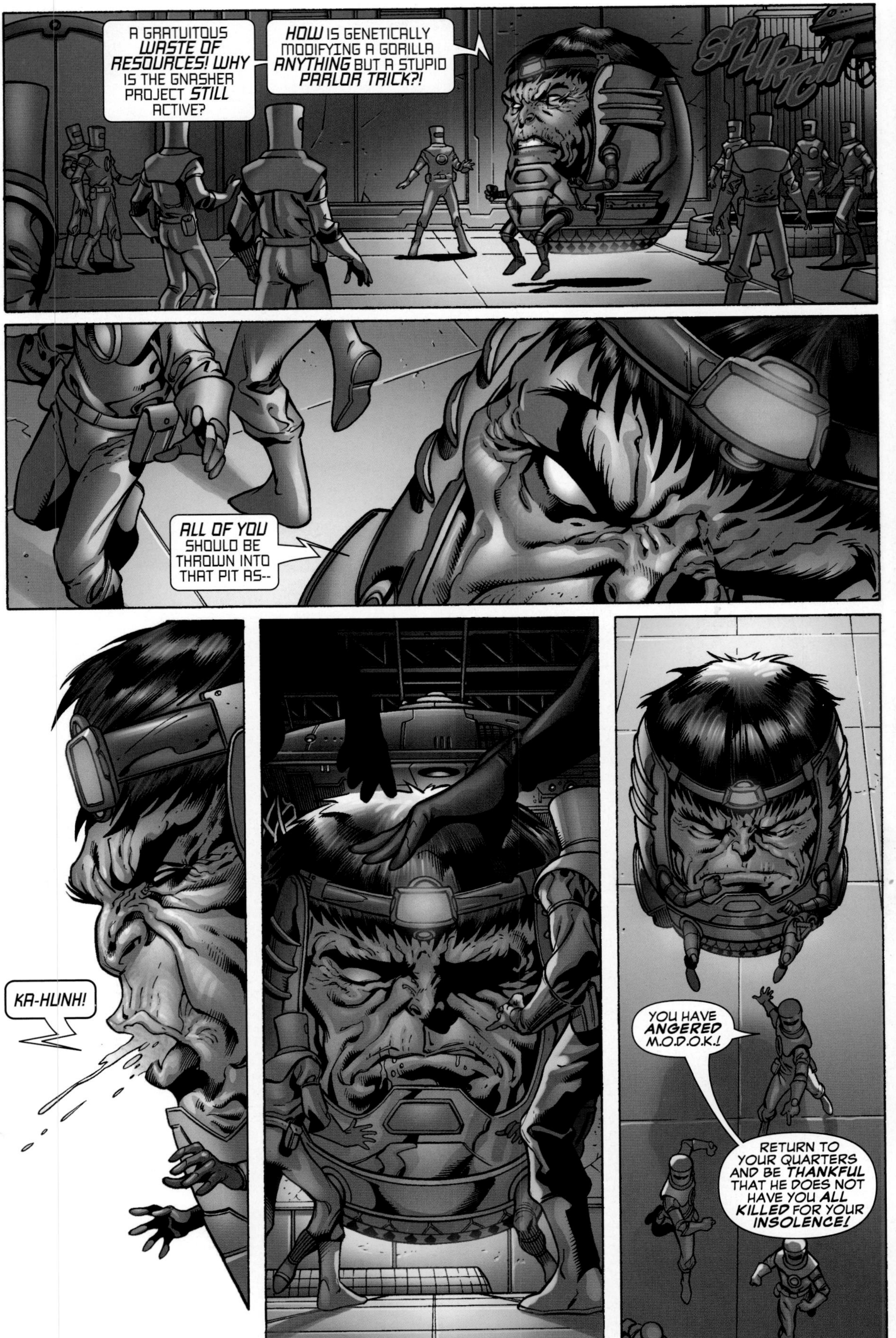
A GRATUITOUS WASTE OF RESOURCES! WHY IS THE GNASHER PROJECT STILL ACTIVE?
HOW IS GENETICALLY MODIFYING A GORILLA ANYTHING BUT A STUPID PARLOR TRICK?!
SPLURTCH
ALL OF YOU SHOULD BE THROWN INTO THAT PIT AS--
KA-HUNH!
YOU HAVE ANGERED M.O.D.O.K.!
RETURN TO YOUR QUARTERS AND BE THANKFUL THAT HE DOES NOT HAVE YOU ALL KILLED FOR YOUR INSOLENCE!

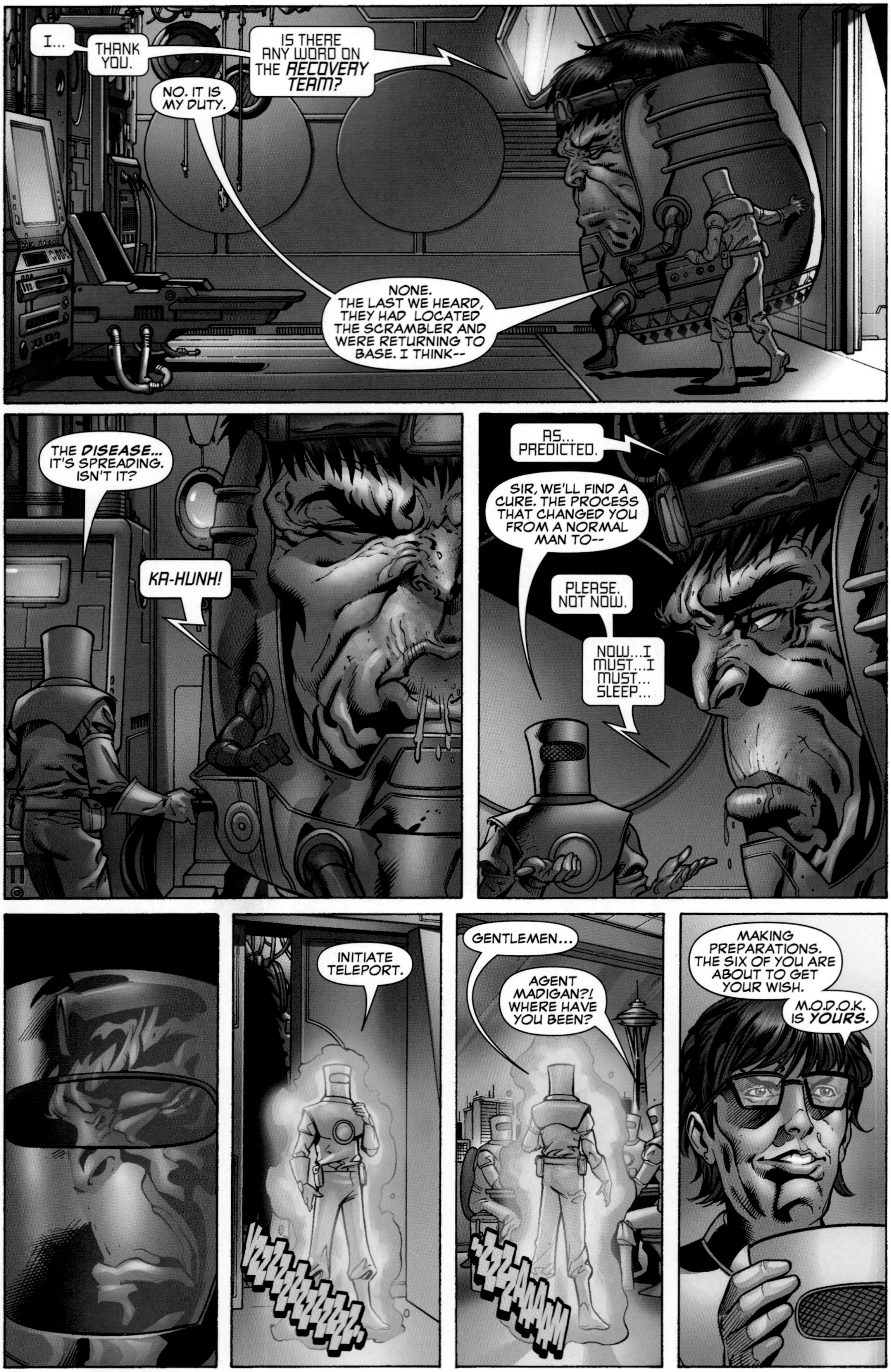

I...
THANK YOU.
NO. IT IS MY DUTY.
IS THERE ANY WORD ON THE RECOVERY TEAM?
NONE. THE LAST WE HEARD, THEY HAD LOCATED THE SCRAMBLER AND WERE RETURNING TO BASE. I THINK--
THE DISEASE... IT'S SPREADING. ISN'T IT?
KA-HUNH!
AS... PREDICTED.
SIR, WE'LL FIND A CURE. THE PROCESS THAT CHANGED YOU FROM A NORMAL MAN TO--
PLEASE. NOT NOW.
NOW...I MUST...I MUST... SLEEP...
INITIATE TELEPORT.
VZZZZZZZZZZZZ
GENTLEMEN...
AGENT MADIGAN?! WHERE HAVE YOU BEEN?
ZZZZAAAAM
MAKING PREPARATIONS. THE SIX OF YOU ARE ABOUT TO GET YOUR WISH.
M.O.D.O.K. IS YOURS.

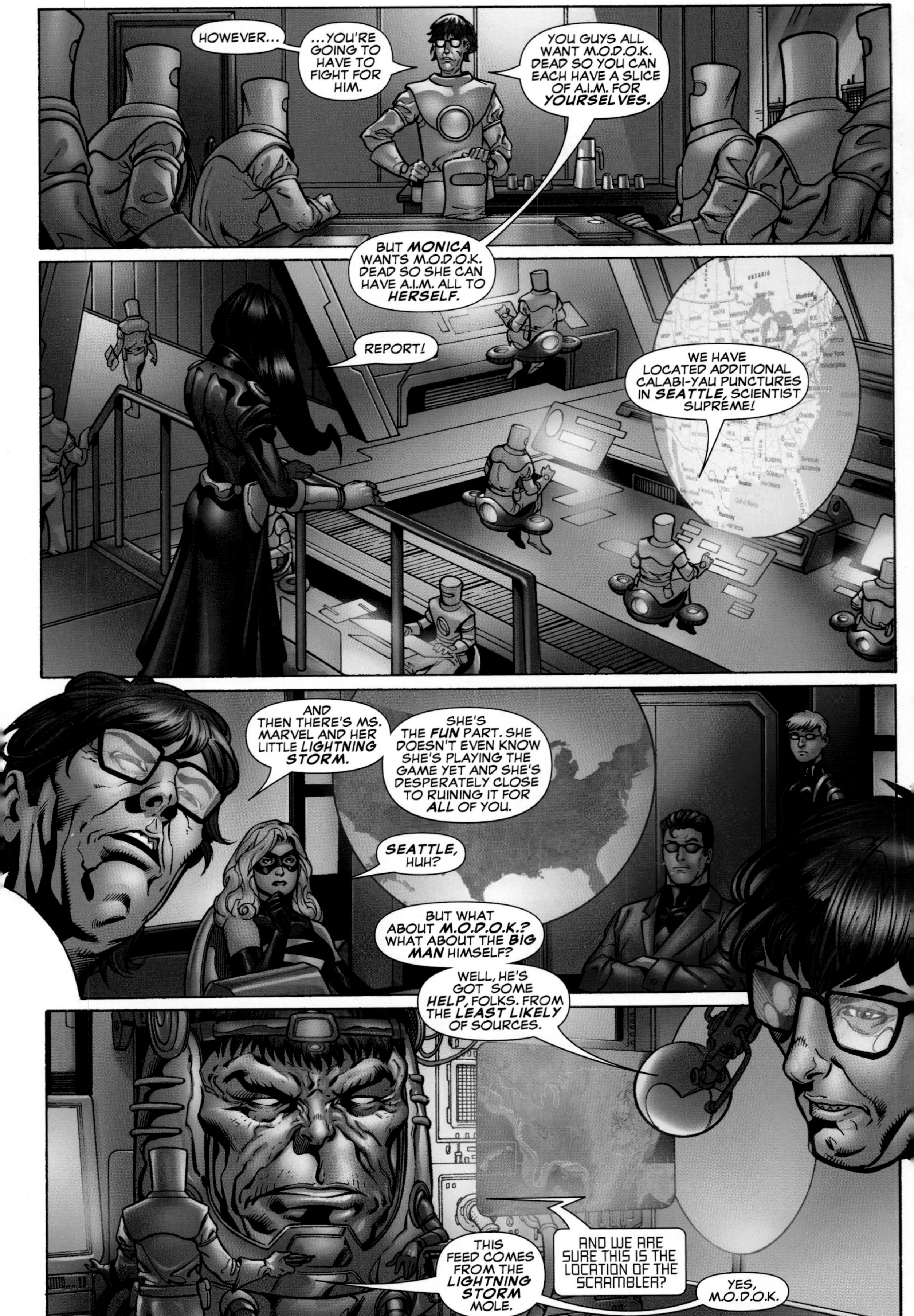
HOWEVER...
...YOU'RE GOING TO HAVE TO FIGHT FOR HIM.
YOU GUYS ALL WANT M.O.D.O.K. DEAD SO YOU CAN EACH HAVE A SLICE OF A.I.M. FOR YOURSELVES.
BUT MONICA WANTS M.O.D.O.K. DEAD SO SHE CAN HAVE A.I.M. ALL TO HERSELF.
REPORT!
WE HAVE LOCATED ADDITIONAL CALABI-YAU PUNCTURES IN SEATTLE, SCIENTIST SUPREME!
AND THEN THERE'S MS. MARVEL AND HER LITTLE LIGHTNING STORM.
SHE'S THE FUN PART. SHE DOESN'T EVEN KNOW SHE'S PLAYING THE GAME YET AND SHE'S DESPERATELY CLOSE TO RUINING IT FOR ALL OF YOU.
SEATTLE, HUH?
BUT WHAT ABOUT M.O.D.O.K.? WHAT ABOUT THE BIG MAN HIMSELF?
WELL, HE'S GOT SOME HELP, FOLKS. FROM THE LEAST LIKELY OF SOURCES.
THIS FEED COMES FROM THE LIGHTNING STORM MOLE.
AND WE ARE SURE THIS IS THE LOCATION OF THE SCRAMBLER?
YES, M.O.D.O.K.

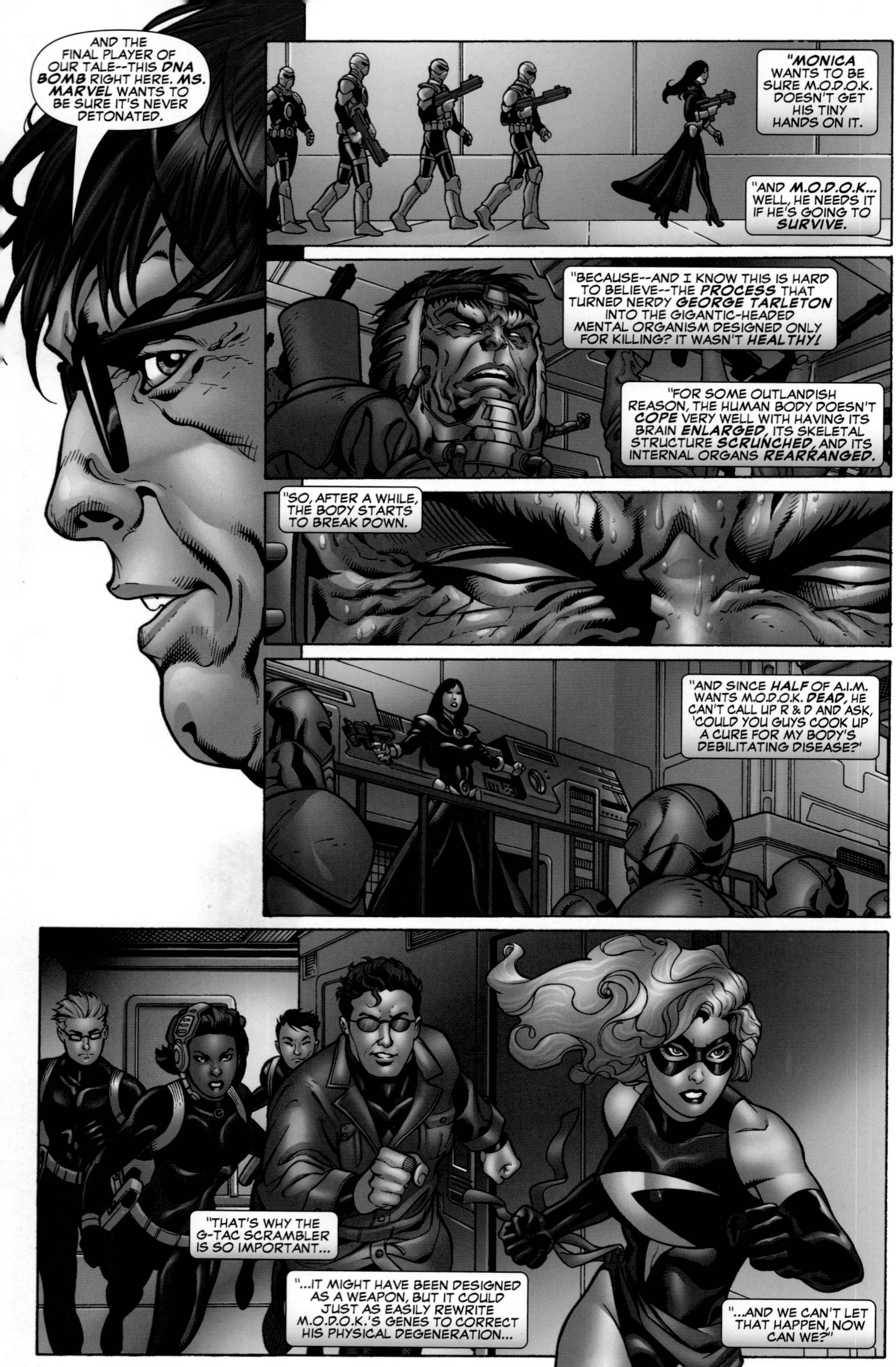
AND THE FINAL PLAYER OF OUR TALE--THIS DNA BOMB RIGHT HERE. MS. MARVEL WANTS TO BE SURE IT'S NEVER DETONATED.
"MONICA WANTS TO BE SURE M.O.D.O.K. DOESN'T GET HIS TINY HANDS ON IT.
"AND M.O.D.O.K... WELL, HE NEEDS IT IF HE'S GOING TO SURVIVE.
"BECAUSE--AND I KNOW THIS IS HARD TO BELIEVE--THE PROCESS THAT TURNED NERDY GEORGE TARLETON INTO THE GIGANTIC-HEADED MENTAL ORGANISM DESIGNED ONLY FOR KILLING? IT WASN'T HEALTHY!
"FOR SOME OUTLANDISH REASON, THE HUMAN BODY DOESN'T COPE VERY WELL WITH HAVING ITS BRAIN ENLARGED, ITS SKELETAL STRUCTURE SCRUNCHED, AND ITS INTERNAL ORGANS REARRANGED.
"SO, AFTER A WHILE, THE BODY STARTS TO BREAK DOWN.
"AND SINCE HALF OF A.I.M. WANTS M.O.D.O.K. DEAD, HE CAN'T CALL UP R & D AND ASK, 'COULD YOU GUYS COOK UP A CURE FOR MY BODY'S DEBILITATING DISEASE?'
"THAT'S WHY THE G-TAC SCRAMBLER IS SO IMPORTANT...
"...IT MIGHT HAVE BEEN DESIGNED AS A WEAPON, BUT IT COULD JUST AS EASILY REWRITE M.O.D.O.K.'S GENES TO CORRECT HIS PHYSICAL DEGENERATION...
"...AND WE CAN'T LET THAT HAPPEN, NOW CAN WE?"

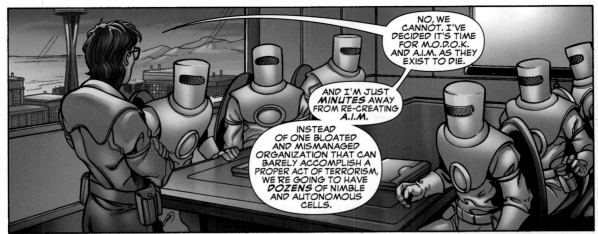

NO, WE CANNOT. I'VE DECIDED IT'S TIME FOR M.O.D.O.K. AND A.I.M. AS THEY EXIST TO DIE.

AND I'M JUST *MINUTES* AWAY FROM RE-CREATING A.I.M.

INSTEAD OF ONE BLOATED AND MISMANAGED ORGANIZATION THAT CAN BARELY ACCOMPLISH A PROPER ACT OF TERRORISM, WE'RE GOING TO HAVE *DOZENS* OF NIMBLE AND AUTONOMOUS CELLS.

ALL CAUSING DESTRUCTION AND HORROR ON AN *INCREDIBLE* SCALE.

FUN, HUH?

NO! THE DEAL WAS THAT YOU WOULD BRING US M.O.D.O.K.! WE HAVE NO INTEREST IN *SEGMENTING* A.I.M.! WE HAVE NO--

THE BEST YOU CAN HOPE FOR IS TO GRAB SOME OF THE SCRAPS THAT FALL TO THE FLOOR. BUT YOU BETTER GET READY, BECAUSE EVERYBODY IS COMING *RIGHT HERE.*

TO THIS.

VERY.

VZZZZZZZZZZZZZ--

VZZZZZZZZZZZZZ--

ROOM.

MS. MARVEL! SO GLAD YOU COULD MAKE IT. NOW THE GANG'S ALL HERE!

KR EE EE ESH

THREAT ASSESSMENT COMPLETE! MS. MARVEL IS PRIMARY TARGET!

SHOULD I TAKE THAT PERSONALLY?

NAH. IT'S JUST A WELL-KNOWN FACT THAT I... KIND OF ROCK.

DARK DOOR IS PRIMED! INITIATE TELEPORT!

VZZZZZZZZZZZZZZZ...

LOCKE! WHERE ARE THEY GOING?!

BACK TO BASE. THEY'RE ALL THINKING THEY DON'T WANT TO BE ANYWHERE NEAR SEATTLE WHEN THE DARK DOOR ACTIVATES.

GREAT.

SIMON, CAN YOU DEAL WITH THESE GUYS WHILE I TAKE THIS NASTINESS SOME-WHERE ELSE?

I DON'T KNOW IF I ROCK ENOUGH TO HANDLE IT.

OHHH, YOU HAVE YOUR MOMENTS.

OKAY. THINK FAST. UNKNOWN DEVICE SO BAD THAT IT SCARES THE GUYS THAT DEPLOYED IT. WHAT DO I *DO* WITH IT?

BAINES, WHAT DO YOU HAVE ON A.I.M. TECH CALLED THE *DARK DOOR?* I NEED TO KNOW WHAT THIS IS AND HOW FAR AWAY FROM CIVILIZATION TO GET IT.

DARK DOOR... DARK DOOR... LET'S SEE...

THE ONLY THING WE HAVE UNDER "DARK DOOR" IS SOME PLANS THAT *CAPTAIN AMERICA* FOUND DURING A LAB RAID.

NOTHING *WE'VE* EVER ENCOUNTERED IN THE FIELD. LET ME BRING THEM UP...

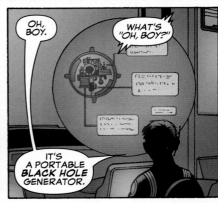

OH, BOY.

WHAT'S "OH, BOY?"

IT'S A PORTABLE *BLACK HOLE* GENERATOR.

WAIT. THIS THING FEELS TOO LIGHT. A.I.M. IS SCREWING WITH US.

THE DARK DOOR IS DESIGNED TO WIPE OUT A CITY AND--

MAYBE SO...BUT *THIS ONE'S* A FAKE.

I DON'T KNOW ABOUT THAT.

POP

I DO.

A.I.M. JUST WANTED TO GET ME OUT OF THE ROOM LONG ENOUGH FOR--

AGENT LOCKE TO MS. MARVEL! SOMETHING *BIG* IS TELEPORTING IN!

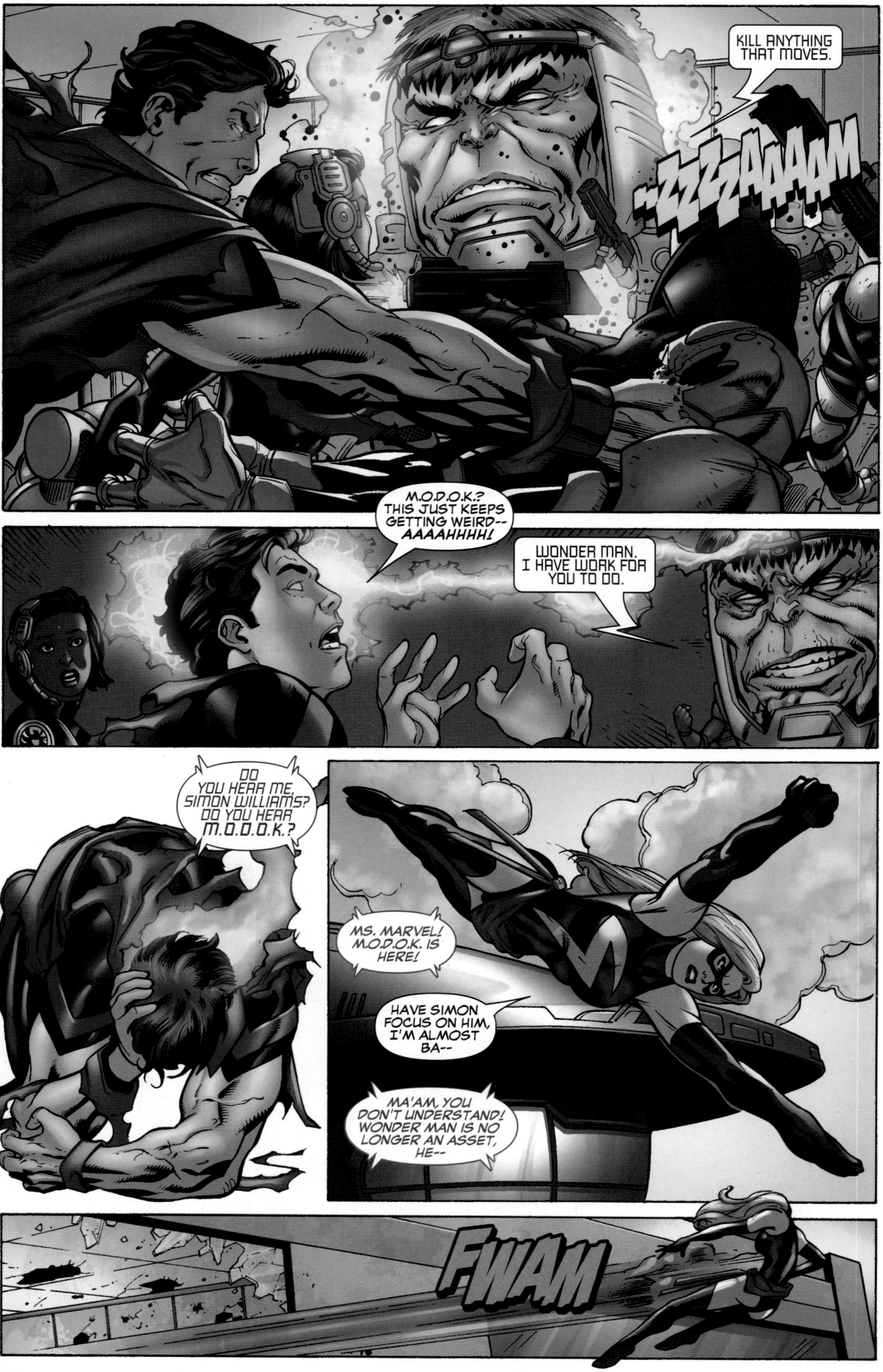
KILL ANYTHING THAT MOVES.
-ZZZZAAAAM
M.O.D.O.K.? THIS JUST KEEPS GETTING WEIRD-- AAAAHHHH!
WONDER MAN. I HAVE WORK FOR YOU TO DO.
DO YOU HEAR ME, SIMON WILLIAMS? DO YOU HEAR M.O.D.O.K.?
MS. MARVEL! M.O.D.O.K. IS HERE!
HAVE SIMON FOCUS ON HIM, I'M ALMOST BA--
MA'AM, YOU DON'T UNDERSTAND! WONDER MAN IS NO LONGER AN ASSET, HE--
FWAM

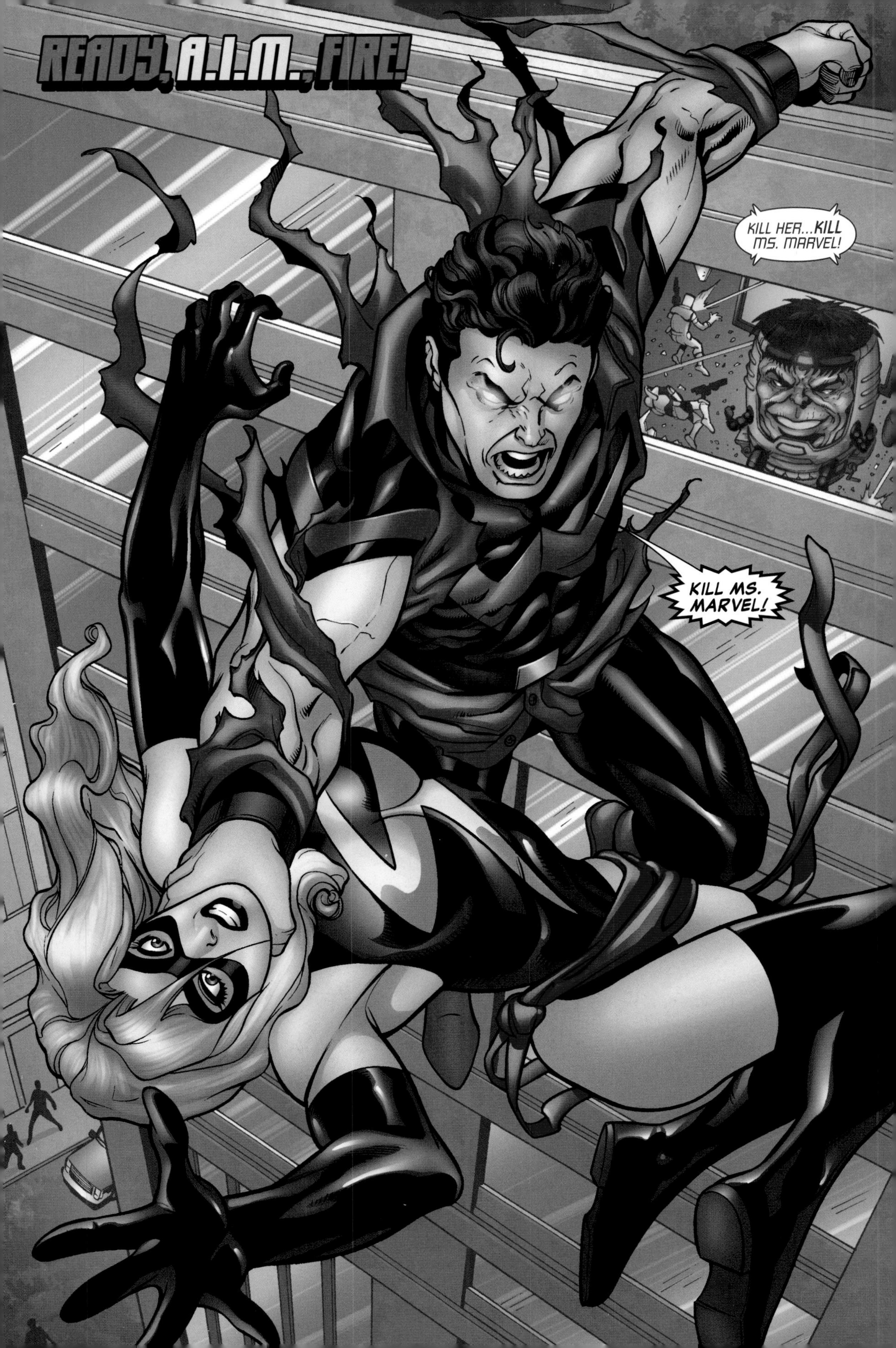
READY, A.I.M., FIRE!
KILL HER...KILL MS. MARVEL!
KILL MS. MARVEL!

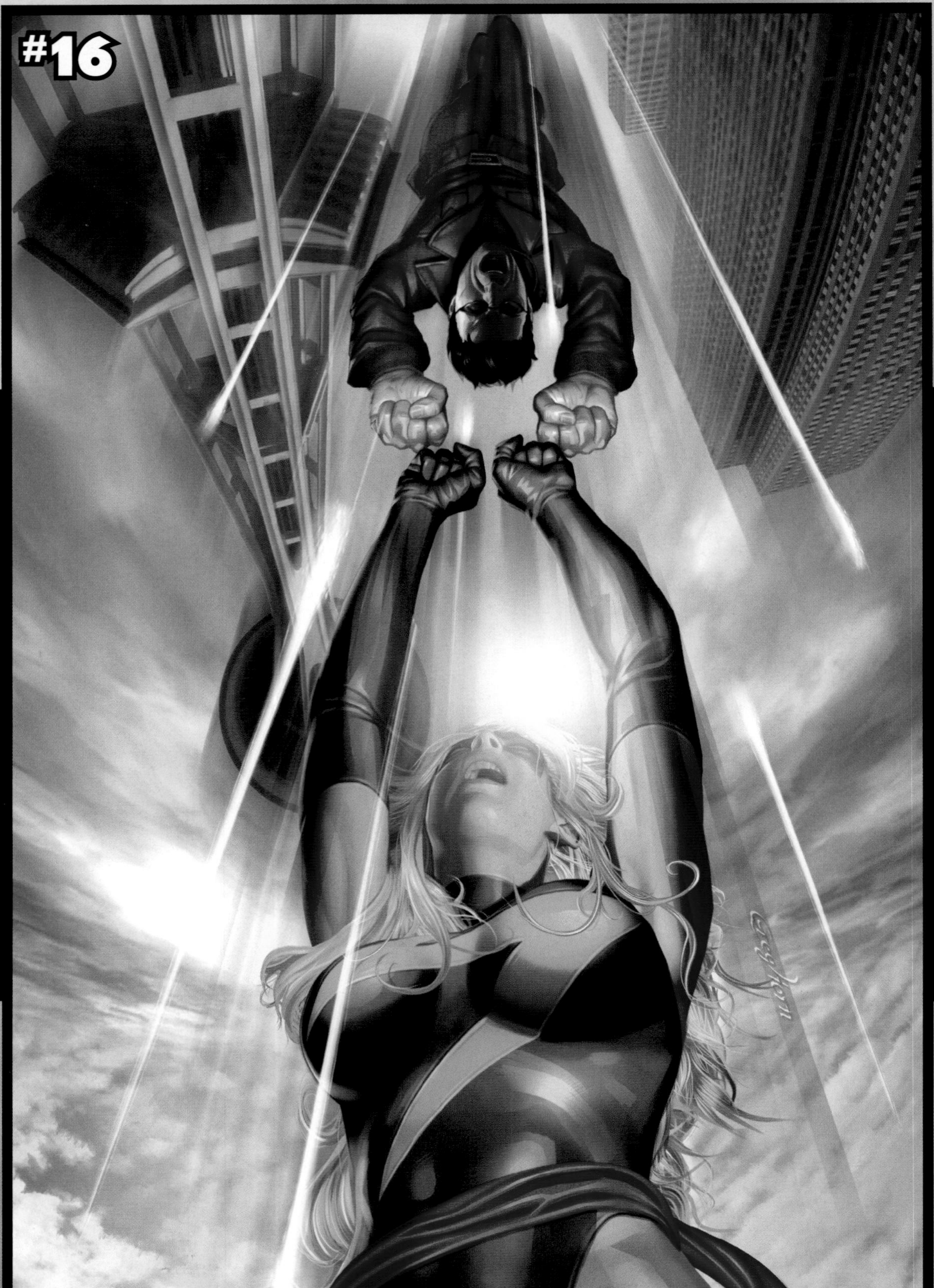
#16

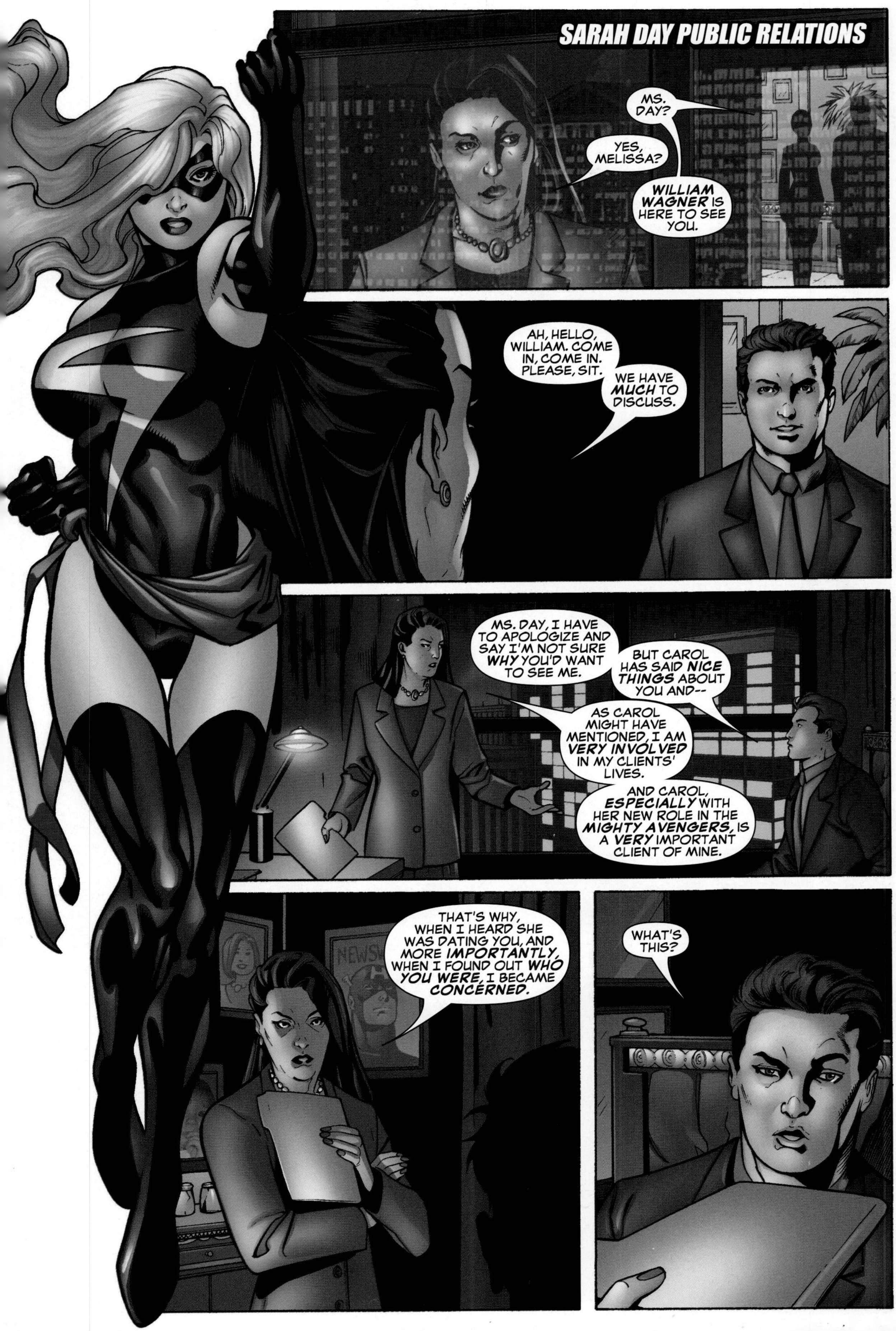
SARAH DAY PUBLIC RELATIONS
MS. DAY?
YES, MELISSA?
WILLIAM WAGNER IS HERE TO SEE YOU.
AH, HELLO, WILLIAM. COME IN, COME IN. PLEASE, SIT.
WE HAVE MUCH TO DISCUSS.
MS. DAY, I HAVE TO APOLOGIZE AND SAY I'M NOT SURE WHY YOU'D WANT TO SEE ME.
BUT CAROL HAS SAID NICE THINGS ABOUT YOU AND--
AS CAROL MIGHT HAVE MENTIONED, I AM VERY INVOLVED IN MY CLIENTS' LIVES.
AND CAROL, ESPECIALLY WITH HER NEW ROLE IN THE MIGHTY AVENGERS, IS A VERY IMPORTANT CLIENT OF MINE.
THAT'S WHY, WHEN I HEARD SHE WAS DATING YOU, AND MORE IMPORTANTLY, WHEN I FOUND OUT WHO YOU WERE, I BECAME CONCERNED.
WHAT'S THIS?

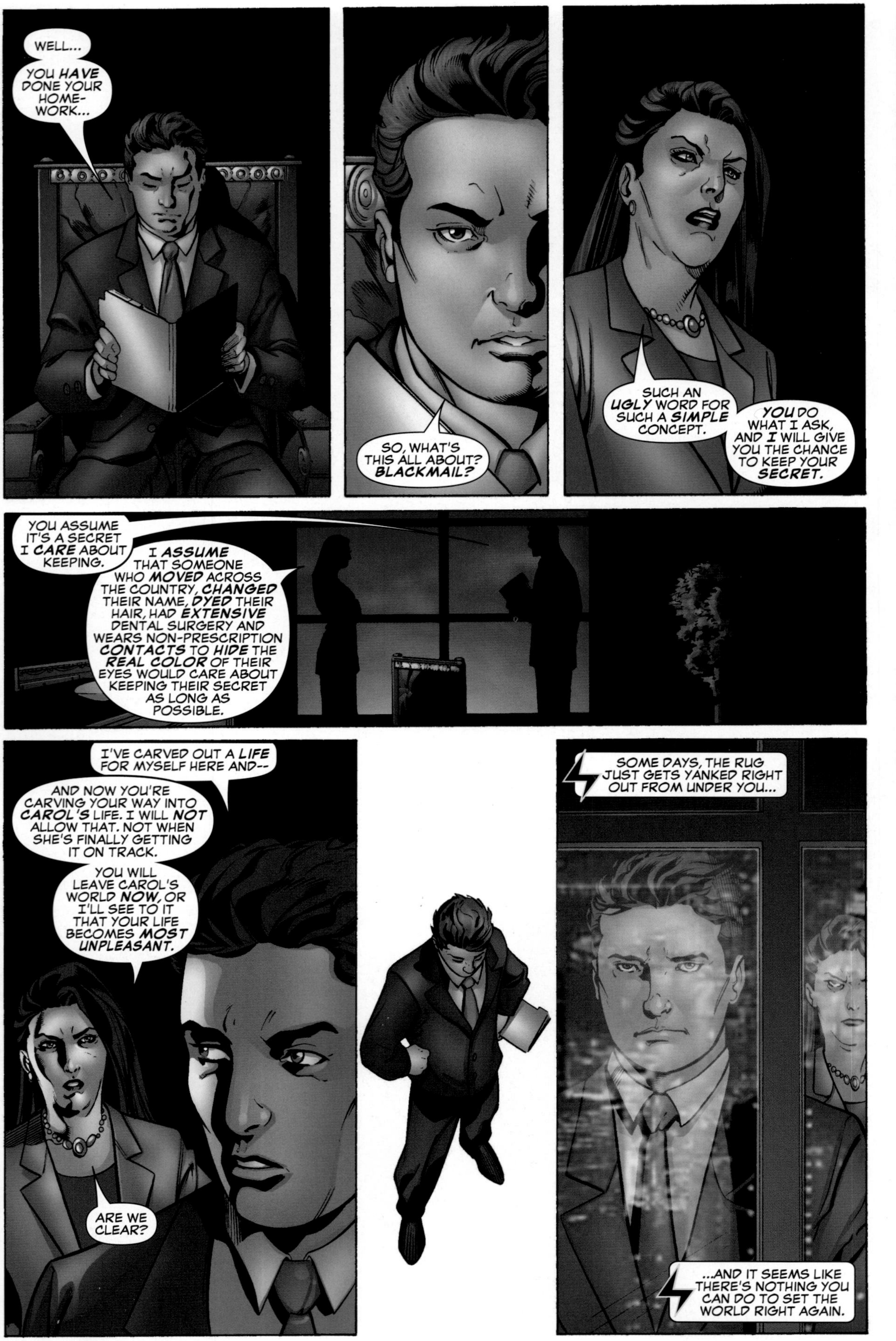
WELL...
YOU HAVE DONE YOUR HOME-WORK...
SO, WHAT'S THIS ALL ABOUT? BLACKMAIL?
SUCH AN UGLY WORD FOR SUCH A SIMPLE CONCEPT.
YOU DO WHAT I ASK, AND I WILL GIVE YOU THE CHANCE TO KEEP YOUR SECRET.
YOU ASSUME IT'S A SECRET I CARE ABOUT KEEPING.
I ASSUME THAT SOMEONE WHO MOVED ACROSS THE COUNTRY, CHANGED THEIR NAME, DYED THEIR HAIR, HAD EXTENSIVE DENTAL SURGERY AND WEARS NON-PRESCRIPTION CONTACTS TO HIDE THE REAL COLOR OF THEIR EYES WOULD CARE ABOUT KEEPING THEIR SECRET AS LONG AS POSSIBLE.
I'VE CARVED OUT A LIFE FOR MYSELF HERE AND--
AND NOW YOU'RE CARVING YOUR WAY INTO CAROL'S LIFE. I WILL NOT ALLOW THAT. NOT WHEN SHE'S FINALLY GETTING IT ON TRACK.
YOU WILL LEAVE CAROL'S WORLD NOW, OR I'LL SEE TO IT THAT YOUR LIFE BECOMES MOST UNPLEASANT.
ARE WE CLEAR?
SOME DAYS, THE RUG JUST GETS YANKED RIGHT OUT FROM UNDER YOU...
...AND IT SEEMS LIKE THERE'S NOTHING YOU CAN DO TO SET THE WORLD RIGHT AGAIN.

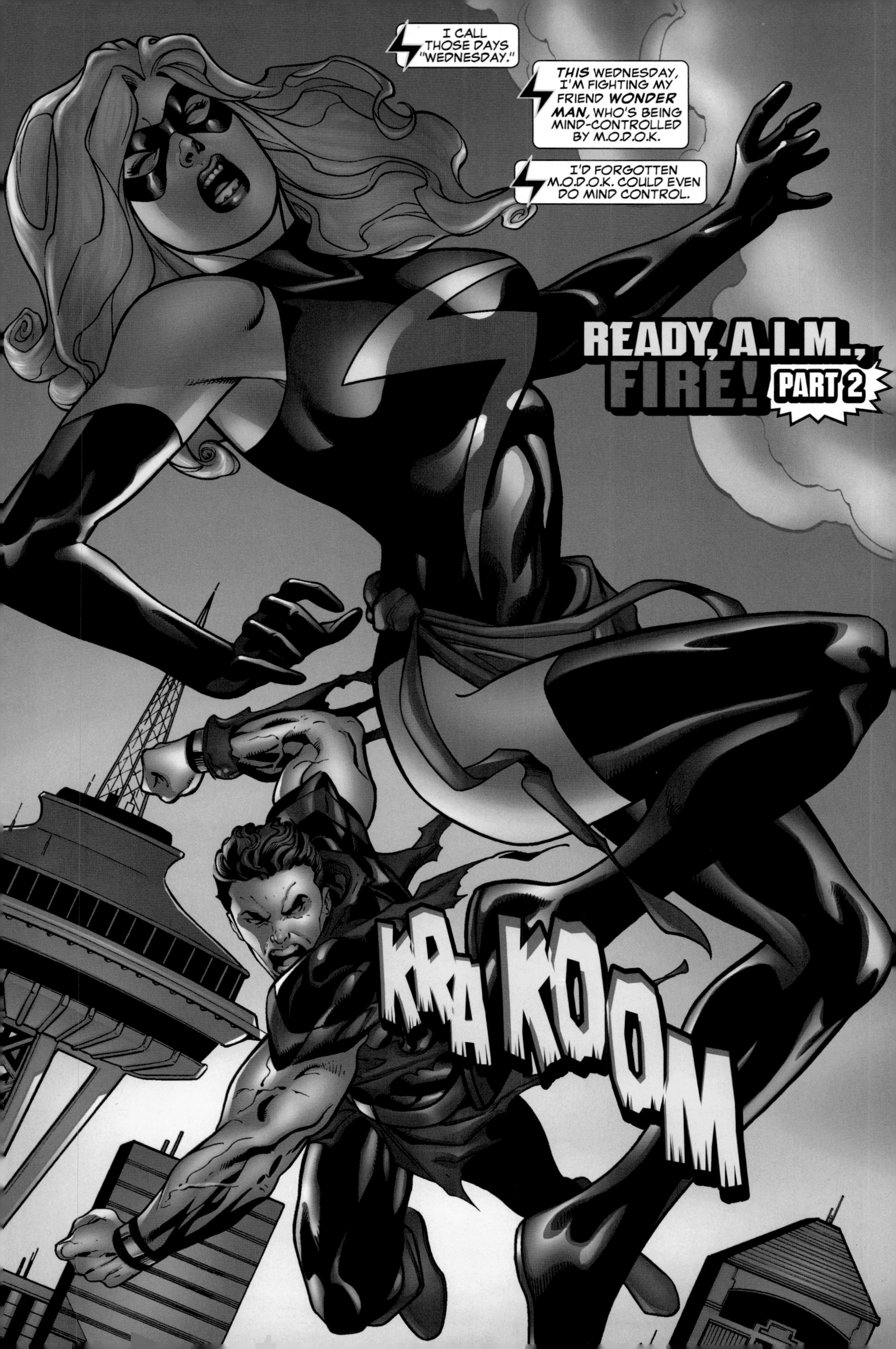
I CALL THOSE DAYS "WEDNESDAY."
THIS WEDNESDAY, I'M FIGHTING MY FRIEND WONDER MAN, WHO'S BEING MIND-CONTROLLED BY M.O.D.O.K.
I'D FORGOTTEN M.O.D.O.K. COULD EVEN DO MIND CONTROL.
READY, A.I.M., FIRE! PART 2
KRA KOOOM

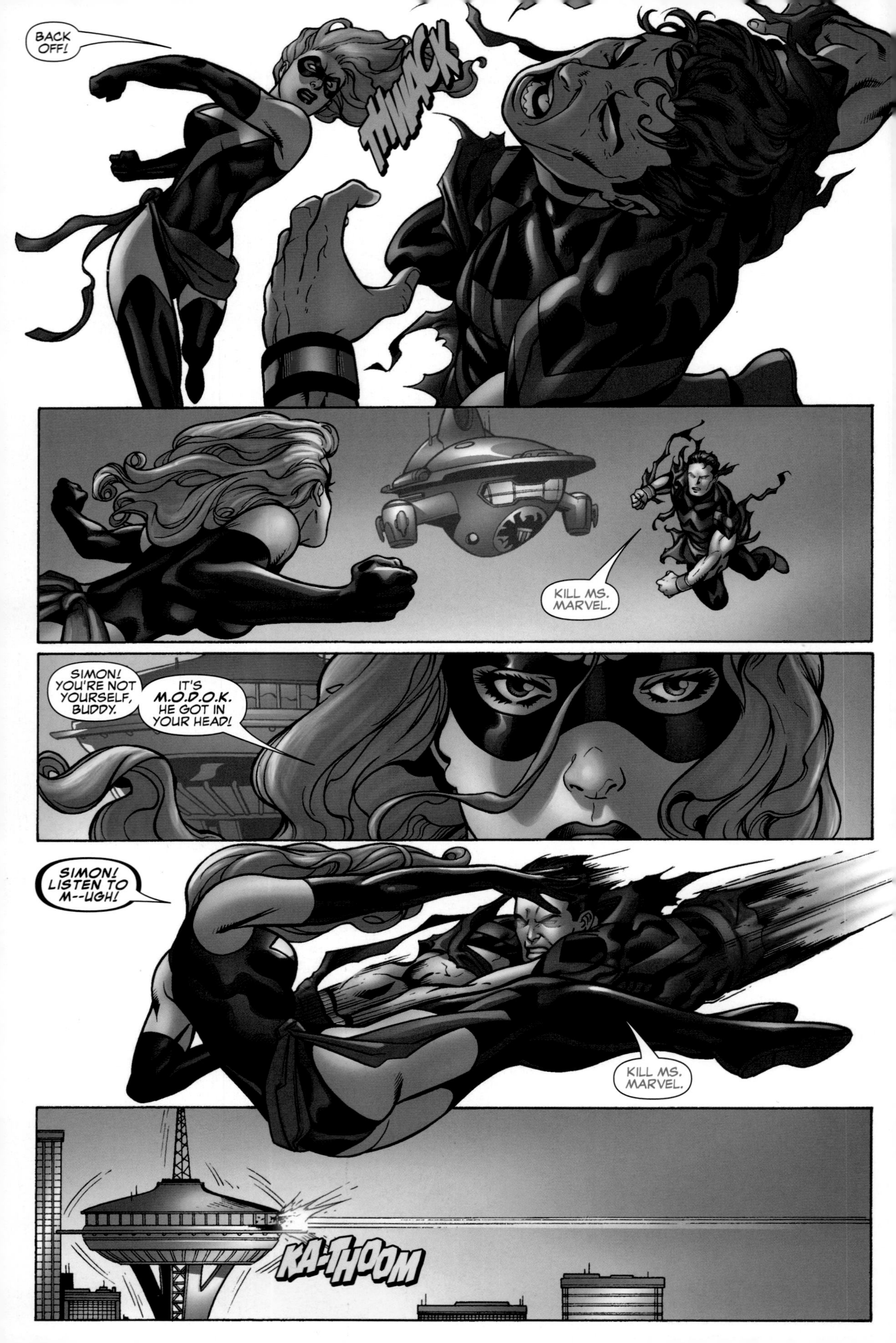
BACK OFF!
THWACK
KILL MS. MARVEL.
SIMON! YOU'RE NOT YOURSELF, BUDDY.
IT'S M.O.D.O.K. HE GOT IN YOUR HEAD!
SIMON! LISTEN TO M--UGH!
KILL MS. MARVEL.
KA-THOOM

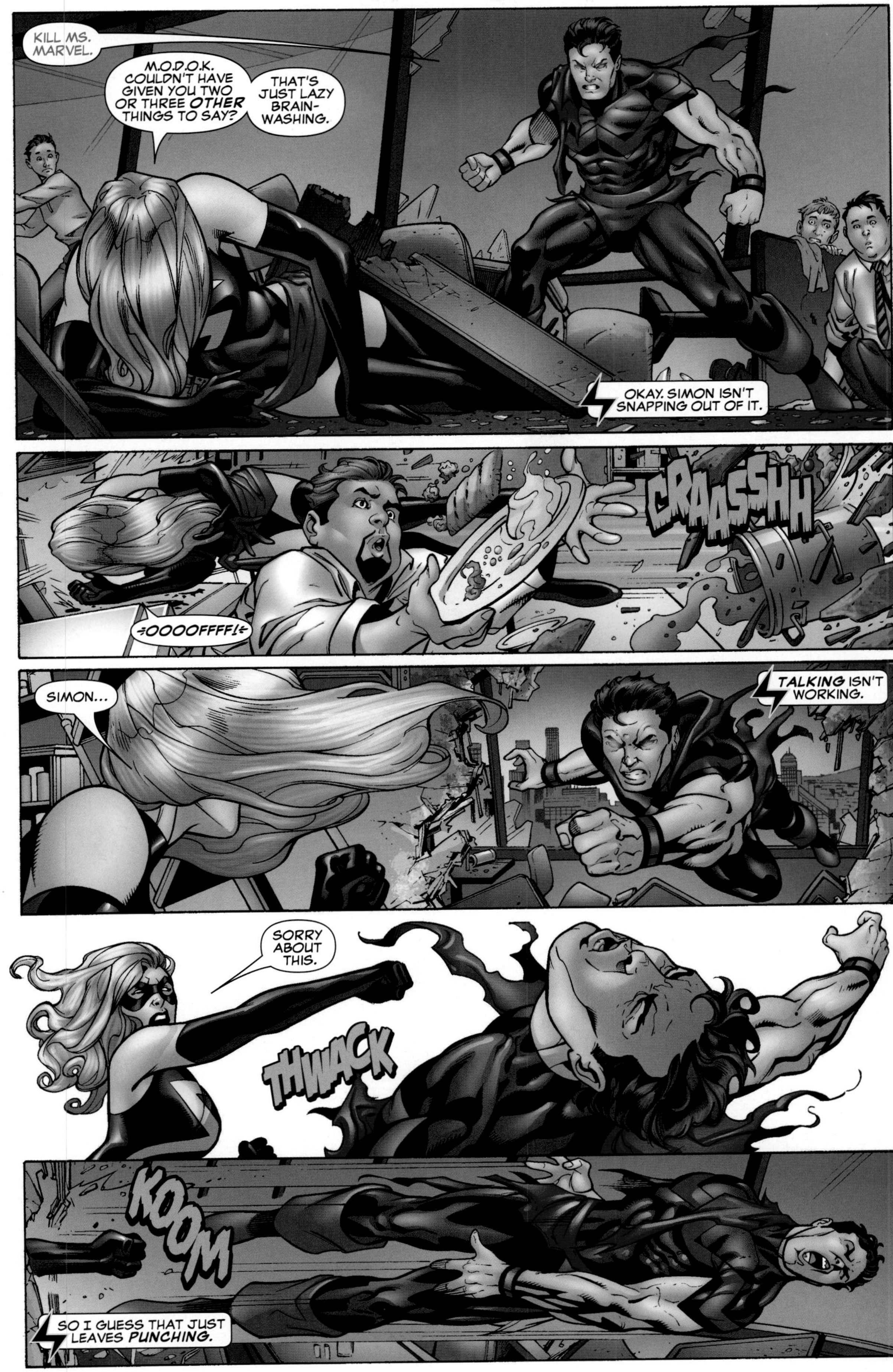
KILL MS. MARVEL.
M.O.D.O.K. COULDN'T HAVE GIVEN YOU TWO OR THREE OTHER THINGS TO SAY?
THAT'S JUST LAZY BRAIN-WASHING.
OKAY. SIMON ISN'T SNAPPING OUT OF IT.
CRAASSHH
OOOOFFFF!
SIMON...
TALKING ISN'T WORKING.
SORRY ABOUT THIS.
THWACK
KOOM
SO I GUESS THAT JUST LEAVES PUNCHING.

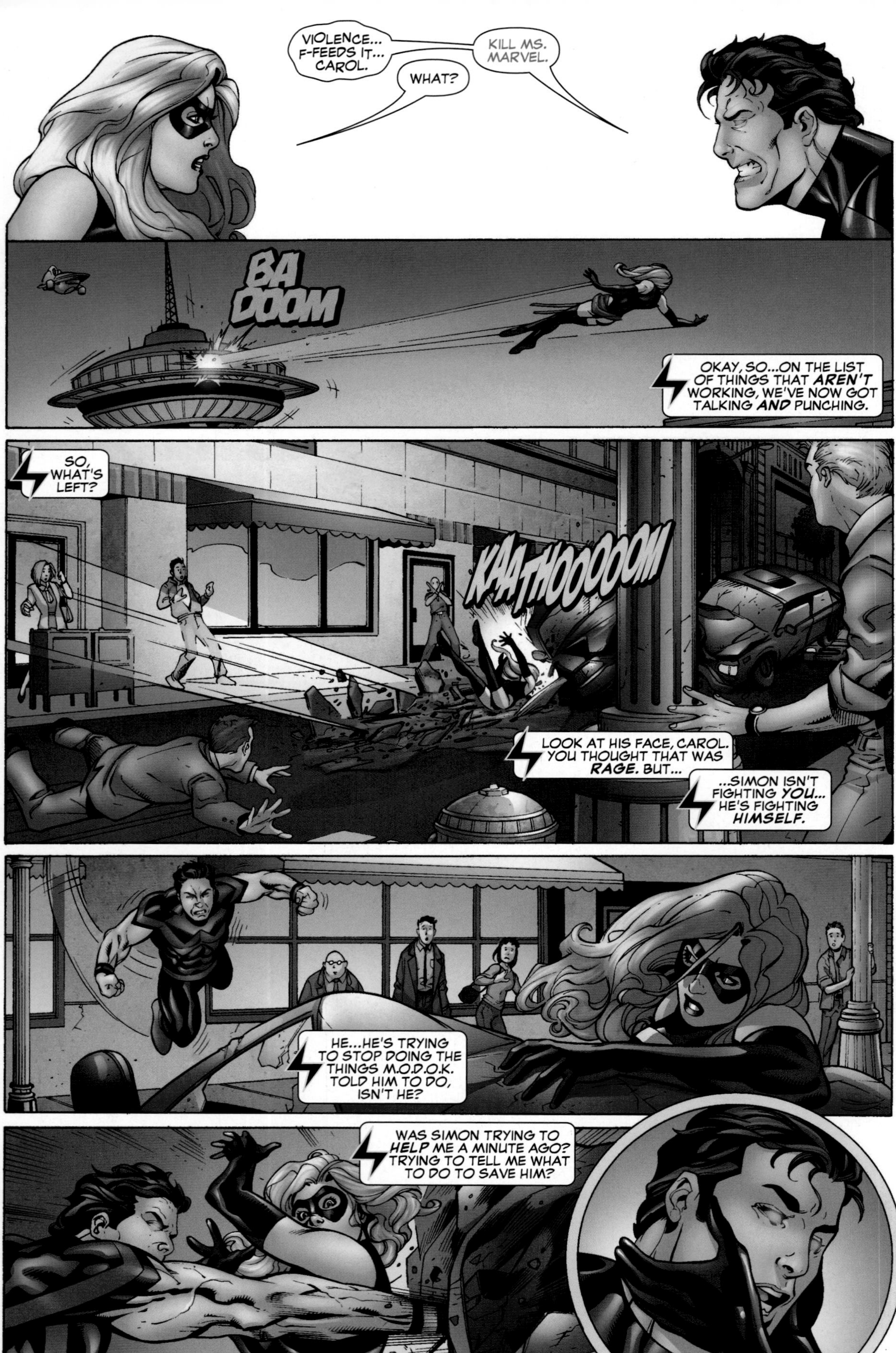
VIOLENCE... F-FEEDS IT... CAROL.
KILL MS. MARVEL.
WHAT?
BA DOOM
OKAY, SO...ON THE LIST OF THINGS THAT AREN'T WORKING, WE'VE NOW GOT TALKING AND PUNCHING.
SO, WHAT'S LEFT?
KAATHOOOOOM
LOOK AT HIS FACE, CAROL. YOU THOUGHT THAT WAS RAGE. BUT...
...SIMON ISN'T FIGHTING YOU... HE'S FIGHTING HIMSELF.
HE...HE'S TRYING TO STOP DOING THE THINGS M.O.D.O.K. TOLD HIM TO DO, ISN'T HE?
WAS SIMON TRYING TO HELP ME A MINUTE AGO? TRYING TO TELL ME WHAT TO DO TO SAVE HIM?
"VIOLENCE FEEDS IT," HE SAID.

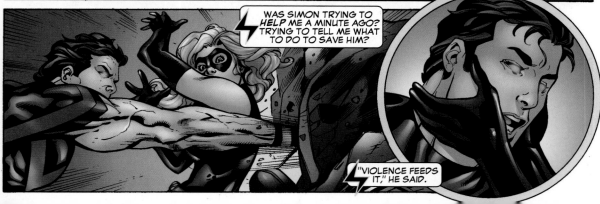

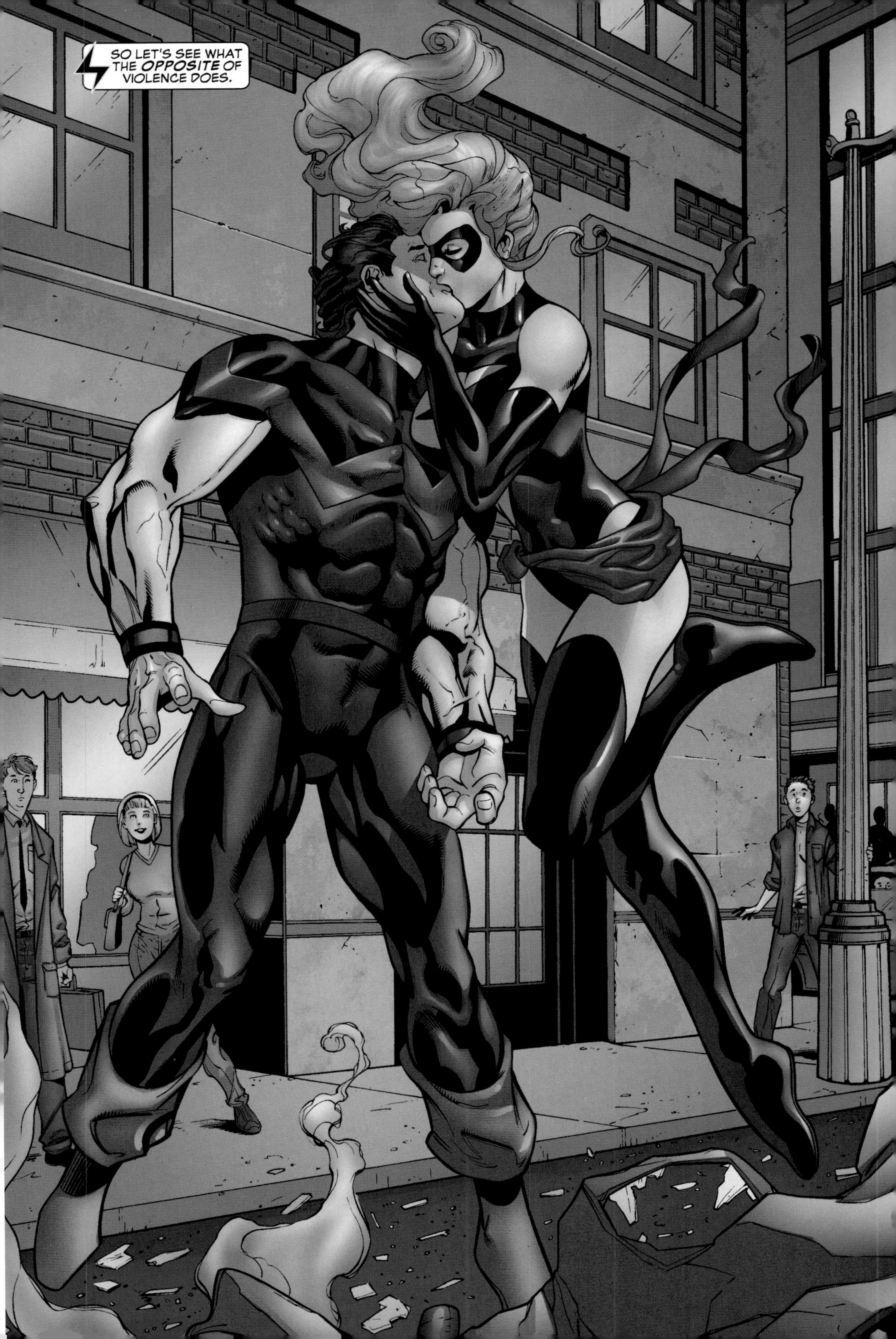
SO LET'S SEE WHAT THE OPPOSITE OF VIOLENCE DOES.

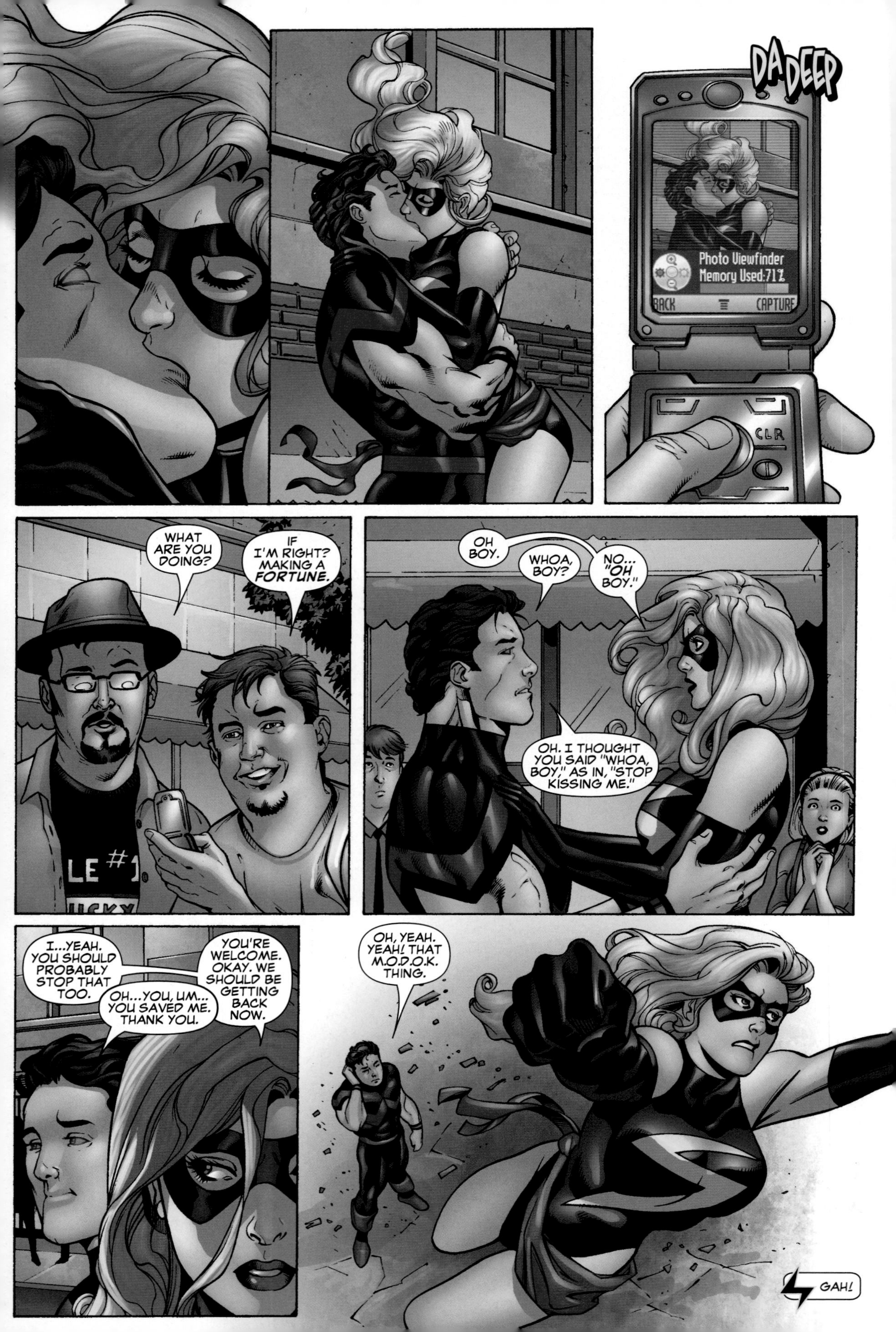
DA DEEP
Photo Viewfinder
Memory Used:71%
BACK
CAPTURE
CLR
WHAT ARE YOU DOING?
IF I'M RIGHT? MAKING A FORTUNE.
OH BOY.
WHOA, BOY?
NO... "OH BOY."
OH. I THOUGHT YOU SAID "WHOA, BOY," AS IN, "STOP KISSING ME."
I...YEAH. YOU SHOULD PROBABLY STOP THAT TOO.
OH...YOU, UM... YOU SAVED ME. THANK YOU.
YOU'RE WELCOME. OKAY. WE SHOULD BE GETTING BACK NOW.
OH, YEAH. YEAH! THAT M.O.D.O.K. THING.
GAH!

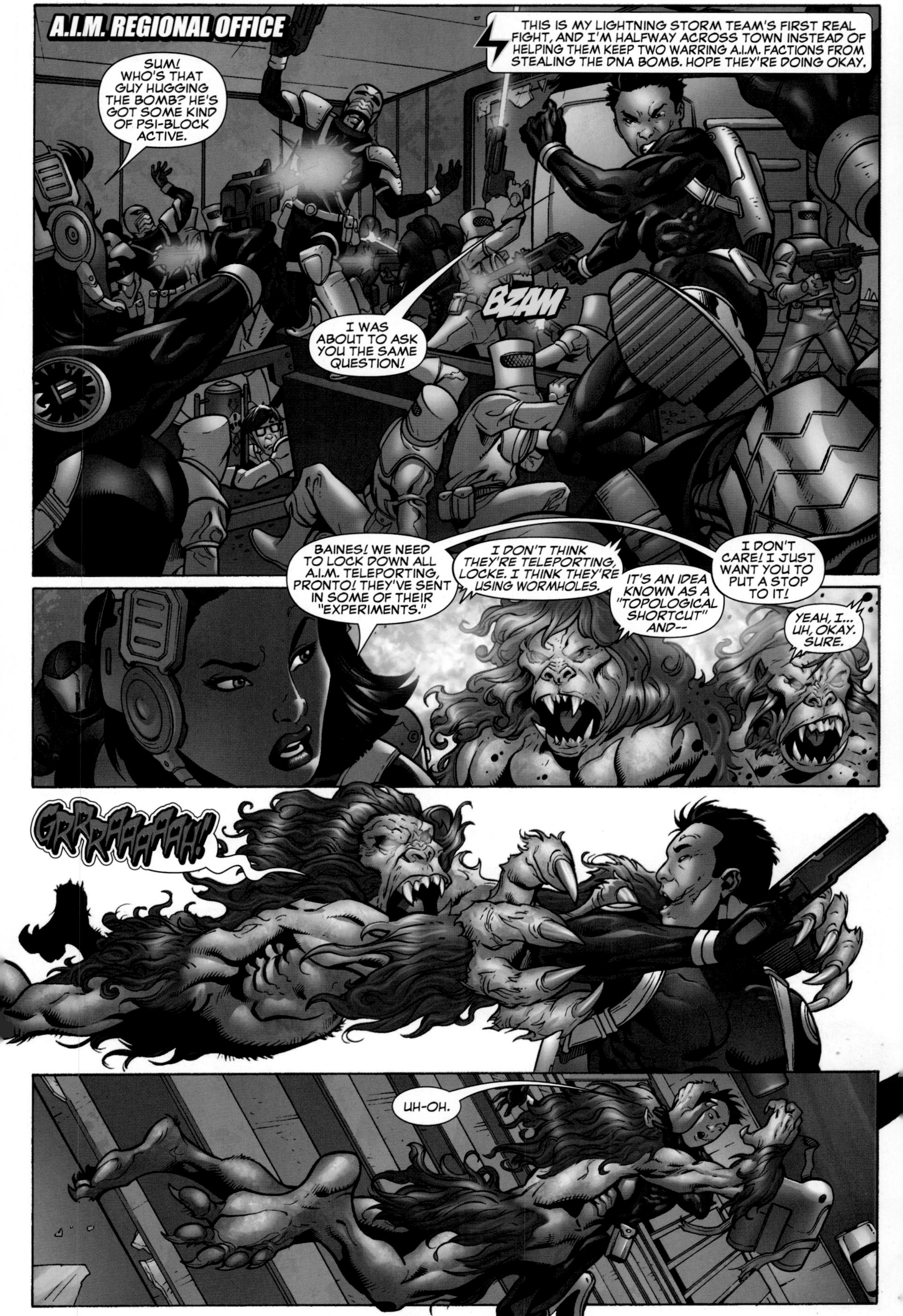
A.I.M. REGIONAL OFFICE
THIS IS MY LIGHTNING STORM TEAM'S FIRST REAL FIGHT, AND I'M HALFWAY ACROSS TOWN INSTEAD OF HELPING THEM KEEP TWO WARRING A.I.M. FACTIONS FROM STEALING THE DNA BOMB. HOPE THEY'RE DOING OKAY.
SUM! WHO'S THAT GUY HUGGING THE BOMB? HE'S GOT SOME KIND OF PSI-BLOCK ACTIVE.
BZAM
I WAS ABOUT TO ASK YOU THE SAME QUESTION!
BAINES! WE NEED TO LOCK DOWN ALL A.I.M. TELEPORTING, PRONTO! THEY'VE SENT IN SOME OF THEIR "EXPERIMENTS."
I DON'T THINK THEY'RE TELEPORTING, LOCKE. I THINK THEY'RE USING WORMHOLES.
IT'S AN IDEA KNOWN AS A "TOPOLOGICAL SHORTCUT" AND--
I DON'T CARE! I JUST WANT YOU TO PUT A STOP TO IT!
YEAH, I... UH, OKAY. SURE.
GRRRAAAAAH!
UH-OH.

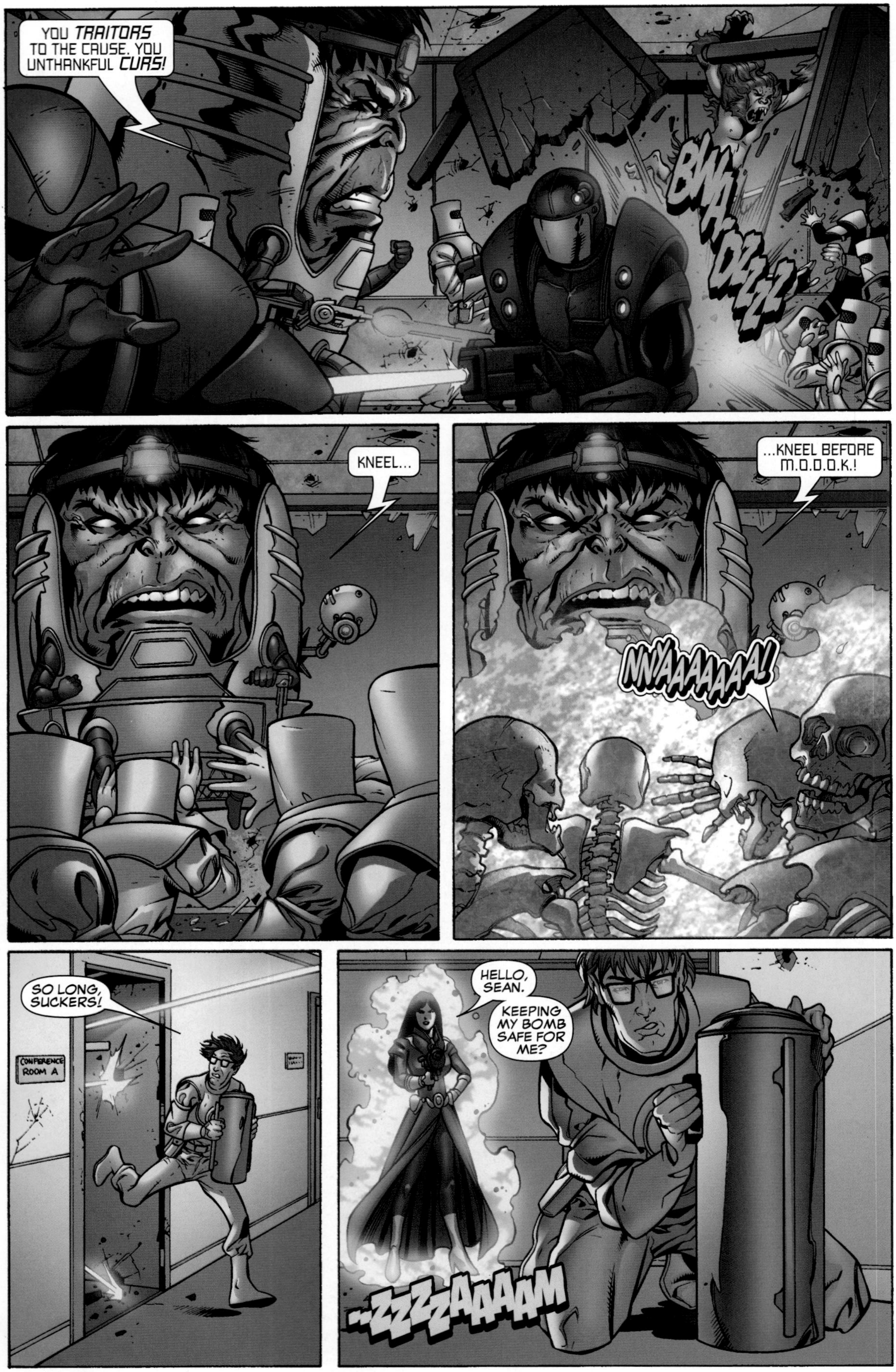
YOU TRAITORS TO THE CAUSE. YOU UNTHANKFUL CURS!
BWA-DZZZZ
KNEEL...
...KNEEL BEFORE M.O.D.O.K.!
NNYAAAAAAA!
SO LONG, SUCKERS!
CONFERENCE ROOM A
HELLO, SEAN.
KEEPING MY BOMB SAFE FOR ME?
--ZZZZAAAAM

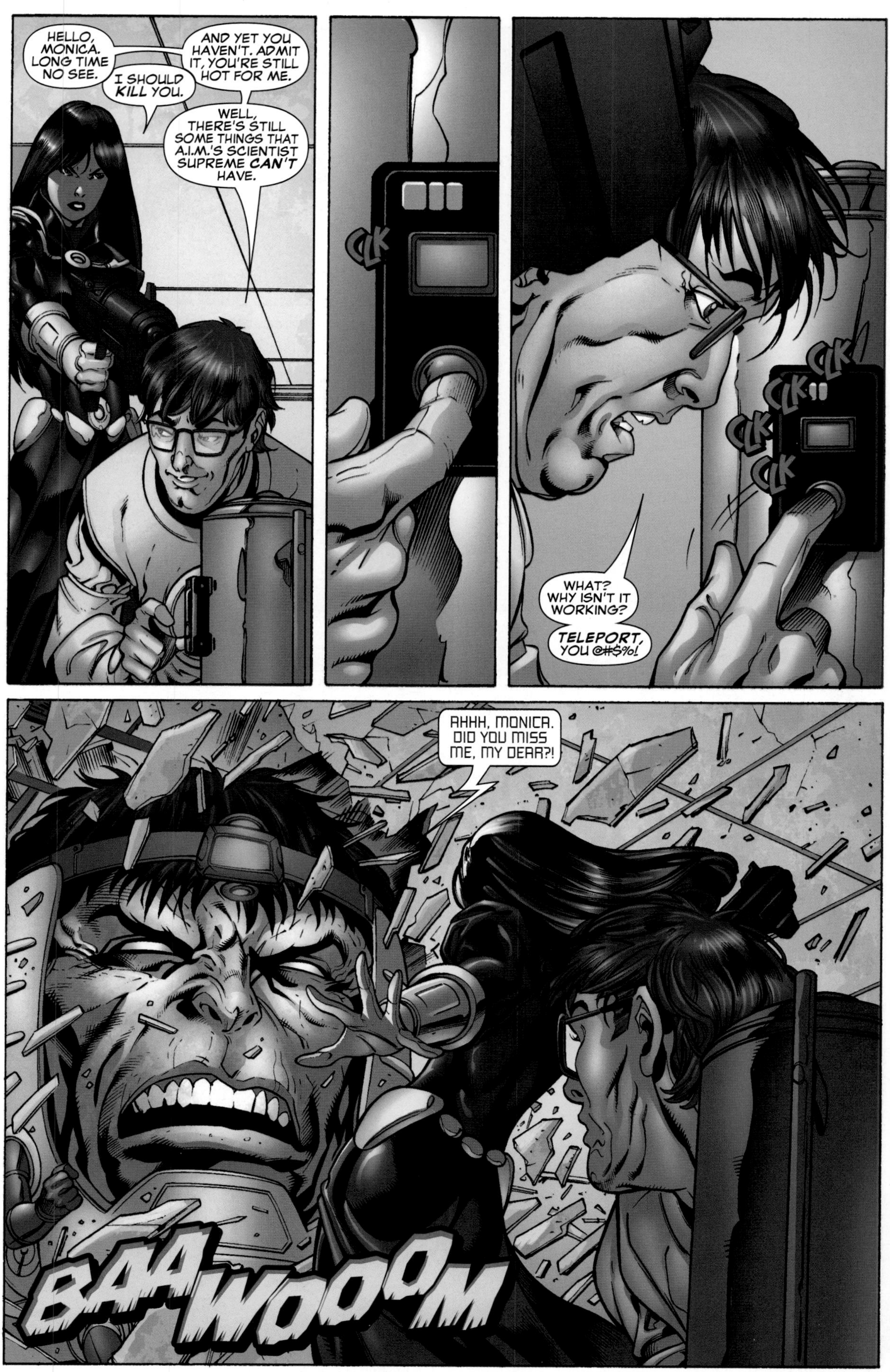
HELLO, MONICA. LONG TIME NO SEE.
I SHOULD KILL YOU.
AND YET YOU HAVEN'T. ADMIT IT, YOU'RE STILL HOT FOR ME.
WELL, THERE'S STILL SOME THINGS THAT A.I.M.'S SCIENTIST SUPREME CAN'T HAVE.
CLK
CLK
CLK
CLK
CLK
WHAT? WHY ISN'T IT WORKING?
TELEPORT, YOU @#$%!
AHHH, MONICA. DID YOU MISS ME, MY DEAR?!
BAAWOOOOM

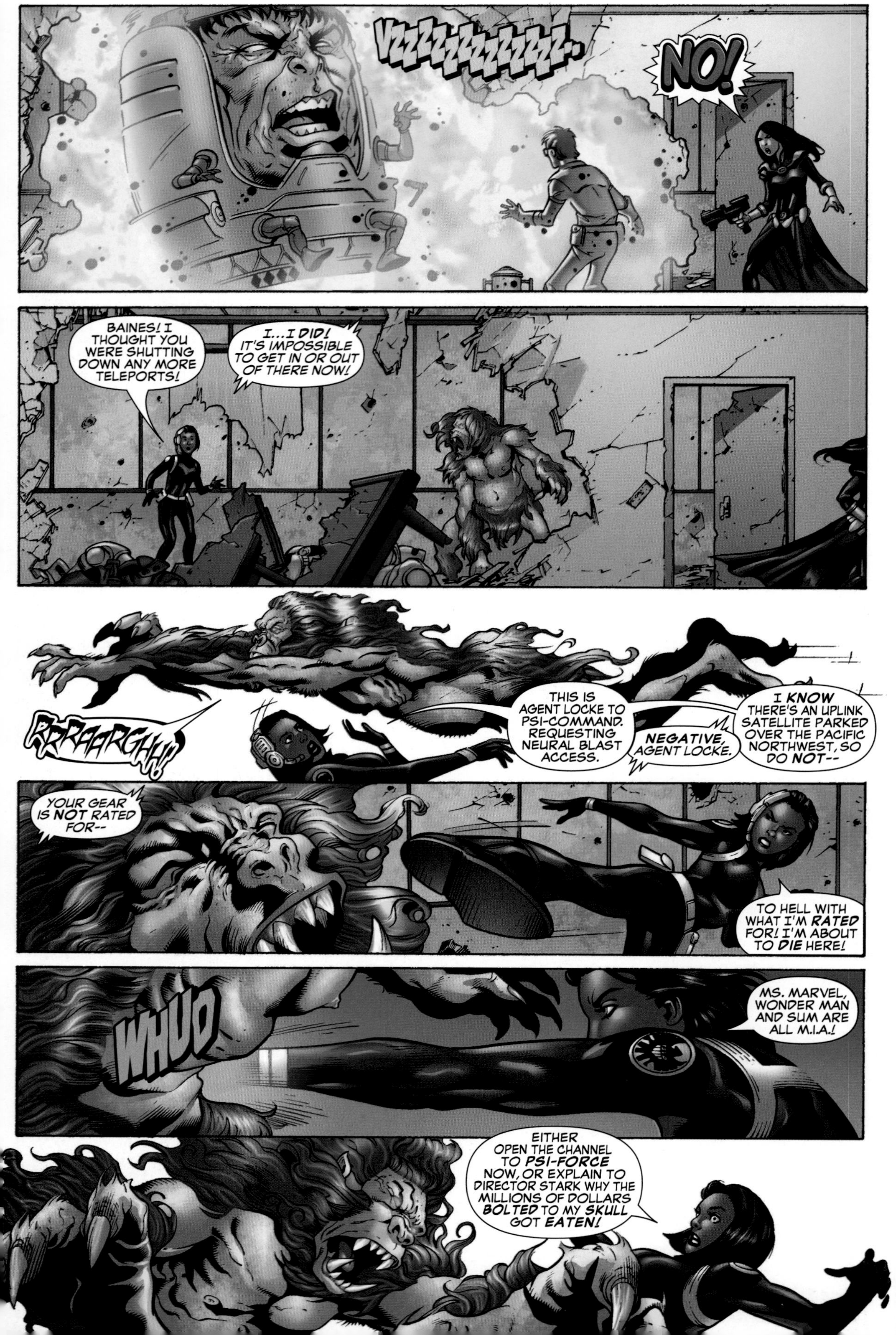
VZZZZZZZZZZZZZZ..
NO!
BAINES! I THOUGHT YOU WERE SHUTTING DOWN ANY MORE TELEPORTS!
I...I DID! IT'S IMPOSSIBLE TO GET IN OR OUT OF THERE NOW!
RRRAARGHH!
THIS IS AGENT LOCKE TO PSI-COMMAND. REQUESTING NEURAL BLAST ACCESS.
NEGATIVE, AGENT LOCKE.
I KNOW THERE'S AN UPLINK SATELLITE PARKED OVER THE PACIFIC NORTHWEST, SO DO NOT--
YOUR GEAR IS NOT RATED FOR--
TO HELL WITH WHAT I'M RATED FOR! I'M ABOUT TO DIE HERE!
WHUD
MS. MARVEL, WONDER MAN AND SUM ARE ALL M.I.A.!
EITHER OPEN THE CHANNEL TO PSI-FORCE NOW, OR EXPLAIN TO DIRECTOR STARK WHY THE MILLIONS OF DOLLARS BOLTED TO MY SKULL GOT EATEN!

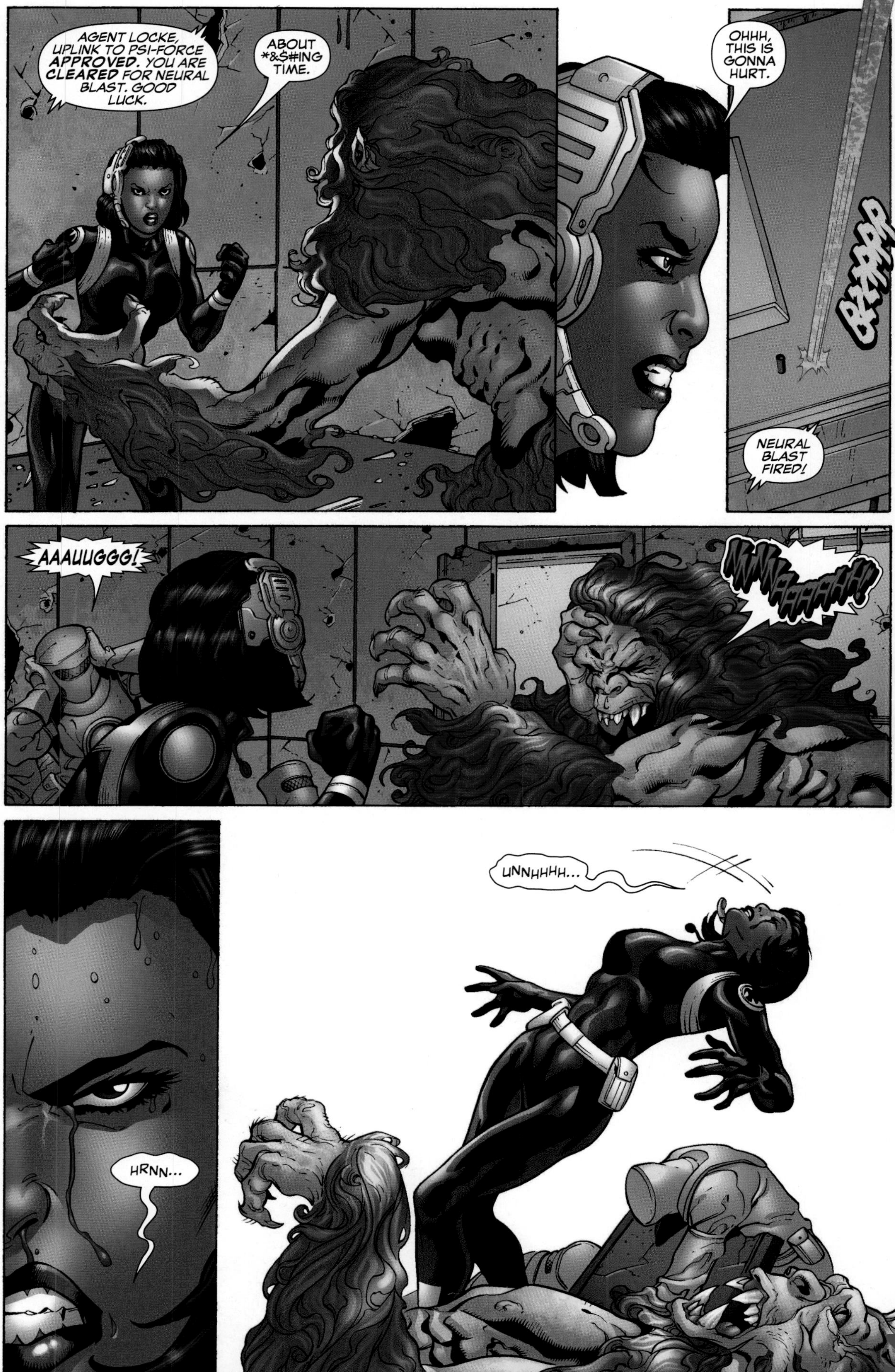
AGENT LOCKE, UPLINK TO PSI-FORCE APPROVED. YOU ARE CLEARED FOR NEURAL BLAST. GOOD LUCK.
ABOUT *&$#ING TIME.
OHHH, THIS IS GONNA HURT.
BZZZZT
NEURAL BLAST FIRED!
AAAUUGGG!
NNNAAAAAHH!
UNNHHHH...
HRNN...

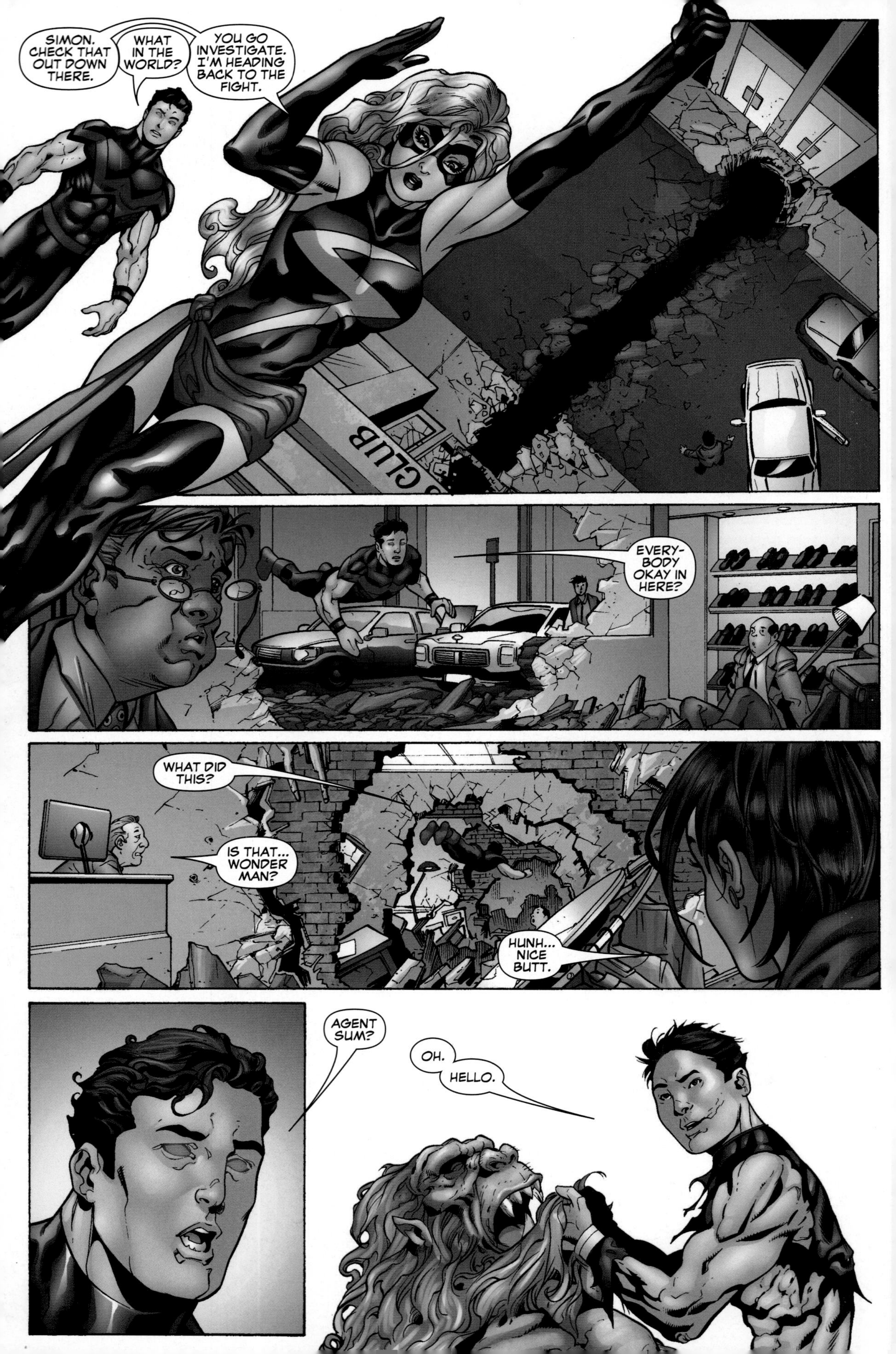
SIMON. CHECK THAT OUT DOWN THERE.
WHAT IN THE WORLD?
YOU GO INVESTIGATE. I'M HEADING BACK TO THE FIGHT.
CLUB
EVERY-BODY OKAY IN HERE?
WHAT DID THIS?
IS THAT... WONDER MAN?
HUNH... NICE BUTT.
AGENT SUM?
OH.
HELLO.

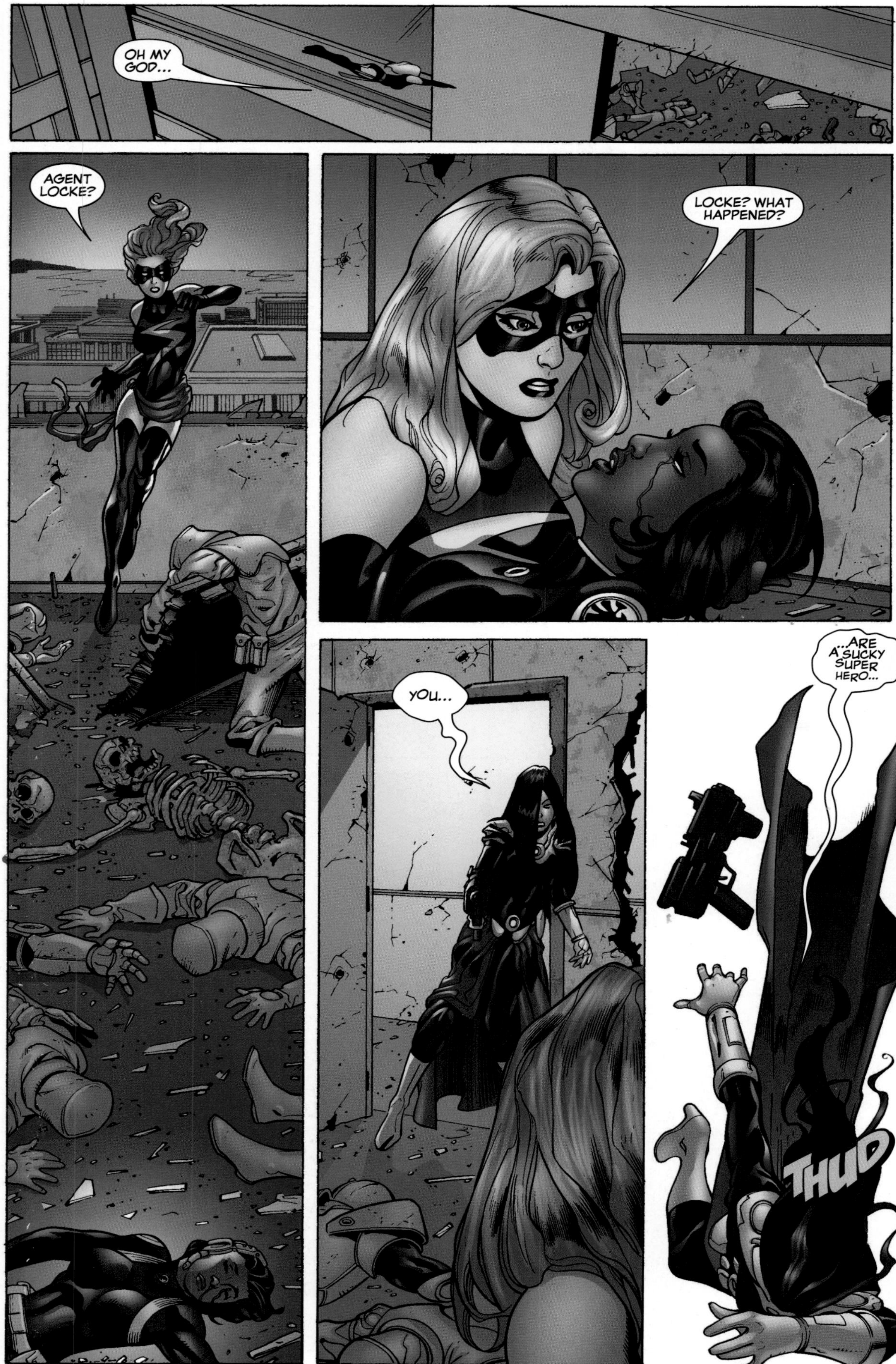
OH MY GOD...
AGENT LOCKE?
LOCKE? WHAT HAPPENED?
YOU...
...ARE A SUCKY SUPER HERO...
THUD

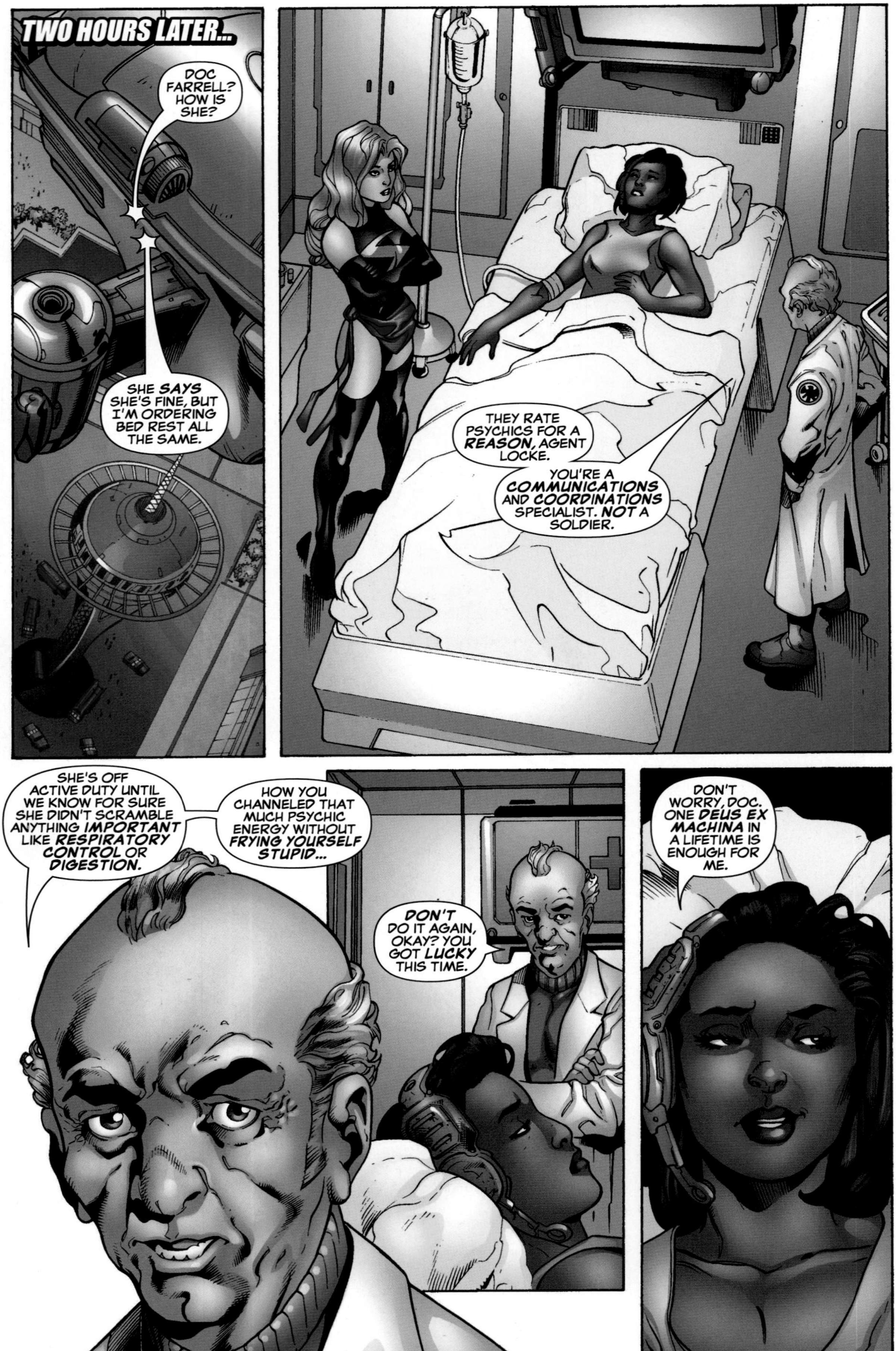
TWO HOURS LATER...
DOC FARRELL? HOW IS SHE?
SHE SAYS SHE'S FINE, BUT I'M ORDERING BED REST ALL THE SAME.
THEY RATE PSYCHICS FOR A REASON, AGENT LOCKE.
YOU'RE A COMMUNICATIONS AND COORDINATIONS SPECIALIST. NOT A SOLDIER.
SHE'S OFF ACTIVE DUTY UNTIL WE KNOW FOR SURE SHE DIDN'T SCRAMBLE ANYTHING IMPORTANT LIKE RESPIRATORY CONTROL OR DIGESTION.
HOW YOU CHANNELED THAT MUCH PSYCHIC ENERGY WITHOUT FRYING YOURSELF STUPID...
DON'T DO IT AGAIN, OKAY? YOU GOT LUCKY THIS TIME.
DON'T WORRY, DOC. ONE DEUS EX MACHINA IN A LIFETIME IS ENOUGH FOR ME.

YOU FOUND IT!

WE FOUND ITS CASING ABOUT TWO MILES FROM THE OFFICE BUILDING.

THERE'S NOTHING HERE BUT THE TRIGGERING MECHANISM.

MINICARRIER 13 HANGAR BAY

ANY TRACE OF SEAN?

NAH. HE'S GONE. SAME WITH M.O.D.O.K.

SO WE LOST EVERYTHING WE CAME HERE FOR.

WE CAPTURED THAT MONICA LADY. NOT EVERY DAY YOU GET TO CALL HOME BASE AND SAY YOU HAVE A.I.M.'S SCIENTIST SUPREME IN THE BRIG.

THANKS FOR REMINDING ME. SHE'S MY NEXT STOP, ACTUALLY.

MIND IF I TAG ALONG?

I--UM, NO. I GUESS NOT.

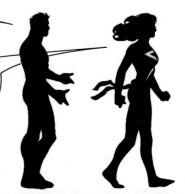

SO...ARE WE GONNA TALK ABOUT WHAT HAPPENED OUT THERE?

WHICH PART? SUM SURVIVING A TWELVE-STORY FALL AND FIGHTING THAT MONSTER BARE-HANDED, M.O.D.O.K. ESCAPING, LOCKE NEARLY KILLING HERSE--

YOU KNOW WHAT I MEAN.

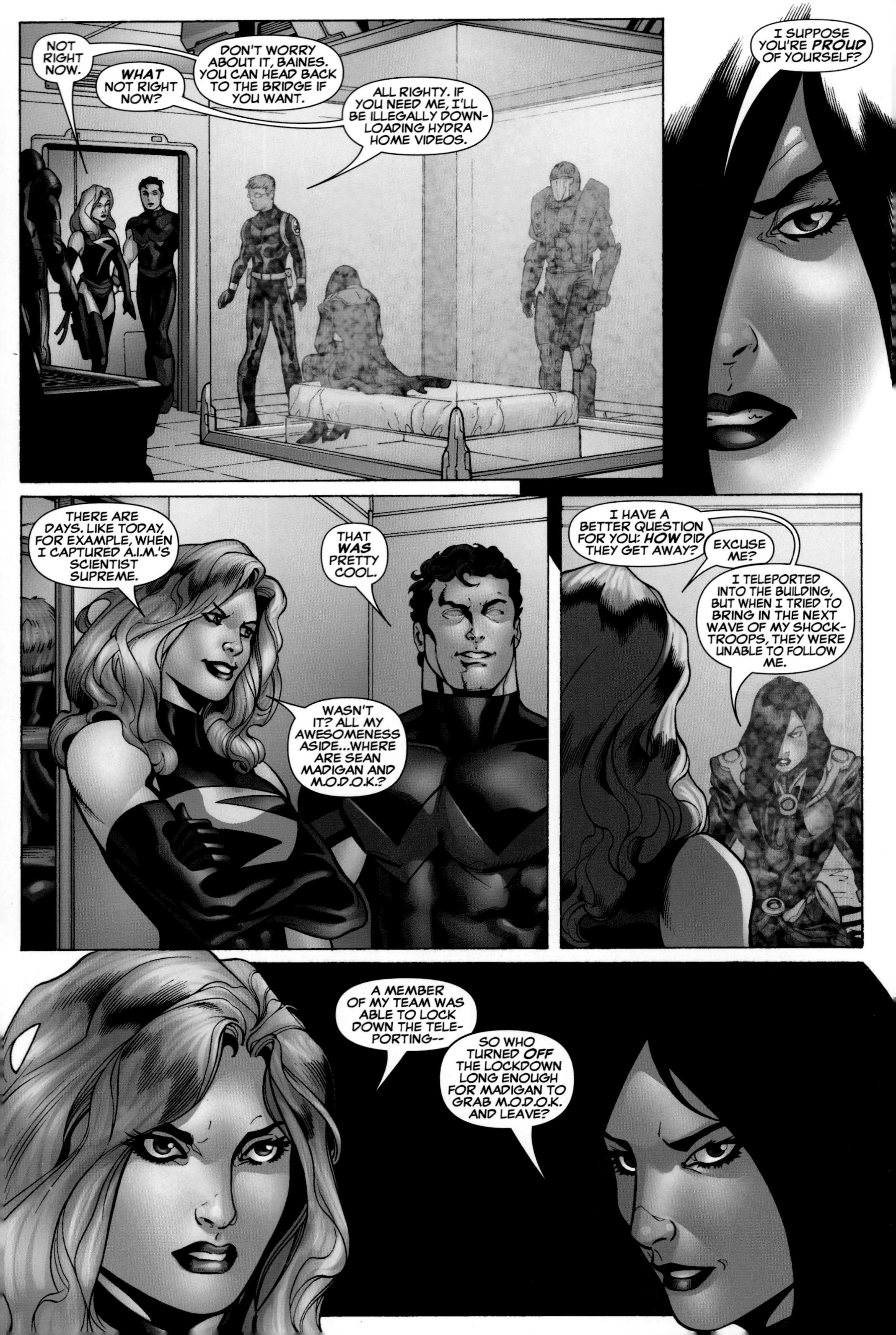
NOT RIGHT NOW.
DON'T WORRY ABOUT IT, BAINES. YOU CAN HEAD BACK TO THE BRIDGE IF YOU WANT.
WHAT NOT RIGHT NOW?
ALL RIGHTY. IF YOU NEED ME, I'LL BE ILLEGALLY DOWN-LOADING HYDRA HOME VIDEOS.
I SUPPOSE YOU'RE PROUD OF YOURSELF?
THERE ARE DAYS. LIKE TODAY, FOR EXAMPLE, WHEN I CAPTURED A.I.M.'S SCIENTIST SUPREME.
THAT WAS PRETTY COOL.
WASN'T IT? ALL MY AWESOMENESS ASIDE...WHERE ARE SEAN MADIGAN AND M.O.D.O.K.?
I HAVE A BETTER QUESTION FOR YOU: HOW DID THEY GET AWAY?
EXCUSE ME?
I TELEPORTED INTO THE BUILDING, BUT WHEN I TRIED TO BRING IN THE NEXT WAVE OF MY SHOCK-TROOPS, THEY WERE UNABLE TO FOLLOW ME.
A MEMBER OF MY TEAM WAS ABLE TO LOCK DOWN THE TELE-PORTING--
SO WHO TURNED OFF THE LOCKDOWN LONG ENOUGH FOR MADIGAN TO GRAB M.O.D.O.K. AND LEAVE?

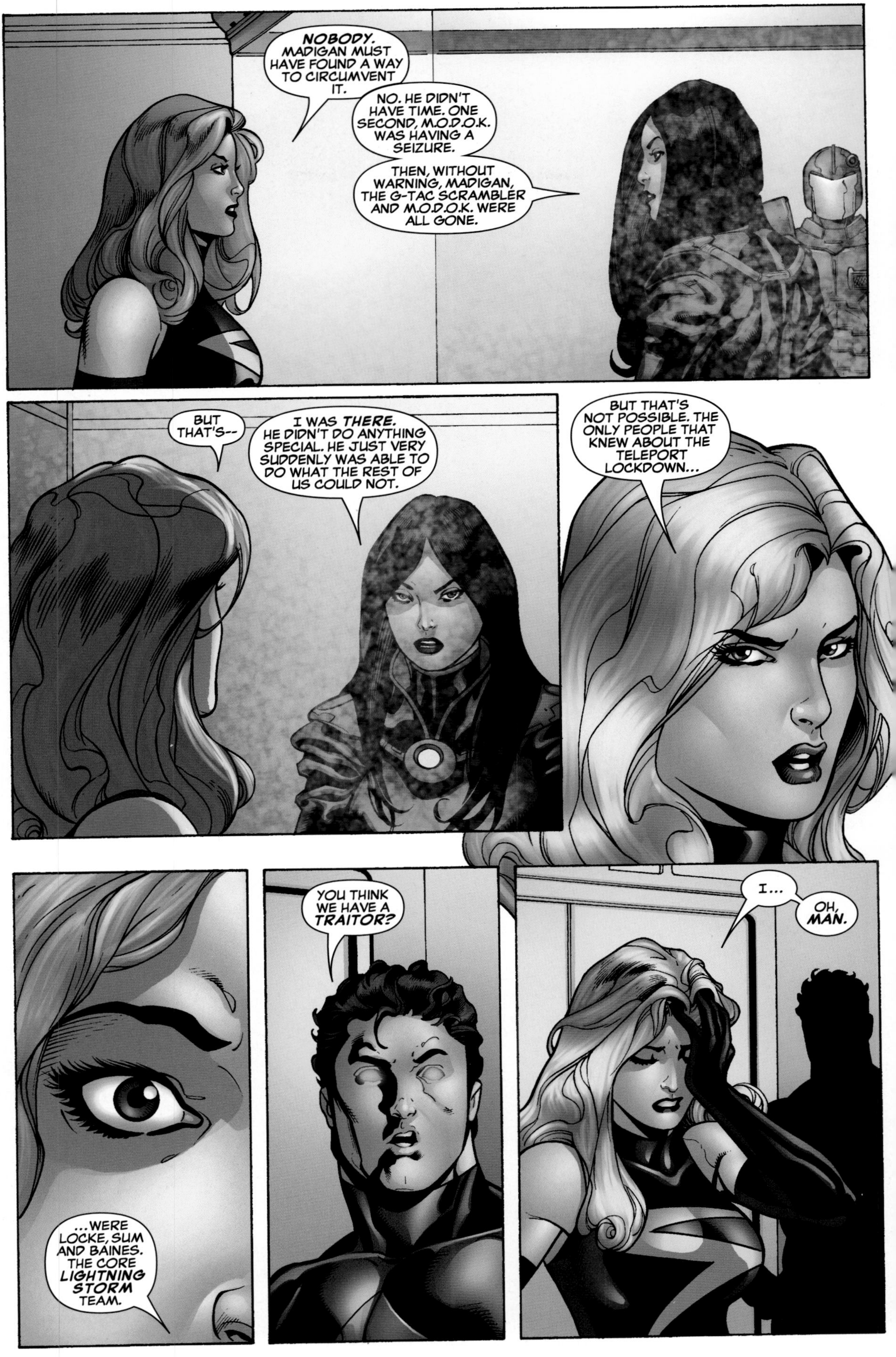
NOBODY. MADIGAN MUST HAVE FOUND A WAY TO CIRCUMVENT IT.
NO. HE DIDN'T HAVE TIME. ONE SECOND, M.O.D.O.K. WAS HAVING A SEIZURE.
THEN, WITHOUT WARNING, MADIGAN, THE G-TAC SCRAMBLER AND M.O.D.O.K. WERE ALL GONE.
BUT THAT'S--
I WAS THERE. HE DIDN'T DO ANYTHING SPECIAL. HE JUST VERY SUDDENLY WAS ABLE TO DO WHAT THE REST OF US COULD NOT.
BUT THAT'S NOT POSSIBLE. THE ONLY PEOPLE THAT KNEW ABOUT THE TELEPORT LOCKDOWN...
...WERE LOCKE, SUM AND BAINES. THE CORE LIGHTNING STORM TEAM.
YOU THINK WE HAVE A TRAITOR?
I...
OH, MAN.

LISTEN CLOSELY. I AM ABOUT TO TELL YOU MANY IMPORTANT THINGS AND I DO NOT HAVE TIME TO REPEAT MYSELF.
M.O.D.O.K. IS DYING. HE HAS BEEN FOR MONTHS, BUT NOT MANY A.I.M. AGENTS KNEW. BUT NOW THAT THE SECRET IS OUT...
...A.I.M. HAS FRACTURED.
POOR OLD MAN... THAT FIGHT REALLY TOOK IT OUT OF YOU, DIDN'T IT?
I HONESTLY CAN'T BELIEVE YOU SURVIVED THAT. IN YOUR CONDITION, IT WAS AN AMAZING EFFORT.
BUT FIGHTING LIKE THAT, AND ALL THE TELEPORTING-- WELL, IT'S A LOT TO THROW AT A BIG-HEADED SICK GUY, RIGHT?
AND M.O.D.O.K.'S SON IS LOOKING TO MAKE IT SHATTER.
M.O.D.O.K.'S SON?
WHY DID YOU THINK WE'VE BEEN PAYING SO MUCH ATTENTION TO A GEEK LIKE SEAN MADIGAN?
BUT I COULDN'T LET THEM CAPTURE YOU.
AT LEAST, NOT YET.
NO. I NEEDED SOMETHING... MORE PUBLIC. SOMETHING MORE DESERVING OF THE MIGHTY M.O.D.O.K.
SOMETHING INVOLVING THE GUTS OF THE G-TAC SCRAMBLER.

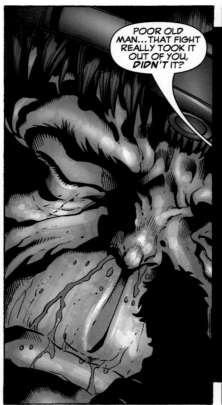

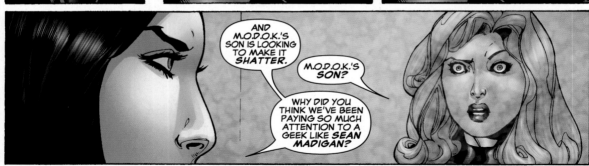

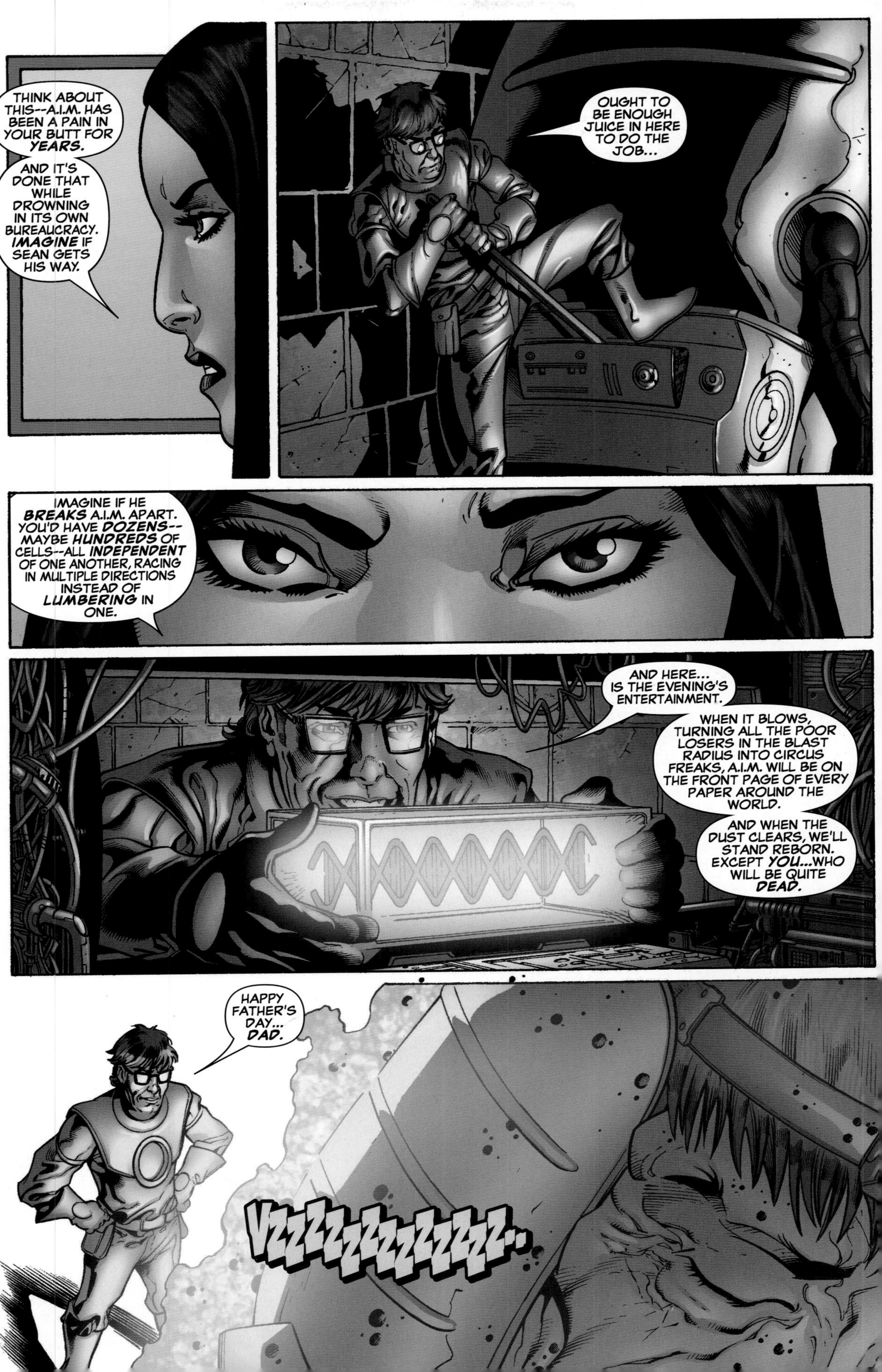
THINK ABOUT THIS--A.I.M. HAS BEEN A PAIN IN YOUR BUTT FOR YEARS.
AND IT'S DONE THAT WHILE DROWNING IN ITS OWN BUREAUCRACY. IMAGINE IF SEAN GETS HIS WAY.
OUGHT TO BE ENOUGH JUICE IN HERE TO DO THE JOB...
IMAGINE IF HE BREAKS A.I.M. APART. YOU'D HAVE DOZENS--MAYBE HUNDREDS OF CELLS--ALL INDEPENDENT OF ONE ANOTHER, RACING IN MULTIPLE DIRECTIONS INSTEAD OF LUMBERING IN ONE.
AND HERE... IS THE EVENING'S ENTERTAINMENT.
WHEN IT BLOWS, TURNING ALL THE POOR LOSERS IN THE BLAST RADIUS INTO CIRCUS FREAKS, A.I.M. WILL BE ON THE FRONT PAGE OF EVERY PAPER AROUND THE WORLD.
AND WHEN THE DUST CLEARS, WE'LL STAND REBORN. EXCEPT YOU...WHO WILL BE QUITE DEAD.
HAPPY FATHER'S DAY... DAD.
VZZZZZZZZZZZZZ..

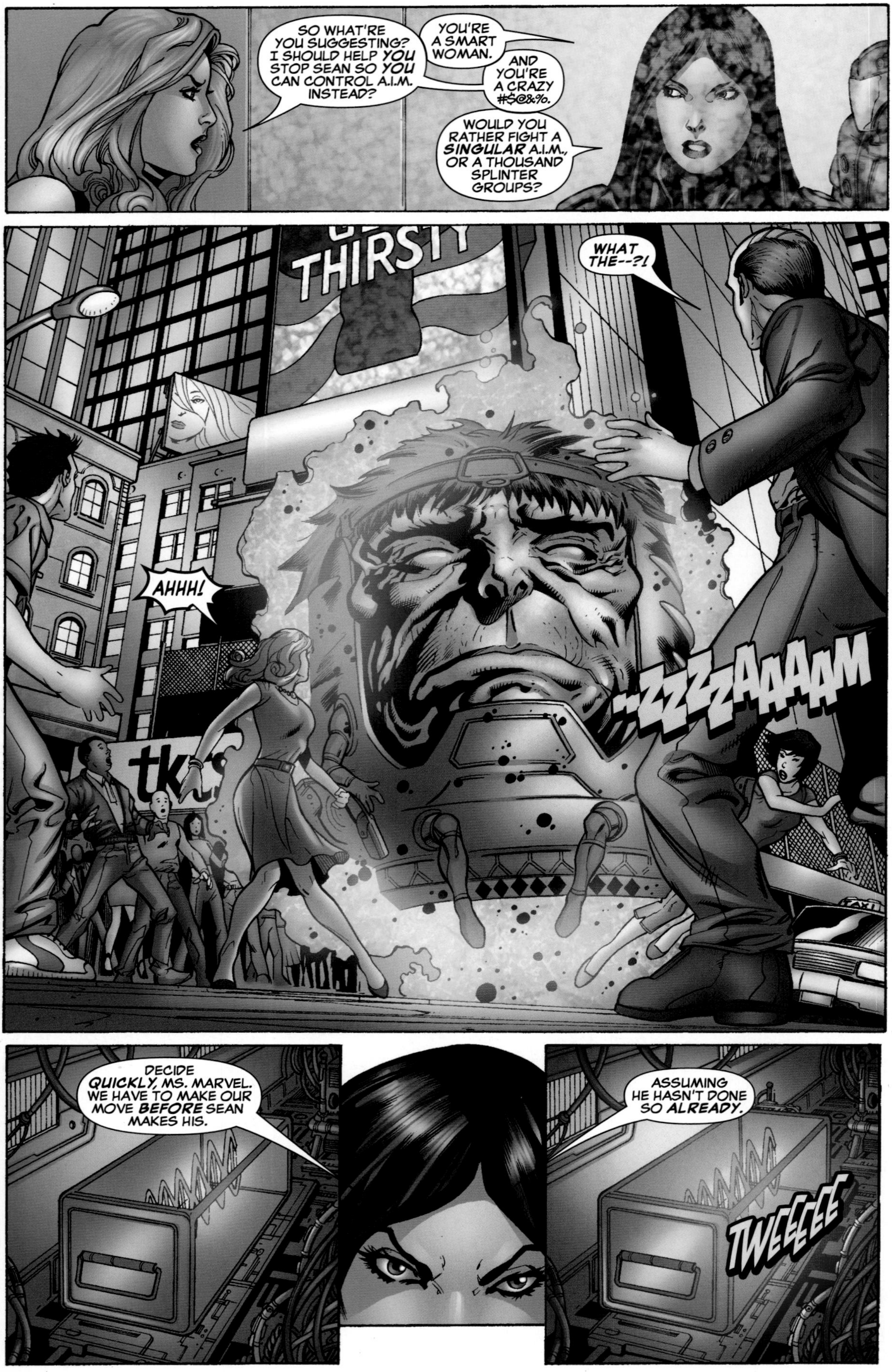
SO WHAT'RE YOU SUGGESTING? I SHOULD HELP YOU STOP SEAN SO YOU CAN CONTROL A.I.M. INSTEAD?
YOU'RE A SMART WOMAN.
AND YOU'RE A CRAZY #$@&%.
WOULD YOU RATHER FIGHT A SINGULAR A.I.M., OR A THOUSAND SPLINTER GROUPS?
THIRSTY
WHAT THE--?!
AHHH!
--ZZZZAAAAM
tk
TAXI
DECIDE QUICKLY, MS. MARVEL. WE HAVE TO MAKE OUR MOVE BEFORE SEAN MAKES HIS.
ASSUMING HE HASN'T DONE SO ALREADY.
TWEEEEE

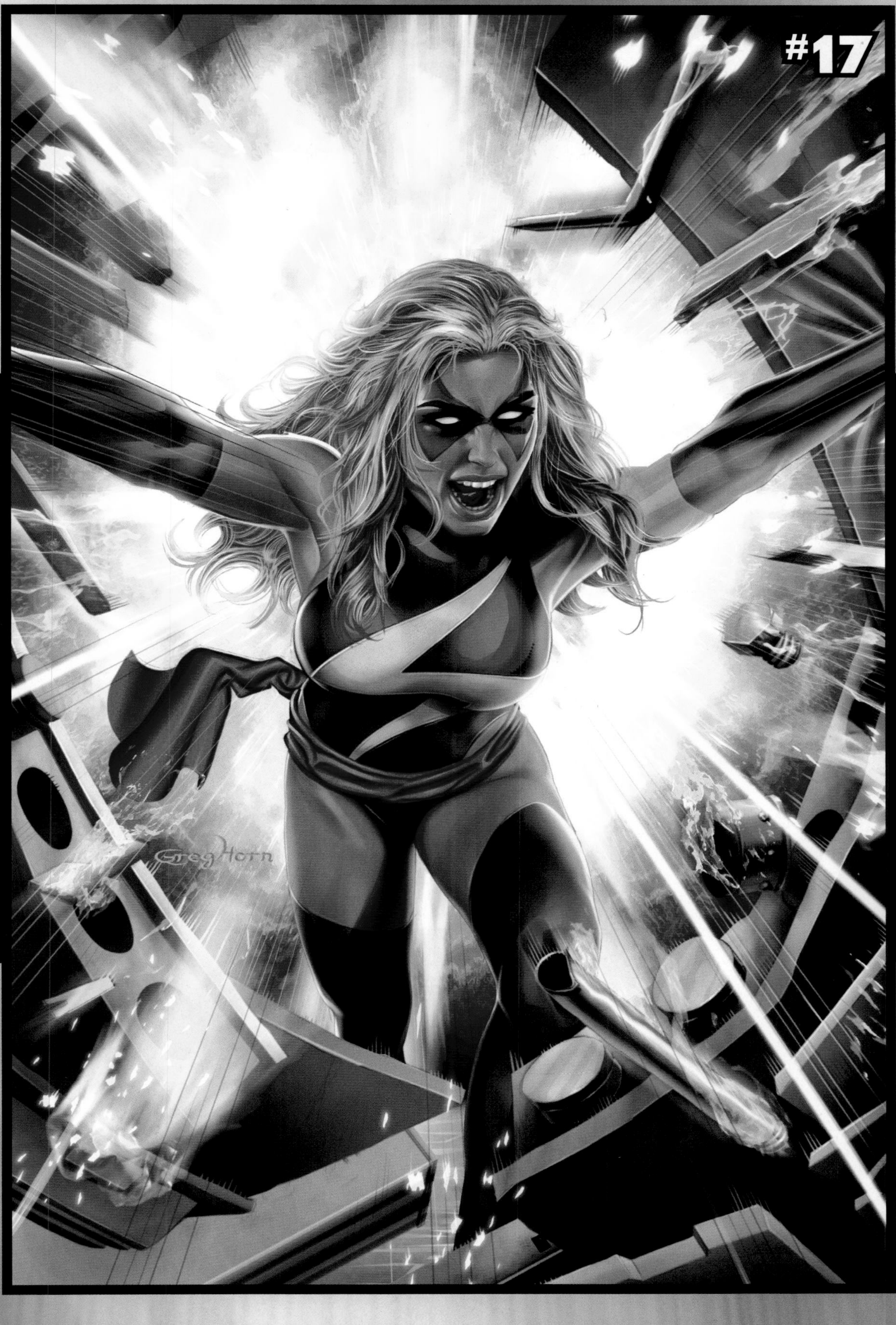
#17
Greg Horn

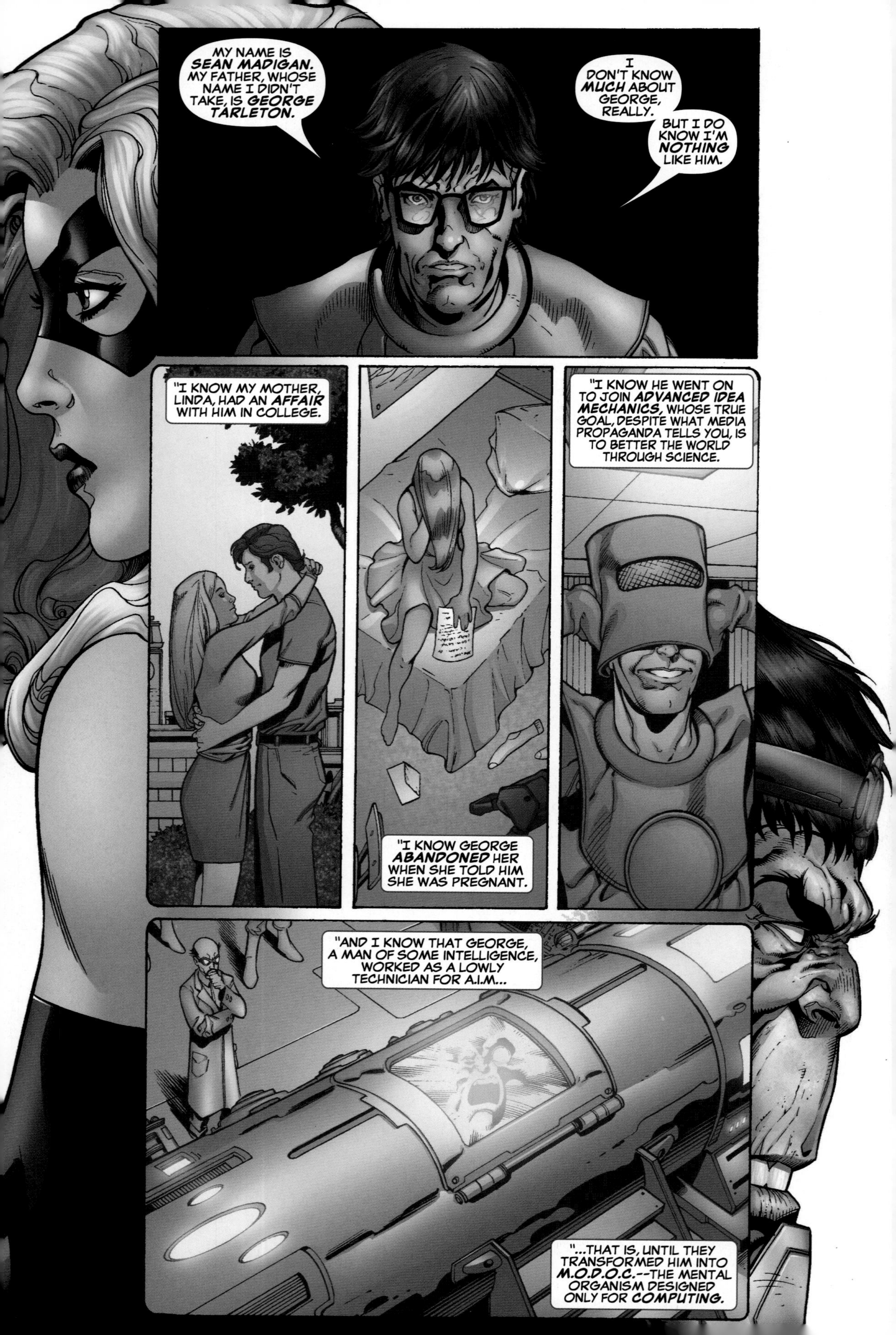
MY NAME IS SEAN MADIGAN. MY FATHER, WHOSE NAME I DIDN'T TAKE, IS GEORGE TARLETON.
I DON'T KNOW MUCH ABOUT GEORGE, REALLY.
BUT I DO KNOW I'M NOTHING LIKE HIM.
"I KNOW MY MOTHER, LINDA, HAD AN AFFAIR WITH HIM IN COLLEGE.
"I KNOW GEORGE ABANDONED HER WHEN SHE TOLD HIM SHE WAS PREGNANT.
"I KNOW HE WENT ON TO JOIN ADVANCED IDEA MECHANICS, WHOSE TRUE GOAL, DESPITE WHAT MEDIA PROPAGANDA TELLS YOU, IS TO BETTER THE WORLD THROUGH SCIENCE.
"AND I KNOW THAT GEORGE, A MAN OF SOME INTELLIGENCE, WORKED AS A LOWLY TECHNICIAN FOR A.I.M...
"...THAT IS, UNTIL THEY TRANSFORMED HIM INTO M.O.D.O.C.--THE MENTAL ORGANISM DESIGNED ONLY FOR COMPUTING.

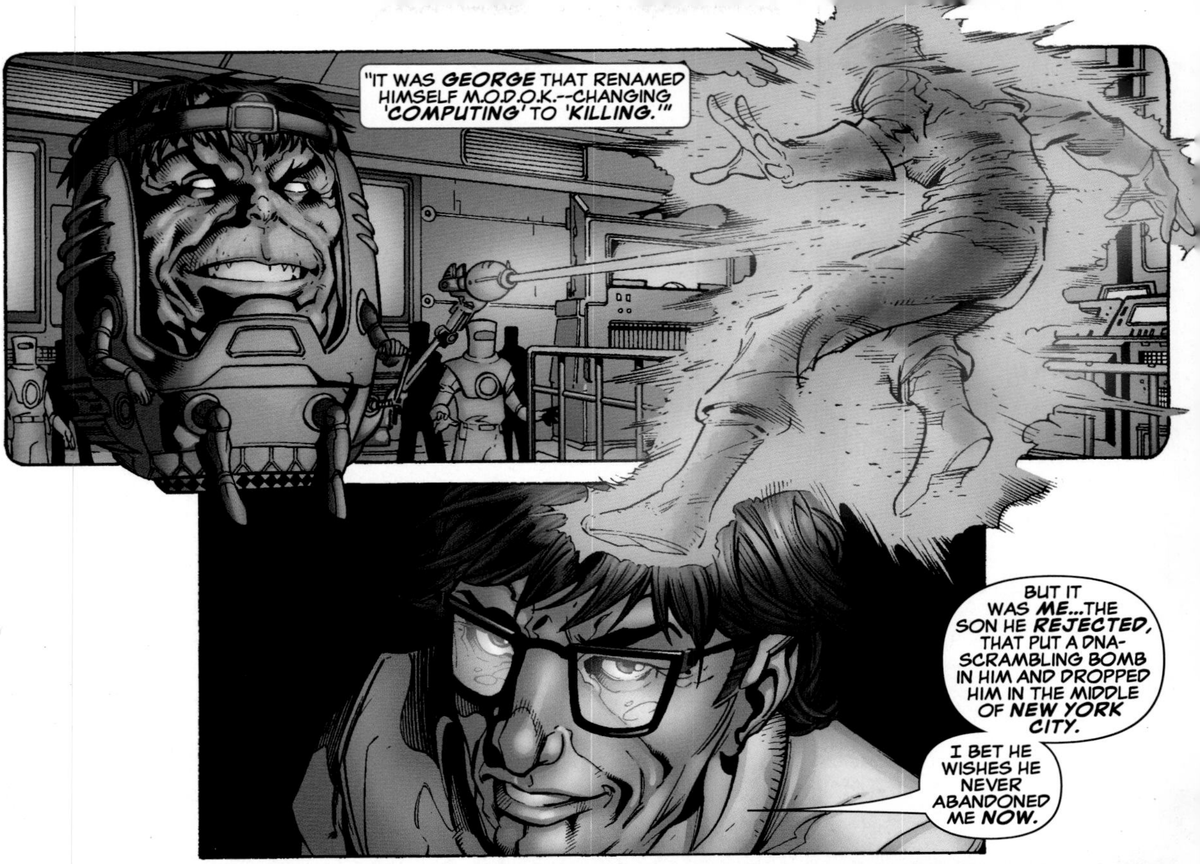
"IT WAS GEORGE THAT RENAMED HIMSELF M.O.D.O.K.--CHANGING 'COMPUTING' TO 'KILLING.'"
BUT IT WAS ME...THE SON HE REJECTED, THAT PUT A DNA-SCRAMBLING BOMB IN HIM AND DROPPED HIM IN THE MIDDLE OF NEW YORK CITY.
I BET HE WISHES HE NEVER ABANDONED ME NOW.

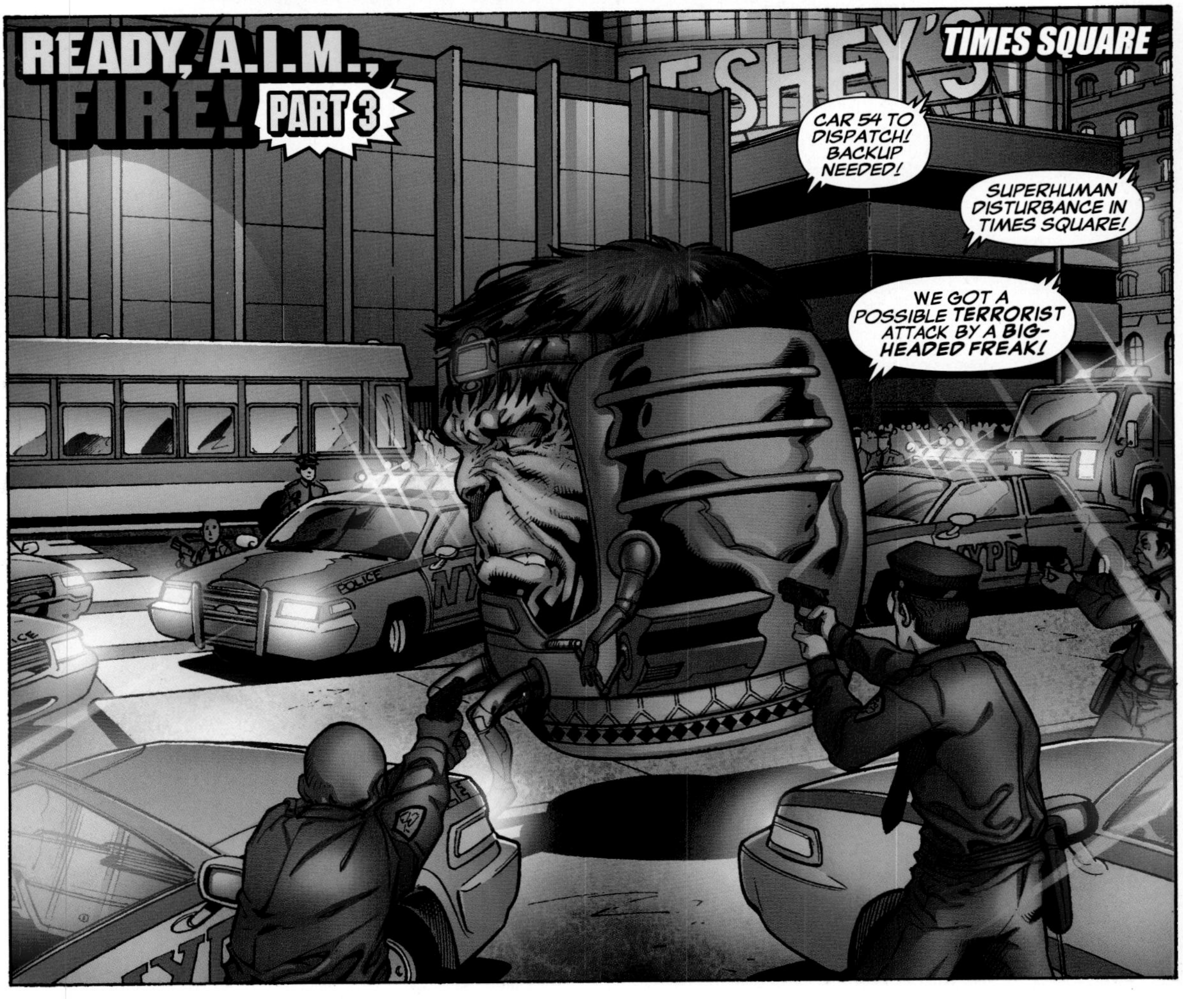
READY, A.I.M., FIRE! PART 3
TIMES SQUARE
CAR 54 TO DISPATCH! BACKUP NEEDED!
SUPERHUMAN DISTURBANCE IN TIMES SQUARE!
WE GOT A POSSIBLE TERRORIST ATTACK BY A BIG-HEADED FREAK!

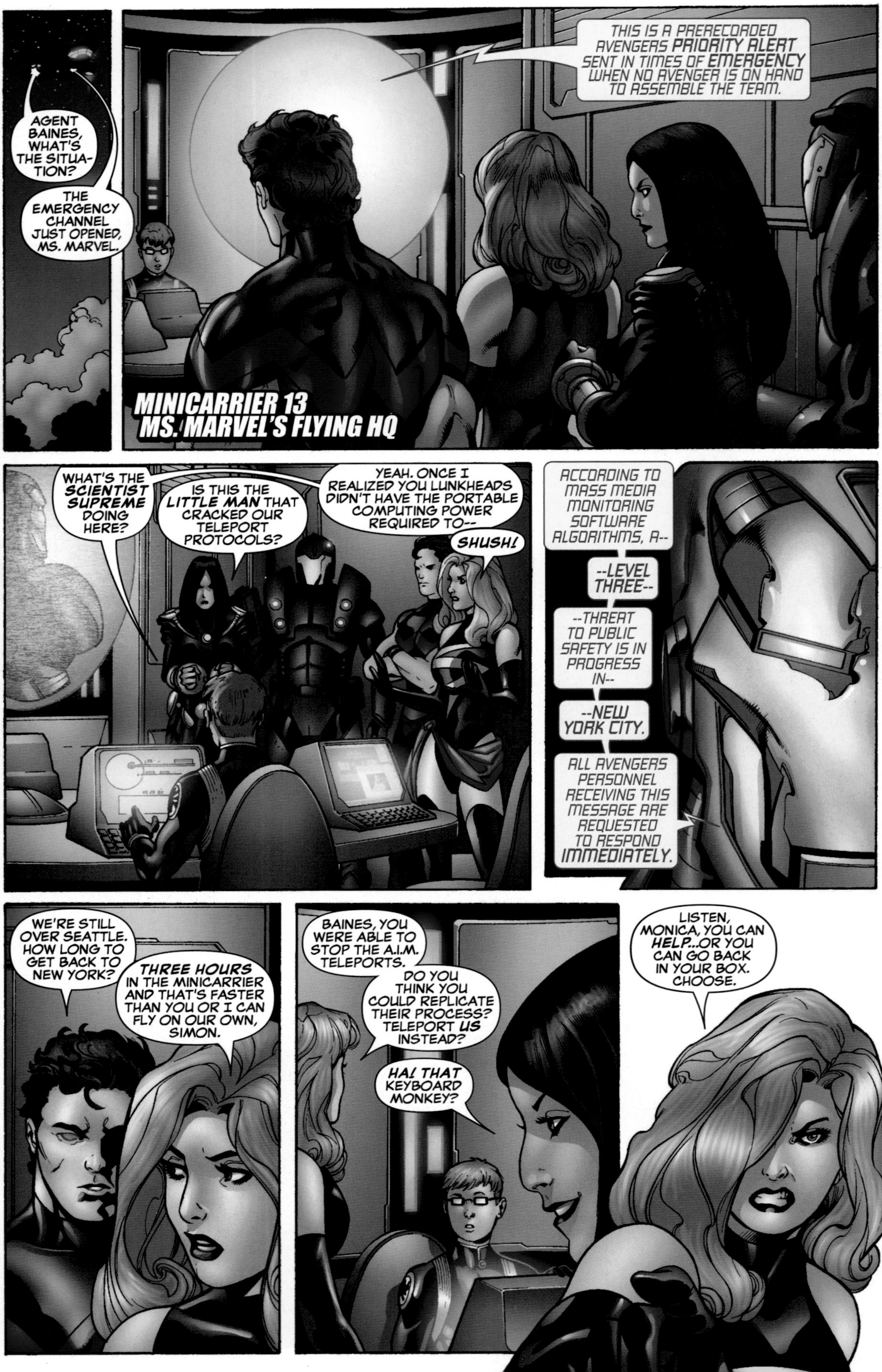
AGENT BAINES, WHAT'S THE SITUATION?
THE EMERGENCY CHANNEL JUST OPENED, MS. MARVEL.
THIS IS A PRERECORDED AVENGERS PRIORITY ALERT SENT IN TIMES OF EMERGENCY WHEN NO AVENGER IS ON HAND TO ASSEMBLE THE TEAM.
MINICARRIER 13
MS. MARVEL'S FLYING HQ
WHAT'S THE SCIENTIST SUPREME DOING HERE?
IS THIS THE LITTLE MAN THAT CRACKED OUR TELEPORT PROTOCOLS?
YEAH. ONCE I REALIZED YOU LUNKHEADS DIDN'T HAVE THE PORTABLE COMPUTING POWER REQUIRED TO--
SHUSH!
ACCORDING TO MASS MEDIA MONITORING SOFTWARE ALGORITHMS, A--
--LEVEL THREE--
--THREAT TO PUBLIC SAFETY IS IN PROGRESS IN--
--NEW YORK CITY.
ALL AVENGERS PERSONNEL RECEIVING THIS MESSAGE ARE REQUESTED TO RESPOND IMMEDIATELY.
WE'RE STILL OVER SEATTLE. HOW LONG TO GET BACK TO NEW YORK?
THREE HOURS IN THE MINICARRIER AND THAT'S FASTER THAN YOU OR I CAN FLY ON OUR OWN, SIMON.
BAINES, YOU WERE ABLE TO STOP THE A.I.M. TELEPORTS.
DO YOU THINK YOU COULD REPLICATE THEIR PROCESS? TELEPORT US INSTEAD?
HA! THAT KEYBOARD MONKEY?
LISTEN, MONICA, YOU CAN HELP...OR YOU CAN GO BACK IN YOUR BOX. CHOOSE.

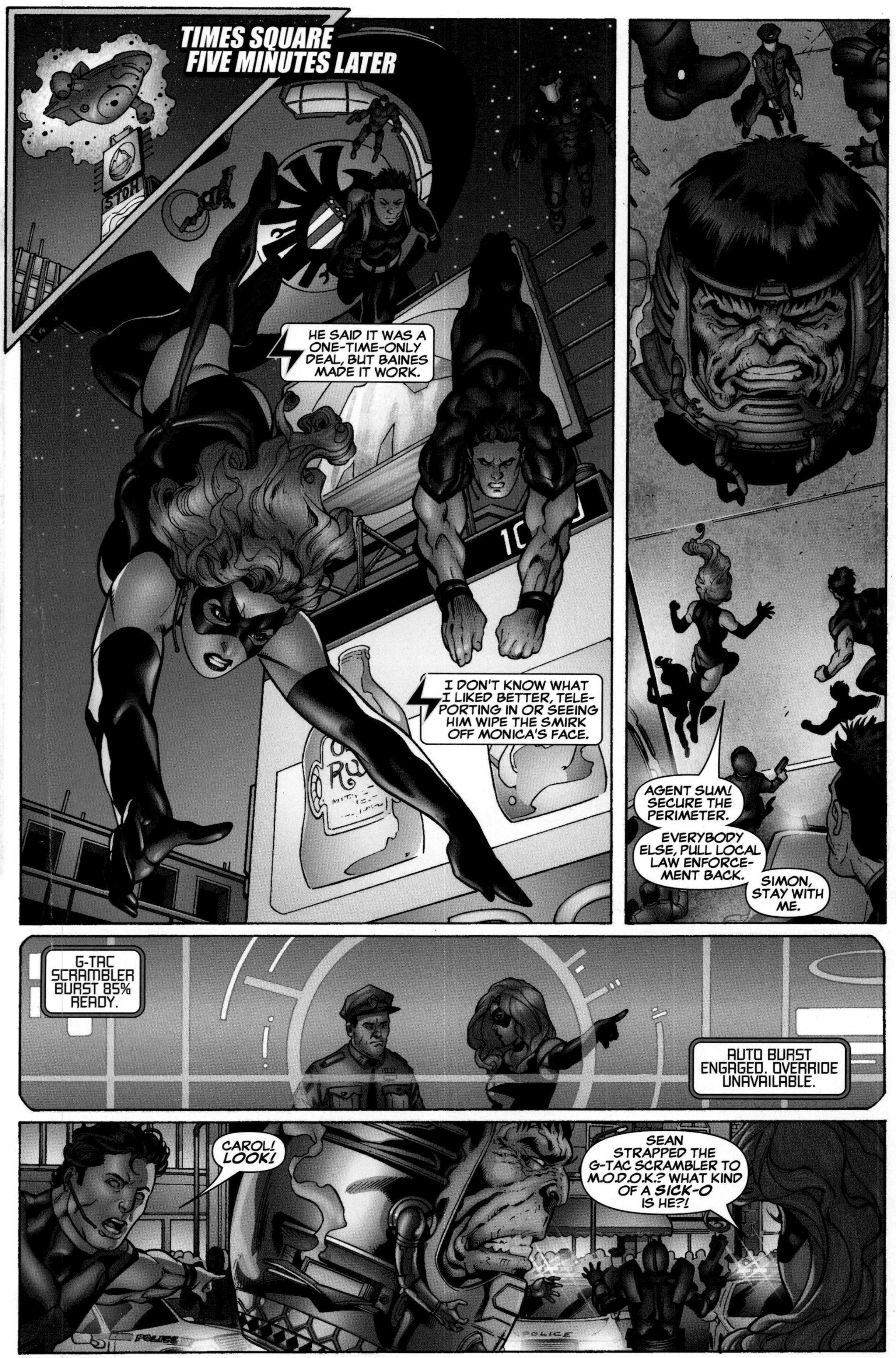
TIMES SQUARE
FIVE MINUTES LATER
HE SAID IT WAS A ONE-TIME-ONLY DEAL, BUT BAINES MADE IT WORK.
I DON'T KNOW WHAT I LIKED BETTER, TELE-PORTING IN OR SEEING HIM WIPE THE SMIRK OFF MONICA'S FACE.
AGENT SUM! SECURE THE PERIMETER.
EVERYBODY ELSE, PULL LOCAL LAW ENFORCE-MENT BACK.
SIMON, STAY WITH ME.
G-TAC SCRAMBLER BURST 85% READY.
AUTO BURST ENGAGED. OVERRIDE UNAVAILABLE.
CAROL! LOOK!
SEAN STRAPPED THE G-TAC SCRAMBLER TO M.O.D.O.K.? WHAT KIND OF A SICK-O IS HE?!
POLICE
POLICE

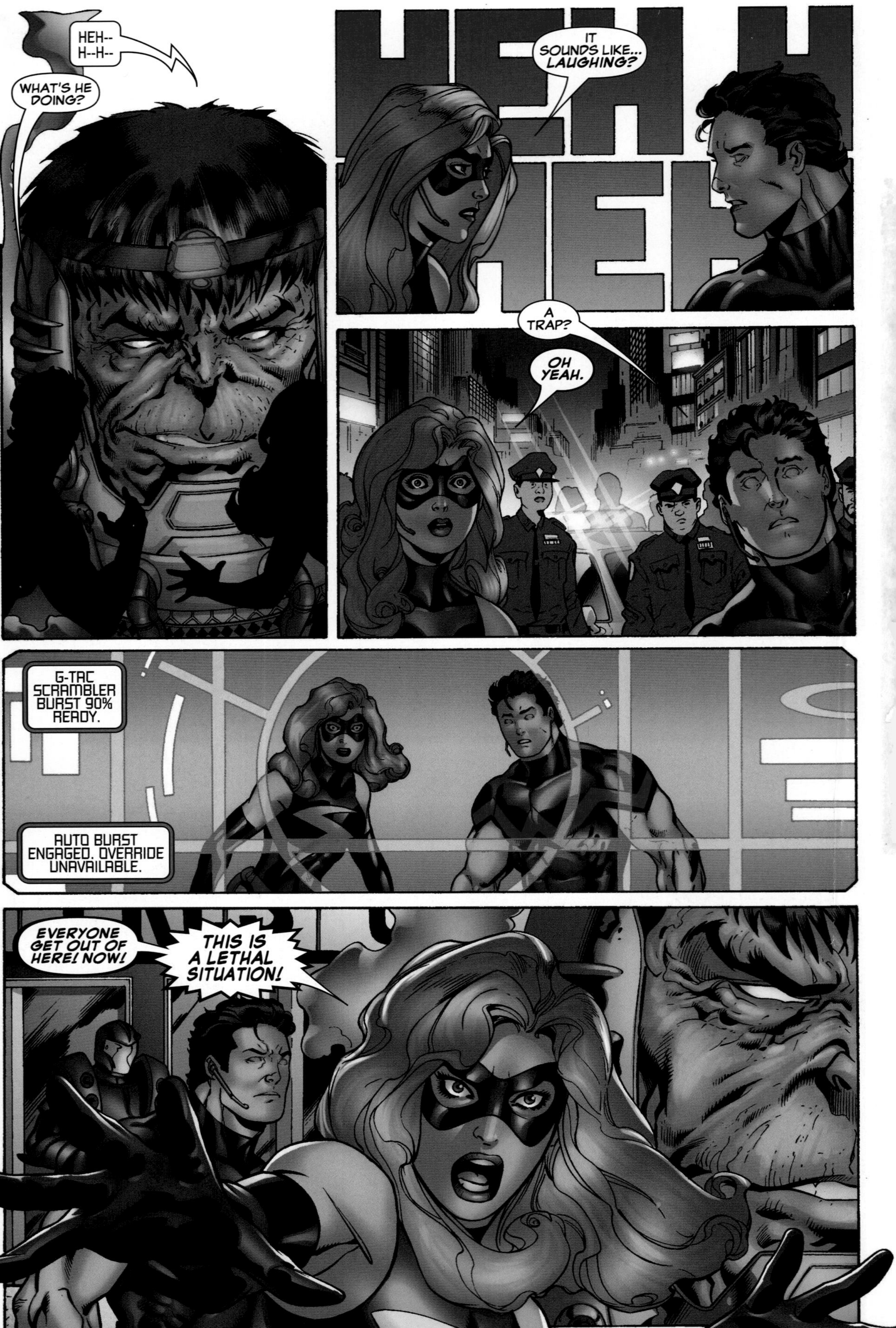
HEH--
H--H--
WHAT'S HE DOING?
HEH H HEH HEH
IT SOUNDS LIKE... LAUGHING?
A TRAP?
OH YEAH.
G-TAC SCRAMBLER BURST 90% READY.
AUTO BURST ENGAGED. OVERRIDE UNAVAILABLE.
EVERYONE GET OUT OF HERE! NOW!
THIS IS A LETHAL SITUATION!

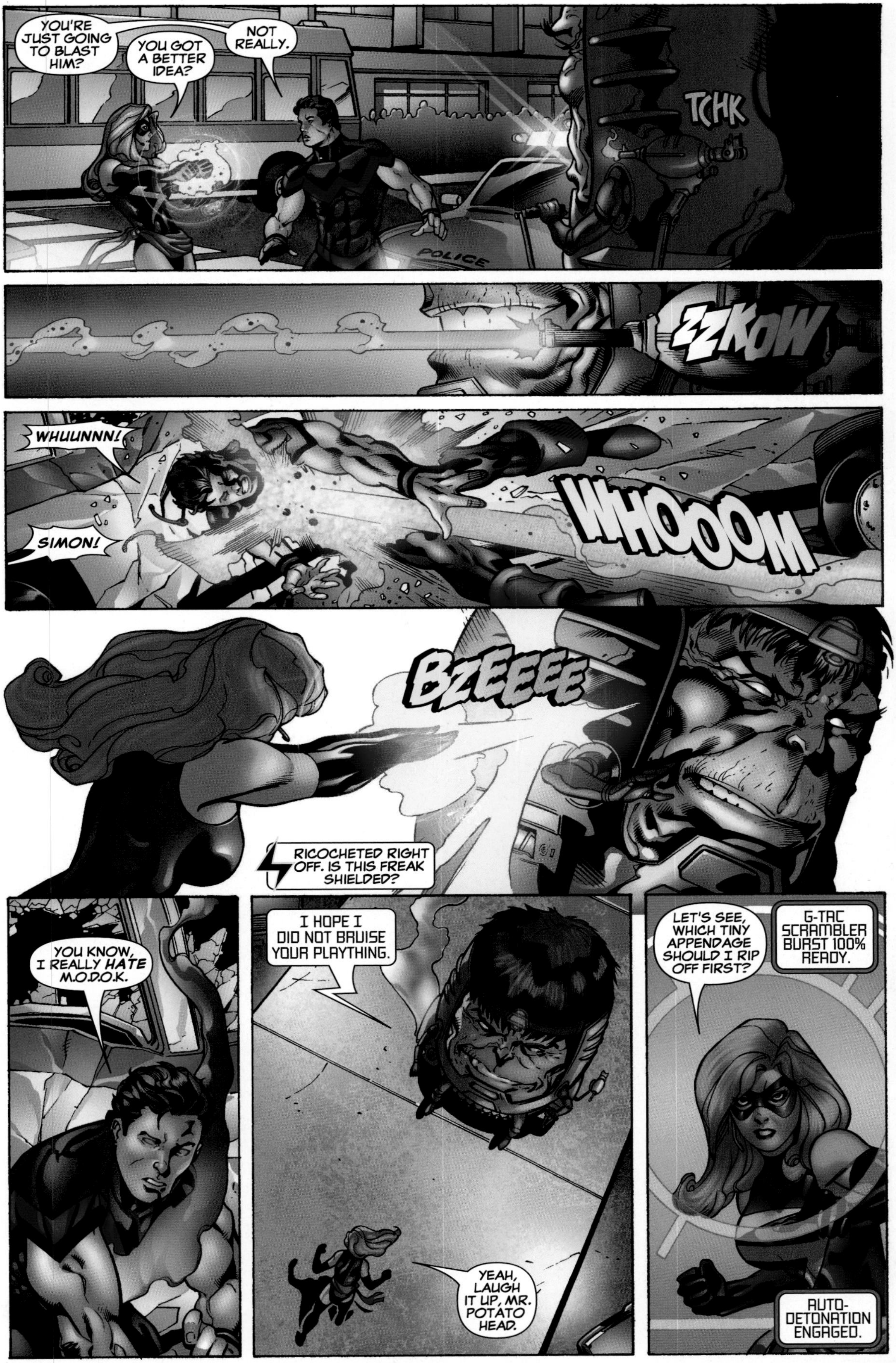

YOU'RE JUST GOING TO BLAST HIM?
YOU GOT A BETTER IDEA?
NOT REALLY.
TCHK
POLICE
ZZKOW
WHUUNNN!
SIMON!
WHOOOM
BZEEEE
RICOCHETED RIGHT OFF. IS THIS FREAK SHIELDED?
YOU KNOW, I REALLY HATE M.O.D.O.K.
I HOPE I DID NOT BRUISE YOUR PLAYTHING.
YEAH, LAUGH IT UP, MR. POTATO HEAD.
LET'S SEE, WHICH TINY APPENDAGE SHOULD I RIP OFF FIRST?
G-TAC SCRAMBLER BURST 100% READY.
AUTO-DETONATION ENGAGED.

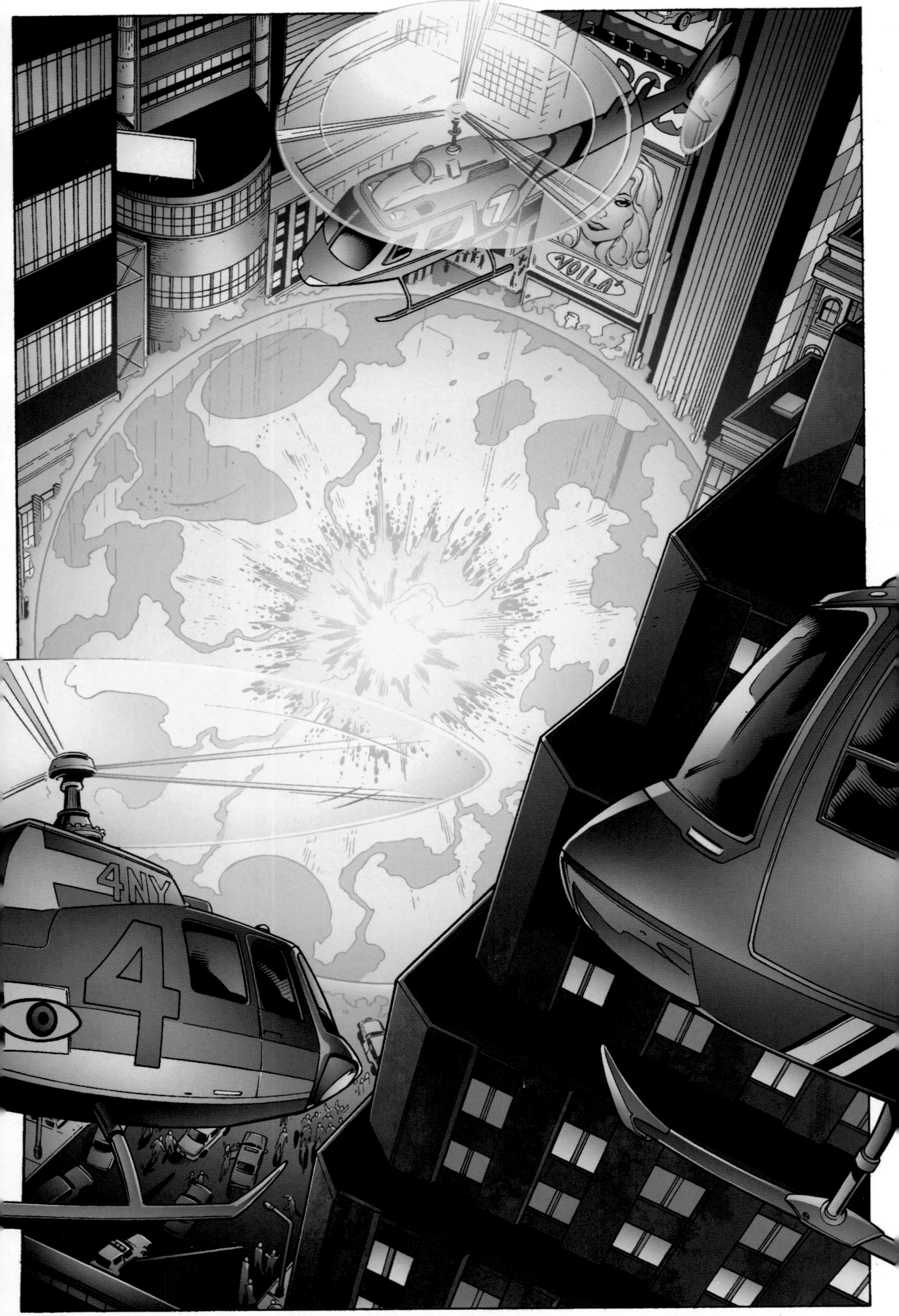
VOILA'
4NY
4

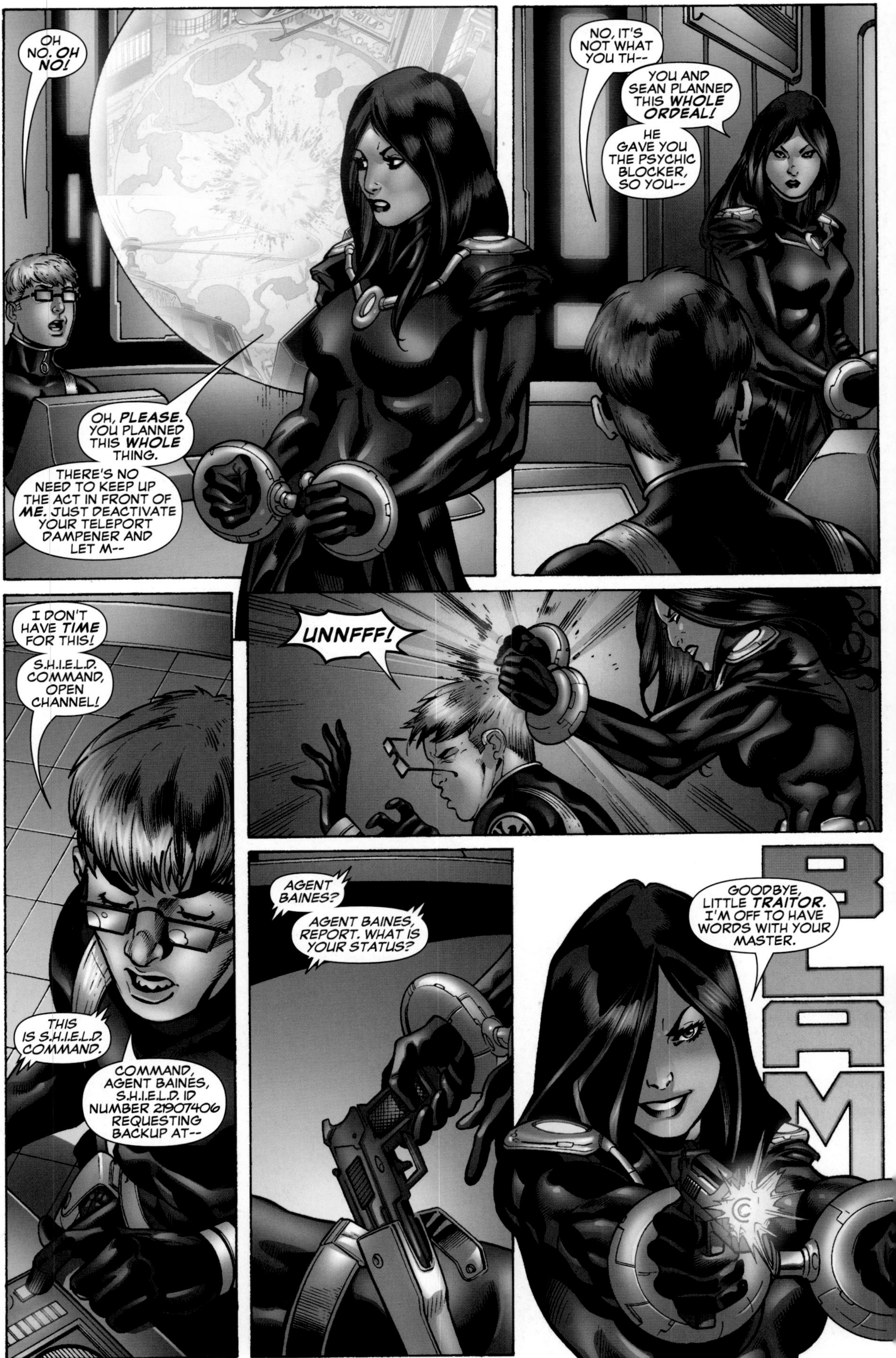
OH NO. OH NO!
OH, PLEASE. YOU PLANNED THIS WHOLE THING.
THERE'S NO NEED TO KEEP UP THE ACT IN FRONT OF ME. JUST DEACTIVATE YOUR TELEPORT DAMPENER AND LET M--
NO, IT'S NOT WHAT YOU TH--
YOU AND SEAN PLANNED THIS WHOLE ORDEAL!
HE GAVE YOU THE PSYCHIC BLOCKER, SO YOU--
I DON'T HAVE TIME FOR THIS!
S.H.I.E.L.D. COMMAND, OPEN CHANNEL!
UNNFFF!
THIS IS S.H.I.E.L.D. COMMAND.
COMMAND, AGENT BAINES, S.H.I.E.L.D. ID NUMBER 21907406 REQUESTING BACKUP AT--
AGENT BAINES?
AGENT BAINES, REPORT. WHAT IS YOUR STATUS?
GOODBYE, LITTLE TRAITOR. I'M OFF TO HAVE WORDS WITH YOUR MASTER.
BLAM

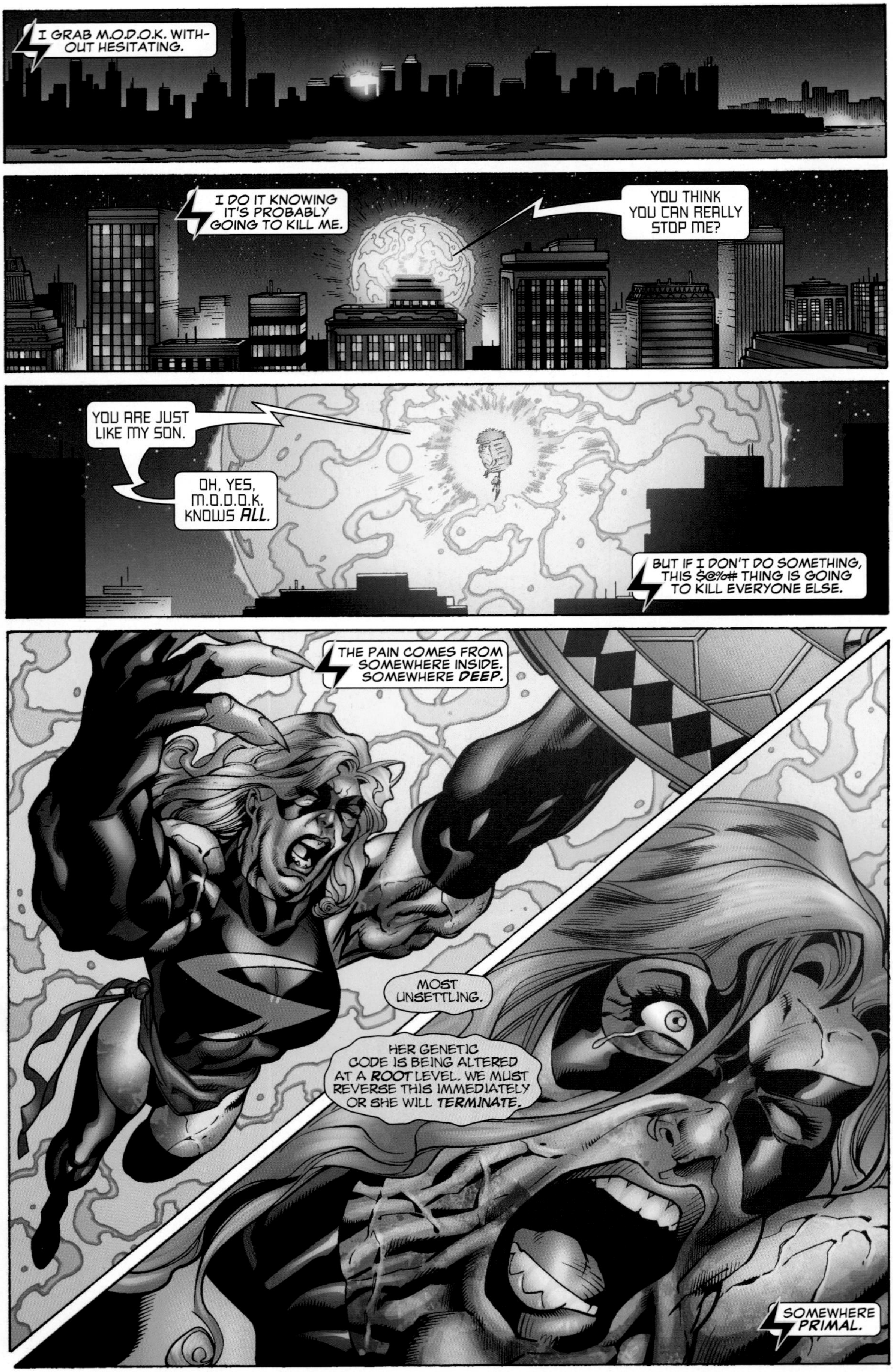
I GRAB M.O.D.O.K. WITHOUT HESITATING.
I DO IT KNOWING IT'S PROBABLY GOING TO KILL ME.
YOU THINK YOU CAN REALLY STOP ME?
YOU ARE JUST LIKE MY SON.
OH, YES, M.O.D.O.K. KNOWS ALL.
BUT IF I DON'T DO SOMETHING, THIS $@%# THING IS GOING TO KILL EVERYONE ELSE.
THE PAIN COMES FROM SOMEWHERE INSIDE. SOMEWHERE DEEP.
MOST UNSETTLING.
HER GENETIC CODE IS BEING ALTERED AT A ROOT LEVEL. WE MUST REVERSE THIS IMMEDIATELY OR SHE WILL TERMINATE.
SOMEWHERE PRIMAL.

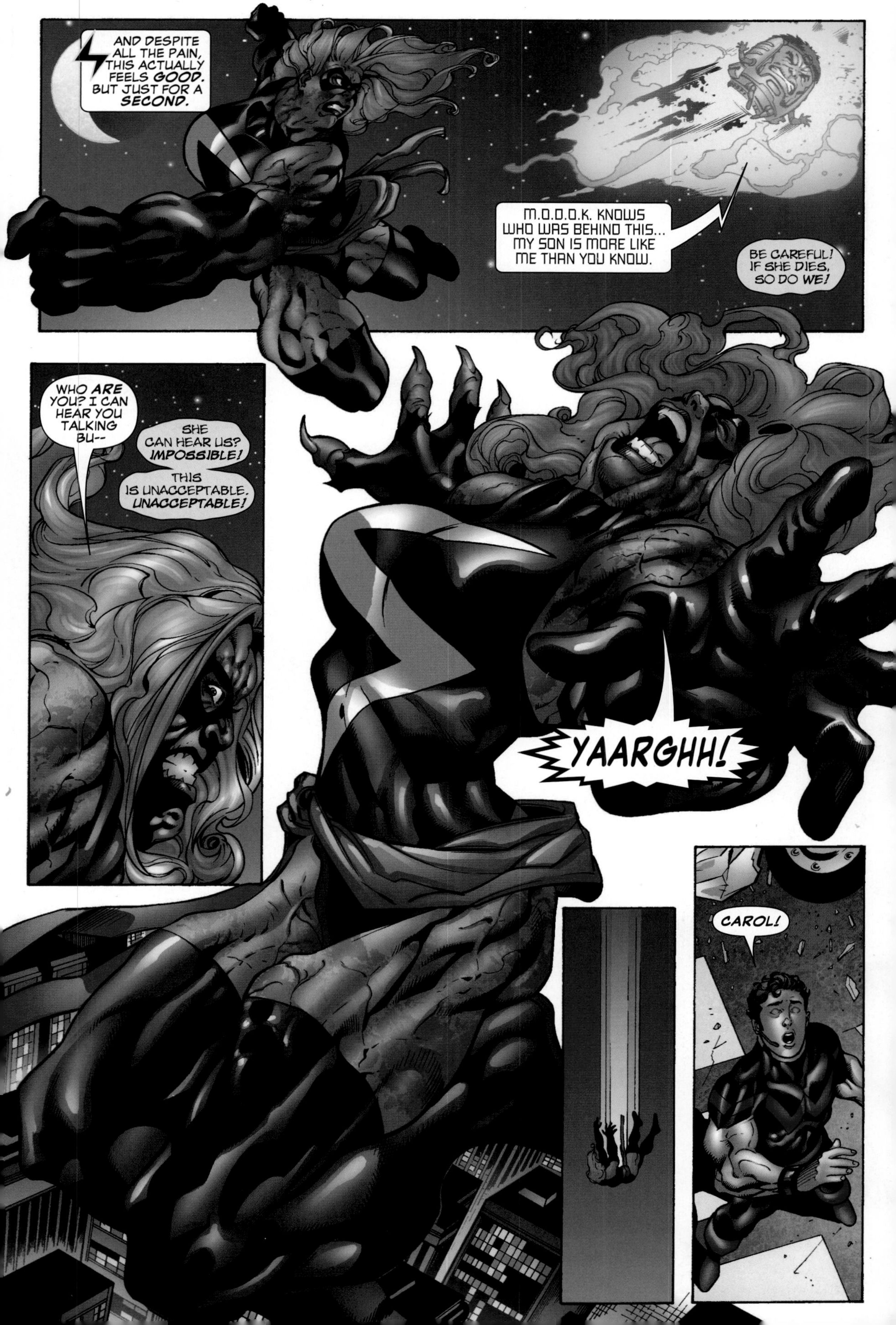
AND DESPITE ALL THE PAIN, THIS ACTUALLY FEELS GOOD. BUT JUST FOR A SECOND.
M.O.D.O.K. KNOWS WHO WAS BEHIND THIS... MY SON IS MORE LIKE ME THAN YOU KNOW.
BE CAREFUL! IF SHE DIES, SO DO WE!
WHO ARE YOU? I CAN HEAR YOU TALKING BU--
SHE CAN HEAR US? IMPOSSIBLE!
THIS IS UNACCEPTABLE. UNACCEPTABLE!
YAARGHH!
CAROL!

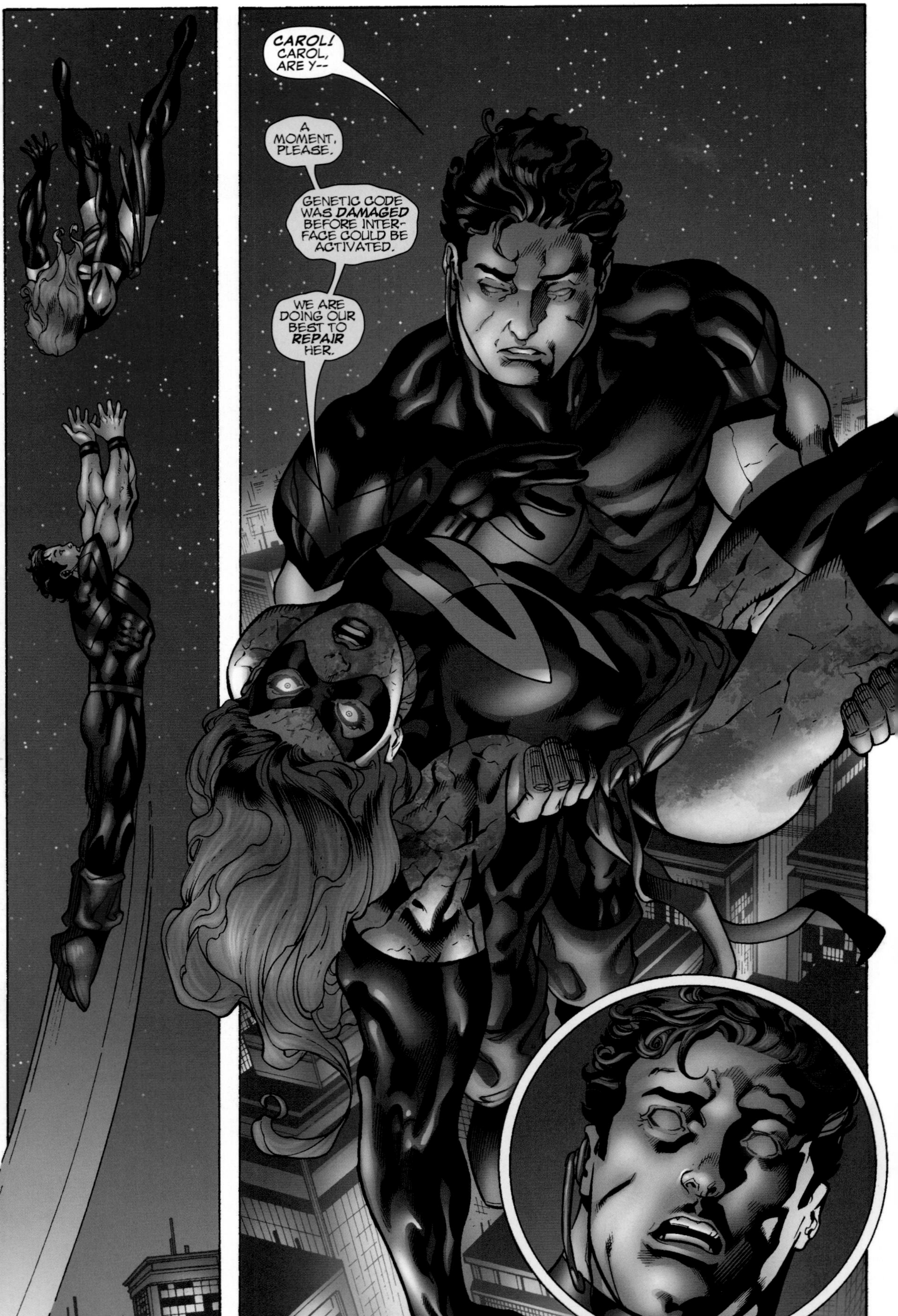

CAROL! CAROL, ARE Y--
A MOMENT, PLEASE.
GENETIC CODE WAS DAMAGED BEFORE INTER-FACE COULD BE ACTIVATED.
WE ARE DOING OUR BEST TO REPAIR HER.

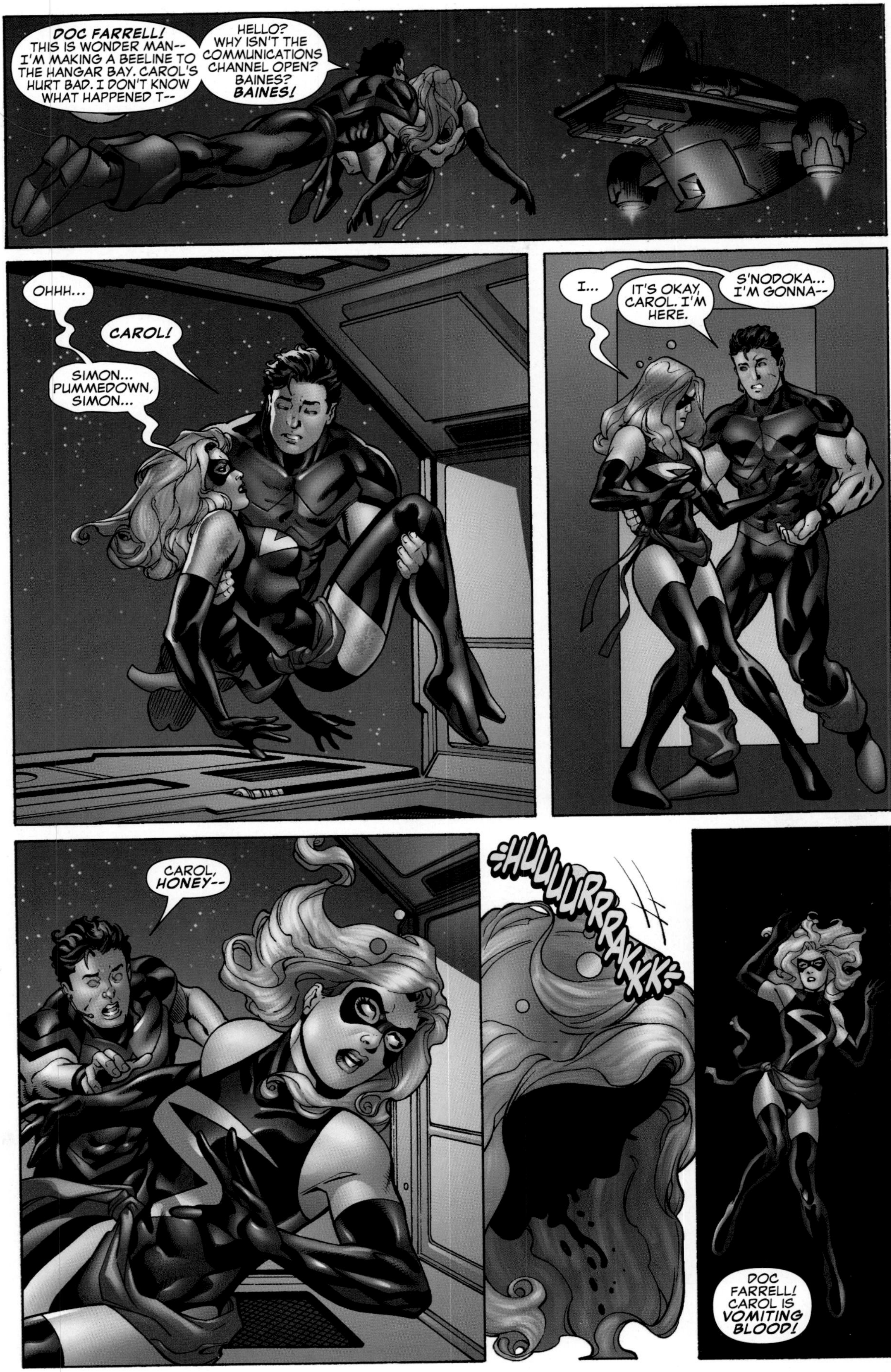
DOC FARRELL! THIS IS WONDER MAN-- I'M MAKING A BEELINE TO THE HANGAR BAY. CAROL'S HURT BAD. I DON'T KNOW WHAT HAPPENED T--
HELLO? WHY ISN'T THE COMMUNICATIONS CHANNEL OPEN? BAINES? BAINES!
OHHH...
CAROL!
SIMON... PUMMEDOWN, SIMON...
I...
IT'S OKAY, CAROL. I'M HERE.
S'NODOKA... I'M GONNA--
CAROL, HONEY--
HUUUURRRAKKK
DOC FARRELL! CAROL IS VOMITING BLOOD!

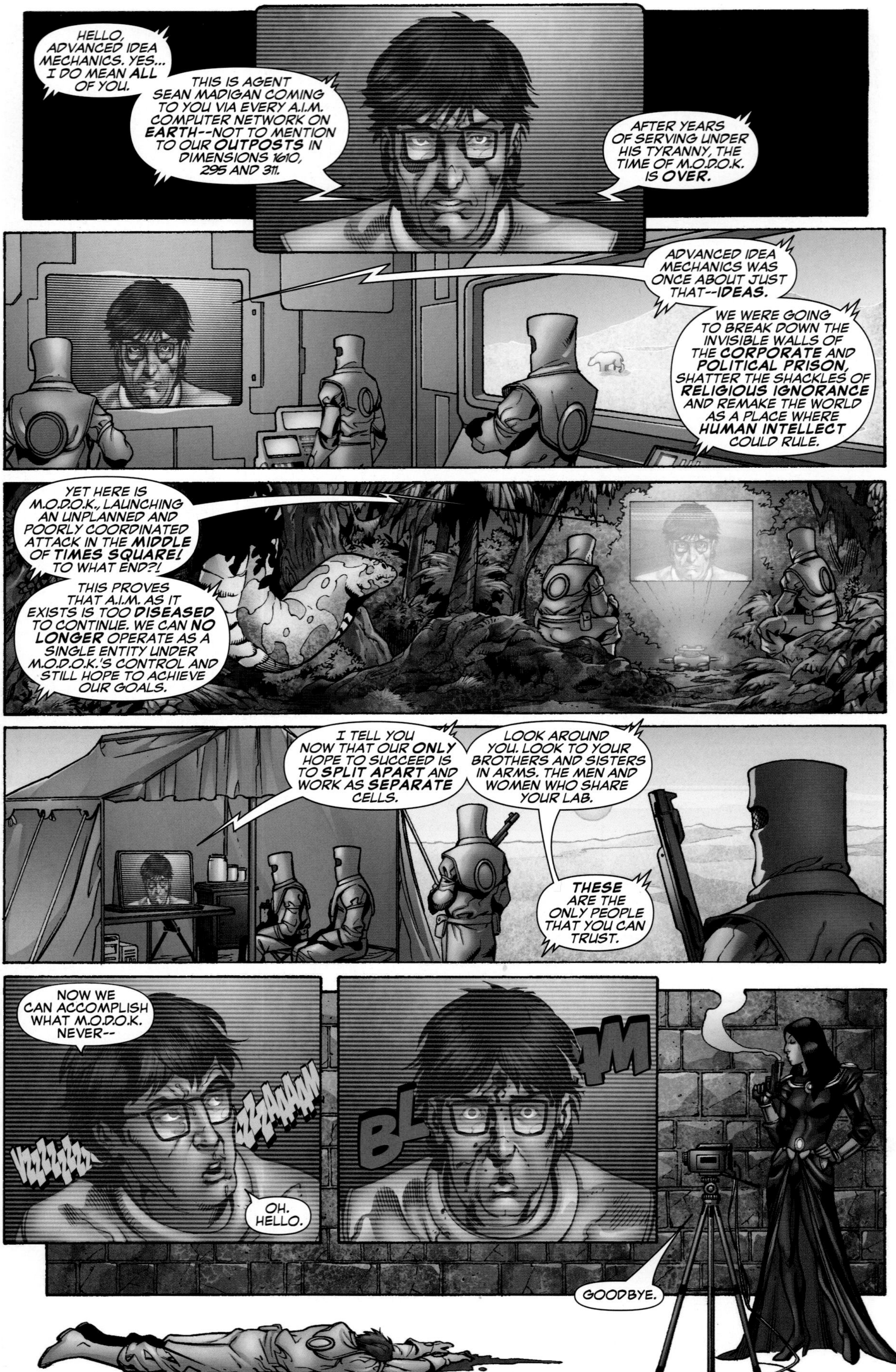
HELLO, ADVANCED IDEA MECHANICS. YES... I DO MEAN ALL OF YOU.
THIS IS AGENT SEAN MADIGAN COMING TO YOU VIA EVERY A.I.M. COMPUTER NETWORK ON EARTH--NOT TO MENTION TO OUR OUTPOSTS IN DIMENSIONS 1610, 295 AND 311.
AFTER YEARS OF SERVING UNDER HIS TYRANNY, THE TIME OF M.O.D.O.K. IS OVER.
ADVANCED IDEA MECHANICS WAS ONCE ABOUT JUST THAT--IDEAS.
WE WERE GOING TO BREAK DOWN THE INVISIBLE WALLS OF THE CORPORATE AND POLITICAL PRISON, SHATTER THE SHACKLES OF RELIGIOUS IGNORANCE AND REMAKE THE WORLD AS A PLACE WHERE HUMAN INTELLECT COULD RULE.
YET HERE IS M.O.D.O.K., LAUNCHING AN UNPLANNED AND POORLY COORDINATED ATTACK IN THE MIDDLE OF TIMES SQUARE! TO WHAT END?!
THIS PROVES THAT A.I.M. AS IT EXISTS IS TOO DISEASED TO CONTINUE. WE CAN NO LONGER OPERATE AS A SINGLE ENTITY UNDER M.O.D.O.K.'S CONTROL AND STILL HOPE TO ACHIEVE OUR GOALS.
I TELL YOU NOW THAT OUR ONLY HOPE TO SUCCEED IS TO SPLIT APART AND WORK AS SEPARATE CELLS.
LOOK AROUND YOU. LOOK TO YOUR BROTHERS AND SISTERS IN ARMS. THE MEN AND WOMEN WHO SHARE YOUR LAB.
THESE ARE THE ONLY PEOPLE THAT YOU CAN TRUST.
NOW WE CAN ACCOMPLISH WHAT M.O.D.O.K. NEVER--
VZZZZZZZ
ZZZAAAAM
OH. HELLO.
BL
AM
GOODBYE.

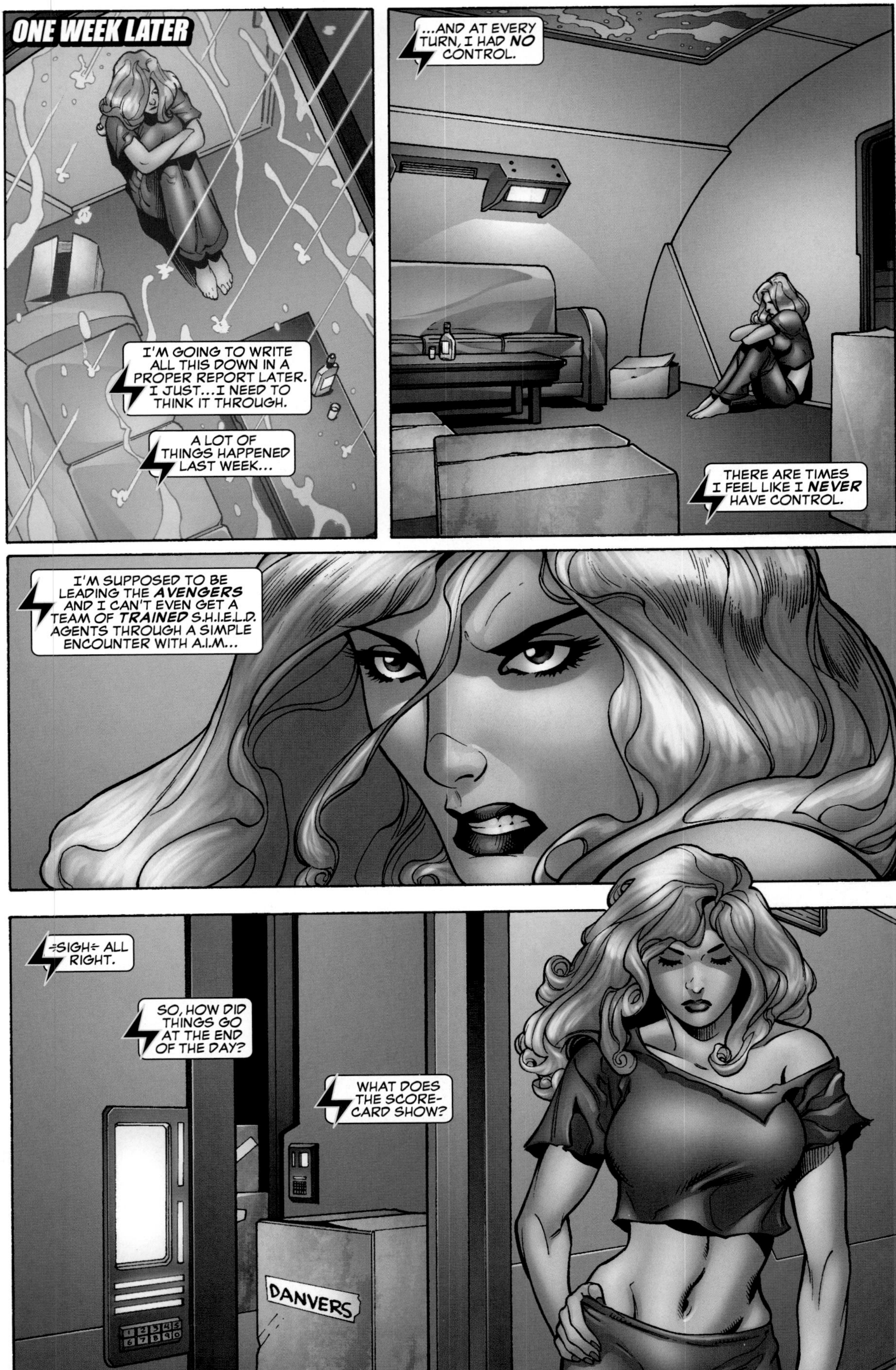
ONE WEEK LATER
I'M GOING TO WRITE ALL THIS DOWN IN A PROPER REPORT LATER. I JUST...I NEED TO THINK IT THROUGH.
A LOT OF THINGS HAPPENED LAST WEEK...
...AND AT EVERY TURN, I HAD NO CONTROL.
THERE ARE TIMES I FEEL LIKE I NEVER HAVE CONTROL.
I'M SUPPOSED TO BE LEADING THE AVENGERS AND I CAN'T EVEN GET A TEAM OF TRAINED S.H.I.E.L.D. AGENTS THROUGH A SIMPLE ENCOUNTER WITH A.I.M...
=SIGH= ALL RIGHT.
SO, HOW DID THINGS GO AT THE END OF THE DAY?
WHAT DOES THE SCORE-CARD SHOW?
DANVERS
1 2 3 4 5
6 7 8 9 0

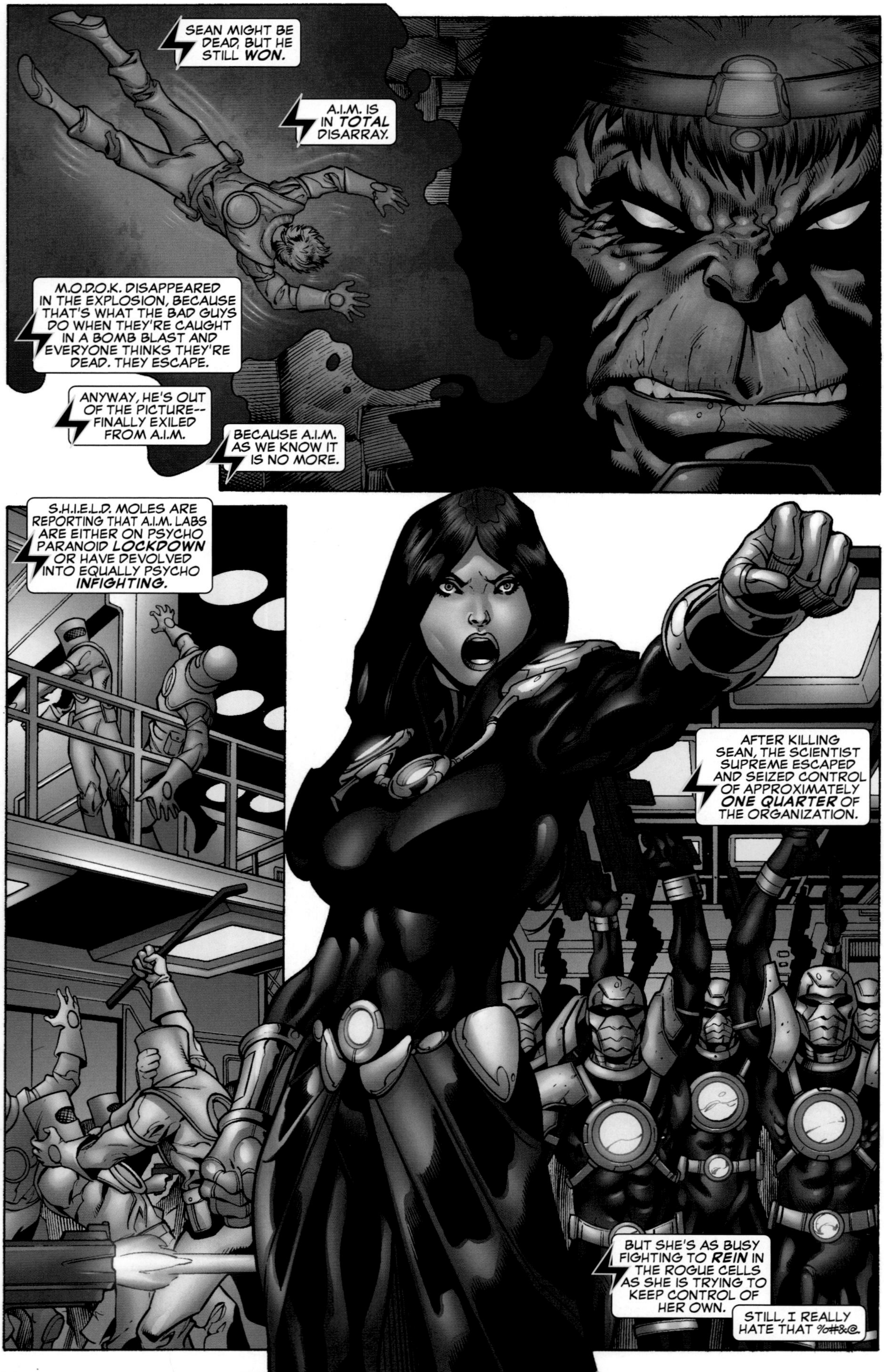
SEAN MIGHT BE DEAD, BUT HE STILL WON.
A.I.M. IS IN TOTAL DISARRAY.
M.O.D.O.K. DISAPPEARED IN THE EXPLOSION, BECAUSE THAT'S WHAT THE BAD GUYS DO WHEN THEY'RE CAUGHT IN A BOMB BLAST AND EVERYONE THINKS THEY'RE DEAD. THEY ESCAPE.
ANYWAY, HE'S OUT OF THE PICTURE-- FINALLY EXILED FROM A.I.M.
BECAUSE A.I.M. AS WE KNOW IT IS NO MORE.
S.H.I.E.L.D. MOLES ARE REPORTING THAT A.I.M. LABS ARE EITHER ON PSYCHO PARANOID LOCKDOWN OR HAVE DEVOLVED INTO EQUALLY PSYCHO INFIGHTING.
AFTER KILLING SEAN, THE SCIENTIST SUPREME ESCAPED AND SEIZED CONTROL OF APPROXIMATELY ONE QUARTER OF THE ORGANIZATION.
BUT SHE'S AS BUSY FIGHTING TO REIN IN THE ROGUE CELLS AS SHE IS TRYING TO KEEP CONTROL OF HER OWN.
STILL, I REALLY HATE THAT %#&@.

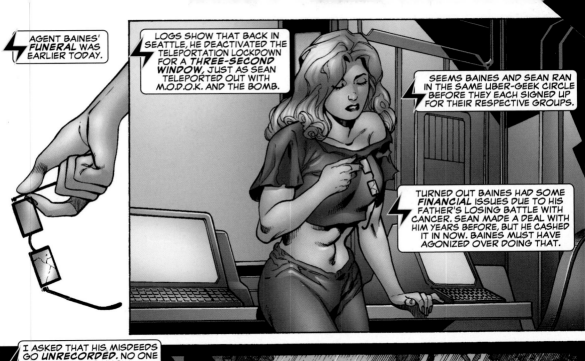

AGENT BAINES' **FUNERAL** WAS EARLIER TODAY.

LOGS SHOW THAT BACK IN SEATTLE, HE DEACTIVATED THE TELEPORTATION LOCKDOWN FOR A **THREE-SECOND WINDOW,** JUST AS SEAN TELEPORTED OUT WITH M.O.D.O.K. AND THE BOMB.

SEEMS BAINES AND SEAN RAN IN THE SAME UBER-GEEK CIRCLE BEFORE THEY EACH SIGNED UP FOR THEIR RESPECTIVE GROUPS.

TURNED OUT BAINES HAD SOME **FINANCIAL** ISSUES DUE TO HIS FATHER'S LOSING BATTLE WITH CANCER. SEAN MADE A DEAL WITH HIM YEARS BEFORE, BUT HE CASHED IT IN NOW. BAINES MUST HAVE AGONIZED OVER DOING THAT.

I ASKED THAT HIS MISDEEDS GO **UNRECORDED.** NO ONE NEEDS TO KNOW.

WHEN I HANDED THE FLAG TO HIS MOTHER...

...SHE NEVER LOOKED AWAY FROM HIS CASKET. NOT EVEN **ONCE.**

SINCE AGENT LOCKE WAS INJURED IN SEATTLE, THE S.H.I.E.L.D. PSI-CORPS PLACED HER ON MEDICAL LEAVE.

THERE HAVE BEEN A **LOT** OF **SURGERIES** FOR HER. A LOT OF **PAIN.**

I SHOULD GO VISIT HER...

...BUT I DON'T THINK SHE'D BE HAPPY TO SEE ME.

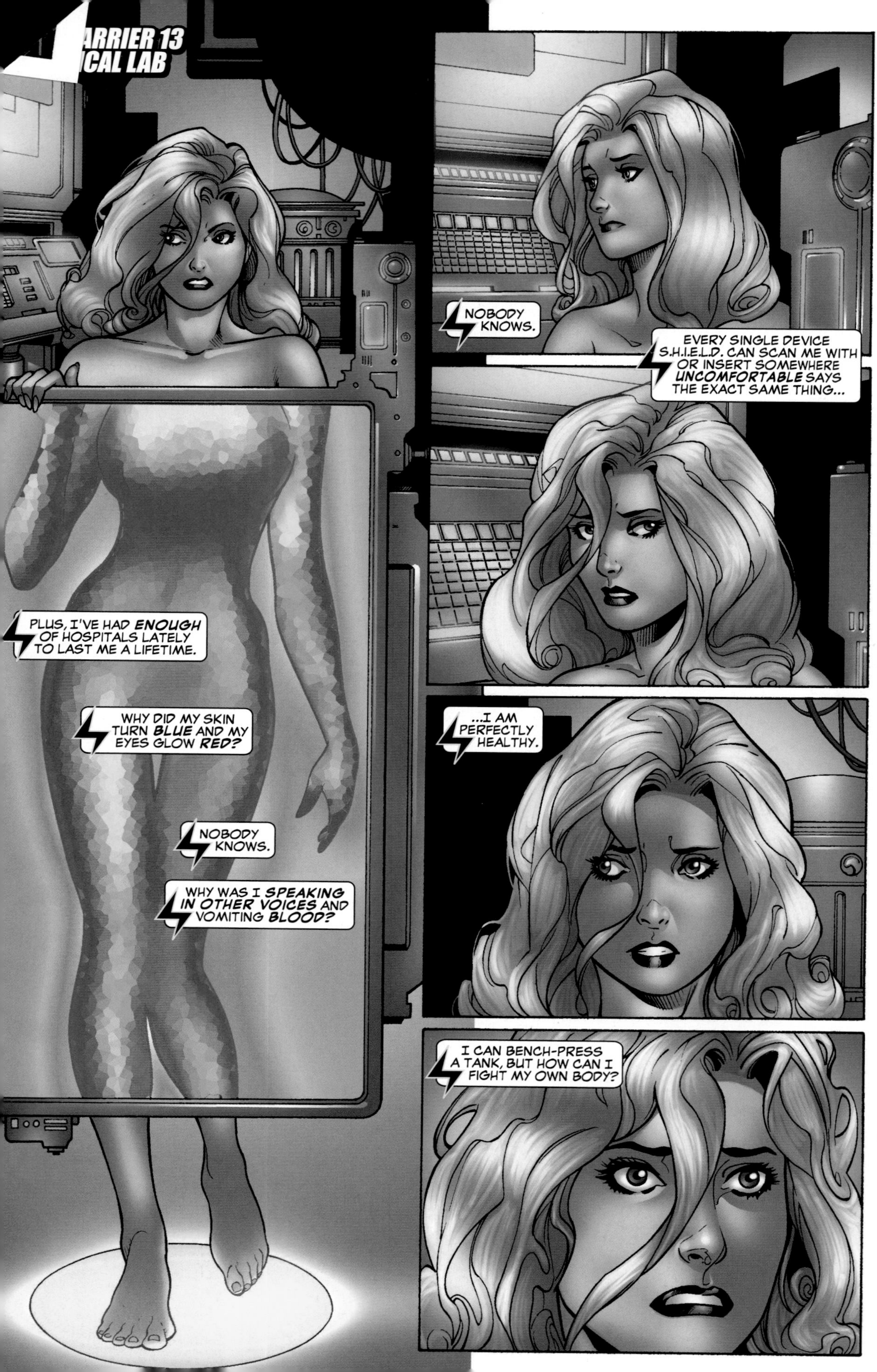
ARRIER 13
ICAL LAB
PLUS, I'VE HAD ENOUGH OF HOSPITALS LATELY TO LAST ME A LIFETIME.
WHY DID MY SKIN TURN BLUE AND MY EYES GLOW RED?
NOBODY KNOWS.
WHY WAS I SPEAKING IN OTHER VOICES AND VOMITING BLOOD?
NOBODY KNOWS.
EVERY SINGLE DEVICE S.H.I.E.L.D. CAN SCAN ME WITH OR INSERT SOMEWHERE UNCOMFORTABLE SAYS THE EXACT SAME THING...
...I AM PERFECTLY HEALTHY.
I CAN BENCH-PRESS A TANK, BUT HOW CAN I FIGHT MY OWN BODY?

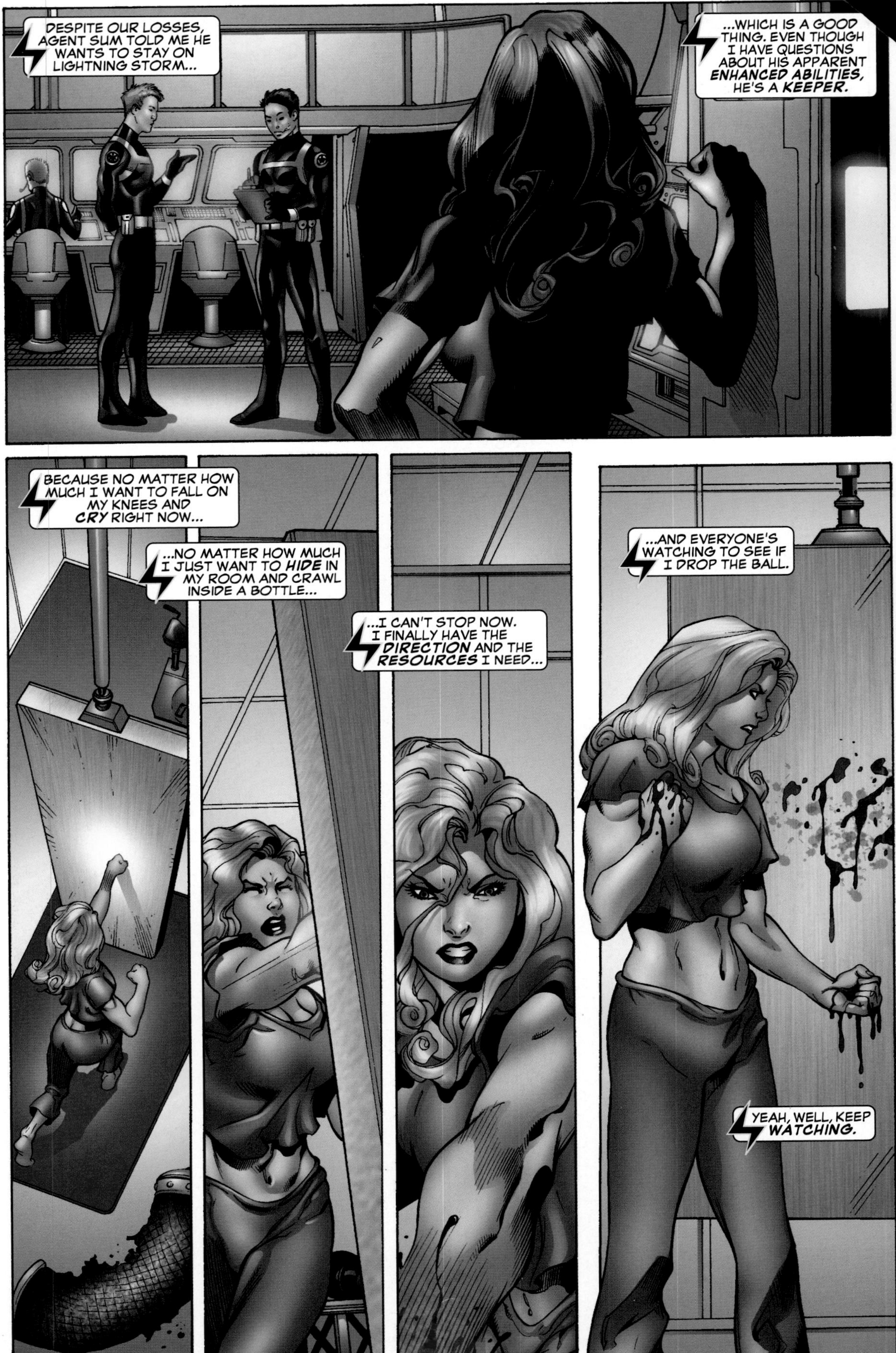
DESPITE OUR LOSSES, AGENT SUM TOLD ME HE WANTS TO STAY ON LIGHTNING STORM...
...WHICH IS A GOOD THING. EVEN THOUGH I HAVE QUESTIONS ABOUT HIS APPARENT ENHANCED ABILITIES, HE'S A KEEPER.
BECAUSE NO MATTER HOW MUCH I WANT TO FALL ON MY KNEES AND CRY RIGHT NOW...
...NO MATTER HOW MUCH I JUST WANT TO HIDE IN MY ROOM AND CRAWL INSIDE A BOTTLE...
...I CAN'T STOP NOW. I FINALLY HAVE THE DIRECTION AND THE RESOURCES I NEED...
...AND EVERYONE'S WATCHING TO SEE IF I DROP THE BALL.
YEAH, WELL, KEEP WATCHING.

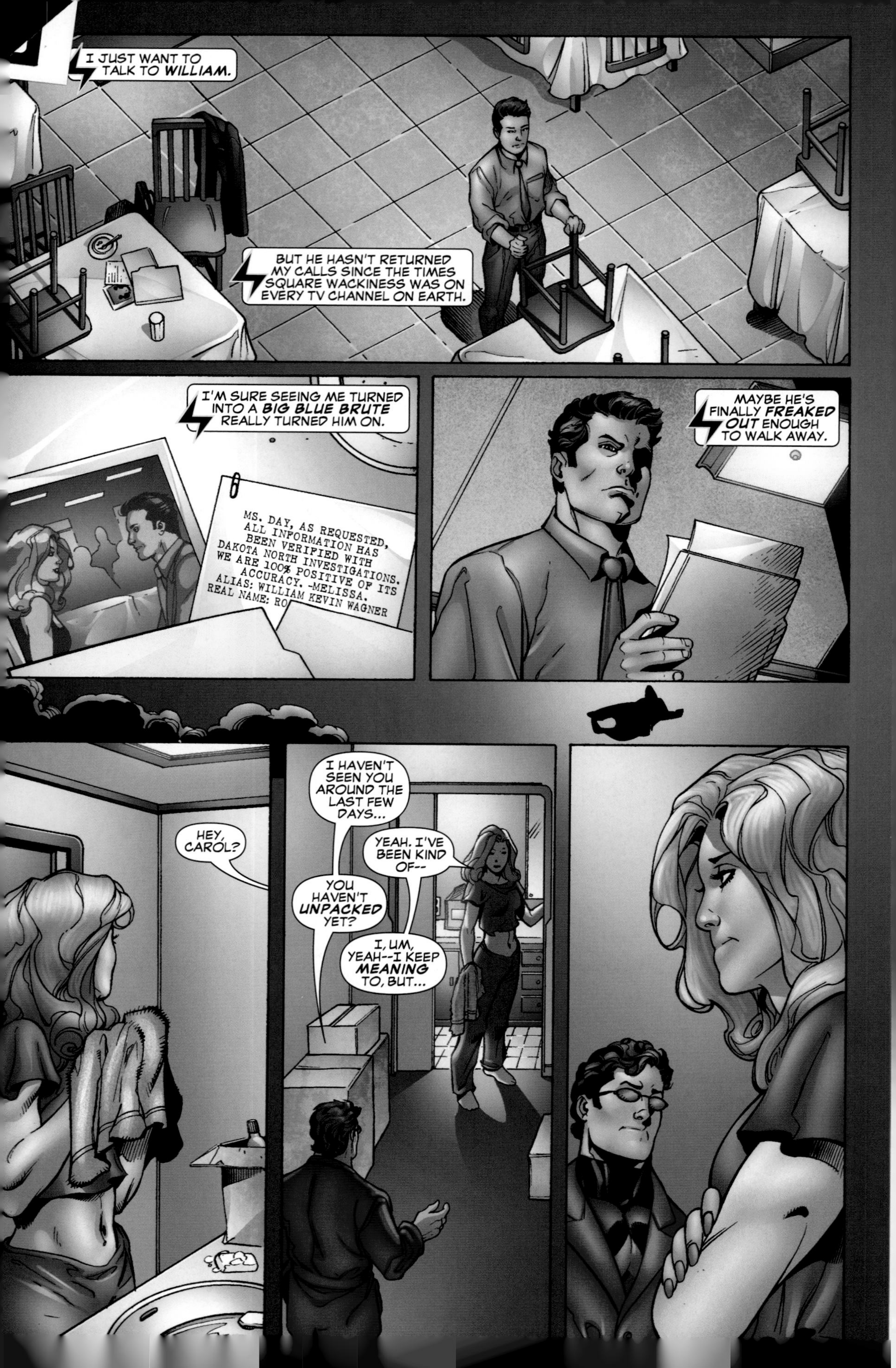

I JUST WANT TO TALK TO WILLIAM.
BUT HE HASN'T RETURNED MY CALLS SINCE THE TIMES SQUARE WACKINESS WAS ON EVERY TV CHANNEL ON EARTH.
I'M SURE SEEING ME TURNED INTO A BIG BLUE BRUTE REALLY TURNED HIM ON.
MS. DAY, AS REQUESTED, ALL INFORMATION HAS BEEN VERIFIED WITH DAKOTA NORTH INVESTIGATIONS. WE ARE 100% POSITIVE OF ITS ACCURACY. -MELISSA.
ALIAS: WILLIAM KEVIN WAGNER
REAL NAME: RO
MAYBE HE'S FINALLY FREAKED OUT ENOUGH TO WALK AWAY.
HEY, CAROL?
I HAVEN'T SEEN YOU AROUND THE LAST FEW DAYS...
YEAH. I'VE BEEN KIND OF--
YOU HAVEN'T UNPACKED YET?
I, UM, YEAH--I KEEP MEANING TO, BUT...

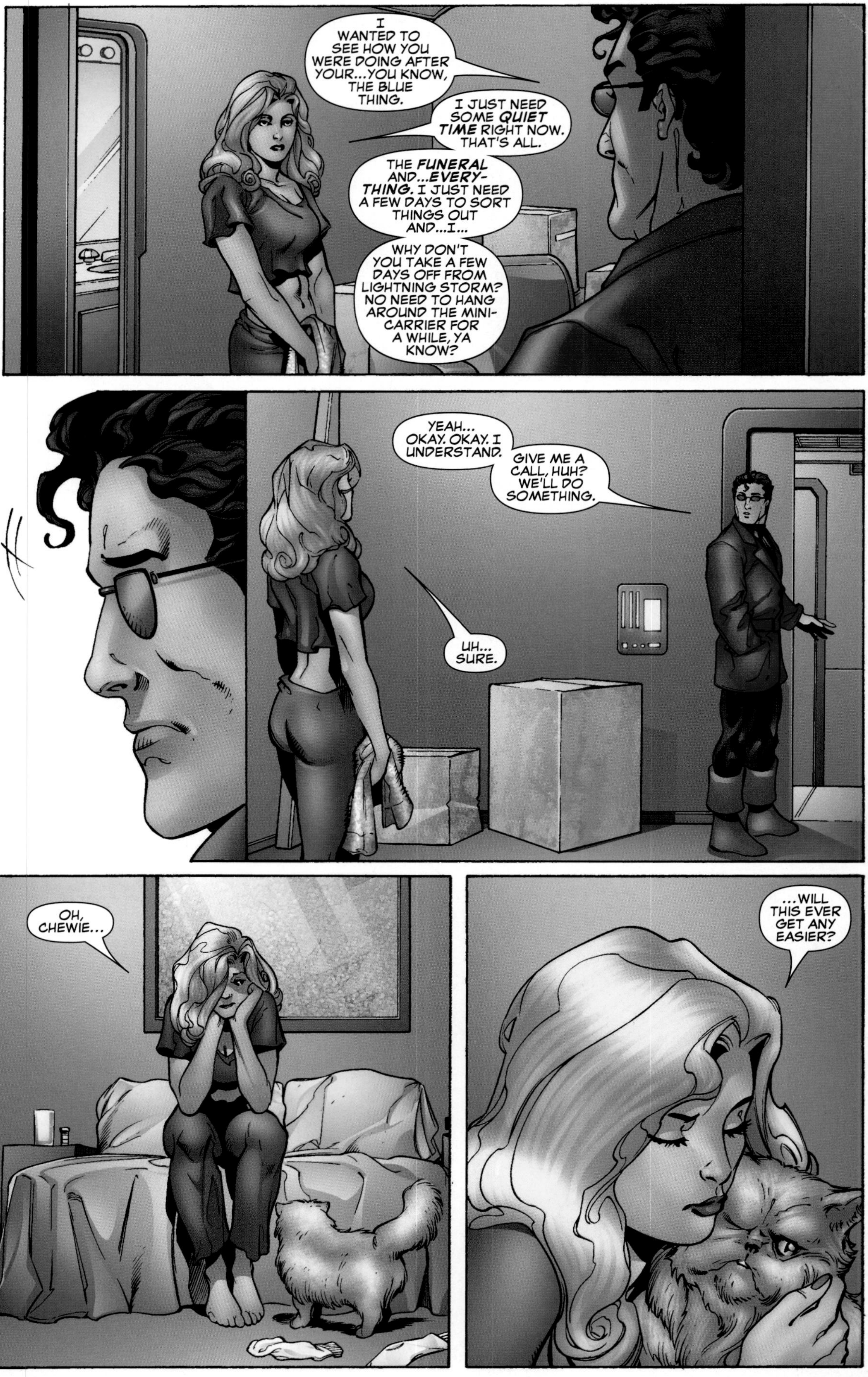
I WANTED TO SEE HOW YOU WERE DOING AFTER YOUR...YOU KNOW, THE BLUE THING.
I JUST NEED SOME **QUIET TIME** RIGHT NOW. THAT'S ALL.
THE **FUNERAL** AND...**EVERY-THING.** I JUST NEED A FEW DAYS TO SORT THINGS OUT AND...I...
WHY DON'T YOU TAKE A FEW DAYS OFF FROM LIGHTNING STORM? NO NEED TO HANG AROUND THE MINI-CARRIER FOR A WHILE, YA KNOW?
YEAH... OKAY. OKAY. I UNDERSTAND.
GIVE ME A CALL, HUH? WE'LL DO SOMETHING.
UH... SURE.
OH, CHEWIE...
...WILL THIS EVER GET ANY EASIER?

ISN'T IT *AMAZING?*

HONESTLY? IT'S SORT OF *GROSS.*

SECRET A.I.M. LABORATORY

HOW CAN YOU SAY IT'S GROSS?

THIS IS *EXACTLY* WHAT MADIGAN WAS TALKING ABOUT!

BIG IDEAS, MAN! CHANGING THE *WORLD!*

I GUESS... BUT I'M NOT SURE SEAN IMAGINED HE MIGHT *END UP* AS ONE OF THOSE BIG IDEAS.

COME ON, THIS LAB WAS *ALWAYS* IN CHARGE OF *REANIMATION* RESEARCH, WASN'T IT?

HAND ME THE M.G. CHIP, PLEASE?

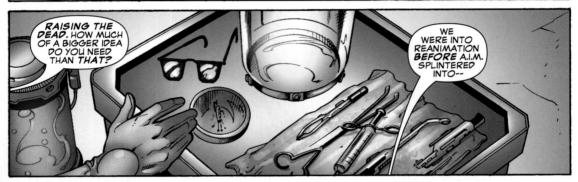

RAISING THE DEAD. HOW MUCH OF A BIGGER IDEA DO YOU NEED THAN *THAT?*

WE WERE INTO REANIMATION *BEFORE* A.I.M. SPLINTERED INTO--

YOU MEAN BEFORE MR. MADIGAN HERE REMINDED EVERY-ONE THAT WE--*ANY* OF US--COULD CHANGE THE WORLD?

THE *TARGOTHS* WERE NEAT TO LEARN WITH, BUT THEY WERE MINDLESS...*STUPID.* THIS, THOUGH...

TAKING WHAT WE LEARNED FROM DOOMSDAY MAN'S NEURAL LINKS...

...CROSSING IT WITH THE REANIMATIVE PROPERTIES OF THE TARGOTH VIRUS...

ACTIVATING THE CHIP--OH, WHAT A *PRETTY* GLOW.

OKAY... FILLING THE SUIT WITH GEL. OHHH, THAT'S *PERFECT.* HE LOOKS GOOD, DOESN'T HE?

HAND ME THE HELMET, PLEASE? NOW LET'S SEE WHAT HAPPENS...

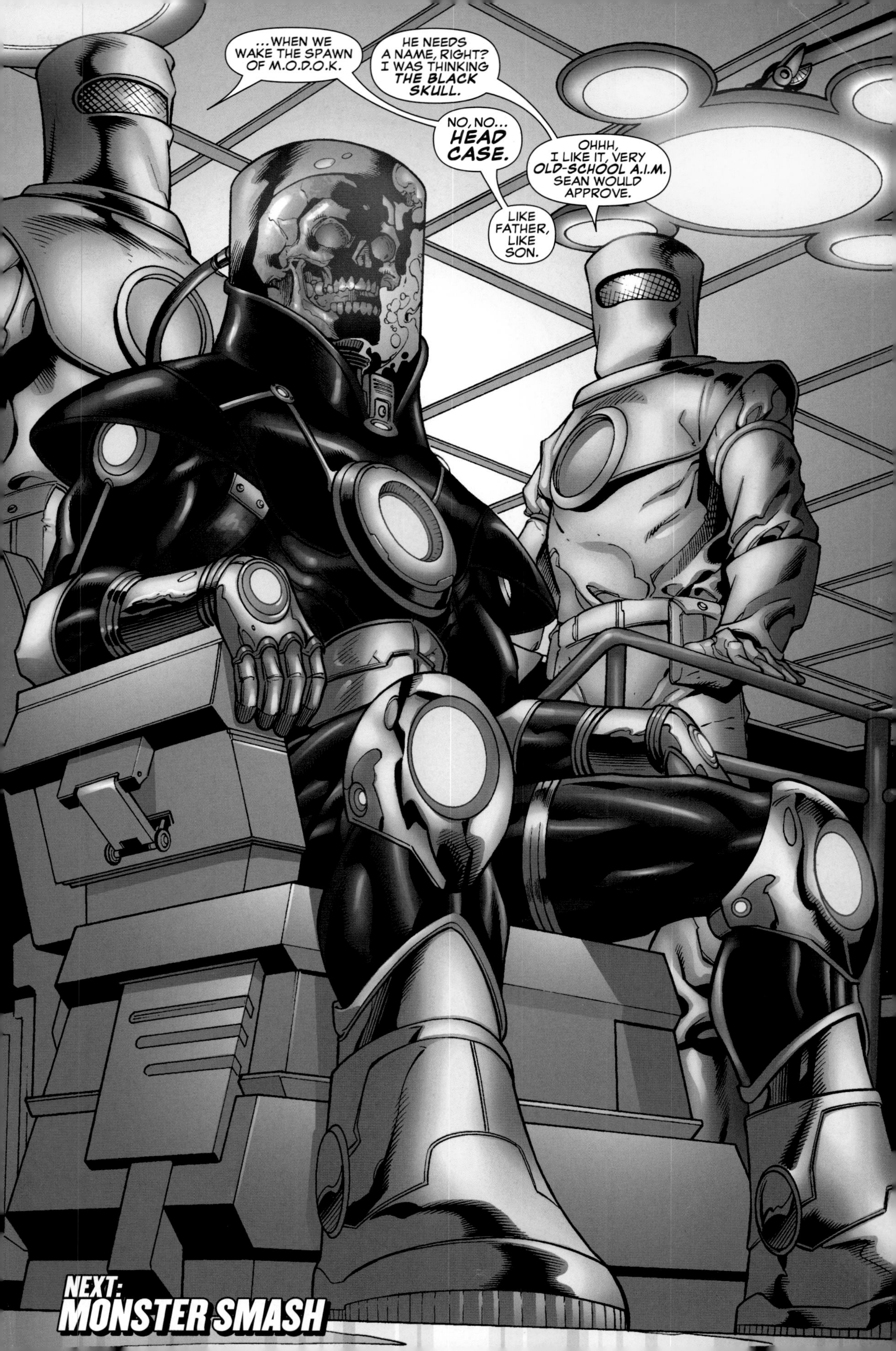
...WHEN WE WAKE THE SPAWN OF M.O.D.O.K.
HE NEEDS A NAME, RIGHT? I WAS THINKING THE BLACK SKULL.
NO, NO... HEAD CASE.
OHHH, I LIKE IT, VERY OLD-SCHOOL A.I.M. SEAN WOULD APPROVE.
LIKE FATHER, LIKE SON.
NEXT: MONSTER SMASH